The Myths of Health Care

Paola Adinolfi · Elio Borgonovi
Editors

The Myths of Health Care

Towards New Models of Leadership and Management in the Healthcare Sector

Foreword by Henry Mintzberg

Springer

Editors
Paola Adinolfi
CIRPA (Interdepartmental Centre for Research in Economics, Law and Management of Public Administrations)
University of Salerno
Fisciano
Italy

Elio Borgonovi
Public Administration and Health Institute "Carlo Masini"
University "Luigi Bocconi" of Milan
Milan
Italy

ISBN 978-3-319-53599-9 ISBN 978-3-319-53600-2 (eBook)
https://doi.org/10.1007/978-3-319-53600-2

Library of Congress Control Number: 2017932085

Printed on acid-free paper

This Springer imprint is published by Springer Nature
The registered company is Springer International Publishing AG
The registered company address is: Gewerbestrasse 11, 6330 Cham, Switzerland

To Graziano, Stefano and Matteo

To Mattia, Milo and Bianca

Wishing that they could live in a healthy and peaceful society

Foreword

Needless to say, it is a great compliment to me and my work on the myths of health care that Paola Adinolfi and Elio Borgonovi have elected to do this volume. I am amazed how much this book contains, and how thorough these chapters are. We publish in parallel, this book based on talks I gave at the University of Salerno at the invitation of Paola Adinolfi, which uses a summary article I did earlier, and my book Managing the Myths of Health Care, which is going to appear around the same time. Too bad we could not have had each other's manuscript, to incorporate with our own views. But the happy part is that the readers will have both, and will thereby be able to probe in greater depth, having the interdisciplinary perspective from Paola and Elio's book. I am confident that having these two books together will shed greater light on the important field of health care, and I hope that we can continue to share our ideas in the future.

September 2016 Henry Mintzberg

John Cleghorn Professor of Management Studies
Desautels Faculty of Management, McGill University, Montreal, QC, Canada

Preface

It can be considered widely held that health care models are significantly conditioned by sets of beliefs which are in turn parts of broader philosophical ideas rooted in the culture of the time. Such beliefs may be more or less true, nevertheless they are vitally important in shaping health care models. Henry Mintzberg identified some false sets of beliefs—he calls "health myths"—which in his view are at the basis of the mess we currently face in health care.

It is indeed difficult for any one individual to see the fallacy of such myths, because they are below the surface. Furthermore, because of their invisibility, they are rarely challenged: debate on health care management is mainly focused on managerial-organizational models, as well as on specific techniques and tools, while discussion on ideas is surprisingly poor. We wanted to fill this gap: without informing Mintzberg, we asked a number of academic and practitioners, equally distributed between supporters and critics, to reflect on the "health myths". We aimed at bringing Mintzberg's myths to light, being open to any possible outcome: either overcoming them or discovering their "Holy Grail".

Among the academics, we invited senior and junior scholars from the field of management, accounting and organization studies, enrolled in CERGAS (the Research Centre for Health and Social Services) at Bocconi University of Milan (Patrizio Armeni, Oriana Ciani, Francesca Lecci, Federico Lega, Marco Morelli, Anna Prenestini, Rosanna Tarricone and Alexandra Torbica) and in CIRPA (Interdepartmental Centre for Research in Economics, Management and Law of Public Administrations) at the University of Salerno, a leading university in the South of Italy for research and action-research on public sector management and health care (Carmela Annarumma, Antonio Botti, Giuseppe Festa, Giuseppe Iuliano, Gaetano Matonti, Rocco Palumbo, Gabriella Piscopo, Paolo Tartaglia Polcini, Alessandra Storlazzi, Aurelio Tommasetti, Massimiliano Vesci). We also engaged academics from the University of Chieti-Pescara (Massimo Sargiacomo), the University of Florence (Mario Del Vecchio), the University of Lazio and Cassino (Lorenzo Mercurio), the Polytechnic University of Marche (Luca Del Bene), the Polytechnic University of Milan (Emanuele Lettieri), the University of Naples "Federico II" (Mariavittoria Cicellin, Gianluigi Mangia, Stefano Consiglio), the University of Naples "Parthenope" (Luigi Moschera), the Second University of Naples (Ettore Cinque, Corrado Cuccurullo, Mario Pezzillo Iacono, Marcello Martinez), the University of Rome (Alessio Santoro, Andrea Silenzi), the University of Sannio (Vincenza Esposito), the University of Venice (Salvatore Russo), and the University of Verona (Giuseppe Favretto). In addition, contributors from Switzerland (Stefano Calciolari) which shows a mixed public-private health care system, Sweden (Evert Gummesson), which shows a largely publicly funded and universal health care system, have been invited, as well as from Ireland (Gerardine Doyle) and the United Kingdom (Michael Drummond) which adopt a mainly Beveridgean health model.

Young promising scholars, bringing their fresh vision to inspire the future shapes of the health care system, have joined outstanding scientists, who can bring a long experience and a deep knowledge of the health care system. Among others, Michael Drummond is considered the founder of Health Economic Evaluation and author of several papers published in leading journals of the field, Editor-in-Chief of Value in Health; Evert Gummesson, Emeritus Professor of Service Marketing and Management at the Stockholm Business School, is an international pioneer in the field of service and one of the fathers of leadership in service. Also, we included eminent scientists from other disciplines: Engineering (Cristina Masella), Medicine (Annamaria Colao), and Philosophy (Matteo Motterlini).

We did not want to confine the discussion to the realm of academic conversation, so we also invited practitioners who cope every day with the challenges of increasingly complex health care systems, able to contextualize their reflections by connecting to concrete examples and practical activities. We included professionals and consultants who had experience in health care organizations: Vittorio Bertelè is a clinical pharmacologist, director of the regulatory policy at Mario Negri Institute; Enrico Coscioni, a renowned heart surgeon in Southern Italy, is advisor for the Campania's Health Systems, among the most problematic regional health services in Italy; Marina Davoli is the scientific director of the Italian National Health Outcome Program and director of the Department of Epidemiology of the Lazio regional health system, another regional health service in deep financial crisis; Chiara Marinacci is fellow of the General Directorate for Health Planning of the Italian Ministry of Health; Maurizio Mauri, a radiologist who was Health Director in some big hospitals in Northern Italy, is now a hospital planner; Joseph Polimeni, after having managed several health care organizations in Central Italy, is currently the State Sub-Commissioner for the financial recovery plan of the Campania Regional Health Service. The consulting industry is represented by Daniela Scaramuccia, who was the Ministry of Health in the Tuscany Region (4.5 million inhabitants), and Alberto Calvo, both affiliates of one of the chief consulting companies operating in the health sector (Value Partners Management Consulting). The pharmaceutical industry is also represented: among the contributors, we invited Maurizio De Cicco, Vice President of Farmindustria, accountable for leading innovation and Agenda talks with the Italian Medicine Agency.

We also invited a general, member of the Italian Airforce (Lt. Gen. Fernando Giancotti), currently Commander of the Air Education and Training Command, who published essays and textbooks on the US Air Force Leadership and a book in Italy widely used for education on leadership and change management.

Finally, we decided to invite key actors in the Italian health care arena, who are in a position to look at the broader system: Francesco Bevere, after having performed as a senior manager in different health care organizations operating both in the North and the South of Italy, and as head of the Health Planning Directorate of the Italian Ministry of Health, is currently the Director in chief of the National Health Agency (the consulting body for the Health Ministry); Renato Botti, after long experience as a senior manager of both for-profit and not-for-profit organizations, is now the chair of the Directorate of Health Planning of the Ministry of Health; Silvio Garattini is one of the most prestigious researchers in the field of pharmacology: in 1963 he founded the Mario Negri Institute, a not-for-profit research institute that is well known in the international scientific community; he was principal investigator of hundreds of studies in this field and was member of several national, European and international committees and regulatory agencies; Walter Ricciardi, Professor of Public Health, is member of the External Advisory Board to the WHO European Regional Director for the development of the European Health Policy, member of the National Committee for the evaluation of the Italian National Health Service, President of the Italian Higher Institute of Health; Maria Grazia Sampietro has long managerial experience in health and social services and is currently the Director in Chief of the Welfare Directorate of INPS (the Italian National Institute for Social Security); Umberto Veronesi is an outstanding oncologist surgeon who developed in late 1970 an innovative and less aggressive approach to breast cancer. He has also top management experience as director of the Italian Cancer Institute based in Milan: in 1982 he founded in Milan the private European Institute for Oncology (IEO). Last but not least, Umberto Veronesi was the Ministry of Health of the Italian Government from April 2000 to June 2001.

We selected the contributors in order to maximize the diversity of perspectives: different cultural backgrounds; different geographical areas; both academic and practitioners (sometimes the two cooperating in the same contribution); senior and junior positions.

A common element to all contributors is having encountered, at a certain point of their professional path, Mintzberg's provocations: some of them participated as discussants to the conferences organized in 2007 and 2010 at the University of Salerno. Others have been mentioning Mintzberg on other occasions, assuming different positions: from those who have been struck on the road to Damascus and fell in love with Mintzberg's theses, to those who were severely critical.

The outcome of this joint effort is presented in the second section of the volume, after an introductory section which includes an outline of health myths, as originally proposed by Henry Mintzberg, a historical analysis of their consolidation over the centuries, as elaborated by the two editors of the volume, as well as an overview of the comments proposed by the invited contributors. In the third section we build on the common points to provide the foundation of a rich, higher order reflection on the current changes and challenges in the health care arena. We conclude our trip into the complexity of health care management with no definitive answers but many questions.

As editors, we are extremely grateful to all the authors for having managed their contributions according to the requested terms and modalities. Academics are busy running their laboratories and classes; moreover, they are rewarded for producing science, rather than for reflecting on such production. Practitioners are also very busy running their organizations. Nevertheless, all the invited authors have unsparingly offered their time and intellectual energy by contributing to our editorial project. We also thank the practitioners and academics missing from the volume who could have legitimately participated in it. In some cases, a collaboration by them was sought but for one reason or another did not occur. In particular we thank Dr. Fulvio Moirano and Profs. Maria Aristigueta, Luca Anselmi and Simone Lazzini, who kindly welcomed our invitation, but could not complete the work. Although the issues involved have been covered by other contributions, we regret having lost the richness of their specific views.

We sought to avoid any possible influence on the content of the contributions (this attempt would anyway have been self-defeating), therefore we provided very poor indications: we just invited the contributors to comment on Mintzberg's article "Managing the myths of health care" (unfortunately, Mintzberg's complete manuscript was not yet available), focusing in particular on one of the myths, and adopting a fluid, discursive approach, without technicalities or specialized language. In some cases, we assisted the authors to elucidate and enlarge upon what they intuitively wanted to contribute. We have learned a lot along the way, so this collaboration has been one of the most rewarding aspects of editing the book.

Coordinating over 60 contributors has indeed been a huge enterprise, and our warmest thanks go to Dr. Rocco Palumbo, a promising young research fellow who unsparingly supported our efforts and put the contributions together.

Finally, our deep thanks to Henry Mintzberg, who inspired our editorial project, in that he tore the veil which constitutes at the same time a shroud and a shield disguising the true reality of health care management. We had the pleasure of meeting him personally, so we had the privilege of knowing him not only as scientist, but also as person. He came to the University of Salerno the first time in 2007, to illustrate his challenging arguments, and we still have a vivid memory of that day. He arrived on time, with a backpack on his shoulders and checked shirt. Moved by the reverent homages from deferent academic and institutional authorities, and the endless standing ovation and round of applause from an overcrowded hall, he felt he should put on a jacket and tie. With his humble smile and his willingness to learn, he was able to floor even the impeccable Chancellor, Prof. Raimondo Pasquino. Before an attentive audience, the Canadian "guru" started to illustrate with disarming simplicity his view on managing health care, highlighting the unescapable conundrums of management and crumbling the intellectual framework of health care management orthodoxy. To us, Henry Mintzberg appeared himself as a conundrum: a complex and provokingly simple scientist, a humble and refined speaker, an irreverent and respectful scholar, a generous teacher and an eager learner.

Fisciano, Italy
Milan, Italy
April 2017

Paola Adinolfi
Elio Borgonovi

The original version of the book was revised: Authors' affiliations have been updated. The erratum to the book is available at https://doi.org/10.1007/978-3-319-53600-2_15

Contents

Contributors

Paola Adinolfi Director of CIRPA (Interdepartmental Centre for Research in Economics, Law and Management of Public Administrations), University of Salerno, Fisciano, Salerno, Italy

Carmela Annarumma Department of Management & Innovation Systems, University of Salerno, Fisciano, Salerno, Italy

Patrizio Armeni Centre for Research in Health and Social Care Management (CERGAS), University "Luigi Bocconi," Milan, Italy

Vittorio Bertelè Laboratory of Drug Regulatory Policies, IRCCS Istituto di Ricerche Farmacologiche Mario Negri, Milan, Italy

Francesco Bevere AGENAS—National Agency for Health Services, Italian Ministry of Health, Rome, Italy

Elio Borgonovi Public Administration and Health Institute "Carlo Masini," University "Luigi Bocconi," Milan, Italy

Antonio Botti Department of Management & Innovation Systems, University of Salerno, Fisciano, Salerno, Italy

Renato Botti School of Management, Italian Ministry of Health, Rome, Italy

Stefano Calciolari Institute of Economics (IdEP), Università della Svizzera Italiana, Lugano, Switzerland

Alberto Calvo Value Partners Management Consulting S.P.a, Milan, Italy

Carlo Canepa Center for Research in Experimental and Applied Epistemology, University Vita-Salute San Raffaele, Milan, Italy

Oriana Ciani Centre for Research in Health and Social Care Management (CERGAS), University "Luigi Bocconi," Milan, Italy

Maurizio de Cicco Chairman of the Board of Directors, Managing Director Roche, Italy; Vice President of Farmindustria, Monza, Italy

Mariavittoria Cicellin Department of Economics, Management and Institutions, University of Naples Federico II, Naples, Italy

Ettore Cinque Department of Economics and Management, Università degli Studi della Campania "Luigi Vanvitelli", Caserta, Italy

Anna Maria Livia Colao Department of Clinical Medicine and Surgery, University of Naples Federico II, Naples, Italy

Stefano Consiglio Department of Social Sciences, University of Naples Federico II, Naples, Italy

Enrico Coscioni Department of Ascending Aorta and Thoracic Surgery, University Hospital "San Giovanni e Ruggi d'Aragona," Salerno, Italy

Corrado Cuccurullo Department of Economics, Universita' degli Studi Della Campania "Luigi Vanvitelli," Capua, Caserta, Italy

Antonio D'Andreamatteo Department of Management and Business Administration, University "G.d'Annunzio" of Chieti, Pescara, Italy

Marina Davoli Director of the Department of Epidemiology ASL ROMA1, Lazio Region, Operational center of the National Outcome Programme for the National Agency of Regional Health Services, Rome, Italy

Luca Del Bene Department of Management, Polytechnic University of Marche, Ancona, Italy

Gerardine Doyle College of Business, University College Dublin, Belfield, Dublin, Ireland

Michael Drummond Centre for Health Economics, University of York, York, North Yorks, UK

Vincenza Esposito Department of Law, Economics, Management and Quantitative Methods, University of Sannio, Benevento, Italy

Giuseppe Favretto Department of Management, Università Degli Studi Di Verona, Verona, Italy

Giuseppe Festa Department of Economic and Statistical Sciences, University of Salerno, Fisciano, Salerno, Italy

Silvio Garattini Directorate, IRCCS Istituto di Ricerche Farmacologiche Mario Negri, Milan, Italy

Lt. Gen. Fernando Giancotti Commander, Italian Air Force Air Education and Training Command, Bari, Italy

Evert Gummesson School of Business, Stockholm University, Stockholm, Sweden

Mario Pezzillo Iacono Department of Economics, Università degli Studi della Campania "Luigi Vanvitelli", Caserta, Italy

Luca Ianni Department of Management and Business Administration, University "G.d'Annunzio" of Chieti, Pescara, Italy

Giuseppe Iuliano Department of Management & Innovation Systems, University of Salerno, Fisciano, Salerno, Italy

Francesca Lecci Department of Policy Analysis and Public Management, Bocconi University, Milan, Italy

Federico Lega Department of Public Policy & Management, SDA Bocconi School of Management, Milan, Italy

Emanuele Lettieri Department of Management, Economics and Industrial Engineering, Politecnico di Milano, Milan, Italy

Gianluigi Mangia Department of Economics, University of Naples "Federico II", Naples, Italy

Chiara Marinacci Health Planning General Directorate of the Italian Ministry of Health, Rome, Italy

Marcello Martinez Department of Economics, Università degli Studi della Campania "Luigi Vanvitelli", Caserta, Italy

Cristina Masella Department of Management, Economics and Industrial Engineering, Politecnico di Milano, Milan, Italy

Gaetano Matonti Department of Management & Innovation Systems, University of Salerno, Fisciano, Salerno, Italy

Maurizio Mauri "CERBA" Foundation (Centro Europeo Ricerca Biomedica Avanzata), Milan, Italy

Lorenzo Mercurio Department of Law, Economics, Management and Quantitative Methods, University of Sannio, Benevento, Italy

Riccardo Mercurio Department of Economics, Management and Institutions, University of Naples Federico II, Naples, Italy

Henry Mintzberg Desautels Faculty of Management, McGill University, Montreal, Canada

Marco Morelli Corporate and Real Estate Finance Department, SDA Bocconi School of Management, Milan, Italy

Luigi Moschera Department of Business and Economics, University of Naples Parthenope, Naples, Italy

Matteo Motterlini Philosophy Department, Center for Experimental and Applied Epistemology, University Vita-Salute San Raffaele, Milan, Italy

Sabina Nuti Management and Healthcare Laboratory, Sant'Anna School of Advanced Studies, Pisa, Italy

Rocco Palumbo Department of Management & Innovation Systems, University of Salerno, Fisciano, Salerno, Italy

Gabriella Piscopo Department of Management & Innovation Systems, University of Salerno, Fisciano, Salerno, Italy

Joseph Polimeni Siena University Hospital, Siena, Italy

Anna Prenestini Centre for Research in Health and Social Care Management (CERGAS), University "Luigi Bocconi," Milan, Italy

Walter Ricciardi WHO Collaborating Centre for Health Policy, Governance and Leadership in Europe, Institute of Public Health, Catholic University of the Sacred Heart of Rome, Rome, Italy

Pasquale Antonio Riccio Health Campus NPO, Naples, Italy

Salvatore Russo Department of Management, University of Venice, Venice, Italy

Maria Grazia Sampietro National Social Security Institute, Rome, Italy

Alessio Santoro Department of Public Health and Infectious Diseases, University of Rome La Sapienza, Rome, Italy

Massimo Sargiacomo Department of Management and Business Administration, University "G.d'Annunzio" of Chieti, Pescara, Italy

Daniela Scaramuccia Value Partners Management Consulting S.P.a, Milan, Italy

Andrea Silenzi WHO Collaborating Centre for Health Policy, Governance and Leadership in Europe, Institute of Public Health, Catholic University of the Sacred Heart of Rome, Rome, Italy

Alessandra Storlazzi University "Suor Orsola Benincasa" - Facoltà di Scienze della Formazione, Naples, Italy

Rosanna Tarricone Department of Policy Analysis and Public Management, Centre for Research in Health and Social Care Management (CERGAS), Bocconi University, Milan, Italy

Paolo Tartaglia Polcini Executive Committee CIRPA (Interdepartmental Centre for Research in Economics, Law and Management of Public Administrations), University of Salerno, Fisciano, Salerno, Italy

Aurelio Tommasetti Department of Management & Innovation Systems, University of Salerno, Fisciano, Salerno, Italy

Aleksandra Torbica Department of Policy Analysis and Public Management, and Senior Researcher, Centre for Research in Health and Social Care Management (CERGAS), Bocconi University, Milan, Italy

Mario Del Vecchio School of Medicine, University of Florence, Florence, Italy; Director of the Observatory on Private Healthcare Consumption OCPS-SDA, Bocconi University, Milan, Italy

Emanuele Vendramini DISES—Department of Economic and Social Disciplines, Catholic University of the Sacred Heart, Piacenza, Italy

Umberto Veronesi European Institute of Oncology, Milan, Italy

Massimiliano Vesci Department of Management & Innovation Systems, University of Salerno, Fisciano, Salerno, Italy

About the Editors

Paola Adinolfi (BA in Bocconi University; MA in Warwick University-Industrial Relation Research Unit; PhD in Birmingham University-Institute of Local Governments) is Full Professor of Organization Studies at the University of Salerno in Italy. Formerly, the Director of the Department of Management & Information Technology, she now chairs the Interdepartmental Centre for Research in Law, Economics and Management of Public Administrations (CIRPA). Since the 2000s, Paola has been directing the PhD programme in "Management of Public Organizations" and the Master course "Leadership in Healthcare Services" (DAOSan), organized by the University of Salerno with Campania Region, University of Naples, and University of Sannio. DAOSan ex-alumni represents a renowned and dynamic community of practitioners in healthcare management in Southern Italy. She has been elected to the board of ASSIOA, the Italian Association of Organization Studies, and of *Azienda Pubblica*, the leading Italian journal on public management, and is a member of other scientific boards and committees in public agencies and academic journals regarding her fields of competence: public management, healthcare management, and organization and human resource management.

Elio Borgonovi is Full Professor of public administration, and healthcare and not-for-profit organization management at Bocconi University in Milan, Italy. After graduating from Bocconi University, he has been a researcher, Associate Professor, and then Full Professor at Bocconi University and Parma and Trento State University. In 1978, he founded the healthcare and social services management research center (CERGAS) and the public administration, healthcare, not-for-profit division at SDA Bocconi School of Management. In his career, he has been Director and President of CERGAS, SDA Dean, President of ASFOR (the Italian Association of School of Management), Vice President of AIDEA (the Italian Academy of Management), member of the board of EFMD (European Foundation for Management Development), and EQUIS (European Quality Improvement System). In the early 1990s, he designed and promoted an innovative 4-year bachelor program at Bocconi on public administration and international organization economics and management, currently GIO (Government and International Organization) Master of Science. Over the last 45 years, he was a member of several advisory boards, committees, and research groups in both public administration and healthcare authority at local, regional, and national levels; and a member of scientific boards of national and international journals. Currently, he is Director of the laboratory on health services performance at AGENAS, the national technical agency for healthcare services.

Part I
Managing in Health Care: Cues and Reflections

Chapter 1
Managing the Myths of Health Care

Henry Mintzberg

1.1 The Myths of Health Care

Myths abound in management, for example that senior managers sit on "top" (of what?), that leaders are more important than managers (try leading without managing), and that people are human resources (I am a human being). Myths abound in what is called the system of health care too, not least that it is a system, and is about the care of health (mostly it is a collection of treatments for disease). Combine these two sets of myths, as is increasingly common these days, and you end up with the mess we now face in the world of health care.

Let us begin with the myths of managing now prevalent in health care and then turn to some reframing that may help to escape this mess.

Myth #1: The health care system is failing. Speak to people almost anywhere in the world and they will tell you how their system of health care is failing. The truth is quite the opposite: In most places in the developed world, health care is succeeding—expensively. In other words, success is the problem, not failure. Consult almost any statistic. We are living longer, losing fewer infants, and so on, in large part because of advances in treatments. The trouble is that many of these are expensive, and we do not want to pay for them—certainly not as healthy people through our insurance premiums or taxes. So health care services get squeezed, and it looks like the system is failing. In fact, as we shall discuss below, the problems are not in the health care services themselves so much as in the consequences of our

Source: Mintzberg H. Managing the Myths of Health Care. World Hospitals and Health Services: The Official Journal of the International Hospital Federation 2012; 48(3):4–7.

H. Mintzberg (✉)
Desautels Faculty of Management, McGill University, 1001 Sherbrooke West, Montreal H3A 1G5, Canada
e-mail: hm@mcgill.ca; henry.mintzberg@mcgill.ca

P. Adinolfi and E. Borgonovi (eds.), *The Myths of Health Care*,
https://doi.org/10.1007/978-3-319-53600-2_1

interventions to fix this ostensible failure. We consider three interventions in particular: social engineering, leadership, and business practice.

Myth #2: The health care system can be fixed by clever social engineering. The system is broken so the "experts" have to fix it: usually not people on the ground, who understand the problems viscerally, but specialists in the air, such as economists, system analysts, and consultants, who believe they understand them conceptually. Thanks to them, in health care we measure and merge like mad, reorganize constantly, apply the management technique of the month, "reinvent" health care every few years, and drive change from the "top" for the sake of participation at the bottom. Do all this and all will be well, we are told. But is it ever? In particular, at this so-called bottom, the real experts struggle to cope with the pressures, not least from these very "solutions," most of which seem to make things increasingly convoluted. What if, instead, we came to appreciate that effective change in health care has to come largely out of the operations, and diffuse across them rather than forced down into them? Consider, for example, the changes in recent times that have made the greatest differences, not only in cutting costs—that is the easy part—but also in improving quality. Day surgeries have to be near the top of that list. This idea came from engaged clinicians, not detached social engineers.

Myth #3: Health care institutions as well as the overall system can be fixed by bringing in the heroic leader. New leadership can certainly help, at least when it replaces a leadership that was worse. But what does effective leadership mean in a field where the professionals have so much of the power? In hospitals, for example, physicians are usually far more responsive to their own hierarchies of professional status than the managerial hierarchies of formal authority. Hence what can be called "heroic leadership," so fashionable now in business (witness the whole system of bonuses), can be bad for health care, let alone for business itself. Far more necessary is what can be called engaging management: managers who are deeply and personally engaged so as to be able to help engage others.

Myth #4: The health care system can be fixed by treating it more as a business. This is a particularly popular prescription in the United States. Perhaps no country on earth treats health care more as a business, or is more encouraging of competition in this field. But given America's current state of performance—far more expensive than anywhere else, with overall quality rankings that are mediocre—shall we take this as testimonial to the wonders of competition and business practices in the field of health care? The United States spends about 31¢ of every health care dollar on administration; Canada, with much less competition and far less of a business orientation in health care, spends about 17¢, and achieves better measures of quality. To quote from an article in the New York Times: "Duplicate processing of claims, large numbers of insurance products, complicated bill paying systems and high marketing costs [plus all the 'paperwork required of American doctors and hospitals that simply do not exist in countries like Canada or Britain'] add up to high administrative expenses" (Bernasek 2007). In the name of competition, American health care in fact suffers from individualization: every professional and every institution for his, her, or itself. So again, let us try it differently: Health care functions best as a calling, not a business; as such, it needs greater cooperation, not competition, among its many players and institutions. Physicians may be well paid, but these are smart people capable of earning large incomes elsewhere. What keeps many, if not most, of them in health care is the sense of service. This applies equally, if not more so, to the nurses, who do not earn that kind of money, and many of the managers too. What happens to health care as a calling when it is seen as "one-stop shopping," hospitals as "focused factories," patients as "customers" and "consumers," and physicians as "industry players" (as described by Herzlinger 2006)?

Myth #5 and 6: Health care is rightly left to the private sector, for the sake of efficiency. Health care is rightly controlled by the public sector, for the sake of equality. Take your choice, according to the country in which you live. In fact, if you live where the services are largely public, you hear a great deal about the private sector (as in Canada now). And if you live where they are largely private, then you hear a great deal about the public sector (as in the recent debates in the United States Congress). That is because, nowhere in the world today can the field of health care function without serious involvement of both government controls and market forces. Many Americans, and not only on talk radio shows, are sharply critical of the role of the state in health care. In two influential publications, Porter and Teisberg were highly dismissive of the state as a player in this field. Their book Reforming Health Care (2006) referred to government-controlled regulations as "never a real solution" (although it certainly is in most developed countries). Concerning the unsatisfactory performance of American health care over many years, they claimed in their related Harvard Business Review article (2004) that "while this may be expected in a state-controlled sector, it is nearly unimaginable in a competitive market." (Again, the facts suggest exactly the opposite.) Of particular importance is that many of the most important services in health care come from neither the public nor the private sector. Canada and the United States sit near the two extremes on this issue, yet the vast majority of hospitals in both countries are in the plural sector, namely in the form of organizations that are owned by no-one (so-called "voluntary" in the United States), and that includes the most prestigious. Efficiency and equality certainly matter in health care, but hardly more so than quality, which often seems to be delivered best by organizations that are autonomous—controlled neither by the state nor owned by private shareholders. Presumably this helps to reinforce the engagement of their professionals with regard to their sense of calling. Of course, all the sectors have a role to play in health care: the public sector, largely to maintain a certain level of equality (as in the new American legislation) as well as in regulation; the private sector, significantly to provide supplies and equipment as well as some of the more routine services; and the plural sector, for the delivery of many of the key professional services, including research. (And the latter might well include pharmaceuticals. In the twentieth century, arguably the three most significant pharmaceutical developments —penicillin, insulin, and Salk vaccine—all came out of not-for-profit laboratories.) The Myths of Measurement and of Scale Measurement is a fine idea, as long as it does not mesmerize the user. Unfortunately, it so often does: both managers who rely on it for control and physicians who believe that being "evidence-based" always has to trump being "experienced-based." Management and medicine alike have to balance these two in order to be effective. Unfortunately, too much of health care at both the administrative and clinical levels has been thrown out of balance by their obsessions with measurement. In the management of health care, the frustration of trying to control rather autonomous professionals has led the administrators and social engineers to a reliance on measurement. And this, it should be noted, is no less prevalent in private sector control by insurance companies and HMOs, etc., than in public sector control by government agencies. The problem with measurement is that, while the treatments exist in standard categories—certain medications for manic depression, particular forms of angioplasty for various heart conditions, etc—their outcomes are often not standard, and therefore can be tricky to pin down by measurement. That is because we as individual patients are not standardized, and so our treatments have to be tailored to our individual needs and conditions. It is often said that "If you can't measure it, you can't manage it." Well, who has ever adequately measured the performance of management? (Don't tell me it can be done by looking at a stock price.) In fact, who has ever even tried to measure the performance of measurement itself? I guess we must conclude therefore that neither management nor measurement can be managed. So what can be done if we cannot rely wholly on measurement? That's easy: use judgment. Remember judgment? Can you imagine medicine without judgment? Well, then, I suggest that you not try to imagine management without judgment either. Measurement favors large scale; in fact scale is measurement. So a society mesmerized by measurement is a society obsessed with large scale. Hence the small hospitals are the ones that get closed. Herzlinger wrote in her 2006 Harvard Business Review article that "Health care is still an astonishingly fragmented industry. More than half of the US physicians work in practices of three or fewer doctors; a quarter of the nation's 5000 community hospitals and nearly half of its 17,000 nursing homes are independent." But what is wrong with that? She added that "You can roll a number of independent players into a single organization…to generate economies of scale." Picture that! Notice the term: economies of scale. Not effectiveness of scale but economies of scale. Too much of the management of health care has come to be about using scale to reduce measurable costs at the expense of difficult-to-measure benefits. I am not trying to make the case that smaller is always more beautiful, only to plead that bigger is not always better. Scale, too, has to be judged, especially for its impact on performance. Health care as a calling works best in units that are as humanly small as the best of technology allows. This, in fact, seems to hold true even in pharmaceutical research. To quote Roger Gilmartin when he was chief executive of Merck: "Scale has been no indication of the ability to discover breakthrough drugs. In fact, it has been the other way—you get bogged down" (Clifford 2000). All of this suggests that it is time for some reframing in the management of health care. What follows is not social engineering so much as a suggested set of guidelines.

1.2 Reframing Management: As Distributed Beyond the "Top"

As noted at the outset, management on "top" is a myth. Aside from that ubiquitous chart, and those famous bonuses, what is management on top of exactly? Indeed, in hospitals, "top" managers often sit on the ground floor (perhaps to be able to make a quick getaway). Seeing yourself on top of an organization all too often means not being on top of what is going on in that organization. Should these top managers have the power to make decisions about the purchase of expensive equipment, independent of the physicians who use them? That hardly makes more sense than leaving those decisions to the physicians themselves. These are not financial decisions or technical decisions but hospital decisions, and so require collaboration on the part of managers and physicians. And, make no mistake about it, involvement in such decision-making places the physicians squarely in the realm of management—as soon as we get past the notion that management is something practiced only by people called managers. Many health care organizations require "distributed management," which means that managerial activities be performed by whoever has the necessary skills, knowledge, and perspective to carry them out most effectively—and that often means collaboratively.

1.3 Reframing Strategy: As Venturing, not Planning

If you want to understand what strategy means in a professional organization such as a hospital, stay away from almost all the strategy books. They tell you about strategic planning from the top; recognize instead strategic venturing at the base. If strategy concerns the positioning of products and services for users, then in a hospital the services are specific kinds of treatments for specific diseases. And where do these come from? Rarely from any "top" management and rarely in any planning process. They come mostly from the venturing activities of professionals: concern about a new disease here, championing of a new treatment there. In other words, the strategy of a hospital is largely the sum total of the many ventures of its professional staff. So here, especially, is where we see distributed management: Professionals on the ground, who are not managers, are responsible for most of the strategic initiatives in health care. Sure there are other, more conventional strategies determined at large—for example, about what services to offer and where to locate them. But much of that is built into the structure and history of the institution. Hospitals may engage in strategic planning, but a great deal of this, in my experience, does not amount to much. Too often it is just another indication of what can be called "the administrative gap"—the disconnect between the machinations of management and the operations of clinicians (Henry Mintzberg 1994, 2007).

1.4 Reframing Organization: As Collaboration Beyond Control, Communityship Beyond Leadership

With management as distributed and the strategy process as venturing, the nature of most health care organizations can be better understood. The prevailing model in business is what can be called the "machine organization": top-down, hierarchically focused, control-oriented, numbers-driven, and outputs-standardized. Managers rule. But a very different model, that can be called the "professional organization," is more common in health care: expert-driven, skills-oriented, and highly oriented to pigeonholing, which means getting the client into the right box (mania, hernia, etc.) so that the most appropriate intervention can be applied. Such pigeonholing describes the great strength of the professional organization as well as its debilitating weakness. The professionals get used to operating in their own pigeonholes, as free as possible of the influence of their own colleagues, let alone the controls of the managers. Unfortunately, as human patients we are sometimes square pegs forced into these round holes. Some of us have this habit of getting illnesses that cut across the disease categories, or worse still, that do not fit them well (as in auto-immune diseases). Then we require interventions that cut across the pigeonholes, which are often resisted by medical specialists used to operating within them. In other words, we need collaboration from people who are mostly inclined to avoid it. How to organize around this problem? The inclination has been to use solutions designed for the machine organization—centrally imposed control systems, performance measures, financial incentives and the like, or else expecting managers up the hierarchy to force the professionals to collaborate. But these hardly work well with independent professionals. Resistance to collaboration in the professional organization will more likely be overcome by drawing on the professionals' sense of calling, and enhancing their organization as a community of service. Put differently, when people are committed to their organization, and not just to their own profession, they are more likely to collaborate effectively. A good sense of this can be had from some comments made by Atul Gawande in one of his New Yorker articles on health care: The Mayo Clinic is among the highest quality, lowest cost healthcare systems in the country. A couple of years ago, I spent several days there as a visiting surgeon. Among the things that stand out from that visit was how much time the doctors spent with patients. There was no churn—no shuttling patients in and out of rooms while the doctor bounces from one to the other. The core tenant of the Mayo Clinic is "The need of the patient first"—not the convenience of the doctors, not their revenues. The doctors and nurses, and even the janitors, sat in meetings almost weekly, working on ideas to make the service and the care better, not to get more money out of patients decades ago Mayo recognized that the first thing it needed to do was eliminate the financial barriers. It pooled all the money the doctors and the hospital system received and began paying everyone a salary, so that the doctors' goal in patient care could not be increasing their income almost by happenstance, the result has been lower costs (Gawande 2009, pp. 14–15).

1.5 Reframing Scale: As Human Beyond Economic

None of the guidelines suggested above are helped by large scale—not community, not engagement, not collaboration, not closing the gap between administration and operations. Nor does large scale help to humanize the practice of medicine. There can, of course, be technical reasons to favor large scale, for example, in order to purchase necessary expensive equipment. This suggests that we should no more reject large scale than embrace it. But the unfortunate fact is that, because of our mesmerization with measurement, far too often we embrace large scale, conveniently forgetting the human factors. Imagine if we made small scale the default position, so to speak—in other words put the onus on the proponents of large scale, in health care institutions as well as in health authorities, to make their case for scale on social grounds, judgmentally as well as numerically, beyond the technical and economic grounds.

1.6 Reframing Managing Style: As Caring More Than Curing

Nursing, focused on care, may be a more appropriate model for managing than medicine, focused on cure. Our health care institutions, in other words, require care more than cure: the engagement of their managers to help them function more smoothly, rather than having the power of heroic leaders to run around fixing things. There was a cartoon once that showed a group of surgeons around a patient on an operation table, with the line "Who opens?" In medicine, we know who opens; in management often we do not—not even if someone should open. That is why management has to be a fundamentally cooperative practice, of a style far from heroic leadership. Managing in health care should be about devoted, continuous, holistic and pre-emptive care more than interventionist, episodic, narrow, and radical cures.

1.7 Reframing Managing Style: As a System Beyond Its Parts

I opened this article with the claim that we do not have a system of health care so much as a collection of disease treatments. Even my own examples have come largely from the latter. (Hospitals, it should be remembered, account for only about 30 percent of health care expenditures.) Especially the promotion of health, but also the prevention of disease, are muscled aside by our focus on the treatment of disease, even though investment in the former can be far more cost-effective. An ad appeared some years ago for SAP Canada, headed "This is not a cow." It showed a picture of a cow, with lines drawn where it would be quartered, with the text: "This is an organizational chart that shows the different parts of a cow." In a real cow the parts are not aware that they are parts. They do not have trouble sharing information. They smoothly and naturally work together, as one unit. As a cow. And you have only one question to answer. "Do you want your organization to work like a chart? Or a cow?" Why can't health care work like a cow: why can it not be a true system of cooperation and collaboration? Note that the parts of a cow are not "seamless." They are distinct, necessarily so. But in a healthy cow, they work together harmoniously. Can this happen in health care? I believe so, and have been working with colleagues for some years to that end. Our management and medical schools at McGill University have teamed up to create a master program for health leadership that seeks to encourage all of these guidelines (www.mcgill.ca/imhl). It brings practicing managers from all over the world in all aspects of health care—hospitals, community care, public health, government ministries, etc., most of them with clinical backgrounds—together in an ongoing forum that meets periodically over a year and a half to address the major issues of health care. These include

- The Gap Issue: How to bring the administration of health care closer to the operations, connecting it for support beyond control?
- The Collaboration Issue: How to get the different parts of health care working in greater cooperative harmony?
- The Engagement Issue: How to enhance engagement through the promotion of human scale beyond economic scale?
- The Sector Issue: What are the appropriate roles of the three sectors, especially the plural sector that sits between the now dominant public and private sectors?
- The Performance Issue: How to balance the intrinsic needs for efficiency, equality, and quality in health care?

We have been especially struck by the natural propensity of managers in such a program to work together on such issues, reaching out beyond their own personal needs and those of their institutions, into their local communities and out to the needs of health care in general. On a number of occasions, groups in the class have brought into our forum key issues of concern in their communities, to enable the class to address them in a process we call "friendly consulting." A group of managers from Quebec, for example, invited the three commissioners of a major government health care commission into the class for a workshop on some of these issues. And two physician managers from Uganda brought our classroom to a conference they organized in Kampala for 60 health care managers from seven African countries, on the subject of how to scale up their management infrastructures. What this has made clear is that an immense amount of energy and goodwill exists in the field of health care, to work collaboratively to render it more effective, on both the local and the global levels. We just need to get past the myths.

References

Bernasek A (2007) U.S. health care debate burdened by ideology: suspicion stalls single payer insurance. International Herald Tribune, p 11

Clifford A (2000) Tyrannosaurus Rx. Fortune 142(10):84–91

Gawande A (2009) The cost conundrum: what a Texas town can teach us about health care. The New Yorker. Retrieved 22 Feb 2010 from http://www.newyorker.com/reporting/2009/06/01/090601fa_fact_gawande

Herzlinger RE (2006) Why Innovation in health care is so hard. Harv Bus Rev 84(5):58–66

Mintzberg H (1994) The rise and fall of strategic planning. The Free Press, New York

Mintzberg H (2007) Tracking strategies…toward a general theory. Oxford University Press, Oxford

Porter ME, Teisberg EO (2004) Redefining competition in health care. Harv Bus Rev 82(6):65–76

Porter ME, Teisberg EO (2006) Redefining health care: creating value-based competition on results. Harvard Business Press, Watertown

Chapter 2
The Historical Evolution of Health Concepts and Approaches: The Challenge of Complexity

Paola Adinolfi and Elio Borgonovi

2.1 Introduction

An adage says that "myth is more potent than history" (Fulghum 1988, p. vii). Indeed, the myths of health care identified by Henry Mintzberg (2012) have proven to be stronger than both history and reality. They have played, and still play, a significant role in affecting health policies and practices, influencing the shapes of health care systems. The belief that the health care system is failing, the assumption that it could be fixed by detached social engineering and heroic leadership, the idea that public health care guarantees equality, while private health care ensures efficiency, the blind trust in the healing role of management models drawn on the for-profit sector, the emphasis on scale and measurement: all these are common prescriptions to cure the illness of current health care systems.

It is interesting to reconstruct, through an analysis of secondary sources, the period and the context in which these ideas emerged, and how they have affected

---

This chapter is a re-elaborated and enriched version of two articles previously published in Health care Analysis. In particular, this chapter is drawn on: Adinolfi, P. (2014). Barriers to Reforming Health care: The Italian Case. Health care Analysis, 22(1), 36-58 and Adinolfi, P. (2014). Philosophy, Medicine and Health care: Insights from the Italian Experience, Health care Analysis, 22(3), 223–244.

P. Adinolfi (✉)
CIRPA (Interdepartmental Centre for Research in Economics, Law and Management of Public Administrations), University of Salerno, Fisciano, SA, Italy
e-mail: padinolfi@unisa.it

E. Borgonovi
Public Administration and Health Institute "Carlo Masini", University "Luigi Bocconi" of Milan, Milan, Italy
e-mail: elio.borgonovi@unibocconi.it

P. Adinolfi and E. Borgonovi (eds.), *The Myths of Health Care*,
https://doi.org/10.1007/978-3-319-53600-2_2

medical and health care models over the course of time, thus leading to the consolidation of what Henry Mintzberg calls "myths."

In this chapter, medical and health care models are diachronically examined to evaluate their relationship to the sets of beliefs identified as myths. This is an innovative perspective, considering that historical analyses of medicine and health care are typically intra-disciplinary and do not touch upon any underpinning foundations. The analytical narrative focuses on the unfolding over the centuries of the various myths. In the limited space available, only a synthetic outline can be presented, with the unavoidable consequence of oversimplifying complex phenomena; such an account is indeed sufficient to show that the sets of beliefs identified by Henry Mintzberg have significantly affected the functioning of health care systems in developed countries. These myths, being strongly conceived on a subconscious level, have had insidious effects on the broad concepts of "medicine" and "management."

In particular, we can say, although bearing in mind the limits involved in the simplification and modelling of complex ideas into schemes, that the myth of heroic leader and the myth of measurement, which emerged in remote historical epochs, have consolidated over the centuries and blended with the other myths, reinforcing one another until assuming the current configuration of coherent frameworks that can be subsumed under the models of "biomedicine" and "scientific management."

2.2 Healers as Heroic Leaders in Archaic Societies

The belief that "not only health but the overall system can be fixed by bringing in the heroic leader" (discussed in Chap. 6) can be traced back to archaic societies, where the healers had the attributes of heroic leaders in the sense intended by Henry Mintzberg. A common element of all the archaic healing cultures—Mesopotamic (3000 a.c.–2000 a.c.), Assyro-Babylonian (1792 a.c.–323 a.c.), Egyptian (3000 a.c.–2000 a.c.), Hebrew (1200 a.c.–550 a.c.)—was the recourse to the heroic figure of healers, who could solve health problems (and also more general problems) with their miraculous virtues and absolute wisdom deriving from their relationship with the supernatural.

Illness was seen as overwhelming and linked to the action of supernatural entities. According to this "theurgical model," divinities, offended by human behavior, allowed malevolent entities to take control of an individual's body or hint it with an object (a caterpillar, a stone, a sting). As a result, healers had to try to calm down the fury of the gods, acting as intercessors by means of superstitious practices, exorcisms, and mass offerings.

Related to the "theurgical" model, was the "magic" model of medicine. Magic was Man's attempt to control, through irrational practices, the shadowy forces around him. Not rejecting the transcendent, the "magic" model acknowledged the validity of experiential remedies (amulets, individual or group rituals, gestures, herbal blends and potions) and conferred ever greater honours to healers.

In this framework, medical care could not be considered from a commercial perspective: healers acted not on the basis of scientific knowledge, but by virtue of a supernaturally endowed gift; therefore they were not trained in the art of medicine, but rather were consecrated by ancestral faith healers, by virtue of a miraculous event linked to their birth or by what was considered a divine calling.

These "heroic leaders" considered Man in his wholeness and showed moral virtues consonant with their relationship with the transcendent. The extraordinary moral standing of healers was not significantly affected by the progressive abandoning of supernatural explanations in favour of a gradual repositioning within the domain of natural causes. Healers were increasingly substituted by schooled professionals who had the same heroic connotation and moral standing apart from the relationship with the transcendent: it is significant that in Babylonian times the Scribes abandoned the incurables while the healers treated them until their death.

2.3 Health Care as Private Profession in Ancient Times

In ancient times, the figure of the healer, who acted by virtue of his relationship with the transcendent, was progressively substituted by that of the private doctor, who acted on the basis of the scientific knowledge, assimilated through a long-lasting training. This evolution coincided with the development of a medical *tekne*, namely a body of theoretical and empirical knowledge managed by professionals, which can be put in relation to a ground-breaking cultural change: the occurrence of a deep fracture between Man and Nature: Man discovered himself to be an external actor able to control, by means of rational thought, the rest of Nature.

Hippocrates was the forerunner of this new approach, which rejected the supernatural and introduced clinical medicine, based on the observation, elaboration and reproduction of natural phenomena. He advocated a rational approach as opposed to the theurgic-magic conception of medicine: any possibility for divinities to provoke illness was refuted, as well as any validity for therapeutic activity aimed at awakening the pity of the divinities, while attention was paid to discovering the natural causes of illnesses. Doctors, endowed with specific intellectual and technical competences, had to address the condition of the patient in each specific situation, from a holistic perspective. The holistic approach typical of theurgic and magic medical models consolidated and led to the concept of complexity, according to which each organism is an open network of relationships and, therefore, a rich variety of elements—diet, psychology, social relations, experiences, hygiene, dreams, etc.—are to be considered when investigating the causes of illness.

Unlike the archaic age, an antagonistic attitude towards illnesses emerged, as proved by the frequent use of metaphors of war related to medicine. This was reflected in the doctor–patient relationship, as summed up in the Hippocratic Oath (the first deontological code of conduct, sworn by doctors and other health care practitioners professing to practice medicine ethically): it reveals how doctors exercised absolute power, making decisions for their patients, not informing them, not considering their preferences, not looking for consensus, not accounting to them (or to anybody) for diagnostic and therapeutic decisions.

Another pioneering figure was Galen, who added to the empirical observation the experimental method, thus further enriching the complex medical model. He suggested the existence of a strict link between physiology, personality and the external environment: for example, he asserted that bodily humours had not simply a biological fluid function, but also depended on the character as well as on the physical and sociopolitical environment.

Summing up, in ancient times there was the consolidation of the complex holistic conception of Man and the emergence of the idea (discussed in Chap. 8) of health care as a private service provided by ad hoc trained professionals. The fruitful merger of the scientific vocation of the Greeks with the efficient organization of the Romans led to the development of clinical medicine and to the construction of the first operating theatres and hospitals—the so-called valetudinaria—as structures of assistance created (prevalently in frontier areas) to treat and heal wounded legionnaires. These were mainly used by rich people to cure their relatives and slaves in a private, commercial framework.

2.4 Divine Engineering in the Middle Ages

The Middle Ages witnessed exploratory trends that went beyond the familiar to enter the sphere of the transcendent. In the Christian conception of the period, the main emphasis was no longer on a mysterious, unpredictable world, nor a knowable and controllable world, but an incommensurably distant God. All this had a marked impact both on medical theory and practice. From a religious perspective, only God, as Creator, could have a full comprehension of the universe, and significant aspects of the world (including illnesses) would forever remain mysterious and uncontrollable by Man.

Illness was seen as a natural occurrence related to the frailty of Man, represented by Adam's original sin and the fall from Eden. The biblical idea of disease was reinstated (substituting the notion of fault with that of sinful behavior). Pain was welcome as a way to amend sins. The new meaning that suffering acquired within the theological perspective stimulated attitudes of resignation and prayer rather than efforts towards treatment: healing was regarded as a function of God's grace.

Along with the rise of this new approach, the health care based on the valetudinaria model was challenged: the first hospitals in the fifteenth century were aimed at providing shelter for sick people who could not privately be assisted, because poor. These hospitals, deficient in terms of structural and hygienic conditions, as well as in terms of quality of care, were richly endowed with sculptures, paintings and works of art. The latter most probably had a therapeutic value: the biographical documents of the epoch show how, in order to lessen suffering, wide recourse was made to paintings of the Crucifixion, while during surgical operations—performed under extremely painful conditions—extracts from the Bible and from the lives of martyrs were read aloud.

Under the control of the Church, a new body of medical knowledge developed, which was detached from the reality of patient and founded on a top-down, unidirectional relationship between patients and doctors. The Church established what could be good or bad for the body and soul, thus expropriating doctors from the faculty of deciding what could be considered useful for healing the sick. Doctors were obliged to remain celibate (until 1452) and to ask for the permission of a priest to be allowed to cure patients (only after verifying that patients had previously confessed their sins, and by adhering to the detached model of health care). Detachment as regards bodily functions derived from the idea that the body was not only the fruit of divine creation but also an obstacle on the path towards God, in conflict with the soul, therefore there was a limit to hygienic procedures which were linked with bodily contact.

This detached model of health care questioned the so-called "popular medicine," a range of consolidated holistic medical and nursing practices focused on a visceral knowledge of body/soul, provided by popular healers such as the barbitonsor, cerusicus, cataract couchers, lithotomists, phlebothomists, herniotomists, booth-surgeons. Holistic healing practices were also carried out by the so-called vetulae (in Latin "old women")—who possessed "first hand" knowledge of the body, due to their experience of childbirth and motherhood and to their daily "routines" for "survival." The knowledge possessed by these vetulae was strongly refused by the Church, which declared that any woman daring to dispense medical care without prior medical education was a "witch" and, consequently, to be condemned to death.

This is the cultural basis of what Henry Mintzberg (2012) calls "the myth of clever social engineering" (see Chap. 5): "the health system can be fixed by experts, not people on the ground, who understand the problems viscerally, but specialists in the air, such as economists, system analysts and consultants." The Medieval doctors can be considered the first "specialists in the air": specialists of sanitas corporis and salus animae, who dispensed a detached, top-down care in conformity with the reigning perspective of the Church—the only faster mother that Science could find (Fielding 1913, p. 112). Later this detached, top-down conception will be consolidated in the development of modern medicine and will pass from medicine to health care, leading to a centralist approach to the administration of care, both at a macro- and a micro-level.

2.5 Mechanism and Measurement in the Modern Age

The modern age was the epoch of secularization: the starting point was not any more God, but Man, with his autonomy and possibility of exercising full control over natural phenomena. In the late sixteenth century, Bacon theorized that, through a "new" science, a powerful understanding of an essentially ordered physical world could be gained. This view was reinforced in the Newtonian mechanistic view of the world and continued to develop in the physical sciences throughout the eighteenth and nineteenth centuries, combined with a triumphal vision of unlimited scientific progress. On the other hand, the medieval dualistic conception of body and soul consolidated during the Renaissance and reached its peak in the eighteenth century with the Cartesian idea of Man as a soul separated from the body and isolated from the external environment. The concept was then widely assumed and explored by many philosophers, from Locke to modern existentialists. Separations and dichotomies became fundamental pillars of modernity.

These ideas had a profound impact on the conception of medicine and of health/illness, stimulating the belief in the possibility of exercising full control over illnesses, with its potential for creating a new order of knowledge that relied on the possibility of measurement.

The ideal of objectivity gradually began to gain ground within medical disciplines, involving a scientific approach to the human body and, at the same time, its separation from subjective factors. While in the Middle Ages the dichotomy body/soul had been resolved by emphasizing the spiritual elements, in modern times there was an increasing focus on the organic components of pathologies. The human body was considered a machine, and health linked to its smooth functioning. A biomechanical approach, based on the application of the laws of physics, mechanics and chemistry to organic processes, took hold within medicine and established the research agenda for three centuries. It led to huge progresses in therapies, but also to an increasingly reductionist concept of medicine and an impoverished notion of the doctor–patient relationship.

In this context, hospitals were the fulcrum of the health care system, designed to pursue research and clinical aims, rather than charity and humanitarianism. They were consequently designed according to the rules of hygiene and hospital engineering, structured in relation to the scientific disciplines and organized in compliance with the bureaucratic hierarchical model. The latter was functional to specialization and research objectives, and favoured the development of clinical knowledge, but produced a focus on diseases rather than on patients, perfectly in line with the scientific conception of medicine and health/illness that had gradually been consolidating.

Hospitals were considered not only a treatment center, but also laboratories for the study of diseases to develop new knowledge and competencies, and, therefore, were completely separated from the daily lives of patients, clearly distinguishing the scientific knowledge (deriving from the academic disciplines) from the "non-scientific" knowledge (deriving from socio-cultural and environmental elements). A series of new techniques were introduced, such as the analytical observation of patients, the recording of a thorough description of their case histories and symptoms, the comparative study of clinical symptoms and anatomical lesions, the statistical recording of syndromes and the measurement of pathological phenomena by means of metric criteria. All these techniques were founded on the myth of measurement (discussed in Chap. 10) which consecrated hospitals as sanctuaries of objectivity and experimental knowledge.

The above trend accelerated during the nineteenth century, encouraged as it was by pharmacological and technological developments. On the one hand, progress in bacteriology strengthened the dualistic notion of illness as a conflict between two opposing entities: the pathogenic micro-organism and the healthy macro-organism (later, the discovery of antibiotics added “therapeutic certainty” to the “causal certainty”). On the other hand, technological progress, notwithstanding its unquestionable benefits, amplified the divide between doctors and patients, further impoverishing their relationship.

2.6 Health in the Twentieth Century

The twentieth century can be considered the century of a new complexity, which has had a profound impact on medical and health care models.

The paradigm of modern science and, in particular, the triumphal vision of progress started to be questioned, as awareness of vulnerability and risks increased, favouring the progressive affirmation of a more complex and moderate relationship between Man and Nature, not in terms of control, but rather of harmony and interdependence. At the same time, the modern conception of Man based on the dichotomy body/soul was being discussed critically, and a more holistic vision of Man as the product of multiple linked factors emerged. Consequently, a new holistic conception of health, in line with the new conception of Man and his relationship with Nature, started to take shape in most Western societies.

This cultural revolution evolved jointly with other developments in the epidemiological field. While acute infectious illnesses declined, new pathologies emerged, generated by complex and combined causes, partly unknown and characterized by no clear pharmaceutical remedy. In addition, the abuse of antibiotics provoked the chronicization of pathogenic processes, and the transformation of the fight against bacteria from a patchy battle to a prolonged war, with neither winners nor losers. The epidemiological transformation promoted the epistemological change of medicine from a criterion of strong causality, typical of infectious diseases, to that of weak causality, typical of chronic degenerative pathologies.

The discovery of X-Rays at the end of the nineteenth century, the technological improvement of diagnostic tests, new and more effective drugs, advanced imaging equipment, the use of sophisticated devices and medical technology for treatment and rehabilitation, on the one hand, helped doctors to be more effective in early diagnosis and treatments, while, on the other hand, generated the risk of anonymous doctor–patient relationships. An increasing number of doctors started to rely more and more on test results, normality range for glycaemia, cholesterol, blood cells composition, blood pressure and others, rather than on their own capacity to consider the patient as a whole. The advancement of technologies pushed towards an extreme specialization, which could be managed in more and more complex delivery organizations, such as the ambulatory with many specialists, the hospital with dozen of specialized units, hundreds of beds for inpatient units and for outpatient treatment, thousands of doctors, nurses, professionals and administrative staff. Doctors, nurses, other professionals, patients and their relatives had to comply to the formal rules of the organization and, because of that, personal relationships became weaker. Continuity of care was not guaranteed and only under certain conditions patients could ask to be treated by one specific doctor.

The twentieth century is also characterized, at least in Europe and Western developed countries, by the development of sickness funds, social insurance funds (voluntary or compulsory), private insurance integrated with national health systems (based on the principles of universal coverage, equity, solidarity), private insurance integrated by public financed programs for poor, elderly and disable people (US). For this reason hospitals and other delivery organizations, public or private, are conditioned by whole-system rules, such as structural and functional requirements, manpower standards in relation to beds, parameters related to funding or reimbursement systems (DRG's, length of stay, typology of treatment/surgical procedure, others).

In this increasingly complex environment, health care is affected by a large number of factors, such as

- Sociopolitical environment, in particular health care models (universal coverage, sickness funds, private insurance, public–private funding and delivery) and health policy (role of prevention, acute care, outpatient treatment, chronic disease, continuity of care, home care);
- Political-institutional processes, in particular priority-setting among different health conditions and the relation between different levels of the institutional system (State, Region, local health organization, hospital, etc.);
- Administrative models, in particular for public authorities, regulators, policy makers;
- Organizational models, in particular the functioning rules of hospitals and other delivery organizations;
- Technology, in particular drugs, equipment for laboratory tests and imaging devices and other medical technologies;
- Professional approaches, in particular new solutions to the specialization–integration challenge, due to the evolution from cure (for acute patients) to continuity of care (for chronic health conditions), from a focus on diseases to a focus on health.

2.7 The New Myths of the Twentieth Century

The transformations linked with scientific-technological developments and the changed epidemiological, socio-economic and political conditions formed the backdrop to the development of the welfare state model. Public rules, state control and financing through general taxation or mandatory sickness funds or social security funds, are considered conditions for guaranteeing universal coverage, solidarity among different groups of population and equity. The idea that health care should be publicized for the sake of equality (discussed in Chap. 9), was launched in the second half of the nineteenth century by Otto von Bismarck and was developed in the period between the two world wars and consolidated after the second world war with the Beveridge reform in the UK and similar reforms in other countries during the 1950s–1970s of the last century. At the core there were a series of demands made by the "Movements for Health," inspired by new ideas emerging in many industrialized countries: the concept of universalism, settled in the throes of the "liberation from need" principles sustained by the Atlantic Charter (1941); of "welfare from the cradle to the grave," as recommended by the Beveridge Plan; and of health considered as "a state of total well-being—physical/psychological/social—and not merely absence of illness," as recognized in the 1948 World Health Organization (WHO) constitution. The peak of the international cultural evolution on health matters was represented by the Alma Ata conference of 1978, which sealed a unifying vision of care for both the physical and psychic health of individuals.

After the 1973 oil crisis, all Western developed countries experimented a double trend: increasing public expenditure (in some of them, increasing public debt) and the awareness of the public bodies' inefficiency. The dimension and the causes of the public sector inefficiency were analyzed both from the theoretical point of view and by empirical research.

From the theoretical point of view, the negative trade-off between the objective of getting short-term political consensus and that of pursuing efficiency and economic sustainability in the long run was underlined. So, public ownership and political power to appoint public and, in particular, health care managers, was considered as the main weakness: low efficiency prevented equity or caused high expenditure and increasing public debt. This theoretical approach was supported by an increasing volume of empirical research which compared the efficiency of public and private hospitals or other delivery organizations. The validity of this comparison is widely commented in this book (Chaps. 8 and 9). The consequences were the spreading of a managerial approach (so-called New Public Management) in the public sector and a new wave of privatizations.

At the beginning of the 1980s, the time seemed ripe for the introduction of "business" in the health care sector, in relation to a series of concomitant factors: the hegemony of Reaganian/Thatcherian-inspired policy; the reformist trend inaugurated by the United Kingdom linked to the diffusion of the New Public Management; the loss of legitimacy on the part of national and local governments following cronyism and the politically influenced degeneration of Health Authorities and organizations; the significant raising of citizens' expectations combined with little trust in public institutions.

During the 1980s and the 1990s of the last century, many European countries approved reforms inspired by the **myth of business** (see Chap. 7), that pushed towards the introduction in public hospitals and other delivery organizations of business-like methodology and techniques such as planning, programming, budgeting systems, managerial and cost accounting, performance management, organizational restructuring, human resources management, rewarding systems. Sometimes economic and financial performance indicators were dominant, sometimes they were better balanced with health performance indicators, but anyway the underlying principle was the positive effect of competition. Market and quasi-market competition was theorized and became the pillar of a trend towards mixed delivery systems, in which public and private (for profit and not-for-profit) hospitals and other delivery organizations compete with each other. Of course, it was acknowledged that the nature of health needs requires public rules, monitoring and control.

The competition among health care organizations and within each organization was also the driver of another trend that took place in particular with the new millennium: the idea, drawn uncritically from the scientific management applied to manufacturing and service sectors, that, in the global arena, dimension is a critical success factor (see Chap. 11). The reduction of unitary costs, the need to invest in new high-cost technologies (for example surgical robots, advanced imaging equipment, etc.), the evolution towards integrated care for larger groups of population, generated the expectation (or the illusion) that big organizations would be the right solution to deal with public expenditure constraints and cost-cutting policies. This idea, at the basis of the **myth of scale**, inspired a wave of mergers and acquisitions in private health care, as well as the dimensional growth of public hospitals and local health authorities. Italy is a very interesting experience for the myth of scale. As highlighted in Chap. 5, the number of the public health care organizations (HCOs) was reduced by 23% over the last decade, with an acceleration in the last five years, especially in regions under cutback plans. Mergers were driven by Regions, willing to play the role of holdings of health care organizations to enhance performance monitoring, especially on the financial side. It is a process of grip back in contrast to the "corporatization" wave which characterized the 1990s: while in the 1990s firm size was determined by the idea of manageability, in the new millennium size increase was decided in the perspective of technical optimization, pursuing abstract benefits without taking into account some hidden costs (such as those related to stakeholder coordination, employee motivation, increased cognitive complexity and the need for shared decision-making).

2.8 The Complexity Trajectory and the Myth of Health Systems' Failure

All the myths that have characterized the history of health care systems must be considered in the perspective of a new trend of complexity, that is already here and that will characterize ever more the immediate future.

On the one hand, we are witnessing increasing scientific progress, which can be intended as the ability to solve problems in order to create, challenge and try to deal with new complexity. Health care systems, in the last quarter of century, have been affected by three main phenomena, which allow delivery of increasingly expensive and successful health treatments (as proved by the improvement of the statistics of life expectancy or infant mortality rates):

1. Development of ICT that provides an enormous capacity of data collection, computing, repository, storage, retrieval and in particular the Internet and digital revolution.
2. Genome discovery and genome sequencing at lower cost in very short time for an increasing number of persons, and consequent gene and cell therapies.
3. Nano- and new materials technologies that provide opportunities for the substitution of organs, nutraceuticals and regenerative medicine.

On the other hand, these trends are generating growing pressures over health care systems, thus giving the idea of their failure (discussed in Chap. 4). More specifically, these trends are

1. Pushing ahead the frontier of knowledge concerning the causes of disease, the prevention of disease and recovery opportunities for damage suffered by people.
2. Giving doctors (and other specialists) increasing power regarding the physical and mental well-being of people. The above trends reinforce the traditional hierarchical relationships and, consequently, a higher trust in the professionality and morality of health professionals is required on the part of patients.
3. Dramatically changing past specialization patterns. The traditional professions and specializations (sectorised by diseases, organs, and procedures, for example cardio- and neuro-surgery) are becoming obsolete and will be destroyed; new interdisciplinary approaches and inter-professional approaches are and will be more and more required to deal successfully with health conditions in different settings (hospital for acute care, post-acute care for outpatients, community care settings, nursing homes, long stay organizations, homecare).
4. Dramatically strengthening patient access to information and knowledge. Discoveries relating to health, positive results of trials for specific illnesses, the availability of new drugs, technology or treatment are widespread through the Internet, more or less in real-time. Dozens of mass media programs on health, hundreds and thousands of websites that propose diagnosis and therapy to everybody, increase the expectations of patients. A growing number of patients privilege self-diagnosis and therapy, or contact doctors asking them to prescribe medical tests and exams, to pushing towards over-prescription behavior. In many cases, patients have not the knowledge to distinguish between websites which give correct (trustable) or incorrect (not trustable) information, between websites accredited or non-accredited by professional and scientific societies, public regulators and authorities. Because of patient pressures, doctors cannot resist because they are worried about the risk of malpractice procedures promoted by patients. The consequence of the digital and advanced therapies and health technology is the so-called "trust trap." The trap arises because, on the one hand, patients who are much more informed than before, trust their doctors less, and on the other they should or must trust their doctors, who have an increasing power over their health.

The increasing pressures generated by the above-mentioned trends give the idea that health care systems are failing, since they are raising the costs of care and, at the same time, they are profoundly changing the relationship between patients and doctors (as well as other health professionals, such as biologists, bio-engineers, nurses), so that the former are not available to pay for the advanced and more expensive care. This dynamics are at the basis of the myth of health care failure.

References

Fielding HG (1913) An introduction to the history of medicine, IV edn. W.B. Saunders Company, Philadelphia, p 112
Fulghum R (1988) It was on fire when I lay down on it. Ivy Books, New York
Mintzberg H (2012) Managing the myths of health care. World Hosp Health Serv 48(3):4–7

Chapter 3
A Plural Analysis of Health Myths: Overview of the Volume

Paola Adinolfi and Elio Borgonovi

In this chapter, we present an overview of the contributions received from academics and practitioners invited to comment on Henry Mintzberg's myths. The chapter is organized around nine paragraphs: each of them corresponds to one of the myths, according to the original Henry Mintzberg's sequence; the last paragraph deals with Gummesson's reflections and related comments.

3.1 Myth #1: The Health Care System Is Failing

All the contributors who comment on Myth #1, i.e. The Health Care System Is Failing, agree that the real issue is not failure, but pressures on the health care system. Because of scientific and technological progress, an increasing quantity of health needs can be successfully met and this trend will be even faster and relevant in the future. In addition, social and political factors influence health expenditure, which has shown a rapid increase since the 2007–08 crisis. Moreover, the health systems have been affected by radical changes from acute care to chronic care, mainly because of an ageing population. So, the paradigm to be adopted is not the level of expenditure as a share of GDP, but the relationships between quantity and

P. Adinolfi (✉)
CIRPA (Interdepartmental Centre for Research in Economics,
Law and Management of Public Administrations), University of Salerno,
Fisciano, SA, Italy
e-mail: padinolfi@unisa.it

E. Borgonovi
Public Administration and Health Institute "Carlo Masini",
University "Luigi Bocconi" of Milan, Milan, Italy
e-mail: elio.borgonovi@unibocconi.it7

P. Adinolfi and E. Borgonovi (eds.), *The Myths of Health Care*,
https://doi.org/10.1007/978-3-319-53600-2_3

quality of services provided and policies to be adopted to contrast inefficiencies, corruption and misuse of resources.

Umberto Veronesi and Maurizio Mauri clarify many examples of the improvements experimented in the recent past and foresee that, in ten years from now, around 80% of present knowledge will be superseded due to the gene therapies, cell therapies, nutraceutical, regenerative medicine and ICT applied to medicine. Therefore, the challenge is economic sustainability, for which they have a twofold proposal: to contrast inefficiencies, corruption, lack of professionality, and to adopt a new paradigm of preventive health care. This paradigm is based on the following characteristics: proactive, predictive, preventive, customized, participatory, and specific.

Mario Del Vecchio points out that the introduction of National Health Systems in Italy and in other countries, jointly with the declaration of health as a human right, has determined a strong increase of expectations for health services. Therefore, higher patients' and general population's expectations are at the same time cause and effect of the lack of satisfaction with the system, creating a vicious circle that differently affects Italian regions and various countries. He highlights the difference between personal experience, that is not bad for the majority of the population, and the criticism towards collective political choice, that is considerated inadequate to priority settings.

Patrizio Armeni underlines different policies that many countries have adopted to deal with the sustainability challenge: co-payments, linear cost cuts, spending review, efficiency gains, and new organizational arrangements. But one of the main factors of the economic pressure on the health system is economic stagnation, in particular in Europe. So, to come out from this trap, he proposes to consider health care expenditure as a driver for a new growth paradigm. Actually, the health chain, from pharma and medical technology industries to better health for patient, can contribute to higher productivity for the whole economy and to increased social value.

In their contribution, Vincenza Esposito, Mario Pezzillo Iacono, Lorenzo Mercurio and Joseph Polimeni, focus on the spending review strategy in the Italian system. They analyze the conditions needed for an effective spending review: knowledge to discover actual inefficiencies, legitimation of committees and authorities in charge of the spending review, and commitment of policy makers, managers and professionals at all levels of the health system. Their conclusion is that spending review cannot be considered as an "emergency," but must be considered a continuous process of reviewing the quality of health care approaches to acute and chronic patients.

3.2 Myth #2: The Health Care System Can Be Fixed by Clever Social Engineering

The second myth assumes that the health care system can be fixed by outside-the-box social engineering through large-scale, top-down, externally driven, out-side-informed approaches. Emanuele Lettieri and Cristina Masella assert that

Henry Mintzberg, on the one hand, confutes the myth of clever social engineering, but, on the other, creates another myth, that health care will be fixed by health care professionals themselves through small-scale, inside-informed, professionally driven, evolutionary approaches, continuously amended in the light of experience. The two authors firmly reject this new myth and propose an alternative integrative approach, drawing on their research at the "Politecnico di Milano" regarding the adoption of Electronic Medical Records and of Integrated Care Pathways: their findings show that relevant and long-lasting changes are likely to occur when outside-healthcare experts and context-wise professionals collaborate in the innovation process, sharing and mediating their visions, core values and positive energies.

Corrado Cuccurullo echoes these arguments, arguing that managing change in health care organizations is not a problem of clever social engineering, but rather a problem of including different internal and external cultures in the change process. So, the over-emphasis on the individuals at the top should be replaced by a broader vision, which values the important roles of middle managers and of outsiders, such as external consultants, patients, suppliers and government. Managers indeed perform as internal catalysers of innovation and their style for driving change is crucial. According to context, different managerial styles could be more or less appropriate to foster innovative change in the health care arena: direction, intervention, education, participation. These styles are not mutually exclusive: they can be combined and recombined over time, and the managers with the greatest ability in managing change are those who have the ability to adopt different styles, or combinations of styles, in different circumstances.

Fernando Giancotti adopts the framework of "the new science of chaos and complexity" to interpret the functioning of health care organizations, thus allowing for a reconciliation of the positions of Lettieri-Masella and Cuccurullo with Henry Mintzberg's demythologizing exercise. The complexity framework does not provide support either to an approach that advocates the supremacy of clever social engineering, or to another one that advocates the supremacy of incremental, small-scale, professionally driven change. Whereas conventional reductionist scientific thinking assumes that we shall resolve all the unresolved issues, complexity theory is comfortable with—and even values—inherent tensions between opposite approaches, that are to be reconciled (and not resolved). Henry Mintzberg himself considers that the complexity and richness of reality does not tolerate unique, extreme solutions, and in the specific case he does not deny the importance of clever social engineering, but rather its mythologization.

In this perspective, Lettieri and Masella's idea that change could be realized by combining the top-down with the bottom-up approach, by relying on sound and dynamic partnerships between outside-healthcare social engineers and context-wise health care professionals, is appropriate to the complexity framework and is also closer to Henry Mintzberg's view than the two authors themselves admit (for the sake of argument, they declare their firm disagreement with Henry Mintzberg's opinion). Also, Cuccurullo is in line with Henry Mintzberg, when he recommends blending and forging over time different and sometimes opposing leadership styles.

Relying on the complexity framework, Giancotti firmly denies that clever social engineering is the panacea to the problems of the health care systems, and proposes developing polycentric structures of high-performance modules well connected with the mainstream of organizational knowledge flowing top-down, bottom-up and throughout. He establishes a bridge to Myth 3, highlighting the overlapping between the two myths, as Myth 2 implies the assignment of big challenges to heroic leaders. One could imagine that a military view of leadership and change management is established on the command and control paradigm, instead the Airforce General strongly criticizes the Myth of the Heroic Leader, whom he colourfully defines as "hopeless bottleneck," contending that health care organizations need an agile and diffuse leadership, able to "trigger the motivational hyper-cycles and a related networking of hearts and minds thus multiplying and boosting the overall capability of the organization." This view of change and leadership is also corroborated by an interesting anthropological consideration. Compared to command and control leadership, diffuse and empowering leadership is more capable of satisfying our ancestral needs and is in far better accord with human nature, which has been shaped during the millennia in between our chimpanzee past and our civilized present. Rather than in contemporary complex societies, we have been ecologically adapted to life in gathering-hunting societies, which lasted an incomparably long period (before different forms of social organization emerged) and therefore constituted the environment where any natural dispositions that we possess even today have evolved: despotic leadership and top-down change was made unsustainable by the material conditions of such societies (such as small groups with little division of labour, cheap exit-options for dissatisfied people, the possibility of building coalitions to put down would-be dominators, little property and difficulty in stockpiling durable resources and exploiting skills for political advantage).

3.3 Myth #3: Health Care Institutions as Well as the Overall System Can Be Fixed by Bringing in the Heroic Leader

As regards the myth of the Heroic Leader, Colao and Riccio assume a collectivist perspective and frame health leadership as a group matter, rather than an individualist concern. They appear in line with Henry Mintzberg when recognizing the need to break away from past associations with what leaders are and how their medical training places limitations on their ability to properly function in a health care organization that is patient-centered with team-based delivery of care. Situational awareness, proactivity, openness, knowledge sharing, followers empowerment and engagement are considered to be the main ingredients of the recipe for effective leadership in health care.

Botti and Tommasetti, reflecting on the importance of leadership skills to fulfil managerial practices in the health care arena, point out the lack of universal recipes. No one leadership style is the best ever (included the engaging distributed style advocated by Henry Mintzberg): leadership effectiveness depends, among others, on the organizational level (macro, meso and micro) and on the management quality (which is strictly linked to leadership at all levels).

Massimo Sargiacomo, while advocating the shift from a hierarchical, leader-centered approach to a shared, consensus-based model, concludes that health care organizations should not neglect the role of key managers and transformational leaders, whose "heroism" may still be a necessary—albeit non-sufficient—condition.

All authors identify a void in the area of leadership in health care, and a need to overcome the traditional hierarchical approach. The pars construens is less convergent. As for the Myth of clever social engineering, the various positions can be read in the light of the complexity theory.

There are a set of circumstances that call for diffuse, engaging leadership that could be identified with those that Langton (1989) has termed "the edge of chaos," an area where there is insufficient certainty to make decisions obvious (as it is in simple linear systems), but not so much uncertainty that the system is thrown into chaos.

In such a framework, Henry Mintzberg's idea of engaging leaders can be agreed if not absolutized (as Henry Mintzberg himself is not willing to do), and further efforts need to be made in order to investigate how and in what circumstances this approach to leadership seems to be working best.

3.4 Myth #4: The Health Care System Can Be Fixed by Treating It More as a Business

All contributors commenting on Myth #4, which states that the health care system can be fixed by treating it more as a business, have two common starting points: the recognition that economic sustainability is a critical issue, and that cooperation is a peculiarity of health care services. There is no need to clarify the first issue, because financial constraints affect not only public finance, but also household purchasing power for health care services both out of pocket and subscription of private insurance. Something more can be said with regard to the second issue, because the contributors argue that market competition cannot guarantee cost containment, appropriateness, effectiveness and quality of care. Moreover, competition can destroy physicians, nurses and other health professionals' motivation and prevent a holistic approach to patients. Rather than an economic or a business-like approach, what is needed is a humanistic one. Nevertheless, it is necessary to introduce and strengthen managerial culture, principles, criteria, techniques and instruments.

Federico Lega, after stating that there is no evidence that the business-like approach produces benefits, underlines that "business-driven health systems cost more and have greater problems in equity in access to health care delivery, variation in outcomes, adverse selection and opportunistic behaviors." If managing the health care system as a business is not the right thing to do, managerial knowledge and consolidated tools can help to do things in the right way. Then he focuses on strategic management, performance management, quality systems, lean techniques, operations management, business planning, human resources management that can be helpful in dealing with a complex and turbulent environment.

Emanuele Vendramini's views are summarized in three words: ambidexterity, professionalism and accountability. Ambidexterity has a twofold interpretation. Firstly, to guarantee good care at present and, in the future, being innovative in terms of technology and clinical pathways. Secondly, to guarantee health care and, at the same time, financial sustainability, a challenge that in the past was much easier than currently. Vendramini relates professionalism to the intrinsic motivation of physicians (and nurses) to treat patients and not to pursue the highest possible remuneration, as happens in market-driven activities. Of course, not all physicians have this motivation but, in general, "for a physician it is important to have the right number of cases (and case mix) to be able to tackle all the different situations and be able to offer a state of the art service." Accountability in health care systems requires clinical involvement and a very sophisticated performance measurement system.

Giuseppe Festa and Enrico Coscioni's main points can be summarized as follows. There is no doubt that economic issues are becoming more and more relevant also in national health systems, in which service costs are covered entirely or mostly by taxation. Nevertheless, economic logic and principles must and should remain ancillary to health issues and to human relationships between health care professionals and their patients. Economic criteria should never become a priority because this will produce what the authors define as defensive economy, that means undertreatment to cope with financial constraints. Defensive economy is the contrary of defensive medicine, that increases cost because of overtreatment. The authors conclude that, while standardization can be a useful tool for better organizing health care structures and systems, personalization remains the pillar of health care services.

3.5 Myth #5: Health Care Is Rightly Left to the Private Sector, for the Sake of Efficiency

The comments on Myth #5, which states that health care is rightly left to the private sector for sake of efficiency, are divided in two parts: one related to delivery of health services and the other related to financing. With regard to the first part of the problem, the first three contributions state that there is no clear evidence that proves that private delivery organizations are more efficient. When they are, private organizations generally pursue higher efficiency without considering the final effect on appropriateness and quality of service for patients. Management models and tools are not restricted to private organizations, but can and must be applied in all complex organizations, both public and private. With regard to the second part of the issue, the suggested mainstream solution is a mix of public and private funding. This solution is not a choice, but, in some way, seems to be inevitable, because of the structural increase of expenditure and the difficulties of public finance in all countries. To overcome this myth a win-win approach for public and private organizations should be adopted.

Aleksandra Torbica and Oriana Ciani's contribution make a comparison between public and private delivery organizations based on three main theories: agency/property rights theory, public choice and organization theories. According to the first, it is likely that private ownership achieves lower costs in service provision compared with their government counterpart. Public choice's central argument is that often politicians pursue their own aims rather than the public interest. Organizational theories focus on the differences of structure between private hospitals and state-owned provider organizations. These three theories are used to discuss the three dimensions of efficiency used in empirical studies: technical, productive (cost) and profit. The authors conclude that the existing empirical evidence does not always support the positive effects of privatization on efficiency predicted by the different theories. Public–private distinction is only one part of a broader and more complex link.

Francesca Lecci and Marco Morelli are very clear and concise in saying that efficiency is not a peculiarity of the private or public sector. It may be that the efficiency issue was raised in the past for private business companies that operate in a competitive market environment, but they analyze many reasons why efficiency is also necessary for public delivery organizations. At present, the cost-management approach is much more related to the availability of information rather than to the nature of organizations (public or private). To support their argument, they mention the cost accounting system introduced in a public-local health organization and in a private hospital (IEO—European Institute of Oncology). Then they move towards the argument that it is important to be clear that what should be measured is not only efficiency and costs but the value for patients, which is the aim of the public system rather than that of private providers. They accept the principle according to which only what is measureable and measured can be improved, but what is really important is the outcome-input ratio (effectiveness) and not the output–input ratio (efficiency). While the latter drives private providers, the first pushes public organizations when social and political pressures are strong.

Michael Drummond and Rosanna Tarricone start distinguishing two components of privatization that are the financing of the system and the provision of services. Drawing on the agency theory, they argue that, because patients do not know the value of services, it may be easier under public financing to prevent escalating costs rather than with private financing. Of course there are many tools to control the increase of costs in the private system, but the profitability objective can push up the prices of services and it may still be more difficult to control the growth of expenditure. Then, the authors turn to HTA as a methodology that can be better applied in National Health Services. Private providers generally use high technology as a proxy for higher quality and higher prices, while national systems are much more interested in evaluating the actual benefit-cost ratio. So, they conclude that the private providers' objective is higher profitability that can be obtained through higher prices rather than higher efficiency or that profitability can be obtained through higher efficiency/productivity without considering appropriateness.

Maurizio De Cicco, Salvatore Russo and Luca Del Bene's contributions debate the other side of the public-private issue. In particular, Maurizio De Cicco, after a very short description of the evolution of the Italian NHS, analyses the role of complementary health care (private social security funds agreed between companies, unions and private insurance). He is convinced that, in Italy and in the European welfare model, public financing is still the keystone for generalized health care. Private financing can be only an additional contribution to support the evolution of health needs. He quotes the situation of innovative drugs that can be easily introduced into the market if some private insurance of social security funds accept to pay for them. His conclusion is that the actual problem is not more efficiency in provision, but a mixed system of financing and provision aimed at promoting innovation.

Salvatore Russo e and Luca Del Bene are interested in financing investment in health care system rather than in financing current expenditure. Starting from the evidence that public health care systems are under financial pressure, they see in the public–private partnership (PPP) one of the possible solutions. This approach was developed under the New Public Management (NPM) practice, that characterized the 1980s and 1990s of the last century. The most common public–private partnerships deal with the building and management of hospitals. Its main benefit is to attract private investment based on the win-win principle. Public delivery organizations can renew hospital technologies they could not otherwise afford and private investors can pursue their profit objective. So, the former can guarantee higher quality of services for patients and the latter can pursue profitability, because they can manage some core and non-core activities, such as facility management for buildings and supporting systems, the thermic heating system, refrigerator system, air conditioning, electrical equipment and plumbing, medical gas supply systems, catering for in-patients and staff, cleaning, disposal of waste material, reception, reservation center, parking and others. Without solving the problem of more efficiency for private institutions, authors recommend PPPs as an institutional formula where equal roles and tasks still meet the value for money.

3.6 Myth #6: Health Care Is Rightly Controlled by the Public Sector, for the Sake of Equality

Myth #6, which states that health care is rightly controlled by the public sector, for the sake of equality, is analyzed from different perspectives: the concept of equity, the comparison between public and private provision, the competition and collaboration challenge, the inadequate policy making and control for drugs and medical device innovation, the role of private not-for-profit organizations and low-cost providers. A common framework is that there are very different levels of analysis: the general principle of Universal Health Coverage that can be guaranteed only by clear public regulation, at least in European countries; the health care policy setting that is increasingly more inadequate, because private interests condition public authorities; the health care delivery process that must be based on collaboration rather than competition and on an integrated approach to patients; last but not least, the rising of a new business model that is private not-for-profit organization, which can guarantee low cost, high quality and customized services.

Andrea Silenzi, Alessio Santoro and Walter Ricciardi's main concern is health system complexity, because it affects the political, social and financial context where it operates. The declaration of the World Health Organization, according to which everyone should have access to quality health services everywhere without financial hardship, is an abstract principle, but must be concretely applied. The financial constraint is a real issue, as the demographic trends show that, by 2050, the 37% of the European population is expected to be over the age of 60, and similar trends towards an ageing population characterize the US and China. Therefore it is crucial to clarify the difference between equity and equality. Their reasoning is that equality means the same services for all, while equity is related to the concept of social justice: people should get the health services they need and fund the health system according to their ability to pay. However, here is the problem for countries that adopted the Universal Health Coverage model, because public authorities have difficulties in setting priorities aimed at guaranteeing equity. To overcome this criticism, the authors' suggestions are to redefine the governance system, in order to involve as many actors as possible, to strengthen the social and political leadership that is a requirement for changing in the management process, to diffuse a greater sense of responsibility for both patients and delivery organizations, to invest in education for health care professionals, to design appropriate policies, to introduce formal systems for monitoring and evaluating the impact of policies.

Anna Prenestini and Stefano Calciolari shortly describe the evolution of public intervention in the 60–70 years. After World War II, many countries converged to establish a relevant role of the public subject in several sectors, included health care. Since 1980, the prescription of fixing major problems by treating such sectors in a more business-like manner became quite popular. This evolution is due to social pressures and financial constraints and is based on the overrating of the positive effect of competition. Then they introduced the debate between competition and collaboration, saying that, for a large part of health care services, the latter is much more beneficial than competition. The cooperation between health care professionals takes different paths: multidisciplinary teamwork, collaboration between specialists of the same disciplines and/or different professions (e.g., between doctors and nurses). The conclusion is that public control is not only a problem of equity but the best way to foster multidisciplinary, multi-professional cooperation and integrated service delivery.

Silvio Garattini and Vittorio Bertelè underline that the health care sector is unique because quality is by far more relevant than other goods or services, so the quality–price ratio cannot be left only to the strategic choice of private providers, which select the most profitable pathologies and interventions. Even if public policies should take care of everybody and, in particular, of rare diseases, often public health authorities do not promote innovation. The authors examine what happens in the pharmaceutical industry, stating that companies try to sell everything they produce. They are not interested in the actual advancement of innovative drugs, as in the last decade only a little more than 1% of over one thousand authorized medicines have offered a real advantage for patients. They support this statement with many examples, drawn from studies carried out in the Mario Negri Pharmacology Institute. In conclusion, for the authors the crucial point is not the alternative between public and private but, is to strengthen scientific knowledge about what is useful for patients and what is not. Equality in health is a mirage that is hard to achieve. Public institutions are the only ones that can aim at this while private institutions have to put other goals first.

Riccardo Mercurio, Stefano Consiglio e Mariavittoria Cicellin introduce a quite different perspective. The real problem is not the trade-off between equality (or equity) of the public sector and efficiency of the private one. A third party, social enterprises, can be the right solution. These private not-for-profit organizations are more flexible than public authorities and less oriented towards profit maximization. The authors' framework is the welfare state reform, which characterized many European countries and is supported by the European Social Innovation Initiative. In recent years, in Italy there has been a flourishing of social innovation in the health care system that provides low-cost services without reducing the quality of care. They analyze six cases that started a project to develop medical group practices involving public and private partners. This is a new business model that helps many people no longer able to afford health care services not guaranteed by NHS. In conclusion, the transformation of patients into customers/consumers, as well as the nature of not for profit that characterizes the low-cost services projects could weaken the role of the state as guarantor of collective public health, transforming health care in a market not distorted by the profit maximization logic.

3.7 Myth #7: Myth of Measurement

Matteo Mario Pietro Motterlini and Carlo Canepa observe that the myth of measurement carries the "rational agent" assumption, and therefore sacrifies, in the name of exact measurement, some reality aspects in terms of their richness, concrete decisional contexts and decision makers' cognitive faculties. The way in which choice options are structured shouldn't modify a rational agent's preferences, but in practice this is not true: small, low-cost, well-devised architectural elements can guide towards virtuous decisions. Therefore, the rhetorical question is: if we accept that what can't be measured can't be managed, what do we really want to measure and manage? The decisions of omniscient and hyper-rational agents, which operate in abstract economic models, or the decisions of human beings made of flesh and bones, with their cognitive boundaries and emotive conditioning, which work in specific "choice environments"?

The Authors propose merging economics with cognitive psychology so that the systematic nature of human irrationality can be taken into account, and policy makers can overtake traditional models that interpret social science in quantitative and abstract terms, and use tools based on evidence. These tools can be elaborated according to evaluative experimental methods, like randomized controlled trials.

Giuseppe Iuliano, Gaetano Matonti, Paolo Tartaglia Polcini and Ettore Cinque, taking into account the criticism of Henry Mintzberg about measurement in health care, examine the accounting literature on the topic, focusing on the academic debate concerning the relevance and usefulness of measurement systems in health care organizations. Once acknowledged the unescapable need for a measurement system in health care, the authors discuss what should be measured and what should not in order to overcome the critic raised by Henry Mintzberg. In their view, the focus should be on the measurement of quality and outcome, and, from this point of view, promising developments may come from Activity Based Costing methods. These methods, which have been experimented at Harvard University, widen the observation of the whole health care processes and more specifically identify their related costs, to be compared with related benefits. The patient care cycle starts from the first pre-operation appointment and ends one year after the day of treatment (Kaplan and Porter 2011). Extending the analysis to one year from the treatment allows for measuring all aspects, even the social outcome and patient experience measures.

Sabina Nuti expands the literary review on the criticalities of performance measurements, examining some negative consequences of performance data use: tunnel vision, sub-optimization, myopia, measure fixation, misrepresentation, misinterpretation. These dysfunctional effects are all result of some violations of the "synecdoche principle," which assumes that the measure is able to satisfy both the conditions of representativeness and accuracy, by precisely representing the whole object. The inability of the indicators to portray the complexity of the evaluated object is at the basis of their bureaucratic use, and, for this reason, Sabina Nuti believes that the risk that administrators and clinicians are obsessed by measurement appears to be still very weak. In her view, the keystone of improvement process in the health care system is physicians' engagement. Professionals and managers "should share a joint accountability for both the outcome and the costs of the care path in which they are involved and not just for the patients they care for or the phases which they are in charge of."

The theoretical framework outlined by the previous authors is complemented by the empirical analysis carried out by Marina Davoli, Chiara Marinacci and Renato Botti, who investigate the challenges of measurement and performance management in practice, by examining the experience of the Italian National Health Service. By illustrating the various government initiatives, such as the monitoring of Essential Levels of Care (LEA), the National Outcome Programme, the

Regulation on Hospital Standards, the authors show how the Italian NHS is currently evolving towards giving greater importance to measurement systems, both process and result oriented, in order to identify areas of inefficiency, inappropriateness and ineffectiveness of services and facilities, while monitoring equity in access and promoting continuous improvement of health care organizations. The authors also identify, in line with Henry Mintzberg, some criticalities related to an automatic and exaggerated use of measurement without judgment. For a better balance between measurement and judgement, they suggest some procedural recommendations, such as: establishing a systematic process of data quality control and a systematic update of measures used, involving different stakeholders, and ensuring transparency of methods and operational definitions, making it possible for all the assessed administrations and/or providers to replicate measures. They also recommend adapting measurement for the different purposes (budgeting, performance management, provider payment mechanism, clinical audit, provider accreditation etc…), thus avoiding automatic applications, and selecting measures taking into account the cost of data collection and reporting, as compared to the measure's impact on quality and outcomes. They add an important dimension to be considered in selecting quality standard measures: the safety of the process of care delivery, based on critical evidence-based practices strongly related to health outcomes.

Francesco Bevere and Paola Adinolfi observe that, despite the growing sensitivity on the issue of expenditure control and health risks, solutions addressing the problem in an integrated manner are yet to be found. The available supply is mainly advisory and is confined to: staff training on costs, risk and quality issues; financial analysis aimed at a better recognition of the benefits produced by the Diagnostic-related-groups; process certifications based on IT modelling; document management procedures aimed at better legal protection.

When going beyond mere document management procedures, inspired by a defensive administrative approach—which adds to the defensive medicine—the typical approach is aimed at identifying the "best practice" for specific processes, or related to specific risk management aspects. In most cases, there is acceptable compliance with one or more "best practice" models, but also a dramatic drop in reliability and consistency when evaluating the process as a whole. Even when managing to achieve full application of the entire treatment process developed in the literature with the input of the relevant national and international scientific associations, there is hardly a context-specific scope of application, involving ICT-based tools, able to create the necessary interconnections across the various clinical and health information systems involved, and promote the analysis of critical areas and possible innovative connections that include all the assets and the subjects involved in the value chain. Moreover, there are no cases of an integrated evaluation of costs, risks and outcomes. The authors add further evidence of the dysfunctional consequences of a piecemeal, simplistic and obsessive approach to measurement, highlighting its negative effects on the spending review carried out in the last few years in many countries.

They recommend developing innovative tools for the analysis and formal modelling of social-healthcare processes, in order to produce integrated (and even inter-organizational) paths featuring an experimental approach capable of accommodating, on the one hand, the established scientific references and, on the other, the local and structural variables related to individual patients, in a complex perspective in which all the relevant dimensions (costs, risks, outcomes) are measured and all actors (including the patient and his/her family, as well as suppliers) are part of a process of creation of health as a value.

3.8 Myth #8: Myth of Scale

The reconceptualization of measurement systems paves the way for overcoming the myth of scale. Scale has been considered a recipe for success over the last 70 years: managers and entrepreneurs realized that "the bigger their estates, the easier it was to gain and sustain a competitive advantage, typically in the form of lower unit production costs, higher overall productivity and access to large R&D budgets" (Calvo and Scaramuccia).

The relevance of the myth of scale in the health care sector is evident for the merging wave occurred over the last decade: as observed by Cuccurullo, in Italy the number of public health care organizations was reduced by 23%, with an acceleration in the last five years, particularly in regions under cutbacks plans. The increase in size is driven by the pursuit of technical optimality, inspired by the myth of scale. As Davoli, Marinacci and Botti observe, the association between volume of activity and outcomes, documented in several systematic reviews, should be combined with a more complex analysis of the specific context, considering the relationship between treatment effectiveness and costs or the geographical distribution and accessibility of health services. The lack of such a contextual analysis can produce acritical and simplistic decisions, as clearly highlighted by Henry Mintzberg (2009, p. 165) "To manage nursing in a hospital seems natural enough. But what about managing nursing in two hospitals, a few miles apart, that have been magically merged on a sheet of paper?." Cuccurullo points out that to date large size has shown more negative effects on patients than positive ones. In the face of abstract benefits, there are, in fact, some hidden costs, related to the increase in the number and diversity of the stakeholders, the increase in the cognitive complexity managers has to cope with, the difficulty for managers in nourishing the motivation of their followers.

Emphasizing the consideration of motivational aspects, Giancotti observes that the small size allows for the fulfilment of human deep, ancestral needs, which have origins in our remote past (dating back to the Palaeolithic), and that the big organization could recover a more human dimension by organizing itself as a network of teams at all levels.

Rocco Palumbo, Gabriella Piscopo and Maria Grazia Sampietro contribute to shedding light on this argument, by examining, from a Complex Adaptive System perspective, the Mayo Clinic case mentioned by Henry Mintzberg as an example of how big health care organizations are able to benefit from the advantages of small dimensions. The authors also contextualize their reasoning on the Italian NHS, showing data on Caesarean-Section rates, which demonstrate how bigger health care organizations may be less effective as compared with smaller ones, not being able to manage quality issues effectively.

Marcello Martinez, Luigi Moschera and Gianluigi Mangia investigate the clash between economies of scale and effectiveness of care: on the one hand, the willingness—at both policy and organizational levels—to realize cost savings pushes toward big structural sizes; on the other hand, small dimensions allow better handling health-related quality issues. The Authors argue that health care organizations should strive for achieving a balance between management and quality, considering that the new ICT technologies relativize the myth of large size as a condition for the pursuit of economies of scale, by removing the supposition that efficiency can be achieved through concentrating many activities into one physical, administrative, technical and organizational structure.

This view is in some way shared by Alberto Calvo and Daniela Scaramuccia, who acknowledge that the pervasive diffusion and low-cost access to technologies have lowered the barriers to entry in any business sector, but nevertheless for some champions of our digital age, in the fields of on-line advertising, social networks, e-commerce (Google, Facebook, Amazon are enlightening examples), scale is still "well in shape, alive and kicking."

According to the two Authors, public interest sectors—such as health care, education, care of the elderly, professional training—show little sensitivity, if any, to economies of scale. The greater the importance of elements such as personalization, local touch and uniqueness, the less relevant the concept of scale. In the health care sector, experience demonstrates that scale is a key success factor when considering back-office processes (administration, procurement, facility management, logistics), or highly standardized and consolidated procedures (such as cardio surgery, breast units), while it is not relevant in the areas in which the individual knowledge of patients is relevant to deliver integrated, personalized services (as in the chronic care or primary prevention), or in which excellent performance is clearly linked to the variable "time to treatment," as in the case of acute myocardial infarction or poly-traumas, where the proper design of the network is far more relevant than scale. Using a complexity lens, we see that Calvo and Scaramuccia, to detect areas in which scale loses its relevance, identify the set of circumstances that call for adaptive behavior, which match what Langton (1989) defines "the edge of chaos."

3.9 Health Myths and Service-Dominant Logic

Evert Gummesson proposes innovative insights into the future shapes of the health care system which are in line with Henry Mintzberg's theses but add the new developments in service theory, particularly the Service-Dominant Logic (SDL). Discussing the need for a transition from "cure" to "care," he explores the implications of "service theory" on the effort to reframe the health care arena. Even though social engineering is needed to boost structural change of health care organizations, the basically human nature of health services should not be neglected. From this standpoint, a greater emphasis should be placed on doing things *with* people, rather than *on* people. Value co-creation and service co-production turn out to be the moral imperatives of healthcare providers, who should not perform as healers of illness, but as enablers of patients.

Drawing on Gummesson's arguments, Gerardine Doyle, Alessandra Storlazzi and Carmela Annarumma merge the SDL and the Health Literacy construct to shed light on the importance of patient empowerment and patient engagement in revisiting the management of the health care service system. Both reject the traditional industrial medical model, to embrace a patient-centered approach to care, where patients and health care professionals perform as partners rather than as, respectively, users and providers. "A managerial approach which pays attention to both health literacy and S-D logic ultimately performs as a strategy aimed at closing that 'administrative gap' mentioned by Henry Mintzberg, which divides 'those who administer and those who deliver the basic services.'

Drawing on recent literature, Giuseppe Favretto, Massimiliano Vesci and Aurelio Tommasetti suggest an integrative interpretation of health care management, which is established on three theoretical pillars: network theory, viable system approach, and SDL. Such an integrative model allows departure from the mainstream logic which currently affects health policies and practices, paving the way for the overcoming of health care myths.

References

Kaplan RS, Porter ME (2011) The big idea: how to solve the cost crisis in health care. Harvard Bus Rev 1271(9):48–64

Langton CG (1989) Artificial life. In: Proceedings of the Santa Fe Institute. Studies in the Sciences of Complexity, vol 6. Addison-Wesley, Redwood City

Mintzberg H (2009) Managing. Berrett Koehler, Oakland

Part II
Going Through Health Myths

Chapter 4
Myth #1: The Healthcare System Is Failing

Umberto Veronesi, Maurizio Mauri, Mario Del Vecchio, Patrizio Armeni, Vincenza Esposito, Mario Pezzillo Iacono, Lorenzo Mercurio and Joseph Polimeni

4.1 Healthcare Systems: Utopia?

Umberto Veronesi and Maurizio Mauri

4.1.1 Innovative Trends in Health care

Many people say that Healthcare Systems are not financially sustainable and so they are all ultimately doomed.

The reason for the increase in spending is largely due to modern advances in medicine and technology: innovation has opened up new possibilities in health care but has also increased costs to the point that the system is at risk of collapse.

The original version of this chapter was revised: Affiliation were updated for M.P. Iacono. The erratum to this chapter is available at https://doi.org/10.1007/978-3-319-53600-2_15

U. Veronesi
European Institute of Oncology, Milan, Italy
e-mail: umberto.veronesi@ieo.it

M. Mauri (✉)
Direttore Generale, Fondazione CERBA (Centro Europeo Ricerca Biomedica Avanzata), Piazza Velasca, 5, 20122 Milan, Italy
e-mail: maurizio.mauri@cerba.it

M. Del Vecchio (✉)
University Bocconi of Milan, Milan, Italy
e-mail: mario.delvecchio@unifi.it; mario.delvecchio@unibocconi.it

P. Armeni (✉)
Cergas, Università Bocconi, Via Sarfatti, 25, 20142 Milan, Italy
e-mail: patrizio.armeni@unibocconi.it

P. Adinolfi and E. Borgonovi (eds.), *The Myths of Health Care*,
https://doi.org/10.1007/978-3-319-53600-2_4

We do not share this pessimistic view, because we think it is important to take the benefits of the enormous progress made in health care into consideration and not just the dynamics of its cost.

Over the last 30 years, we have witnessed some major changes in diseases afflicting human health, including the eradication of smallpox, the sharp decline in polio and tuberculosis, the drastic reduction in HIV death rates, and the continuing increase in the number of patients winning their battle against cancer.

Generally speaking, there has been a remarkable increase in life expectancy thanks to improvements in economic and social conditions, as well as advances made in health care. These changes were made possible by the revolution in the equipment used for diagnosis and therapy and the restructuring of research and healthcare facilities.

There is no question that the latest therapies that are available for treating cancer, hepatitis, retinopathies and many other conditions, are very expensive but they have also given rise to some extraordinary improvements in human health, such as:

- vaccinations, enabling us to wipe out smallpox and polio and resulting in cures for many patients;
- proton pump inhibitors, used to cure ulcers and gastric conditions, avoiding the need for surgery, once commonplace, and resulting in fewer cases of stomach cancer;
- surgical radiology, such as hemodynamic therapy, frequently used instead of heart surgery to correct heart conditions with small stents;
- antiviral drugs, enabling us to control AIDS and avoiding the need for extremely expensive hospital admissions;
- psychiatric drugs that have made it possible to close mental asylums;
- new imaging techniques (CT, MR, PET, ECO, etc.) that have made the human body transparent and have eliminated the need for the formerly common practice of "exploratory laparotomy".

These innovations have all led to today's upward trend in spending, but they have also given us huge improvements in terms of the costs/benefits (in terms of health) equation.

What's more, if we expand our outlook to the future, there can be no discussion as to the extraordinary innovations we are witnessing today at all levels: scientific, technological, financial, demographic, epidemiological, institutional, cultural, social and political. Just consider four revolutions, which we can recap as: new findings in the post-genomics era, biomedical technology, information technology (ICT), and the patient centrality ethic.

V. Esposito (✉) · L. Mercurio · J. Polimeni
Department of Law, Economics, Management and Quantitative Methods,
University of Sannio, Via delle Puglie, 82, 82100 Benevento, Italy
e-mail: vincespo@unisannio.it

M. P. Iacono
Department of Economics, Università degli Studi della Campania "Luigi Vanvitelli",
Caserta, Italy

As far as the first revolution is concerned, it is worth pointing out the scientific discoveries brought to us by genome research, such as transgenic plants, modified animals, cloning, etc. In medicine, the deciphering of the human genome, whose sequencing was completed in 2001, generated fundamental knowledge for our understanding of degenerative diseases that are the greatest ailment affecting human health today. Finding a solution to the majority of health problems is left to the skillful application in clinical practice of the findings of research, especially genetic and epigenetic research, and their adaptation to individual cases/patients.

Today, it is already possible in many cases to identify the genetic and molecular mechanisms causing diseases, to predict the probability (predictive medicine) of being affected by a disease and to safeguard human health before a condition occurs. Therapies can be "customised" for individual patients (healthy or not) predicting, for example, a person's response to drugs and implementing precision medicine. Some studies estimate that new discoveries over the next 10 years will change more than 80% of what we know now, the methods we use for diagnosis and treatments, but most of all will have an impact on prevention and lead to a radical rethinking of how we approach clinical practice.

With regard to the revolution in biomedical technology, methods of functional or molecular imaging are being developed in addition to the morphological imaging technology of recent years. We will see the consolidation of a new, conservative approach to surgery based on the shift away from the principle of what is the "maximum tolerable (in terms of being invasive)" to what is the "minimum needed". This is also thanks to the development of new techniques in surgery, the use of robots, new types of advanced radiotherapy that are less harmful to the surrounding healthy tissue, for example using particles such as protons or ions, or focused ultrasound.

Nanotechnology, modern pharmacology, biological therapies and regenerative medicine are also part of this revolution.

The revolution in the information technology used in health care has given us controllable and reliable systems for managing a mass of information, promoting the balanced development of the procedures used for prevention, diagnosis, treatment and rehabilitation, the integration of different medical professions and continuity of care in different settings (acute hospital admissions, outpatient-based health care in non-hospital facilities, health care delivered at home). IT and related technologies must be centred on the patient and on his needs, so that he becomes the "focus" of the reorganisation of patient care: it will become increasingly possible to take a holistic approach, treating the patient as a whole instead of his organs or his ailments. It will become possible to have an electronic medical record with a person's complete medical history, useful information on his health, his genome and gradually including information on his epigenome. Bespoke analysis techniques and technologies will also make it possible to process health care-related big data and assess the effectiveness of treatments for homogeneous groups of patients.

The fourth revolution, the ethical revolution, can be described as the "comeback of humanism" where the person is the focus of processes designed to aid prevention, diagnosis, treatment and rehabilitation, balancing the logic of specialisation or hyper-specialisation that has been prominent in recent decades. The patient/public becomes a "stakeholder", taking an active rather than a passive role in his own health care, so he is no longer merely a receiver of a service but a participant in the decision-making processes affecting his own health and the health of the community at large. Greater public awareness, changes in regulations and modes of practice (such as privacy standards or the new code of ethics of physicians), have contributed to a Copernican revolution impacting on the fundamental rights of a person/patient that we can sum up as follows: scientifically valid treatment, prompt treatment, second opinion, privacy, knowing the truth about a disease, being informed about therapies, refusing treatment, stating consensus in advance, not suffering, respect, dignity.

4.1.2 A New Paradigm in Health care

Summing up, these revolutions will lead to the emergence of a new paradigm marked by the shift away from the concept of advanced disease to that of "preventive health". A paradigm of a new medical approach with the following characteristics:

- proactive or taking the initiative, anticipating Healthcare needs in order to provide a more timely and effective response;
- predictive, estimating the probability of developing certain diseases;
- preventive, avoiding an illness or treating it as soon as it first appears for best results, also in terms of quality of life;
- customised, where therapy is "tailor made" to take a person's physical and psychological situation into consideration;
- participatory, involving and empowering patients in the care processes affecting his health;
- specific, considering the individual variability in a person's genes, environment and lifestyle.

These trends will shift the focus of attention away from people who are ill to people who are in good health.

The current patient-care model will change and become a model that puts more emphasis on all of the stages prior to the onset of a disease and on new methods and techniques of treatment should a disease be contracted, bringing superior results in terms of effectiveness, efficiency, real and perceived quality and safety. Since these trends are structural, we should ask ourselves whether it is possible to have Healthcare Systems that are effective, fair, efficient, up to date with modern medicine and sustainable in terms of their cost. This is only realistically achievable if we successfully eliminate the main dysfunctions that exist today: questionable political choices, managers without sufficient knowledge or skills to handle the complexity of the system, physicians and other healthcare personnel who often pay scant attention to the actual needs of patients or to ensuring they are treated in an appropriate manner, the uncontrolled increase in the expectations of the general—and not always well-informed—public, endemic corruption in sectors generating trade and business worth significant amounts. This is by no means prevalent behaviour because positive conduct prevails among many policy makers, managers and other healthcare professionals in the healthcare systems in many countries, who are also motivated, skilled and pay great attention to the needs of patients.

Action needs to be taken in six areas in order to keep Healthcare Systems healthy.

New patient-care models where the focus of health care is shifted away from hospitals to the local area, close to where people actually live, and separating highly complex therapies (carried out at hospital) from prevention, diagnosis and simpler treatment (carried out at other facilities in the local area or at home). This will reduce the number of acute care beds, which will be concentrated at a smaller number of hospitals that have the latest technology and can offer higher levels of patient care. There will be an increase in the number of Healthcare and Welfare Clinics handling diagnosis and treatments, without the need to stay in hospital, and more treatment will be carried out at home with health care personnel working together to safeguard the delivery of healthcare services in and out of hospital. This means that there must be a review of funding criteria, reducing the quota allocated to hospitals and increasing the amount assigned to other services.

Only therapies that have been scientifically proven to be effective will be made available. In order to curb spending, it will be important to avoid using methods, drugs and medical services whose efficacy has not been proven or those which have a higher cost yet have the same degree of efficacy. Some studies estimate that less than 50% of services today have proven benefits. Scientific or clinical knowledge alone is not enough if we are to achieve this goal; instead, physicians and other healthcare professionals must be trained/motivated/induced/encouraged to focus on aspects of management (programmes, time, efficacy, efficiency, quality and costs), i.e. ensuring the procedure and delivery is appropriate and that everything necessary is provided with the exception of anything superfluous. Regulations and tools are also needed in order to cut spending on defensive medicine by putting adequate safeguards in place for physicians and healthcare professionals, and lowering consumerism in health care resulting from misconceptions or the promise of miracle cures made by those exploiting their position of trust.

Introduction and gradual consolidation of the logic of total quality and continuous improvement, remembering that this leads to a reduction in costs and not an increase. It is not uncommon to find that poor quality and unsafe practice has a higher cost in terms of health care and welfare because they lead to complications requiring expensive treatment.

Continuous improvements in quality can be achieved by promoting the following factors: skilled professionals who are competent and up-to-date, boosting their interpersonal skills and empathy by offering them specific and ongoing training; facilities that are innovative and not outdated; an organisation that optimises its available resources, increasing the level of culture and information about health care offered to patients.

The promotion of responsible conduct throughout the system, with regard to the nature of needs, the quality of delivery and services, costs. One aspect of promoting responsibility concerns appropriate lifestyles for preventing or delaying the manifestation of a disease (primary prevention) and awareness and participation in campaigns promoting early diagnosis (secondary prevention).

In order to achieve this, communication campaigns and testimonials by famous sports—or entertainment personalities should be promoted. Health Care services generating significant positive externalities should be promoted and supported. One example is vaccination, as this not only benefits the person vaccinated but society in general too, since it prevents other people from being infected by contagious diseases.

4.1.3 Concluding Remarks

Innovation of models of organisation that, for a complex system such health care, must pursue excellence in management and achieve the correct use of limited resources compared to the structural expansion of needs and demand. The organisation's strategies and policies, decision-making and executive processes and its administrative procedures, have to be rebuilt starting from the holistic observation of the patient, achieving an interdisciplinary and interprofessional approach, and abandoning traditional methods revolving around the division and specialisation of duties and roles. In this context, innovation should impact both on the organisation within the facility (such as a hospital or local health care authority) and throughout the health care delivery network as a whole, which should distinguish between its role as a provider of services on the one hand and its roles related to funding, programming and the procurement of goods and services (centralised, wherever possible, to achieve economies of scale and specialisation) and control on the other. The delivery network must be based on the integration of public and private facilities, patient care at acute hospitals, local facilities and health care delivered at home, sharing and safeguarding access to information in order to guarantee the best response is offered to meet the patient's needs. It should also include rationalisation, closing or converting small hospitals, whose level of activity is not able to guarantee patient safety, into local (or neighbourhood) hospitals, and the concentration of funding required for the latest technological equipment at hospitals that are able to achieve economies of size, scale, purpose and specialisation.

These models of organisation must include governance structures that allow for the professional autonomy of physicians (and other non-medical professions), responsible for delivering the proper care, and striking a correct balance with their managerial responsibilities, and the correct use and organisation of resources at the different levels in the organisation (central, local health care authorities, hospitals, welfare and health care centres, departments, wards, etc.).

Finally, organisational models should allow for the integration of staff occupied in research, training and patient care, in order to promote the rapid passage from the development of knowledge to the improvement of the quality of life.

Ethically speaking, we may agree with the concept that you can not put a price on the value of life, but in tangible terms health care always comes with a price tag.

Starting from the consideration that the first resources available are those that are not wasted, we should underline that increasing the level of spending for prevention helps to reduce the higher future cost of diagnosis, treatment and rehabilitation. This link can be proven by applying methods of discounted cash flow or net present value. What's more, safeguarding the principles of universal coverage and equity of care that are the foundations of the National Health Service does not automatically imply that the only funding available is through taxes levied by the State. Funding can be raised via regional or local taxes, or through forms of cost-sharing, such as prescription charges, subscribing to private solidarity funds or private insurance coverage, provided the quality of services is high. The public may be willing to bear such charges if they perceive they will be receiving something with a high value.

If we set aside the ideology that was behind the setting up of National Health Services last century, we can state that a National Health Service that guarantees universal coverage may well be founded on a combination of public and private funding, and public and private care providers who have equal dignity, equal duties and equal rights (when providing similar services to the public), assessed for the appropriateness, efficacy and efficiency of their delivery of care.

To conclude, we could claim it is not true that Health Care Systems are too expensive, but it may also be that too much attention has been focused on the increase in spending in recent years, without considering the even faster increase in the quantity and quality of care and, above all, without really tapping into the potential for retrieving resources by combating corruption, inefficiency and waste.

4.2 Health Systems: Too Important to Fail

Mario Del Vecchio

4.2.1 Introduction

Almost everywhere in the world, citizens and patients receive health care services through complex systems in which public intervention (regulation, financing and provision) plays a substantial role. From this point of view, health care systems and their results are more the consequence of an intentional design than the outcome of an "invisible hand" sustaining and regulating atomistic market mechanisms. If provision and allocation of services of such an importance for people's life depend on collective decisions achieved through explicit (democratic) procedures, not surprisingly health care systems are subjected to close scrutiny by public opinion. At the same time and very often, health care is one of the most popular topics in the public debate as well as one of the hottest issues in the political arena. However, as Henry Mintzberg suggests, debates and decisions hardly reflect the "actual reality" of health care systems, emphasising their problems and underestimating the contribution they give to our better and longer lives. The result is a pressure towards a change that, even when needed, cannot well distinguish what functions, and must be preserved in the process of change, from what actually fails and needs to be fixed.

Why do societies tend to not recognise the real value of their health care systems and what can be done in order to have debates and decisions based more on facts and evidence? These questions are really difficult to be answered. The aim of this contribution is, having in mind the Italian experience, just to offer some considerations on the topic without any ambition to develop a comprehensive analysis.

4.2.2 Health care: An Expanding and Differentiating Universe

The dramatic expansion of health care domain and its potentialities is one of the possible reasons behind a growing dissatisfaction with health care and the demands for change to the systems. This expansion occurs, and can be interpreted, along different dimensions.

The most important component is the amount of new procedures and treatments that scientific and technological progress make available for improving and restoring health. Opportunities (and costs) for health systems can come from many different kinds of innovation. In oncology, new expensive drugs are transforming what in many cases used to be a lethal disease in a chronic condition. Advances in nutraceuticals raise new hopes for the prevention of age related pathologies like the Alzheimer's disease. As the area of what can be useful for human health constantly enlarges, budget constraints tend to impose tighter criteria to payers, public and private as well. The result is a widening gap between traditional expectations to receive everything that can add something to health (every effective treatment) and what can actually be delivered by health care systems (treatments effective enough to be considered as reasonably cost-effective).

Moreover, such an expansion is also in part a cause, and in part an effect, of a blurring distinction between health care and well-being domains that is led not only by new discoveries and by medical progresses. A shift from acute to chronic diseases (the new global pandemic), changes in individuals' behaviours and attitudes (from patient to consumer), changes in health care industry (e.g. diffusion of low cost–high quality providers) are just some of the factors transforming the nature of the patients' interaction with their health care systems. For most people contacts with health care services are no longer related to catastrophic events, but they have become part of everyday's life, so their interaction with health systems is changing from merely being episodic to a more continuous relationship, if not dependency.

According to an extensive survey on health status and health services consumption of the Italian population, regularly conducted every five years by the Italian National Institute of Statistics (ISTAT 2014), during the previous year: 72% of the population bought at least one pharmaceutical product, 51% had seen a specialist, 49% had a blood test, 36% had an imaging test, 9% experienced a hospital admission and 7% experienced a surgical procedure. Moreover, most popular and less expensive services show a significant portion of private financing (mostly of it on an out-of-pocket basis). Thus, even if the Italian National Health System (INHS) in principle provides universal coverage for all health care needs, about 30% of pharmaceutical expenses have been borne by households; 40% of visits was entirely paid by patient and an another 22% was partially paid (co-payment). Analogous figures for lab tests are 13% (entirely paid) and 33% (partially paid); while for imaging they are, respectively, 23 and 32%. For rarer and more expensive events, such as admissions, private contribution is negligible (less than 1%).

Italian data tell us to what extent certain areas of health care have become object of ordinary consumption processes and experiences. At the same time they show how hard it can be for a public system to cope with a growing and enlarging demand. The debate around the role of voluntary health insurance in universalistic systems testifies that problems are not limited to specific countries (Thomson et al. 2015). In this perspective, dissatisfaction with the system—expressing either as voice (people complaining for waiting times in the public sector) or exit (private consumption of services already included in the "public basket")—may be the result of a fundamental difficulty that a society has in making explicit choices about what can and should actually be provided under collective responsibility. In fact, the more the consumption of health care becomes similar to that of any other good or service, the more the difficulties grow for societies to draw clear-cut and agreed upon lines separating collective from individuals' responsibilities. Therefore, individuals may feel they have the right to receive all services, provided they pertain to the health domain, while public systems cannot cover the new, larger, health universe to the same extent as they did in the past. As long as the inevitable rationing of the more popular, and sometimes less effective, services is more the result of implicit mechanisms (waiting lists) than of explicit (political) decisions, it is almost fatal that the public opinion tends to look at the missing part, overlooking how significant is the part of health needs that health systems are still able to cover.

4.2.3 Public Opinion, Media and the Political Debate

Public attitudes towards health care systems are the result of different mechanisms and subjected to many influences. Analysing the paradoxical coexistence among Canadians of a strong support of their health care model, on the one hand, with a growing dissatisfaction with health care policy and a demand for radical changes, on the other, Soroka et al. (2013) propose to look at the issue considering two different dimensions. The first one is the source of the attitudes towards a health care system that can be either a direct personal experience or something like a "collective experience", that is the perceptions that individuals have of the beliefs or experiences of others. Both sources influence attitudes, but their relative importance depends on the specific question asked to individuals. From this point of view, a judgement about the quality of interactions with doctors is likely to be influenced by different and more personal sources than a judgement about the quality of the system in general. A second dimension distinguishes between retrospective and prospective attitudes. People have attitudes about the past and the future, and they may differ, as well as they may exert an influence one on the other. Thus, if the past is the natural basis for any future attitude, expectations about the future may, in turn, have an autonomous influence on the attitudes about the past.

Building with the two dimensions a two-by-two matrix results in a four-fold distinction of attitudes on health care: personal retrospective, personal prospective, collective retrospective and collective prospective. Only personal retrospective attitudes are likely to be predominantly driven by personal experience, while the others incorporate different, but significant, shares of perceptions provided by "external sources." Among such external sources, media content as well as messages prevalent in the political arena play an important role in educating citizens and shaping public opinion. Political messages are conveyed and interpreted by media, and, in turn, how media frame health care-related issues influence the political agenda. Therefore, what is usually referred to as public opinion attitudes about health care (in Henry Mintzberg words: people telling us that their health care system is failing) is the result of complex interactions among individuals' personal experiences, analyses and messages circulating in the political environment, media representation and interpretation of a given health care system.

Usually, opinions based on personal experiences with health care services are more positive than those based on external sources. A recent extensive survey about EU public perceptions of the quality of health care (European Union 2014), shows that the older the respondents, the more likely they are to say the quality of health care in their country is good, and the same is true of respondents with higher education levels. It is well known that, for different reasons, both categories have higher than average utilisation rates of health care services. Unfortunately, five years of economic crisis and increasing pressures on public budget may have worsened individuals' personal experiences in many countries. In Italy, since the beginning of economic crisis, public health care expenditures have been stabilised after two decades of uninterrupted and substantial growth. This has implied, in certain regions in particular, the implementation in the public sector of severe cost-cutting policies accompanied by a lengthening of waiting times for visits and diagnostic procedures. According to Censis (2014) 53.4% of respondents are prepared to wait longer before receiving ambulatory services and 48.1% during the previous year had decided to opt for private services, because of the waiting times. The same research shows that negative attitudes on the quality of their regional health system are growing: only 5.5% of citizens think that it has increased (11% in 2011), 38.5% think that it has decreased (29% in 2011) and 56% think that it has remained the same (60% in 2011). The main reasons behind negative judgements are waiting lists and waiting times for ambulatory services, that is, reasons probably more linked than others to personal experiences.

Besides a probable worsening of personal experiences in an area critical for consensus such as that of ambulatory services, external sources are at work. In particular, the prevailing political narrative about INHS may have contributed to diffuse dissatisfaction in the public opinion. An analysis of how problems related to health care are framed and communicated in the Italian political environment is still to be carried out. However, especially at national level (in Italy health care is under the responsibility of regional governments), politicians tend to describe (and public opinion is aligned to such vision) health care as a sector where expenditures are out of control and a lot of resources are wasted. It is not the case to discuss here the actual efficiency levels of the INHS, but it is clear that the larger the efficiency gains potentially exploitable in the system are the lesser is the necessity for structural changes that are always dangerous in terms of consensus. It is easier to tell public opinion that the needed cuts in the public health care budget would not have any impact on levels of services than to readjust expectations about provision of public services. Moreover, the "rhetoric of wastes" shifts the responsibility towards others actors such as regional governments, public managers and to a less extent towards professionals.

Media, traditional and new as well, not only convey and amplify political messages, but substantially contribute to the formation of public opinion, often in a negative direction. One of the few researches about media and health care in Italy (Del Vecchio and Rappini 2010) confirmed the notion that newspapers devote a substantial coverage to health care issues, especially in local pages, but showed also, how they pay a selective attention to negative events. News that can best fit the image of a health care system in crisis are preferred to more positive news that risk to contradict the popular vulgata of an ever present *malasanità* (scandals and bad functioning) characterising the INHS, vulgata that readers expect, and in part want, to be confirmed by the printed pages.

4.2.4 What Can Be Done to Better Support Healthcare Systems and Their Achievements?

The undoubtable achievements of health care systems are not so easily recognised by public opinions in modern societies, while public debates and the dynamics of consensus tend to ignore facts and evidence, at least in the short term. Traditional approaches to the welfare state need to be changed, and not only for economic reasons, but public support for structural changes is weak, and the economic crises makes resistance to change stronger.

Capabilities to change in any society depend on many factors. The possibility for the same societies to recognise the real value of their health care system too depends on many factors. Henry Mintzberg suggests that an indispensable and preliminary element in order to preserve such important systems is a sensible diagnosis and tells us that wrong diagnoses, as well as wrong therapies (myths), are widespread. The diffusion of myths is not an exclusive responsibility of the scientific community, but scholars and researchers have a definite responsibility. Not only they should produce better evidence and analyses, but they should also feel a stronger responsibility for the diffusion of sound analyses and their correct utilisation.

Health care systems are a fundamental part of social systems and, in this perspective, we can hardly confine ourselves to what Weiss Hirschon (1991) defined as data and findings. In certain occasions, the spreading of ideas (the framing of problems and issues) and even playing some role in the political arena (advocacy) may well be part of our responsibilities as scholars towards the collectivities we belong to.

4.3 Are Healthcare Systems Failing?

Patrizio Armeni

4.3.1 Introduction

Health has impressively improved over the last century. OECD health statistics (2015) show that since 1970 there has been a generalised, although not homogeneous, improvement in health conditions (e.g. cancer rate survival, vaccination rates, quality of in-patient care) in the OECD Countries. However, most health care systems are nowadays facing a variety of challenges.

The most economically advanced countries are capitalising the positive impact of health technologies and organisational innovations introduced in the last century with a substantial increase in life expectancy. In 2015, people live on average 5.2 years longer (OECD 2016) than they did in 1990 in the Big-5 European countries and +4.3 years in the U.S. At the same time, due to a low birth rate, population in these countries is ageing. The proportion of people aged 65 or more is 19.9% in the EU Big-5 and 14.8% in the U.S., showing a dramatic increase compared to 1990 (+5.3 points and +2.3 points, respectively, OECD 2016). Consequently, we are experiencing a higher incidence of chronic-degenerative diseases, with intensified health and social care needs, requiring a parallel increase of health-related resources. Moreover, scientific progress and technological innovation are generating opportunities which translated in higher perceived needs, putting additional pressure on costs. In developed countries, longer life expectancy and ageing (which is also affecting pension funding) coupled with technological innovation are often considered to be the drivers of unsustainability of health care systems.

A similar conclusion, but drawn from different arguments, is often proposed for developing countries. There, the fast growing number of inhabitants, associated with increasingly widespread prevention policies (often funded by foreign non-profit organisations), better hygienic conditions and more informed and educated populations require governments to drive the evolution of health care systems from minimal or rudimental institutions to complex and effective systems. This change is similar to the one experienced in the past by developed countries, but with the significant difference that nowadays spill-overs and interdependencies are much more evident, pushing these countries to adopt a faster pattern of evolution which is not necessarily their natural/sustainable one. Such pressure could stretch the mechanisms required for a balanced growth.

Focusing mainly on developed countries, it is possible to analyse the current challenges more in-depth with three arguments. First, the uncertainty of the relationship between life expectancy/ageing and health expenditure; second, the evolution of public coverage and the role of co-payment; third, the role of the health care sector as a driver of economic growth.

4.3.2 The Uncertainty of the Relationship Between Life Expectancy/Ageing and Health Expenditures

The literature has extensively analysed the relationship between life expectancy, ageing and health expenditure. To date, no ultimate evidence is available on this topic. According to the setting and the methodology used in the various studies that have tried to shed more light on this relationship, results vary considerably, ranging from the evidence of a positive relationship (longer life and ageing lead to increased expenditure) to neutral or even negative ones (e.g. Chernichovsky and Markowitz 2001). This lack of consensus is due, mainly, to (i) the uncertain causal direction; (ii) the presence of many possible mediators and/or moderators and (iii) the influence of end-of-life costs. We will present some examples. With respect to the causality issue, Meerdin et al. (1998) report a positive correlation between health-related disabilities and health care resource utilisation. Lichtenberg (2004), instead, finds an opposite direction of causality between public health expenditures and longevity. Zweifel et al. (2005) support the hypothesis of a two-way direction of causality between ageing and health expenditure. As for the end-of-life treatment costs, they have been recognised as a crucial influencing factor (Lubitz and Riley 1993; Garber et al. 1998; Hogan et al. 2001). In fact, after assessing the costs incurred during the last year of life, the relationship between longevity and health care expenditure can turn non-significant (O'Neill et al. 2000). In this light, life expectancy and ageing both tend to shift costs over time rather than to increase them. Other studies have found non-significant or mixed evidence (Getzen 1992; O'Connell 1996; Barros 1998). This is a signal that the relationship, if one exists, is affected by many possible confounding factors (not necessarily exogenous). We tested a longitudinal mediation model using WHO historical data to assess the relationship between life expectancy in t, health expenditure in t + 1 and life expectancy in t + 2: we found that there is a significant mediation for both directions of causality (we inverted the mediator and the independent) but the mediated impact was always low in magnitude (around 1%) and the incremental explanatory power was low (+2%), leaving the explanation of the increase in both expenditure and life expectancy to other factors. Such variety supports the idea that longevity and ageing can be related to health expenditure, although the relationship is neither ineluctable nor necessary because many factors can influence it. Therefore, a pure fatalistic approach under which health care systems will probably collapse due to increased life expectancy and ageing per se is too simplistic.

4.3.3 The Evolution of Public Coverage and the Role of Co-payment

Beyond the longitudinal relationship between the potential demographic causes of unsustainable health care, the simultaneous relationship between needs and resources requires attention, too. It is true that, nowadays, many health care systems are trying to reduce public expenditures with different strategies, including linear cuts, efficiency gains, new organisational arrangements, etc. The diffusion of spending reviews and cost-containment actions is due to the simultaneous increase in needs and stagnation of the amount of resources available for public expenditures. Health care systems based on public universal coverage are challenged since cost-cutting policies, paired with increasing needs, generate the threat of rationing. Provided that a gap between needs, opportunities and resources exists and that such gap is unavoidable, a shift between public and private expenditure is to be expected. However, in many cases there is evidence that the shift is absent or partial (e.g. Armeni et al. 2015a, on pharmaceutical expenditures) and the amount not explained by the shift is mainly due to patients' renunciation (Armeni et al. 2015b). The latter is a notable evidence of under-treatment, a circumstance that could produce a negative rebound effect on financial sustainability itself in the long run. To prevent such negative loop, a change in the perceived meaning of co-payment could play a major role, as well as the satisfaction of emerging or uncovered needs obtained through parallel market mechanisms (e.g. sharing economy). The sharing economy, whose benefits and conditions would require extensive attention, is only cited here as one of the potential and innovative solutions for activating the latent value in an economic system (e.g. Hamari et al. 2015). However, in a health care system, there are many services (e.g. surgical interventions with advanced technologies, access to innovative drugs etc.) where the sharing economy has a limited potential of penetration. To offer a solution to the gap between opportunities and resources, the role of co-payment can be revised. Nowadays many public systems adopt a dichotomist approach to co-payment: either the service is covered by public expenditure or it is completely private (or with fixed proportions of co-payment). The possibility of an upgrade is often seen as unequal. In particular, co-payment now acts as a pure buffer of expenditure cuts, generating regressive inequalities. Such positioning could drive to unsustainability, because it follows the illusion of unrestricted public coverage under growing needs. In fact, under the current dichotomy between fully covered services and fully out-of-pocket ones, patients are either convinced that they can access services for free (while they might be required to wait) or they are forced to access the services paying the full cost out-of-pocket (so they often renounce). A different option is to let co-payment work as a premium price and, consequently, as a driver for the diffusion of innovation. For instance, public coverage could be focused on programmes and technologies showing appropriate value for money for the general population (evaluated through processes like the Health Technology Assessment); instead, programmes, solutions and technologies excluded from public funding could be proposed as possible "upgrades" for patients able/willing to pay the extra cost. Instead of extending public coverage, whose impact is to lengthen the time to patient access (which is actually a form of rationing), governments should be concerned with defining what the public sector can cover immediately for everyone and which services can be provided as "extras" or as "upgrades." The latter can be still offered in a public setting, only applying the extra cost to the patient, who will perceive it as a premium price. Under an economic perspective, the "extra/upgrade" approach, compared to the "dichotomist" public/private rule, would represent a Paretian improvement, since more people could pay for the upgrade, reducing under-treatment, with no surcharge on public expenditure. In conclusion, the current gap between needs and resources requires a rethinking of the meaning of "public universal coverage" towards the more realistic "publicly sustainable universal coverage", where the best publicly affordable quality is offered for free and any upgrade falls under the area of well-being instead of health care.

4.3.4 The Role of the Healthcare Sector as a Driver of Economic Growth

A last important argument to support the idea that health care is not necessarily pushing countries towards collapse is the evidence that the health care sector is an important driver of economic growth and that there is a mutual causality between quality of the health care sector and economic growth. Ageing and longevity are demanding more resources for health care but these circumstances can create the opportunity of a growing sector instead of just representing a threat for public systems. A "healthy" health care system attracts investments by companies, stimulates human capital formation and ultimately generates value. The expansion of partnerships with the private sector testifies that health care is not only a weight for the system, but also a driver of economic growth. Many studies have investigated the relationship between health care quality and expenditure and economic growth, showing evidence of a positive and often bidirectional relationship (e.g. Baldacci

2004; Bloom et al. 2004; Ogungbenle et al. 2013). Looking at health care in an economic development perspective highlights its potential positive influence on interdependent industries. To show how a high-quality health care system holds the promise to positively influence the broader economic system, we can highlight at least five crucial interdependencies. The hypothesis we want to support is that investing in health care is not a pure deadweight cost, but that it is productive for the whole economic system. Firstly, the health care system has important spill-overs with the research system. A "healthy" health care system creates opportunities for research in the domains of science (e.g. medicine, pharmacology, engineering, etc.), management (e.g. how to efficiently organise services, testing innovative organisational arrangements to unfold latent dimensions of value, etc.) and policy (e.g. how to rethink the role of co-payment). The amount of research produced is a benefit for the health care system, generating a positive loop between investing in health care and investing in research. Secondly, the industries selling products and services to the health care systems represent an important interdependency too. The pharmaceutical industry, the medical device industry and the number of service providers are often seen as "cost generators" for a public health care system. However, beyond representing an important job market for local graduates, firms selling products and services to the health care system are an opportunity for enhancing the quality and specificity of the solutions on offer. The geography of new business development of pharma and medical device companies testifies that investments in health care also attract investments in these industries, contributing to economic growth. The greater the willingness to invest in innovative products and services, the greater the opportunity for local and global firms to grow, bringing fresh resources to an economic system. Thirdly, the public health care systems are becoming increasing complementary with private providers, either for-profit or not-for-profit. The sustainability of a whole health care system will be increased by the capacity of private providers to find business opportunities that do not increase public expenditures. The sharing economy and the revisited role of co-payment can play a major role, but also the ability of the public sector to efficiently drive the evolution between internal production and externalisation can gradually improve the overall efficiency of the system. Fourthly, health care systems are increasingly open to the international market. The efficiency of a system can be reached by accessing the international production system, where excess demand and productive capacity can be matched. Moreover, this trend is an incentive for national systems to find and invest in their distinctive excellences to attract foreign demand. Such trend is nowadays growing but still very limited (e.g. in Italy, the net value of international mobility has been around 150 million euros in 2013). Finally, a "healthy" health care system is also attractive in terms of education. Students and executives can be attracted by a health care system showing the traits of excellence, bringing non-financial economic resources (e.g. knowledge) into the system.

In conclusion, we should be conscious of the challenges that health care systems are facing, but we should also reject fatalistic and purely pessimistic views. In this short contribution, we have presented three arguments to reflect on the real nature of the challenges and on the latent opportunities concealed by the same challenges.

4.4 Behind the Clichés. Spending Review and Organisational Change in the Italian NHS

Vincenza Esposito, Mario Pezzillo Iacono, Lorenzo Mercurio and Joseph Polimeni

4.4.1 Introduction and Aims

The link between healthcare needs and services paid by the public and private healthcare system has been the key focus of studies and analyses which, over time, have given rise to very extensive and in-depth management literature (Henry Mintzberg 2012).

One of the trends that unite more strongly the experience of public administration reform in Europe is that of rationalisation and reduction of operating costs of their own organisational models, often labelled as Spending Review (SR) (Porter and Teisberg 2006). These reforms have two main purposes: to contain public expenditure and to increase the efficiency and effectiveness of public administrations (Esposito et al. 2015).

Of course, the key issue is whether and to what extent it is possible to cut costs without reducing service quantity and quality (Mercurio and Adinolfi 2005).

Twenty-first century healthcare systems face many problems which are independent of resource availability, and often result in an over-medicalisation of society: the variability of processes and outcomes, increased risks for patients, wastage, the system's inability to boost value, inequalities and the inability to prevent disease.

In Italy, in particular, coinciding with the financial and economic crisis of recent years and the strong need to limit public expenditure and stay within the budget, there is a lively debate in political, social, media and academic spheres on the subject of SR in the health sector. Mentioning SR is right and to be expected, however, it should be stressed that reducing costs does not in itself ensure a continual virtuous cycle where there are both efficiency and the ability to meet the increasingly strong and diverse needs of the community (de Belvis et al. 2012). SR applied to health systems must be the highest expression of a method of managerial and organisational change based on planning skills, managerial and leadership abilities, as well as on management models and assessment, monitoring and evaluation techniques.

In particular, SR in the health sector must start with the political, managerial, professional and social awareness that health care is perhaps the only market affected by supply and is one of the main sources of consumerism among citizens. It is an extremely complex market at the centre of numerous stakeholders' interests: politics (National, Regional and Autonomous Provinces), public and private health care companies, managers, healthcare professionals and citizens, but also the pharmaceutical and biomedical industry, scientific associations, unions, professional colleges, patients' associations, etc. In this regard, SR must not be seen as a mere cost-cutting mechanism, but as a methodological approach to redesign models, practices and organisational and management tools in the health sector, taking into account the complexity of the stakeholders involved and the lack of homogeneity among the solutions adopted at local level.

Our goal is to provide a reflection on the approach to SR in the Italian National Health Service. After presenting an analysis of the concept of SR in a framework of organisational change (van der Voet 2014), the focus will be on the methods of its actual implementation in the Italian health sector, to then conclude with some final considerations on the need to find a new systemic and holistic approach to SR in the medium to long term.

4.4.2 Moving Beyond the Myth of Measurement

Following the development of a set of political, economic, technological and regulatory factors over the past few decades, public systems have undergone major changes to innovate and improve the efficiency of their equipment. Indeed, as the context within which public organisations operate has changed, an overall need for transformation has risen to ensure the delivery of innovative and high-quality services to groups of users with varying and increasingly complex demands. The approach to productivity and efficiency in public action has thus come alongside with the growing demand to effectively guarantee the rights of individuals and promote the development of communities with careful planning and regulation.

At the same time, the recent economic and financial crises are increasing the complexity faced by public management and demand addressing the approaches and action models for SR, but also—more broadly—of the need to change the organisation of public systems (Mercurio and Martinez 2010).

When reflecting on SR action models, it is clear how crucial it is to focus on the relationship between (a) the outputs and outcomes that an administration intends to achieve and (b) the characteristics and quantity of the resources it uses.

Indeed, the most successful SR interventions are planned with a clear strategic mission and encompass the approach to organisational change (be it incremental or radical) of the working processes of public action. The development of an SR process requires a proper overview of the organisational activities and the expected, declared, assessed and measured results in relation to the contextual conditions, specialist knowledge and, not least, the cultural values that arise in the specific organisational structure. In short, an SR programme should always be seen as the component of a broader "strategy", stressing the importance for the organisation to adopt a well thought out managerial/directional tool to ensure the programme is successful. Indeed, the will and strength of the need to "rationalise" expenditure are not sufficient to make a lasting impact on the actual running of organisations over time.

In any process of change management, the essential backdrop that creates the conditions for change to be successful is to have a shared vision: an end goal expressed clearly and consistently for the benefit of all stakeholders involved in the process itself. A future vision for an organisation investing in change must have a managerial culture made up of a clear implementation schedule, individuals to be involved in various types of partnerships and initiatives, and the costs and benefits to be negotiated at the outset or during the implementation of the programme. A sensible vision of the change process can help to build a common base of knowledge, legitimacy and commitment between the stakeholders involved in the project, thereby reducing any inevitable resistance. Moreover, there must be a strong planning phase: a phase where the specific goals of the change are "interpreted", modelled and adjusted—from the initial structural and relational conditions—to achieve the much-needed harmonisation between the various items of expenditure of the given organisational structure.

However, this kind of change process rarely provides effective and lasting responses—compared, for example, to targets aimed at reducing the running costs of a public organisation—if they are top-down and, especially, if they are enacted uniformly to different administration populations.

4.4.2.1 The Role of Managerial Practices for Organisational Change

Aside from the importance of the planning processes mentioned above, the truly essential resource in any change in management processing often proves to be managerial competence when managing "emerging" organisational models (van der Voet 2014). Managers' awareness and competence are essential to interpret these patterns and to make a lasting impact on the running of administrations and, in turn, on their actual spending levels. These skills and behaviours must go along with "professionalism" when effecting change and building management support tools, as well as distinct leadership qualities and negotiation skills. To make an explicit reference to the Italian health sector, it should be noted that purchases are made by Local, not Regional or National Authorities. Furthermore, there is clear disparity among and within regions and individual Local Health Authorities.

4.4.2.2 Instability of Conditions and Mistrust

The expected resistance of pre-existing organisational models to the "threat" of change can often be seen in concrete experiences in Italy, together with some very critical factors: the turbulence of the political/institutional context, the conflict between management and political commitment, and the public's underlying mistrust.

The sudden and unpredictable changes in control groups and how authorities are managed, the impact of developments in the political and institutional context, managerial behaviours geared towards building alliances and coalitions to achieve results and programmes, often create a deafening "background noise" that surrounds and restricts initiatives aimed at change. The implementation of organisational development projects are often hampered by the constant "reshuffling of cards" that change the "rules of the game" and political power that controls and determines the changes that are actually pursued.

More often, the weakness of local politics has been complemented by that of regional government bodies that often passively support the SR choices made at national level, yet without producing legislation and/or guidelines to tangibly facilitate their implementation.

Therefore, there seems to be a strong resistance to change at all levels of government, whereby the rational and formally shared topics of SR clash with two other systems of power, exercised in a negative form: the propensity not to decide and to preserve structures established over time, for which it is all too easy to raise "tactical" arguments.

This is the widespread expression of "dual power" in public organisations. This critical situation, especially at an early stage, makes it very difficult to quickly acquire the information needed to identify both the stakeholders and the main steps of the process being analysed. In other cases—despite the legitimate and widespread demands for innovation, which often naturally support identifying subjects, content and the expected results of the change—the current internal dynamics between political governance bodies and management are complicating the formalisation and legitimisation of the commitments.

4.4.2.3 Legitimacy and Significance of Standards for Reviewing Costs and Assessing Performance

A final significant factor for the structuring of an SR meta-model, which can tangibly support the effort to rationalise costs in the health sector, is the availability of structured information on standard values and other performance indicators.

Being a process of change, every SR intervention, for reasons explained above, must be accompanied by a clear definition of the "end goals", a strategic vision, but above all, concrete outcomes and target indicators of technical and operational performance. In this regard, every target provided in the start-up phase of an SR intervention (such as those relating to overall cuts in specific categories of running costs), in addition to being a real restraint to the process of change, is also an external factor that guides the more general policies and organisational choices of a given structure.

The need to reduce costs relating to a specific service or operational area has spread like wildfire across all areas of the organisation. To stem this risk, two key contextual factors may come into play. On one hand, the process of change can be facilitated by the introduction of institutional and independent organisations (observatories, authorities, agencies, research centres) with structured data sources relating to specific performance standards and cost categories related to SR (such as the performance data sources in health care which can be a clear factor in establishing the standard costs of a service or staff costs). On the other, the same benefit can be taken from central government measures which have transparent mechanisms to enable technical adjustments of targets set—or rather imposed—by SR. Regulatory provisions that allow some flexibility to establish target values and indicators which are more in keeping with policies and, above all, with the specific organisational conditions and context.

In other words, these two additional components may compete to create an "institutional infrastructure" that can support the rationalisation of government bodies' organisational models. The autonomy and reputation of third parties that could help to measure and assess, at national level, the desired performance standards—compared to families of well-defined work processes—serve as quality assurance factors in the evaluation process.

4.4.3 The Scope of the Spending Review in the Italian National Health Service

In the current climate, the Italian National Health System is at the centre of conflicting pressures: on one hand, the need for spending cuts and, on the other, the constantly growing demand for personal care services.

In Italy, health spending is between 70 and 80% of regional spending and is currently worth around 110 billion euro. The critical point, as mentioned above, is whether it is possible to reduce spending without compromising services (Armeni and Costa 2015).

Excluding the "health services" and "staff costs" items, the spending perimeter, quickly attacked in the National Health Service, has shrunk to around 30 billion euro. These are supplies and services ranging from medicinal products to diagnostic materials, lab coats for doctors, cleaning services, canteens, heat and maintenance.

The recently adopted solutions were made up of three types: centralised purchasing; adopting standard costs; the ability to renegotiate contracts (concerning "personal" expenses).

Therefore, the rationalisation of healthcare costs focuses on purchases by setting reference prices and establishing price "observers": these are areas where there seems to be real margins to boost the systems' efficiency and make savings. And where, typically, corruption can be endemic, which is perhaps the worst form of inefficiency among government bodies. The recent ISPE-Sanità White Paper, for instance, estimated that 23.6 billion euro was wasted in relation to corruption in the health sector in 2013.

Returning to the subject of the SR policies adopted, centralisation—i.e. concentrating the purchasing function for an ASL/AO leader or dedicated institution—aims to take advantage of public market power and seek economies of scale when managing purchases and staff specialisation. Centralisation requires standardising the needs and consumption processes. Standard supplies, like medical products, can be consolidated relatively easily. If the same logic is applied to services, including those which appear simpler such as cleaning, where the costs depend on the context in which the services take place, the situation seems much more complex. Setting out standard costs requires a single classification of purchase items, supply contracts and production processes with which these goods are used to provide the service. On this subject, standard prices should only be seen as benchmarks and points of reference, rather than a formal requirement laid down by law. A recent resolution by the National Anticorruption Authority set the reference price of several consumer goods in hospitals. ANAC prices are based on a survey conducted between March and May 2014 on a sample of 283 administrations. For now, the focus has only been on "syringes", "cotton wool" and "patches", which cost just a few cents per piece but which are used a great deal. It is difficult to say how much they impact spending: as part of SR, the estimate for the entire category of medical equipment was over 5 billion euro a few years ago, 4.5% of current public health spending. All prices should, however, be extended to cover all expenses for the purchase of goods and services.

Yet what has been lacking is a more "micro" perspective of the purchase issue: purchases are made by Local, not Regional or National Authorities. Furthermore, there is clear disparity between and within regions and between individual Local Health Authorities. As such, the subject of management skills (and meritocracy) is a fundamental element which cannot be ignored.

4.4.4 Final Considerations

SR cannot be seen as an "emergency" activity due to the crisis, but requires taking action "step by step" on the purchasing processes and "production" processes especially, while addressing redesigning organisational practices and models. Boosting efficiency by offering better services is a medium-term goal; it requires structural measures that are not dictated by urgency and above all requires investments: redefining the service network, redesigning care processes, staff training and computerisation. It is necessary to adopt system actions and far-reaching structural policies, which set clear goals and go beyond the cost of syringes or cotton wool. In other words, SR should not take on the role of a system of extraordinary corrective measures, but rather should be integrated within the entire process of redesigning culture, organisational models and practices, as well as management performance, so that it can become a systematic tool used to seek the most efficient and effective ways to ensure the Essential Levels of Care throughout the country.

A sustainable health system—regardless of its nature (public, private or mixed) and share of GDP allocated to health—is not possible without adequate investment to improve the production of knowledge, its use by professionals, and the governance of the process to transfer healthcare knowledge. This is because most of the waste is due to the difficulty in transferring research into clinical practice and into the organisation of the health services.

The first step is undoubtedly to realign the diverging and often conflicting goals of the various stakeholders. Policies to protect the Italian National Health Service require adequate healthcare (re)programming. This must start with people's care and social needs while involving all categories of stakeholders and taking into account the epidemiology of diseases and illnesses, efficiency, suitability and cost-effectiveness of existing health care and services—a fundamental "triangulation" which has never before been applied in Italy.

It is also essential to use the knowledge in all policy, managerial and professional areas that affect people's health and to reduce imbalances in information among citizens.

Lastly, more broadly speaking, one cannot fail to point out that one of the levers for the reallocation of healthcare costs based on the actual needs of the community can be found in information and prevention policies. This involves significant investment at an early stage but produces significant economic and social benefits in the medium and long term. With this in mind, it may be possible to improve the effects of the reorganisation of the health systems, especially in the long term.

References

Armeni P, Costa F (2015) La spesa sanitaria: composizione ed evoluzione. In CERGAS (eds) L'aziendalizzazione della sanitaà in Italia. Rapporto OASI 2015. Egea, Milano

Armeni P, Jommi C, Otto M (2015a) The simultaneous effects of pharmaceutical policies from payers' and patients' perspectives: Italy as a case study. Eur J Health Econ 1–15. doi:10.1007/s10198-015-0739-0

Armeni P, Costa F, Sommariva S (2015b) I sistemi sanitari in una prospettiva internazionale. In: CERGAS (eds). L'aziendalizzazione della sanità in Italia. Rapporto OASI 2015. Egea, Milano

Baldacci EB (2004) The impact of poor health on total factor productivity. J Dev Stud 42:918–938

Barros P (1998) The black box of health care expenditure growth determinants. Health Econ 7:533–544

Bloom DE, Canning D, Sevilla J (2004) The effect of health on economic growth: a production function approach. World Dev 32(1):1–13

Censis (2014) Out of Pocket e tempi di attesa: indagine sui Servizi Sanitari Pubblici e Privati. Research for RBM Salute

Chernichovsky D, Markowitz S (2001) Toward a framework for improving health care financing for an ageing population: the case of Israel. NBER Working Paper 8415

de Belvis AG, Ferrè F, Specchia ML, Valerio L, Fattore G, Ricciardi W (2012) The financial crisis in Italy: implications for the health care sector. Health Policy 106:10–16

Del Vecchio M, Rappini V (2010) Aziende sanitarie e stampa quotidiana: una proposta di analisi. In: Cantù E, Anessi Pessina E (eds) L'aziendalizzazione della Sanità in Italia: Rapporto Oasi 2010. Egea, Milano, pp 433–464

Esposito V, Mercurio R, Martinez M, Pezzillo Iacono M, De Nito E (2015) Bridging spending review and change management in Italian public administrations. Law Econ Yearly Rev 4 (2):337–351

European Union (2014) Special Eurobarometer 411. Patient safety and quality of care

Garber AM, McCurdy TE, McClellan ML (1998) Medical care at the end of life: diseases, treatment patterns, and costs. NBER working Paper 6748

Getzen TE (1992) Population ageing and the growth of health expenditure. J Gerontol Soc Sci 47: S98–S104

Hamari J, Sjöklint M, Ukkonen A (2015) The sharing economy: why people participate in collaborative consumption. J Assoc Inf Sci Technol. doi:10.1002/asi.23552

Hogan C, Lunney J, Gabel J, Lynn J (2001) Medicare beneficiares' costs of care in the last year of life. Health Aff 20:188–195

Istat (2014) Indagine multiscopo Condizioni di salute e ricorso ai servizi sanitari. Istat, Roma

Lichtenberg FR (2004) Sources of US longevity increase, 1960–2001. Q Rev Econ Finance 44:369–389

Lubitz J, Riley GF (1993) Trends in medicare payments in the last year of life. New Engl J Med 328:1092–1096

Meerdin WJ, Bonneux L, Polter JJ, Koopmanschap MA, Van der Maas PJ (1998) Demographic and epidemiological determinants of health care costs in Netherlands: cost of illness study. BMJ 317:111–115

Mercurio R, Adinolfi P (2005) La clinical governance, possibile soluzione ai fabbisogni di integrazione nelle aziende sanitarie. Mecosan 53:67–80

Mercurio R, Martinez M (2010) Modelli di governance e processi di cambiamento nelle public utilities. FrancoAngeli, Milano

Mintzberg H (2012) Managing the myths of health care. World Hosp Health Serv 48(3):4–7

O'Connell J (1996) The relationship between health expenditures and the age structure of the population in OECD countries. Health Econ 9:573–578

O'Neill C, Groom L, Avery AJ, Boot D, Thornhill K (2000) Age and proximity to deaths as predictors of GDP care costs: results from a study of nursing home patients. Health Econ 9:733–738

OECD Health Data, 2016 (last access: 7th July 2016)

Ogungbenle S, Olawumi OR, Obasuyi FOT (2013) Life expectancy, public health and economic growth in Nigeria: a vector autoregressive model (VAR). Eur Sci J 9:210–235

Porter ME, Teisberg EO (2006) Reforming health care. Harvard Bus School, Harvard

Soroka S, Maioni A, Martin P (2013) What moves public opinion on health care? Individual experiences, system performance, and media framing. J Health Polit Policy Law 38(5):893–920

Thomson S, Figueras J, Evetovits T, Jowett M, Mladovsky P, Maresso A, Cylus J, Karanikolos M, Kluge H (2015) Economic crisis, health systems and health in Europe: impact and implications for policy. Open University Press, Maidenhead

van der Voet J (2014) The effectiveness and specificity of change management in a public organization: transformational leadership and a bureaucratic organizational structure. Eur Manag J 32(3):373–382

Weiss Hirschon C (1991) Policy research: data, ideas, or arguments? In: Wagner Peter et al (eds) Social sciences and modern states. Cambridge University Press, Cambridge, pp 307–332

Zweifel P, Steimman L, Eugster P (2005) The Sisyphus syndrome in health revised. Int J Health Care Finance Econ 5:127–145

Chapter 5
Myth #2: The Healthcare System Can Be Fixed by Clever Social Engineering

Emanuele Lettieri, Cristina Masella, Corrado Cuccurullo and Fernando Giancotti

5.1 Fixing Healthcare Systems Through Innovation

Emanuele Lettieri and Cristina Masella

5.1.1 Introduction

Can we—or anyone else—disagree sincerely with this demythologizing exercise carried out by Henry Mintzberg? In conferences, meetings and teaching classes we discuss emblematic cases from all the most developed countries about ambitious, top-down, advised-by-experts plans of action aimed at fixing the healthcare ecosystem that actually fell very short of their promise. In many of these cases healthcare professionals are depicted as indifferent—if not resistant—to any request

E. Lettieri (✉)
Politecnico di Milano, Piazza Leonardo da Vinci, 32, 20133 Milan, Italy
e-mail: emanuele.lettieri@polimi.it

C. Masella
Department of Management, Economics and Industrial Engineering,
Politecnico di Milano, Lambruschini 4/B, 20156 Milan, Italy
e-mail: cristina.masella@polimi.it

C. Cuccurullo (✉)
Department of Economics, Universita' degli Studi Della Campania
"Luigi Vanvitelli", Via Gran Priorato Di Malta, Capua, CE, Italy
e-mail: corrado.cuccurullo@Unina2.It

F. Giancotti (✉)
Air Education and Training Command, Italian Air Force, Lungomare Nazario
Sauro, 37, 70121 Bari, Italy
e-mail: giancottif@gmail.com

P. Adinolfi and E. Borgonovi (eds.), *The Myths of Health Care*,
https://doi.org/10.1007/978-3-319-53600-2_5

of change that do not come from them. These anecdotes should probably confirm that socially engineered, "silver-bullet," solutions are not able to promote long-lasting improvements in health care and are likely to be rapidly abandoned.

Looking back to our research on the "management innovation" in healthcare ecosystems at Politecnico di Milano, three examples offer specific empirical evidence that Henry Mintzberg might be on the right direction. They are (i) the institutionalization of telemedicine-based services in the professional daily practice; (ii) the implementation of Health Technology Assessment (HTA) programs at the National/Regional levels in Italy; and (iii) the adoption of knowledge management initiatives in hospitals.

5.1.2 Some Evidences of Management Innovation

In telemedicine, social engineers have paid extensive efforts to redesign the current delivery of care through ICT-enabled innovations, and yet the expected positive impacts on the whole system are still to come (Whitten et al. 2010; Zanaboni and Lettieri 2011). Vice versa, changes were brought about by small-sized, focused initiatives that originated from entrepreneurial physicians since they were able to communicate the "value" of the innovation and thus involve all the relevant professions (other physicians, nurses, healthcare assistants, technicians, etc.).

About HTA, while social engineers—such as the National Institute for Clinical Excellence (NICE) in England and the other National Agencies—implemented top-down, rational approaches to legitimize decision-making in a time of severe resource constraints, physicians engaged in other initiatives—such as the recent Choosing Wisely Movement (Volpp and Loewenstein 2012; Cassel and Guest 2012)—that through incremental, bottom-up, context-wise, and socially agreed discussions, advance professionals' action toward cost-effective choices.

As regards knowledge management, social engineers developed top-down, advised-by-experts initiatives—such as the development of sophisticated knowledge information systems, the enrollment of Chief Knowledge Officers, the adoption of organizational practices as job rotation, interrupting meetings, etc.—to organize knowledge flows within and outside hospitals (Mura et al. 2013; Edmondson 2004). Despite these efforts, results fell short of the promises since knowledge sharing is an individual, discretional behavior that managers cannot mandate and that healthcare professionals have to self-organize.

Given such evidence, should we argue that bottom-up (professionals endorsed) approaches overtake top-down (socially engineered) ones? With these—and many others—examples in mind, our first answer would be "Yes, we do fully agree with Henry Mintzberg."

However, our position is different and in this chapter we would like to deploy our arguments to explain why we do firmly disagree. In framing our thoughts, we will start from the myth itself and from four concepts that need to be rhetorically discussed. They are "social engineering", "system", "fixed," and "clever".

We start from the concept of "social engineering" because its definition—or better, our interpretation of this discipline and its historic development as well as its impacts on our societies—is critical to contextualize the boundaries and the implications of our arguments. Among the many definitions, we refer to the one provided by Weinberg (1991) in his essay on the tension between social engineering and technologies. In his view, "social engineering aims at inventing the social devices—usually legal, but also moral and educational and organizational—that will change each person's motivation and redirect his activities along ways that are more acceptable to the society" (p. 42).

Henry Mintzberg debates change at the "system" level. The healthcare system—as professional setting—results from the composition of structures, processes, reward systems, and people practices that have been consolidated in decades. Relevant, long-lasting changes are likely to occur along complex, not-predictable evolutionary trajectories that transform incrementally the inner components and mechanisms of the healthcare system. Can disruptive blueprints of the surface level actually generate rapid, pervasive, coherent changes in all the lower level components?

Answering this question obliges to reflect on the concept of how healthcare systems should be "fixed."

In this regard, Popper (1961) introduced the difference between utopian and piecemeal social engineering. While the former advocates a revolutionary approach, the latter prefers an evolutionary one. In this regard, utopian social engineers would propose to construct health care from scratch—in other words, they would pursue the "canvas cleaning" approach to the reconstruction of society argued by Plato—since current failures can be fixed only by making a big leap forward. Vice versa, piecemeal social engineers would propose to change health care one step at a time since policy makers do not have a blueprint of health care that should be achieved to provide patients with superior services. Among the two approaches, Popper endorses the latter since a complex social system—such as health care—requires a form of social engineering that is small-scale, incremental, and continuously amended in the light of errors and experience.

As a consequence, two questions deserve an answer: "Which approach should be preferred in the peculiar context of health care? Does Henry Mintzberg consider one of them more 'clever' than the other?"

In assessing the problem, Henry Mintzberg seems to agree with Potter's view that local, incremental, inside-informed innovations should be preferred to utopian, large-size, outside-informed ones. He claims a contraposition between expert, cross-industry knowledge that comes from outside the specific health care landscape (i.e., outside-healthcare social engineers) and expert, context-wise knowledge that is developed incrementally within the healthcare landscape itself. Henry Mintzberg stands for the latter because outside-healthcare experts, beyond any rhetoric, ignore the history and the socially agreed emergent evolutions of the social system they aim at transforming from scratch.

In providing his arguments, Henry Mintzberg surprisingly overlooks to address the innovation process itself and the main implications of its main phases, determinants, and peculiarities. The consequence is the creation of another myth—i.e., that health care will be fixed by healthcare professionals themselves through small-size, inside-informed, professional-driven, incremental approaches.

Our researches at Politecnico di Milano disconfirm this new myth and suggest another perspective that we deploy in the following.

It is widely accepted within the academic community that the innovation process can be divided roughly into three phases—i.e., creativity, socialization, and implementation—that have different triggers, sources of knowledge, and dynamics. Despite these phases are conceptually separate, they need to converge for an innovation to occur.

Creativity—or idea generation—is a divergent process in which a variety of ideas are generated, and then explored, when unexpected ideas or perspectives stimulate new associations. Socialization—or idea evaluation—is a convergent decision-making process through which selecting the most interesting ideas. In a nutshell, "idea generation is expected to produce novel ideas, whereas idea evaluation is expected to improve the quality of ideas" (Harvey and Kou 2013, pp. 348–349). Finally, implementation is the process of gaining targeted professionals' appropriate and committed use of an innovation. In other words, innovations have been fully implemented only once they are institutionalized in new organizational routines.

These phases require the combination and recombination of different perspectives and different bodies of knowledge in order to produce significant change. In this regard, can we agree sincerely that healthcare professionals will outperform in all of them?

5.1.3 Discussion and Conclusions

Our researches on two recent changes in the healthcare domain do not provide support to this claim.

With respect to the adoption of Electronic Medical Records (EMRs), physicians had different roles along the (still undergoing) innovation process. While they were not the trigger of this significant change/innovation, their involvement had been essential in socializing the various proposals in order to identify the most promising ones and in legitimizing the implementation phase. And again, while physicians devoted their attention to "automatize" their paper-based knowledge repositories, they did not really engage in "obliterating" the knowledge silos that prevent hospitals to develop evidence-based managerial practices. Our researches show that even if physicians as well as other healthcare professionals are the preferable vehicle for institutionalizing new practices, they could fail in perceiving the urgency and the scope of what has to be changed to fix health care at the organizational or system level.

About the limited diffusion of Integrated Care Pathways in hospitals, it emerges that physicians could also fail in the phase of socializing the preferable ideas as result of the existing professional tensions toward local, mono-specialty improvements. Even if any physician would agree with the value and urgency of delivering care through cross-specialty approaches, physicians appear unable to organize such boundary-cutting pathways and rely definitely on hospital middle managers—e.g., the Quality Offices in our experience in Italy—or external consultants to move forward. The professions in health care favor the preservation of dominant strategies, values, and routines and limit—when they do not preclude—innovation and change. Routines preserve continuity in behaviors that are reinforced by professional norms and internal social structures that are resistant to change.

Our past researches do not provide support neither to an approach that advocates the supremacy of context-wise professionals in fixing health care nor to another one that advocates the supremacy of outside-the-box social engineers.

What emerges clearly from our studies is an egg of Columbus: relevant and long-lasting changes in health care are likely to occur when outside-the-box social engineers and context-wise professionals collaborate along the three phases of the innovation process, sharing—and mediating—their visions, core values, concerns, and positive energies.

A straightforward example comes from our studies on the development of greening strategies in hospitals in England. While it is evident for all industries that environment protection is an urgent issue, the healthcare ecosystems of many of the most developed countries are still indifferent to this debate.

Healthcare professionals are resisting to the allocation of shrinking financial resources to other stakeholders—such as the Environment—instead of the citizens/patients. The adoption of greening strategies in hospitals and of greening behaviors by professionals required a disruptive change of the well-established core values, professional identities, and routines in the British healthcare ecosystem. In this regard, physicians and the other healthcare professionals would have never been the trigger of such a big change that is successfully happening in England. The new ideas came from the National Healthcare System–Sustainable Development Unit (NHS–SDU) that acted as a "social engineer" in defining the expect goals and the trajectories of this system-wide disruptive change. However, the unit acknowledged the need of engaging into numerous, dedicated publicly open conversations with the representatives of health care with the aim of aligning "the theoretical, utopian change" to the actual contingencies of the context that would have been affected by it. These consultations helped refining the original blueprint and identifying, among the number of proposals, the most promising in terms of relevance and feasibility. The emerging concerns about this change were addressed by knowledgeable, from-the-outside experts which provided healthcare professionals with encouraging experiences of similar changes already occurred in other industries and about the strategies and initiatives implemented to detect and overcome potential dark side effects. Finally, the NHS–SDU co-designed the implementation strategies jointly with professionals in order to create motivation, abilities, and opportunities at both the organizational and individual levels. Their perspective was that changes are likely to fail not as result of their disruptiveness, but as result of managerial interventions that are unable to create the premises for changing. In this regard, the normative actions in terms of taxation and incentives were complemented with a number of initiatives—e.g., the establishment of Sustainability Managers as new facilitating organizational roles, dedicated training sessions, etc.—orchestrated by the Hospital Human Resource Management Units aimed at creating a collective commitment to change and at facilitating professionals in engaging organization citizenship behaviors toward the environment.

Concluding, we believe that the current economic, demographic, social, and technological megatrends are creating a bundle of opportunities for rethinking the delivery of care as we know it. Professionals and social engineers—such as politicians, consultants, technology-suppliers, and academicians—have the temporal co-responsibility of putting in place new models, tools, and policy recommendations that protect the needs of future generations. In this view, we hope that future research will gather additional evidence that health care could be fixed by the diffusion of "smart" collaborative approaches between social engineers and professionals which complement each other along the phases of the innovation process to produce significant, positive differences for citizens/patients.

5.2 Change and Innovation in Health care

Corrado Cuccurullo

5.2.1 Introduction

Myth #2 of Henry Mintzberg comes from the widespread perception that the healthcare system in the industrialized countries is not economically sustainable ("broken") and, therefore, there is the need that a group of experts and not of practitioners identifies the right solutions to fix it.

The recurrent element of these repairs is driving the change from the "top" (the one best way!). Experts are expected to produce the best strategies as well as step-by-step guidelines for carrying out the change in the health care so that the practitioners could not get them wrong. In this way, the health sector is subject to a never-ending process of change both at the level of the industry as at the organizational level. What occurs is a disconnection between what is approved and what is happening on the ground.

Italy is a very interesting experience for the Myth #2. At the organizational level, we observe (i) processes of constant reorganization aimed at the better use of resources, partly because of the hiring freeze that has lasted for many years and (ii) the introduction and refinement of tools for performance measurement and management. At the level of the whole industry, change is more evident for the merging wave in place. The number of the public healthcare organizations (HCOs) was reduced by 23% over the last decade, with an acceleration in the last five years, especially in regions under cutback plans. Mergers are driven by Regions wanting to play the role of HCOs holding to ensure better performance monitoring, especially the financial one. It is a real process of grip back in contrast to the "companization" process during the 1990s. The paradigm is completely different. If in the 1990s firm sizes were determined by the idea of manageability, today's size increase is driven by the pursuit of technical optimality (the scale). The economic benefits, expected by this process, are slow to emerge, while negative effects on patients are substantial. HCO mergers pursue abstract benefits and do not take into account some hidden costs. First, there is a risk on actors' coordination, especially the external ones. The expansion of the firm boundaries may not mean an increase in the population served, but it can result in increasing the number and diversity of external stakeholders. The case of the Local Health Authority (LHA) of Trento is paradigmatic. The provincial LHA has a catchment area of just over 550,000 inhabitants. This size is not dramatic in terms of operational complexity, but the LHA CEO has to face 217 mayors of small towns. This is problematic! In addition, internal complexity intensifies because business combinations broaden the diversity of internal professional groups and cultures. This raises organizational tensions and makes difficult efforts to ensure the unity of intent along with an efficient and effective operational functioning. Second, another risk concerns the cognitive complexity that emerges from dimensional enlargement. This complexity has consequently the increasing organizational tensions which top management has to govern. It is inevitable to reduce the amplitude of direct supervision as mechanism of control. Thus, it requires a growth in middle management positions and responsibilities. Each strategic choice in HCOs should be shared with the broad range of actors who play a significant role in operations. This presupposes a patient action by top management aimed at building the conditions for sharing decision-making assumptions before, and decisions, then, between actors with different interests and goals. If the resources of time and attention that management can make available to this delicate process are not sufficient, risks of strategic stall can emerge, with management proceeding in the absence of shared goals (lack of strategic consensus), or of change dilution, that is goals are not realized in the expected time and permanently postponed. Third, there is a risk that concerns the internal and external stakeholders' motivation because top management must be able constantly to nourish it around the whole organization goals. Any institutional rearrangement always involves strategic and organizational changes. Thus, top management must be aware that change has to be managed continuously. Top management must convince and motivate with perseverance over time internal and external parties that are by nature oriented to defend their own interests and perspectives, even distorting the managerial processes and operating systems. The expansion of the firm boundaries, increasing the number and the diversity of stakeholders, ends up increasing the risk that top management cannot effectively perform its function.

So from above this question arises, if these "reparations" do not match the expectations, is it possible to reverse the paradigm, assuming that the change emerges from the bottom?

5.2.2 Clash of Interests

The starting point of any reflection is based on the kind of context in which we must bring change. HCOs as professional service organizations in a regulated industry are typically pluralistic organizations shaped by the divergent goals and interests of different groups, each of which has sufficient power bases to ensure that their goals are legitimate to the strategy of the organization. The most obvious consequence is the continuous tension between strategizing and organizing. Strategizing refers to those planning, resource allocation, monitoring, and control practices and processes through which strategy is enacted. The pluralistic organization produces conflicting strategic objectives and goals in its attempts to respond simultaneously to multiple, shifting, competing or contradictory environmental demands. Organizing can be defined as the creation and use of structural practices and coordination processes by internal stakeholders to enact the organization's identity, culture, and interests. In pluralistic settings, multiple interests emerge from different organizational groups and these are associated with fragmentation of organizational identity and multiple subcultures.

Strategizing in pluralistic contexts raises the problem of enacting a multiplicity of conflicting strategic goals simultaneously. This situation arises from the competing legitimate demands of powerful stakeholders. A goal cannot be pursued either before or at the expense of another target. Following contradictory or incompatible goals—simultaneously—produces conflict. For example, HCOs must pursue multiple strategic objectives of quality in clinical practice, facilitating medical research and teaching, demonstrating value for money and resource efficiency (to satisfy government demands), and responding to required professional codes of conduct and pressures from health service users. Strategies to maximize resource utilization (e.g., beds, medical equipment, and medical staff) might compromise patient care strategies. As strategic objectives are legitimate to important stakeholders, HCOs cannot afford to follow clinical practice at the expense of resource efficiency. The reverse process is not suitable, too.

Organizing tensions are typical in the public sector and not-for-profit organizations, which develop different bureaucratic organizing practices and processes to cater to the interests of autonomous knowledge workers and cope with their administrative pressures. Within professional organizations, the operative core is the key organizational component. Professionals use their knowledge, skills, and attitudes, which they have acquired over long periods of academic education, training, and experience. Because in HCOs the application of medical standards in specific situations implies autonomy and discretion, professionals can make themselves relatively independent of the organization in which they work. So organizing within HCOs is characterized by professionals who are autonomous and who significantly decouple their daily work from HCOs' organizational management structures. As a consequence, management in HCOs has only limited opportunities to guide and control the implementation of organizational change within the operative core because, on this level, professionals have the autonomy to decide if and how they are going to engage with change. Therefore, no social engineering is able to limit this autonomy. Typically, pluralism in professional organizations manifests itself at the broadest level as tensions between professional and managerial cultures and interests, but the medical world is fragmented in many diverse subcultures too. Moreover, organizing tensions increase during turnaround or cutback period.

Extreme internal and external pluralisms in HCOs often generate a destructive association between organizing and strategizing. When multiple strategic objectives cannot be aligned, and organizing pulls are diverse and unable to be accommodated, or are in active conflict with strategic objectives, the organization is pulled in too many directions to resolve the multiple demands upon it, requiring major change, or failing that, leading to organizational breakdown. Sometimes pluralism favors an imbalanced mode between organizing and strategizing, creeping up on organizations without managerial recognition of its sources or implications. The imbalanced mode occurs when strategic objectives are blocked by organizing practices, such as HR systems and incentives that deflect attention from some goals towards others, while some strategizing practices emphasize the interests of some parts of the organization at the expense of others, raising conflict between subcultures and identities. This leads to block strategic and organizational change. To mitigate clashes of interests, management must support an interdependent association, which involves mutual adjustment to generate alignment between strategizing and organizing. The accommodation of interests requires frequent and ongoing dialog among organizational actors. The term dialog is used advisedly here, rather than communication, which too often indicates a top-down dissemination of goals, rather than a two-way discussion process that surfaces different interests and tries to establish common ground, by placing these interests within the wider context of multiple goals and interests. The different characteristics and managerial implications for action, as well as the potential risks of these different modes of association between strategizing and organizing, are illustrated in Table 5.1.

5.2.3 Managing Change in Pluralistic HCOs

Managing change in the healthcare industry and organizations is not a problem of clever social engineering. It is necessary to include different internal and external cultures in change processes, differently from the traditional view that overemphasizes individuals at the top of an organization. The "strategic leadership" approach has more to do with creating strategy, or with control rather than the management of change in the specific change context.

According to the top-down approach to manage the strategy and strategic change, middle managers are implementers. Indeed, they are not passive actors, but they play multiple roles. If participating in formulating the strategy, or if sharing strategy only cognitively too, middle managers are able to propose adjustments and reinterpretations of the strategy. They have a crucial role for change because they

Table 5.1 Managing modes of association between strategizing and organizing

	Characteristics	Strategizing practices…	Organizing practices…	Potential risks	Action for managers
Destructive	Proliferation of interests and goals which are mutually exclusive	…produce **vagueness or stall**	**…fragment the organization**: each group attempts to realize its interests by appropriating the organization's strategic resources	– Continual adjustment to multiple internal and external demands may result in **lack of focus** on any specific goal – Pluralistic tensions may be incommensurable, so that the organization is always on a **destructive path**	**Identify competing goals** and interests and **map the trade-offs and prioritizing** that these involve
Imbalanced	The organization is continually in a catch-up cycle as it adjusts either strategizing or organizing practices in response to unintended consequences that give rise to more unintended consequences	**…are too homogeneous to accommodate the legitimate identities and interests** of multiple organizational constituents, deflecting these interests and generating conflict	**…privilege some strategic goals** over others by enabling the interests of some organizational constituents to dominate those of others	If managers adopt a reactive approach to strategic and organizational demands, waiting to see outcomes before adjusting commensurable practices, they will **exacerbate the vicious cycle of catch-up**	– **Synchronize change programs** to match organizing practices and strategizing practices – **Avoid singular or inflexible strategizing and organizing practices**, which are too rigid to accommodate mutual adjustment

(continued)

Table 5.1 (continued)

	Characteristics	Strategizing practices…	Organizing practices…	Potential risks	Action for managers
Interdependent	Ideal type	**…enable response to different strategic objectives** without marginalizing the interests of different organizational constituents	**…are consistent with the identities and interests of different organizational constituents** without blocking the realization of strategic objectives that are not particular to any one group	– Excessive demands on top management time and attention **overstretch their capacity** – **Difficult to maintain the high levels of flexibility in incentive, planning and monitoring systems**, which tend to become rigid and rule-based over time – **Difficult to maintain the close managerial contact** required as the organization grows and/or becomes more geographically diverse	– **Frequent dialog** with organizational constituents to ensure recognition of their interests and help them to place interests in the wider context – **Adjust strategizing and organizing practices, even marginally**, as often as quarterly in order to ensure they continue to reflect interests and agreed goals and targets – Ensure **information systems provides quality and timely feedback on performance** towards each of multiple goals

Source Adapted from Jarzabkowski and Fenton (2006, p. 643) are in day-to-day contact with aspects of the organization and its environment and can advise senior management on what are likely to be blockages and requirements for change. Moreover, they are a bridge between top management and members of the organization at lower levels, such as doctors and nurses, and translate the change initiatives in locally relevant way.

Along with middle management, even the "outsiders" can play an important role for change. New management can increase the diversity of ideas, break down cultural barriers to change and increase the experience and the capacity for change. Consultants bring similar benefits and are typically facilitators of change processes. Other actors can be powerful influencers of change, such as patients, the government, and suppliers.

All of these actors have the potential to act as change agents on HCOs, and all of them can impede change. Therefore, the style of management for driving change is crucial (Table 5.2). Different styles are likely to be more or less appropriate according to context. For example, in HCOs, direction does not fit. It involves the use of personal managerial authority to establish a clear strategy and how the change will occur. HCOs, due to the pluralistic nature, find the following styles more effective:

1. Participation in the change process, that is, the involvement of those affected by strategic change in the change agenda.
2. Education involves the explanation of the reasons for and means of strategic change. This might be appropriate when the problem in managing change is because of misinformation or lack of information and if there is adequate time to persuade people of the need for change.
3. Intervention, that is, the coordination of and authority over processes of change by a change agent who delegates elements of the process to project teams or taskforces.

Table 5.2 The style of management for driving change

Style	Means/context	Benefits	Problems	Circumstances of effectiveness
Participation	Involvement in setting the strategy agenda and/or resolving strategic issues	Quality of decisions	Time consuming	Incremental change
Education	Group briefing	Overcoming lack of information		
Intervention	Project teams or taskforces	Involvement takes place	Risk of perceived manipulation	
Direction	Use of authority to set direction and means of change	Clarity and speed	Risk of lack of acceptance	Transformational change
Coercition	Explicit use of power			Crisis

Source Adapted from Johnson et al. (2009)

Styles of managing change are not mutually exclusive. For example, clear direction on overall vision might aid a more collaborative approach to more detailed strategy development. Education and communication may be appropriate for some stakeholders. Participation may be appropriate for groups in parts of the organization where it is necessary to build capability and readiness. Different organizational stages require different styles of managing change or different styles to suit different managers' personality types. However, those with the greatest capability to manage change may have the ability to adopt different styles in different circumstances.

In conditions of heterogeneous social worlds, managerial tools are the common platform that practitioners adopt or devise to translate, negotiate, debate, triangulate, and simplify in order to work together. Socially, tools provide a common language (common syntax). Language reflects a way to represent meaning and intention. Tools provide also semantic boundaries that permit to translate different meanings into a shared framework. Finally, managerial tools are suitable for users and transform their common interests in consensus and action, orienting their behaviors (pragmatic boundaries).

5.3 Health care, Complexity, and Change

Fernando Giancotti

5.3.1 Mythology and Health care

A recent book of Yuval Harari identifies myths as the instrument through which small groups of individuals could get beyond collaboration in small numbers, establishing visions and behaviors allowing large-scale synergic interaction. According to this interpretation, through shared religious, social, political beliefs, people refer to some common "imagined order," which exists actually just in the imagination of the beholder and strongly influences individual behaviors and therefore collective action toward functioning tribes, towns, cities, organizations, states, empires, and so on. Apart from the different nuances and meanings that the word "myth" can assume, such a perspective can frame Henry Mintzberg's discussion on myths about health care as a system and the way to "fix" it and makes it even more intriguing to me. That is also because to do it we must explore beyond and well before the myths, looking at the nature of Man and Nature, and then because we should try to imagine a better myth to inform collective action in order to provide a more efficient and satisfactory healthcare system. Intriguing and very challenging, also because it has to be done in a few pages, it took me forty years to understand it! We will then focus immediately on two main conceptual frameworks to show why "social engineering" in a reductionist sense is a recipe for failure for fixing a healthcare system in particular, and any complex system anyway. The two frameworks come then from the questions: who are we indeed, beyond and before myths? What is a healthcare system beyond and before current myths? Thereafter, we will try to propose a better myth to fix things, based on a long journey through concepts and many, many facts and failures and a few successes…all that had very little to do (fortunately, in a sense!) with healthcare systems, but a lot with the ancestral and existential issue of the effectiveness of the collective action.

5.3.2 Who Are We Indeed?

We generally see ourselves as very smart, sophisticated creatures, who dress smart or elegantly, use smartphones and all kinds of amazing technologies. We drive smart cars, go everywhere in the world in a few hours, perpetually connected through social media, with a universe of information at our fingertips, powerful computers everywhere in our lives and much more; we have rights and guarantees, even if we think never enough and then…we are many billions: sure quite a successful species! But…are we really so smart? Let's investigate through an "imagined" time machine.

If we clock back 20 years, smartphones, social media, powerful computers, and low-cost airlines disappear. Traveling back, we would see continuous thriving conflict, millions of deaths, widespread violence, mass migration, terrorism, and huge sufferance of the people in many astonishing ways, continuously surprised by events and dynamics generally out of control.

If we go back 200 years we get to a basically agricultural economy, our wealth pro-capita drops by a factor of many hundred times, and pretty much the same for the exchange of good and services, information, and ideas. Only very few dress elegantly, most of the people see only the place where they are born, poverty, diseases, and early deaths are the norm. Very few, the same who dressed fancy, would rule the nations, mostly through coercion. In between, industrialization produces huge wealth through a steep technological gradient and specialization and its new-born culture falls in love with itself, comparing the world to the wonderful machines it is producing: a complicated mechanism that can be built and fixed through good engineers and mechanics; only to be shocked beyond understanding by its own bloody failures and the constant generation of unintended consequences for that "engineering"; such as in the first place the horrible wars of the 1900s, dozens of millions of deaths, marked by genocide and ferocious dictatorships, and then painful social problems and environmental disruption; our "measure of success," the billions of people we got to, becomes threatening overpopulation, and much more. Any good history book is full of the challenges, unprecedented in scale and intensity, produced by this era of humankind. The absurd and yet solidly rational MAD, Mutual Assured Destruction through nuclear annihilation during the Cold War is a paradoxical and yet a powerful symbol of this, well captured by a famous movie from the sixties: Dr. Strangelove.

If we go back about 10,000 years and beyond, we find a whole different world. Throughout the planet Earth small bands of hunter–gatherers roam their environment, almost everywhere from the icy north to the hot equatorial latitudes. The hunting business imposes its rules, which regulate all hunting animals: few individuals in any given hunting territory to allow prey sustainability, a nomadic lifestyle to follow wandering herds and explore new grounds and, for social species, a deeply cooperative hunting process, to multiply effectiveness and therefore maximize survival chances. Thus, a small number of people, living a hard and dangerous life, hunting, eating, defending together against many threats, often saving each other's lives would develop the deepest conceivable relation of interdependence and trust among living beings, affection and emotion based, forced into it by huge evolutionary pressures. The same pressures developed specific modes of enhancements for the effectiveness of the collective action: a fundamental one is leadership, since in highly challenging environments, adaptive coordination of the cooperation makes the difference between success and failure, between survival and extinction. The very first needs to which leadership had to correspond then were in a sense "operational," synergizing efforts and delivering guidance, but also social, ensuring sustainment of group cohesion. That is done maintaining the very balance that allows the miracle of cooperation: the one between the interest of the individual and that of the group. In my view, the maintenance of this dynamic equilibrium is in fact what we call ethics, applied. What scholars call "perception of justice and fairness in the organization" is then a need as deep as the ancestral group human relations: it is the perception of that balance or again of applied ethics, which could be defined as the very glue of collective action. It is not a case that administering justice was a leadership responsibility, until the French Revolution, and still is in a more limited form.

If we go back past 10,000 years, to the very first common ancestor that we share with the apes, following scarce fossil evidence and genetic studies, we eventually get to about 7,000,000 years ago.

Since that time, at first as gathering–scavenging creatures, with a human gait and a small, ape-like brain, then as hunters in the last 2,000,000 million years circa, we have always lived in the small group pattern we just discussed. So, if 200 years may seem a lot in relation to our next vacation or even to our far away retirement, they are in fact nothing in relation to evolutionary times. 10,000 years as well are a tiny fraction of our phylogenetic history: even if we consider only our hunting past, we get to 0.5%. We are then biologically the same as our hunting ancestors of many thousand years ago and the deep needs we have are rooted in our evolution. We would still deeply need group interaction, effective leadership, close and engaged leaders, collaboration and attention to people, perception of justice, and fairness in our social contest, through shared ethics, which has statistically ensured our survival. Nowadays, our social, cultural, and organizational models place us far away from those needs, even though since the Tayloristic era rediscovery of the "School of Human Relations" up to the latest "Emotional Intelligence" theories, we have been unknowingly trying to go back to the affective relation patterns fundament of the effectiveness of the collective action and therefore of our survival as a species.

Today, our everyday environment is most often characterized by individualism rather than intense group life; far away leaders, bureaucratization rather than collaboration; and by often critical perception of justice and fairness, i.e., the ethical issue, because of superficiality, depersonalization, and fragmentation of relations, with consequent lack of trust. You do not know most of the people you interact with; how can you trust them?

Indeed, if we are who I have cursorily described, and neglect establishing a system based on teams who fulfill those deep needs, we do not achieve high performance and organizational well-being. And even if a healthcare system does not fail (see myth #1), it will still be costly and underperforming, and underperforming because costly. This understanding comes not only from an anthropological perspective, but also from looking at the military world, from large-scale operations to small unit leadership, in actuality and in history. It is not a case that the Israeli Defence Force, one of the most effective of the world, is deeply imbued by such concepts.

5.3.3 Healthcare Systems (HCS): A View from a Different Perspective

One definition of HCS I like among several is “the organization of people, institutions, and resources that deliver healthcare services to meet the health needs of target populations.” Stop and think for a moment, picturing the millions and millions of elements of such a system and to the innumerable interactions among them. Patients, doctors, nurses, support and administrative personnel, managers, suppliers and logistics, infrastructures, tools and instruments, and much more interact in constant flux 24/7 through processes, activities, exchanges of information, services, goods, and emotions. They do so in a multidimensional network of feedback loops, feeding inputs into millions of elements and receiving elaborated outputs by as many others, through incommensurable, very complex dynamics… Stop and think some more…you may have now a feeling of a system at work.

But what kind of system? Let us answer a few questions to try to identify some taxonomical characteristics. First, are HCS open systems which exchange matter, energy, information? Yes. Open in that they interact with the society at large, institutions and exchange a lot, inside and outside of the system. Are they evolutionary? They do change through time, through internal dynamics, for example professional competence growth, external inputs, and legislation, not always according to the established policy goals and often in a spontaneous fashion. That answers the next question about linear behaviors: HCSs do exhibit nonlinear behaviors, since output is not immediately and reliably related to input and the path followed by events is seldom exactly the planned one. Our last question is about the existence of networked feedbacks. Our mental reconnaissance of a HCS, picturing it, and trying to grasp its functioning tells us definitely yes, networked feedbacks are at the core of the operations of a HCS.

We can now classify our system. Even though there is no single formal definition, studies of nonlinear dynamical systems converge in outlining the concept of complex adaptive systems (CAS) as "open, non-linear evolutionary systems, such as a rain forest, that are constantly processing and incorporating new information" (Sanders 1998). Gandolfi (1999) defines CAS as "an open system, formed by numerous elements interacting in a nonlinear manner, which constitute a single, dynamic and organized entity, able to evolve and adapt to the environment."

We think that, following our rather fast and necessarily shallow discussion, we can state that Healthcare Systems are Complex Adaptive Systems (CAS). If we share this view, we can then assume that it does exhibit characteristics and behaviors of CAS, i.e., impossible to know all about them; made up of many complex elements; driven by nonlinear relationships; built up of parallel, redundant processes; impossible to forecast; decentralized, information dense, and resilient. This has many implications for the construction of a better myth to fix things and make them work more effectively and efficiently.

We have asked ourselves: "who are we indeed, beyond and before myths? What is a healthcare system beyond and before current myths?" The myths we have looked beyond are the ones which have built an organizational culture forgetting who we really are and which have confused a very complex organization, a living organism of living beings, with a machine, establishing linear fixes and systems to manage it, measuring and rewarding nonlinear processes with a linear logic, thus bringing it to a sustained but unsustainable underperformance.

Is there then a better myth to bring to bear on Healthcare Systems, to support the noble enterprise of enhancing humankind's health?

5.3.4 General Guidelines to Better Mythology

Part of the answer is in the "noble enterprise" part of the question itself. It is rediscovering the value dimension of motivation to perform collectively. A widely diffused, destructive myth, often held as self-evident truth, is that people care only about money and that money drives all. That happens very often, but the huge misunderstanding is that the urge for money is the fundamental root of behaviors, while it is rather an effect of a void of other values and rewards. This void comes from structural and cultural drivers which are largely born from a lack of understanding of very relevant factors, which we have tried to identify in our discussion. I observe every day amazing and very effective motivational drives which have nothing to do with money. That does not mean that money is not relevant for any individual, on the contrary, it is relevant for all. But at the systemic level it is not the main motivational factor, and not understanding that can be very costly, not only for the wages that top managers get, but for the consequences of a money-only-driven management and its metrics and bonuses.

So promoting and rewarding values related to the common good is one of the basics to give heed to, especially appropriate dealing with HCS. That is also related to some deep inclinations that evolution has bred in our genes and that any human culture has always tried in some way to promote.

Then, leveraging the inborn drivers of the collective action is another powerful enabler of its effectiveness. Of course culture has a great influence on modes and contents of the group interaction, but when nature and culture align, the effect is multiplied many times. High-performance groups work within this alignment: as special forces squads in hostile territory are the closest thing to the hunter–gatherer group roaming a dangerous savannah, with plenty of large predators and many risks, or the icy steppe of the Paleolithic Europe. The highest technology fighter squadron operations rely on very tight bonds among the members, also expressed on the ground through very strong esprit de corps, while in the air tactics are based on complex and highly cooperative action, where initiative and everybody's contribution is expected, very much like in the ancestral hunting of buffaloes or of the huge cave bear.

So our next myth should establish a system based on teams who fulfill our deep needs for a group and for a meaning that goes beyond our own self, as well as for good leadership and teamwork. A system networks these teams through values and solid exchanges, which organizes flat, keeping the strategic leadership close to the operators, making sure to get their information, feed-back and ideas. A system where intense communication throughout the organization is normal, and rewards, metrics, and even sanctions are built to promote the values and not greed, short-term achievements or unintended consequences, from looking at the tree and not seeing the forest. Leadership as a system of leaders at all levels, well beyond the hopeless bottleneck of the "heroic leader," becomes the enabler of actual high performance, sustainable results and organizational well-being. This "fractal leadership" building up a structure of high-performance modules well connected with the mainstream of corporate knowledge flowing top-down, bottom-up and throughout, not only increases the results of the single organizational element, but multiplies and boosts the overall capability of the organization, starting from the decision-making process to all the relevant ones.

Unintended consequences, fractals, and system of systems lead us back to the so-called "new science of complexity and chaos" framework, to see what operational indications we can draw from it. We can say that a HCS is a Complex Adaptive System and it exhibits its typical behavior. To change a complex system, we cannot rely on a linear, mechanistic approach; its non-linear dynamics defeat classical social engineering, as we see so far from the gap between intentions and results. We cannot forecast it precisely, cannot determine it, and we must try to influence it. To manage change in a complex system we must then first leave alone "heroism," wear our "Humbleness Cap" and try to understand the fundamental modes and content of the significant transactions at the various levels of the system. Then we should try to figure out the influencing factors which steer modes and contents toward the desired state for each level, reconnoitering the system to understand where we should apply these influencing factors, defining subareas of highest effect to concentrate resources and make the enterprise cost-effective. Applying multiple vectors, in a sense, on various "centers of gravity" of the system, starts to push it in a direction. The very fundamental level to influence according to this "complex system methodology" has been discussed in the previous paragraph. Establishing policies, a culture, and procedures to promote the diffused quality leadership, communication, and "fractal organization" is in my opinion a necessary intervention to redefine a new HCS paradigm, well before and more important than any new regulation, rewiring of diagrams and change of plates on doors. Focusing a little further a possible intervention at the methodological level, we should carry out a holistic reconnaissance of the whole CAS, through quality analysis and proceed then through successive operational approximations, since long time planning is not reliable for CAS. We should seek out a set of influencing factors, intelligently chosen and innovative if need be, to be declined through projects focused at the same time on different "centers of gravity," redundant so to maintain momentum if some fail and synergic to trigger the network of collateral exchanges that can produce so much value, beyond planning and expectation. All projects should then be informed and maintained in a coherent direction by a new Mission and Vision, defined according to our anthropological needs. The results should be reassessed periodically and managed flexibly, and…many more hints could be discussed about interaction with complex systems if time and space on paper allowed.

The conceptual map for change management planning for HCS could now be drawn according to the discussed guidelines, which cannot be in this short paper but it is a fascinating challenge for the next one. Let us consider this a first approximation and draw a (partial, humble and temporary) conclusion.

I think that my comment to the Myth #2, "The healthcare system can be fixed by clever social engineering", is by now quite clear: "social engineering" in a reductionist sense is actually a recipe for failure for fixing a health care system in particular, and any complex system anyway. I spilled over to the myth #3, "Healthcare institutions as well as the overall system can be fixed by bringing in the heroic leader." A "heroic leader" alone has very little chance to change the complex world around himself, unless able to trigger the motivational hypercycles and a related networking of hearts and minds and able to produce a diffused, systemic leadership throughout the organization, from the very top to the ones leading just themselves. The only silent heroism we would really need and not only in HCS, would be from the ones engaged in unleashing the huge, rewarding potential that humans in a truly shared collective endeavors can express through their collective action, establishing a new, comprehensive paradigm, where terms like "social engineering" and "heroic leader" would prompt a smile or a twinge of historical interest, for example when we think of Hammurabi's code or the faces Mussolini made during his "heroic" speeches.

References

Cassel CK, Guest JA (2012) Choosing wisely helping physicians and patients make smart decisions about their care. JAMA 307(17):1801–1802

Edmondson AC (2004) Learning from failure in health care: frequent opportunities, pervasive barriers. Qual Saf Health Care 13(6):3–9

Gandolfi A (1999) Formicai, imperi, cervelli. Introduzione alla scienza della complessità. Torino, Bollati Boringhieri

Harvey S, Kou CY (2013) Collective engagement in creative tasks: the role of evaluation in the creative process in groups. Adm Sci Q 58(3):346–386

Jarzabkowski P, Fenton E (2006) Strategizing and organizing in pluralistic contexts. Long Range Plan 39(6):631–648

Johnson G, Scholes K, Whittington R (2009) Fundamentals of strategy. Pearson Education Limited, England

Mura M, Lettieri E, Radaelli G, Spiller N (2013) Promoting professionals' innovative behavior through knowledge sharing: the moderating role of social capital. J Knowl Manage 17(4):527–544

Popper K (1961) The poverty of historicism. Routledge Classics

Sanders TI (1998) Harnessing complexity: organizational implications of a scientific frontier. Simon & Schuster, New York

Volpp KG, Loewenstein G (2012) Choosing wisely low-value services, utilization, and patient cost sharing. JAMA 308(16):1635–1636

Weinberg AM (1991) Can technology replace social engineering? In: Thompson WB (ed) Controlling technology: contemporary issues. Prometheus Books, Buffalo, NY

Whitten P, Holtz B, Nguyen L (2010) Keys to a successful and sustainable telemedicine program. Int J Technol Assess Health Care 26(2):211–216

Zanaboni P, Lettieri E (2011) Institutionalizing telemedicine applications: the challenge of legitimizing decision-making. J Med Int Res 13(3):e72

Chapter 6
Myth #3: Healthcare Institutions as Well as the Overall System Can Be Fixed by Bringing in the Great Leader

Anna Maria Livia Colao, Pasquale Antonio Riccio, Antonio Botti, Aurelio Tommasetti, Massimo Sargiacomo, Antonio D'Andreamatteo and Luca Ianni

6.1 Health Leadership: A Group Matter

Anna Maria Livia Colao and Pasquale Antonio Riccio

The original version of this chapter was revised: For detailed information please see Erratum. The erratum to this chapter is available at https://doi.org/10.1007/978-3-319-53600-2_14

A. M. L. Colao (✉)
Department of Clinical Medicine and Surgery, University of Naples Federico II, Naples, Italy
e-mail: colao@unina.it

P. A. Riccio
Health Campus NPO, Via Martucci, 80121 Naples, Italy
e-mail: pasriccio@gmail.com

A. Botti (✉) · A. Tommasetti
Department of Scienze Aziendali—Management e Innovation Systems, University of Salerno, Via Giovanni Paolo II, 132, 84084 Fisciano, SA, Italy
e-mail: abotti@unisa.it

M. Sargiacomo (✉)
Department of Management and Innovation Systems, University of Salerno, Viale Pindaro, 42, 65127 Pescara, Italy
e-mail: massimo.sargiacomo@unich.it

A. D'Andreamatteo · L. Ianni
Department of Management and Business Administration, University "G.d'Annunzio" of Chieti, Pescara, Italy

P. Adinolfi and E. Borgonovi (eds.), *The Myths of Health Care*,
https://doi.org/10.1007/978-3-319-53600-2_6

6.1.1 Introduction

The recent global crisis has turned the spotlight on national health systems, and Italy in particular, which is undergoing serious difficulties, has once again seen the reigniting of the debate on the sustainability of its national health system.

Economic and structural reasons have led to reflections on whether what has been built by the Italian community over the past 50 years, oriented towards providing health care to everyone, can still be sustained.

It is precisely in times like these, when historically there is a strong demand for change, that we feel the need for references in large sectors of society able to guide, steer and improve processes. The organization of health systems is no exception, and in fact, especially for the reasons given above, these systems are steadily investigating methodologies to ensure qualitatively acceptable results, notwithstanding a substantial decrease in funding.

The challenges that healthcare decision-makers are faced with today are due to factors that previously were not taken into account or were not always foreseen: population growth, an increase in population age and a consequent upsurge in chronic diseases (we all live longer and the number of elderly people to be taken care of by healthcare systems keeps rising), the rationalization and modernization of the structures along with the adoption of newer and appropriate devices.

These are the factors and scenarios, not experienced before, which healthcare systems have been facing in years of debate on how the structures should be organized for the better, and how best to guide them, i.e. its leadership.

In this regard, Henry Mintzberg has addressed the problem of rethinking and reorganizing health care, by identifying and refuting some of the myths that often accompany the reflections regarding health systems. One of these refers to solving the problems of any system, including health systems, by entrusting it to a great leader.

6.1.2 Contextualizing Leadership in Health care

Notwithstanding a certain tendency to escape the issue, one cannot help but acknowledge that all systems, in addition to needing guidelines and basic principles, also need leading figures in order to achieve lasting goals.

The need is all the more pressing given the particular aim of the health system, i.e. patient care, and taking due account of the ever increasing need to implement health policies that cut costs without compromising the quality of use. In health care a management system based on the figure of a leader and not merely bureaucratic "managers", each operating within their own sector, is essential.

The nature of the end "product" of such a "corporation" or system, featuring a strong ethical connotation, i.e. the curing of a person, makes things even more difficult together with the constant need for models aimed at achieving the goals in a responsible and precise manner. Such models can, in our view, be conformed to only when relying on a clear and shared leadership.

In fact, leadership contributes:

- to maintain the level of commitment and pressure required of the participants of the various working groups;
- to consolidate group and corporate membership working towards bringing the team closer together;
- to assess and collect the needs of team members.

A leadership, to be defined as such, is dynamic and creative by nature: it not only records and replicates processes, but must be able to modify them, make difficult decisions and identify the overall goals for each single operational area.

To assess the compliance of processes and outcomes with goals, the leadership can use specific tools able to measure the performance and activities of the members involved.

The organizational and operating data systems are, in fact, key in understanding, for example, as regards any person in charge:

- his/her ability to generate synergies between services and the sectors they belong to
- his/her effective contribution to achieving the goals of each sector and those of the general body
- his/her ability in cooperating in the management and/or coordination of their sector
- the degree of satisfaction concerning the work carried out, working methods and remuneration.

However, for the analysis of these evaluation criteria it is absolutely necessary that the leader is also ready to make decisions in apparent contrast with the reports of the evaluators.

Of course, for this writer, leadership is such only when it can make decisions and face problems when they arise, and it is even more so in a complex area such as the operation and management of health systems, where the health of people is at stake.

6.1.3 The Role of Leaders in Health care

This consideration leads us to seek what features and peculiarities leaders and protagonists of health systems ought to have, also taking into account the context in which they are called to work.

A leader is such, in fact, if he/she is acknowledged as a guide and often this does not happen thanks only to his/her charisma, but when human groups and communities share a common vision, common values, common rules, sharing the aim of becoming organized hierarchically and above all accepting and respecting this structure.

In fact, as important and often decisive the figure of the leader may be, he/she is still part of a binary "system" in which the other subject is the community which the leader is called to guide.

Over the years, the sociological but also philosophical debate has brought the attention on the different components that make for a successful leader–community relationship, and also in the management of health systems we would like to point out a few features that this relationship should have:

- knowledge of the status quo
- awareness and sharing of goals
- shared vision
- attitude towards change
- awareness of the role that the healthcare system plays in the life of people.

Before planning and organizing the work, a good leader must contribute with his/her own action and then his/her own example, to create among all the staff (from the nearest to the farthest in the hierarchy) a community spirit aimed at clear, distinct targets towards which it is worth addressing all efforts.

The leader should do his/her job avoiding a dictatorial-paternalistic approach, trying instead to build a relationship with his/her workgroup in the name of sharing, but should also not shy away from the decision-making responsibilities that the role assigned to (or conquered by!) him/her calls for.

In health, in fact, from the management of a department to that of an entire hospital, one cannot avoid responsibilities, especially since at stake there is not a product or the simple satisfaction of a patient, but the health of a person.

In the name of this assumption, the increasing complexity and reorganization of hospitals and health systems in general is essential in favouring the spread of a management based on shared leadership practices.

From the availability of increasingly accurate technological tools, useful for diagnostics, to the involvement of many medical and specialist profiles, supported by other health figures, leaders must adopt an approach as open as possible to discussion and aimed towards helping each member of the system define his/her role, tasks, goals and responsibilities.

An example may be the management of an emergency, such as the hospitalization of a patient who has suffered a stroke, which involves many profiles from the head of a Complex Operative Unit to hospital volunteers.

In other words, leaders must be able to direct their management towards an increasingly interdisciplinary model capable of transcending paternalistic or even authoritarian stances.

In fact, shared leadership is fully accomplished when leaders:

- do not order staff members "what to do", but share operational and strategic goals, leaving a certain amount of autonomy of action for each staff member. That is particularly true if we consider that "coercion" and authoritarianism are not the only negative aspects of a "paternalistic" management, as in fact what often happens is that staff members will merely wait passively for their leaders' orders and completely lose autonomy of action resulting in action stagnation;

- promote and support sharing within the organization;
- promote planned or spontaneous team building activities: leaders, in fact, should not fear bonds within the work group, but should instead support them wherever possible.

A leader should also pursue his/her efforts through constantly reviving, not only in medical staff but all staff involved, the founding spirit behind the Hippocratic Oath: human life is a supreme good to be safeguarded with the commitment and behaviour appropriate to the solemnity that such an important goal carries.

This would help create valid reference points by operating not on the fear of a penalty (which a good system must nevertheless include!), but on a strong team spirit that we could almost call "common purpose".

A concept that provides a hierarchically oriented structure, with an acknowledged leader and in which, holistically, each member perceives their work as vital for the reaching of goals as if they were the "vocation" of their team and their work.

Based on these assumptions, the doctor–patient relationship would acquire greater importance: it should never be lost sight of and it goes without saying that for its peculiarity it is defined and re-defined continuously in relation to the players involved.

In the health system, a leader who does not take into account this relationship should never consider goals as fully achieved because, although it is true that the results should be pursued according to effectiveness and efficiency, it is equally important not to forget the specific and human status of each single patient. In relation to this status, in fact, pre-established patterns or actions cannot be applied.

This is the direction which, especially in recent years, seems to have been followed, for example, in the re-organizational structuring initiated in hospital centers and according to which management has stirred towards the creation of Departments as large and homogeneous as possible.

It is in these very contexts that the assertion of leadership at every organizational level becomes essential, because this is the only type able to combine the expectations of organization boards as regards effectiveness and efficiency, the management of the staff/employees and, most importantly, user satisfaction.

Consider for example, the research and clinical activities addressing rare diseases, working approaches, whose focus and goal are the patient, are spreading, but their key feature should be the interdisciplinary approach.

In recent years, notwithstanding the increase of multidisciplinary approaches, we have in fact also observed interdisciplinary types of organization through which, from the physician to the biologist, nurses, data-managers and the patient's direct involvement, all take part in the common goal of care.

It is important to note that in health care the interdisciplinary approach is of greater importance with respect to the multidisciplinary approach: in the latter model we can in fact see individuals operating exclusively within the range of their abilities, whereas in the former model we find, at the core, a cooperation aimed at a common goal, toward which the various professionals work, each according to their skills.

6.1.4 Conclusions

In health care, it is the awareness that "at the center of all goals there is the patient", not the search or the assertion of personal principles, to ensure the growth of work teams and the continuity of care. All this thanks to the fundamental support of a responsible sharing of information and actions. One example can be found in the management of a hospital discharge. If everyone worked with responsibility and shared aims, the information collected will be essential and decisive in the continuation of care, and will facilitate the work of the physician or workgroup called to take care of the next phase of a patient's treatment.

Moreover, it should be noted that collaboration and sharing are also what hold together the physician–patient relationship.

This relationship is crucial in the achievement of goals and in the credibility of a health system. The key element in the physician–patient relationship, on the side-lines of all the considerations made earlier, appears to be one of the qualities necessary for the establishing of a shared leadership: communication.

Given the condition of each patient, the first thing that he/she looks for in a physician is the constant clarity on what action to take, the evolution of the disease, disease history, on how similar cases were dealt with, on the best way of dealing with the world around them.

Efforts are, therefore, needed towards the spreading and use of a shared leadership able to stimulate all the professional profiles involved in the processes to perform their tasks with the highest level of attention, responsibility and openness to ensure an approach as inclusive as possible towards the patient. In order to guide the system aiming at common goals, every leader needs to acknowledge that the best strategy does not involve coercion but teamwork, in addition to the right dose of decision-making.

Human history teaches us that we can win only if united, and the optimization of health systems is one of the most exciting challenges that human beings will have to face over the next 20 years. United.

6.2 Leadership and Management

Antonio Botti and Aurelio Tommasetti

6.2.1 Leadership and Management Practices

As Barnes and Kriger (1986) have said, there is no good all-purpose definition of leadership. In support of this statement, the authors refer to the studies of Burns (1978) and Bass (1981) who maintain that there is no common set of factors, traits or processes that identifies the qualities of effective leadership. The definition of leadership ranges between two extremes: the leader who is a hero-person and the leadership as a set of personal attributes (energy, charisma or style). In between are the contingency theorists who argue that leadership depends upon anything, from task conditions to subordinate expectations. Barnes and Kriger (1986) highlight that all of these approaches are valid, however on their own they are insufficient, as none:

- deals very well with the complexities that arise from the fact that managers are both leaders and followers, given the very nature of organizational hierarchies;
- contends with another fact of organizational life—that informal social networks exert an immense influence which sometimes overrides the formal hierarchy. A person's formal job status may be clear in the hierarchy, but that is only one part of an organization's network of relationships. Less formal network ties often dominate the role behaviour of an individual or group.

Personal approach and cognitive style are factors that influence corporate management. Those who embrace the "rational" approach believe that formal analysis—the systematic study of issues—can help organizations make better decisions (Langley 1995). In contrast, some scholars (Henry Mintzberg 1989, Peters and Waterman 1982) have criticized the "rational" approach: for example Peters and Waterman (1982) highlight its degree of abstraction from reality, its inability to deal adequately with non-quantifiable values, its lack of flexibility and bias against experimentation culminating in a tendency for paralysis.

Managers appear to fluctuate between two extremes: on one hand they assume arbitrary decisions without systematic study; on the other hand they tend to collect more information than strictly necessary for decision-making retreating "… into abstraction and conservatism that relies obsessively on numbers, analyses, and reports ("paralysis by analysis")" (Langley 1995, p. 63). Consequently, the critical issue is how to combine rationality and efficiency. Langley (1995) states that leadership style and cognitive style can affect the quantity of analysis. A highly directive leader will ignore analytical studies, insisting on his or her own viewpoint and, in the long term, this leadership style will discourage analyses. At the opposite extreme, a highly consensual leader might encourage numerous studies and analyses that could easily increase the decision-maker's confusion. Another impacting factor is a leader's cognitive style which can also condition their decision-making processes. Many people are naturally intuitive, while others are more analytical. In making decisions, the former require less information, consequently, the risk of paralysis by analysis is highest for analytical managers. Langley (1995) reaches similar conclusions to those of Barnes and Kriger (1986); the author defines leadership styles not as better but as different. Sometimes "…more directive leadership prevented diverging opinions from degenerating into vicious circles", other times—as in Eisenhardt (1989)—we find "… the superiority of "qualified consensus", in which top managers first attempt to develop consensus among interested parties, air all views, and then impose a decision that accounts for these views" (Langley 1995, p. 68).

The fact that no one leadership style is the best ever, stems from the extent of organizational complexity depending on the diversity of organizational forms and interactions among organizations that are evolving. This degree of complexity is particularly evident in healthcare organizations.

6.2.2 Health System and Complexity

The Health System is a complex adaptive system where any modifications in one component of the system require changes in the other components to guarantee balance and sustainability in the system. In this context, the term "complex" connotes diversity, i.e. numerous connections within a series of elements. In the same definition, the term "adaptive" suggests the idea of change, resulting from experience while the term "system" symbolizes the idea of a set of connected or interdependent things.

Economics and management theory are concerned with real life, dealing with interactions, context and other evolving dimensions. Such conditions imply that corporate leaders and managers should create sustainable systems by virtue of their capacity for viability. Traditional management theories focus on the predictable and controllable dimension of management. However, they lack consistent elements of management. Complexity science invites us to study all the aspects of organizations including those that are unpredictable. In line with Holder and Ramagem (2012), our approach highlights the need to deal with management in the Healthcare System from a systems perspective.

In many parts of the world, the Healthcare System is organized at various levels and it is widely recognized that the management system occurs at three different levels" (Holder and Ramagem 2012): macro (Health Systems), meso (Health Services) and micro (Clinical Management). Holder and Ramagem (2012) in discussing the World Health Organization (WHO) conceptual framework for building leadership and management skills, conclude that there are "appropriate competencies" specific to each of the three levels of management at:

- macro level, leaders and managers have to govern global health problems and agendas, consequently they require negotiating skills to take part in global health governance;
- meso level, the objective is integrated health care delivery services, so managers require competencies to manage strategies for integrated health service delivery networks to improve coordinated care as well as the efficiency and the effectiveness of service delivery;
- micro level, integrated health service delivery is based on a model of care organized around processes. At this level, management capacity is focused on the efficiency and effectiveness of the processes.

6.2.3 *The Quality of Management*

The quality of management is one of the key determinants of developmental outcomes in all sectors. Numerous studies highlight that efforts to improve management quality can also ameliorate health outcomes. Dorgan et al. (2010), in a study of 1194 hospitals in the United Kingdom, report a strong relation between hospital-specific management practices, quality of hospital patient care and productivity. Their research shows that improved management practices in hospitals are associated with significantly lower mortality rates.

The case of Nairobi hospital (Mailu 2010) is a specific example of how better leadership and management practices can improve outcomes in the healthcare sector. The Nairobi Hospital was risking closure due to low growth, increasing costs for care and high staff turnover. Process improvement, investment in infrastructure, quality of care improvement and firm organizational decision-making was how Dr. Mailu and his team resolved the problem (Mailu 2010). They convinced the hospital board of the importance of using ICT, outsourcing non-core business functions, making investments and empowering the workforce. Cost containment and efficient management practice prevented the closure of the Nairobi hospital. Dr. Mailu was personally involved in hospital turnaround so he was able to help engage others. Dr. Mailu's commitment involved persuading the staff of the Nairobi hospital to focus their attention on the hospital's problems and in devising a road map for turnaround. The case of Nairobi hospital supports the argument that positive results depend on multiple factors and indicates that management quality and leadership are closely connected. Dr. Mailu and his team evidenced management quality for example, when convincing the hospital board of the negative consequences of particular managerial choices. Subsequently, Dr. Mailu's leadership facilitated decisively the implementation of decision-making relevant to the rescue of Nairobi hospital.

6.2.4 *Some Cues from the Italian Experience*

Normally, Italian General Practitioners work alone with limited facilities and equipment. However, some years ago, several healthcare organizations started to put specific strategies in place (Heller 2004), in order to:

- encourage cooperation among General Practitioners
- use managerial tools.

General Practitioners are wary of adopting managerial tools because they think their professional autonomy would be reduced. Confidence between General Practitioners and the managers of healthcare organizations (Leese and Mahon 1999) and guaranteed clinical autonomy (Warwicker 1998) are factors that would facilitate the acceptance of innovation. Heller (2004) analyzed three cases of Italian healthcare organizations and stated that in most cases, the managers of healthcare organizations and the Union of General Practitioners played a critical role in introducing innovations. The top management of healthcare organizations pushed for innovations and involved General Practitioners through their Unions. This evidences a style of leadership that is in part managerial and in part cooperative.

The Italian Central Government, the Regions and other stakeholders are currently discussing a Reform in which General Practitioners are to liaise and cooperate with other General Practitioners, Paediatricians or Medical Specialists. However, the incentive schemes to support such innovation have not yet been defined. Warwicker (1998), in analyzing the relationship between General Practitioners and Central Government in Great Britain and the 1980 and 1990 Reforms, detects two crucial aspects. The first is summed up in terms of empowerment and control: General Practitioners became fund-holders and their activity assessed according to numerous indicators. The second is an attempt to reduce substantially clinical autonomy by defining in more detail contractual duties with respect, for example, to health promotion. This combined with financial incentive schemes to achieve immunization targets. Furthermore, the 1990 General Practitioners contract introduced constraints over prescribing and the status of General Practitioners changed from that of Family Practitioner Committees to Family Health Service Authorities (Warwicker 1998). The reason for the change was the shift from an administrative to a managerial body. However, a new contract and financial incentives were required. Barretta (2008) analyzed potential determinants for promoting a mix of cooperation and competition among Italian healthcare trusts. He pointed out the pivotal role of a regulatory body in encouraging a propensity for inter-organizational cooperation/competition. This perspective underlines that environment and rules affect management style. Many authors believe that the characteristics of an organization can influence management style. Henry Mintzberg (1979) defined healthcare trusts as "professional bureaucracies" to underline the role and behaviour of professionals.

Villa et al. (2009) analyzed three innovative design projects that reorganized patient flow logistics around patient care needs, at three Italian hospitals. The authors highlighted a critical aspect "… to manage and overcome some cultural barriers especially on the physicians' side. In fact, especially in the transitional phase, physicians (at least some of them) have complained about "wandering" to and from inpatient units located on different floors of the building as well as about having to share spaces and resources with other colleagues and specialties" (Villa et al. 2009, p. 162). In the study, the critical role of communication is underlined: "…it is important for hospital management to convey the message that changes in patient flow logistics have been made around patient clinical needs and it is the physician that retains final control over the patient's clinical history" (Villa et al. 2009, p. 163). In the case of the three Italian hospitals, all made changes under strong external pressures posed by Regional health authorities (Villa et al. 2009). This further element confirms the critical role played by regulatory bodies and their influence on management.

6.3 When Leadership Meets Change: Some Insights

Massimo Sargiacomo, Antonio D'Andreamatteo, Luca Ianni

6.3.1 *Introduction*

An imperative for healthcare organizations worldwide is the need to change, as claimed by important institutions and leading healthcare systems. For example the Institute of Medicine in the US called in 1999 for a major effort to make health care safe, recognizing the role of leadership for effective improvements (Kohn et al. 2000). The UK government announced in 2010 a new season of reforms to "liberate" NHS and realize a system run from the bottom-up, through putting patients at the heart of policies and actions, focusing measurement and evaluation principally on clinical outcomes and empowering health professionals (Great Britain and Department of Health 2010). Building this new vision requires the development of a new kind of leadership (Ham et al. 2011).

Undoubtedly, for health care to be fixed, good leadership and management are strategic factors. Synthesizing, the leadership style of healthcare managers deeply affects the behaviour of staff at all levels, determining better output and outcome for workers, patients and users as well as for the whole organization, and enhancing a virtuous circle of continuous improvement (Sargiacomo 2003).

6.3.2 *The Different Shades of Healthcare Leadership*

Earlier studies about management and leadership date back to the beginning of the past century. Fayol in 1929 was the first to depict the function of executives, stating that "to manage is to forecast and plan, to organize, to command, to co-ordinate and to control" (Fayol 1949, p. 6), thus laying the foundation for next meaningful studies about management. Barnard, among the first, highlighted, in 1938, the features of leadership distinguishing it from management. According to the author leadership is a question of faith: "… the power of individuals to inspire cooperative personal decision by creating faith: faith in common understanding, faith in probability of success, faith in the ultimate satisfaction of personal motives, faith in the integrity of objective authority, faith in the superiority of common purpose as a personal aim of those who partake it" (Barnard 1968, p. 259). More recently, Zaleznik (1977) pointed out that both management and leadership are necessary within organizations, but they relate to very different kinds of people according to their attitudes towards goals, conceptions of work, relations with others and sense of self. Exactly leadership is the quality needed to promote and drive change within organizations. Kotter (2001) expanded on this idea and claimed that management is coping with complexity, while leadership is coping with change, a very essential role of organizations operating in turbulent external environments. Even though managers and leaders perform the same tasks, e.g. deciding, creating networks of people and monitoring the performance, they do it in a very different way. Managers set plans for the future, organize and staff to allow implementation and ensure achievement through controlling and problem solving. Leaders, on the contrary, set directions, try to align people towards and keep them motivated and inspired.

Another leading body of the literature has emphasized the role of vision, passion and enthusiasm of charismatic leaders crystallized in the theory of transformational leadership (Burns 1978; Bass 1985) that focuses much more on change than past theories. The leader would be an out-and-out change agent champion enhancing involvement of staff towards new patterns of action. Even though this vision is powerful to highlight the effects of leaders onto the environment in which they operate and the role of followers, the risk to overestimate its possibility of success remains (Yukl 1999). Kotter himself (1995) explained a reason why important change initiatives fail: leaders would forget transformation is a process that advances by steps and takes much time, not a discrete event. Following, on the contrary, a well-established pattern of change would rise the likelihood of succeeding.

Certainly, these interpretations improve the understanding of leadership and the relations between leaders and followers, but the risk is to spread and exalt a vision of "heroic" leadership. On the contrary, in order for organizations to face the modern challenges, a more useful theorization would be the so-called shared/distributed leadership, that discusses leadership as an emergent property of a group or network of interacting individuals (leadership is a cohesive activity not a sum of individual contributions), a phenomenon whose boundaries are opened to a plurality of actors and groups and whose results stem from the huge variety of individual expertise distributed across the organization (Bennett et al. 2003).

As stated, healthcare organizations need good management and good leadership, as well. But what kind of leaders and managers? Doubtless, thinking about change at a system level and major transformations, the role of the top management is of paramount importance. The managerial behaviour of CEOs and their style of leadership are strategic to achieve expected performance and innovate within the healthcare organizations (Sargiacomo 2001, 2003). Consistently, the following considerations relate to General Managers (CEOs) of public healthcare organizations but, mutatis mutandis, they can be applied to other leadership positions at different levels (at middle and lower level or external—Region or State). Actually, without claiming to be complete, the idea that CEOs of institutions with an "heroic" style can effectively manage organizations and systems complex by definition is difficult to be a priori sustained for at least three reasons: the features of healthcare organizations, the environmental constraints to the action and the resistance to change embedded in the organizational culture.

6.3.3 *The Challenges of Healthcare Leadership*

Admittedly healthcare organizations are professional bureaucracies, i.e. they are "expert-driven, skills-oriented, and highly oriented to pigeonholing" entities (Henry Mintzberg 2012, p. 6), where a repertory of standard programs is applied to fit with the contingent situations (needs of patients to be satisfied). As for others organizational ideal-type, disadvantages or critical issues can affect the functioning of the structure and its performance (Henry Mintzberg 1993). For example the supervision of professionals (clinicians and nurses in primis) by managers may be difficult, especially when the latter do not belong to the profession. Limited flexibility of the structure impacts negatively upon innovation and contributes to the difficulties in policies of change. Finally, "pigeonholing" not always is the perfect mechanism to match patient's needs (e.g. for patients affected by multiple or chronic diseases). These limits depend on the peculiar characteristics of professional bureaucracies: beyond the formal hierarchy, power of people within the organization is based on competence (the power of the "expert") and professionals within the operating core take advantage of a large autonomy and discretionary power. Relatedly, staff in health care has a vast range of roles and different professional backgrounds, so it is difficult to manage it as a whole. Again and consequently, professionals are usually resistant to control and change.

Moreover, the external environment influences the organizations (Lega 2005). For example there are multiple expectations from external relevant stakeholders (e.g. State, Region or Local health authorities for hospitals), expressed through formal agreements, plans and programs to set strategic lines, assign budgets or oblige to recovery and turnaround. Generally and regardless the public or private nature of organizations, the sector is over regulated and accordingly the scope for actions at the lower level is doubtless limited. Yet, the influences of the political sphere are undeniable as they shape the policymaking process, as well as that of external professional associations upon the human resource management practices (e.g. for the role they have in the standardizations of competencies).

Furthermore, the healthcare system is affected by some relevant changes. In relation to the health profession, Waring and Bishop (2010) stressed the increasing standardization of clinical practices (e.g. the diffusion of evidence-based guidelines and audit regimes), the reconfiguration of clinical work and professional boundaries in an era of new emerging patterns in hospital organizational design (e.g. the care-focused hospital) and the stratification of professional groups (co-option of professionals in managerial roles to direct the change). These changes are not accepted without resistance by clinical communities (Borgonovi 2004, 2005). Generally, within the domain of professionalized public service organizations, radical top-down change initiatives may not be the easier solution.

What is more, the resistance to change can affect individuals interested in preserving the status quo for a variety of reasons. Eccles (1994), for example, identifies the following causes of individual resistance: problems not understood; other preferred solutions; feeling that the proposed solutions will not work; unacceptable personal costs; inadequate rewards; fear of not succeeding; threats to existing equilibrium; questioning of existing sources of influence and control; diffidence towards new values and practices; unwillingness to change; diffidence towards the reasons why management wants to change; other interests more valued; reduced career opportunities and power.

A further consideration about change is that for improvements to be successful, especially for radical projects at a system level, it takes a long time before achieving sustainable outcomes. Accordingly, strong commitment is needed to sustain over time such projects, first of all by the CEOs. On the contrary, policymakers and consequently General Managers usually look for quick gains. Yet, there is a high turnover in the latter position and, as a result, sustainability of change is difficult to achieve (in Italy the average tenure as General Manager is of little more than three years—Guerrazzi and Ricci 2013).

Given these premises the proposition of Henry Mintzberg cannot be challenged. The above factors can explain why it is extremely difficult for an "heroic" leader to drive and impose the expected change. Put in other words, the charisma of the leader and its power may be a necessary but a non-sufficient condition. Earlier studies confirm this assertion. Indeed, a study conducted in a hospital setting highlighted that "a reliance on "strong leadership" by itself is a weak basis for transformational organizational change in large, complex and professionalized organizations" (McNulty and Ferlie 2004, p. 1407). Rather, alternative ways should be found to enhance change from the operating core, with a bottom-up approach more consistent with the nature of managerial work in public organizations.

Consequently what is important is to shift from a centrally imposed change approach, even directed by a great leader, to a more "shared" one, where "organizational leaders have to negotiate rather than impose new policies and practices" (Ham 2003, p. 1979). Reversing the statement of Henry Mintzberg: healthcare institutions as well as the overall system may be fixed by bringing in the "facilitating" leader and spreading distributed management and leadership. Obviously the meaning is not to reject the role of institutional policymakers and General Managers, but to create the organizational readiness conditions to enhance change and the likelihood of better performance and, consequently, to build different organizational cultures supporting and valuing the contribution of all. This kind of culture should promote interprofessional collaboration and synergies both within and outside the organization, spread the diffusion of skills in healthcare redesign and enhance accountability at all levels.

This kind of leadership is more likely to fit with the challenges that healthcare organizations are facing to date. The constraints and pressures the system face urge the need to innovate and improve performance by means of adequate asset, knowledge and disease management systems (Lega 2011). Indeed, as Lee stated, the healthcare system still requires major shifts (Lee 2010): effective articulation of vision and values, organizing for performance, developing a measurement system, building effective teams, improving processes, as dismantling cultural barriers. Of course, this requires a shift in the mindset. If the "heroic" leader at the top level cannot fix the system, on the other hand health professionals have to embrace the "new" role of leader. This could not be easily achieved, but as Bohmer claimed: "the only realistic hope", to fix health care "is for existing general hospitals, clinics, and physician practices to redesign themselves" (Bohmer 2010). In other words—to put it simply—a new era has to come. It is worth extending to all the modern healthcare systems the following statements concerning the UK NHS: "The NHS requires complicated leadership arrangements with negotiated authority between clinicians and professional managers, between clinicians from different professional backgrounds, across one NHS entity to another and for innovations and change projects that involve different directorates" (James 2011, p. 19). The effort should be more than bringing into play leaders on the top capable of engaging people from below (Heifetz and Laurie 1997). Healthcare organizations should enhance distributed leadership to face present complexity and challenges, but cautiously without totally rejecting the role that key managers and transformational leaders can have.

References

Barnard CI (1968) The functions of the executive, vol 11. Harvard University Press, Cambridge, MA (First published in 1938)
Barnes LB, Kriger MP (1986) The hidden side of organizational leadership. Sloan Manag Rev 28 (1):15–25
Barretta A (2008) The functioning of coopetition in the health-care sector: an explorative analysis. Scand J Manag 24:209–220
Bass BM (1981) Stogdill's handbook of leadership: a survey of theory and research, rev edn. The Free Press, New York
Bass BM (1985) Leadership and performance beyond expectations. Free Press, New York
Bennett N, Wise C, Woods PA, Harvey JA (2003) Distributed leadership: a review of literature. National College for School Leadership
Bohmer RM (2010) Fixing health care on the front lines. Harvard Bus Rev 88(4):62–69
Borgonovi E (2004) Ripensare le amministrazioni pubbliche: tendenze evolutive e percorsi di approfondimento. Egea, Milano
Borgonovi E (2005) Principi e sistemi aziendali per le pubbliche amministrazioni. Egea, Milano
Burns JM (1978) Leadership. Harper & Row, New York
Dorgan S, Layton D, Bloom N, Homkes R, Sadun R, Reenen JV (2010), Management in healthcare: why good practice really matters. McKinsey & Company and the London School of Economics and Political Science
Eccles T (1994) Succeeding with change: implementing action-driven strategies. McGraw-Hill, New York
Eisenhardt SK (1989) Making fast strategic decisions in high-velocity environments. Acad Manag J 32:543–576
Fayol H (1949) General and industrial management. London: Pitman (Firs published in French—Administration industrielle et generale, Paris, 1929)
Great Britain, Department of Health (2010) Equity and excellence: liberating the NHS [Norwich]: Stationery Office
Guerrazzi C, Ricci A (2013) La struttura e le attività del SSN. In: CERGAS (ed) L'aziendalizzazione della sanità in Italia. Rapporto OASI 2013. Egea, Milano, pp 112–181
Ham C (2003) Improving the performance of health services: the role of clinical leadership. Lancet 361(9373):1978–1980

Ham C et al (2011) The future of leadership and management in the NHS: no more heroes. Report by The King's Fund
Heifetz RA, Laurie DL (1997) The work of leadership. Harvard Bus Rev 75:124–134
Heller L (2004) Change management nelle cure primarie: l'influenza delle leve aziendali sull'evoluzione degli strumenti manageriali per la medicina generale. In: Anessi Pessina E, Cantù E (eds) L'aziendalizzazione della sanità in Italia. Rapporto OASI 2004. Egea, Milano, pp 405–429
Holder R, Ramagem C (2012) Health leadership and management competencies: a systemic approach. World Hosp Health Serv 48(3):9–12
James KT (2011) Leadership in context lessons from new leadership theory and current leadership development practice. In: Commission on leadership and management in the NHS. The King's Fund
Kohn LT, Corrigan JM, Donaldson MS (2000) To err is human: building a safer health system, vol 627. National Academies Press, Washington
Kotter JP (1995) Leading change: why transformation efforts fail. Harvard Bus Rev 73(2):59–67
Kotter JP (2001) What leaders really do. Harvard Bus Rev 79(11):85–98
Langley A (1995) Between "Paralysis by Analysis" and "Extinction by Instinct". Sloan Manag Rev 36(3):63–76
Lee TH (2010) Turning doctors into leaders. Harvard Bus Rev 88(4):50–58
Leese B, Mahon A (1999) Management and relationships in total purchasing pilots. Relevance for primary care groups. J Manage Med 13(3):154–163
Lega F (2005) Organizational design and development for health care services. McGraw-Hill, Milano
Lega F (2011) Oltre i pregiudizi e le mode: natura e sostanza dell'innovazione organizzativa dell'ospedale. In: Cantù E (ed) L'aziendalizzazione della sanità in Italia: rapporto OASI 2011. Egea, Milano, pp 504–522
Mailu C (2010) The Nairobi hospital. In: The global business school network, 5th annual conference. http://www.gbsnonline.org
McNulty T, Ferlie E (2004) Process transformation: limitations to radical organizational change within public service organizations. Organ Stud 25(8):1389–1412
Mintzberg H (1979) The structuring of organizations. Prentice-Hall, Englewood Cliffs
Mintzberg H (1989) Mintzberg on management: inside our strange world of organizations. Free Press, New York
Mintzberg H (1993) Structure in fives: designing effective organizations. Prentice-Hall, Michigan
Mintzberg H (2012) Managing the myths of health care. World Hosp Health Serv Off J Int Hosp Fed 48(3):4–7
Peters TJ, Waterman RH (1982) In search of excellence. Harper & Row, New York
Sargiacomo M (2001) La misurazione dell'impegno lavorativo dei direttori generali delle Aziende Usl. Mecosan 10(40):31–51
Sargiacomo M (2003) Comportamento manageriale e best-practices nell'azienda Usl. Giappichelli, Torino
Villa S, Barbieri M, Lega F (2009) Restructuring patient flow logistics around patient care needs: implications and practicalities from three critical cases. Health Care Manage Sci 12:155–165
Waring JJ, Bishop S (2010) Lean healthcare: Rhetoric, ritual and resistance. Soc Sci Med 71 (7):1332–1340. doi:10.1016/j.socscimed.2010.06.028
Warwicker T (1998) Managerialism and the British GP: the GP as manager and as managed. Int J Pub Sect Manag 11(2–3):201–218
Yukl G (1999) An evaluation of conceptual weaknesses in transformational and charismatic leadership theories. Leadersh Quart 10(2):285–305
Zaleznik A (1977) Managers & leaders: are they different? Harvard Bus Rev 55:67–78

Chapter 7
Myth #4: The Healthcare System Can Be Fixed by Treating It More as a Business

Federico Lega, Emanuele Vendramini, Giuseppe Festa and Enrico Coscioni

7.1 Some Remarks Beyond Ideology and Fashion

Federico Lega

7.1.1 Introduction

In recent years, the number of advocates for a more business-like management of health care organizations has significantly increased.

Starting from the '90s, the debate on the benefits of treating health care as business has intensified (EOHSP 2009, 2011; Mladovsky et al. 2012; Thomson and Mossialos 2004). The emergence of the New Public Management (NPM) paradigm

F. Lega (✉)
Department of Public Policy & Management, SDA Bocconi School of Management, Rontgen 1, 20136 Milan, Italy
e-mail: federico.lega@unibocconi.it

E. Vendramini (✉)
DISES—Department of Economic and Social Disciplines, Università Cattolica del Sacro Cuore, via Emilia Parmense, 84, 29122 Piacenza, Italy
e-mail: emanuele.vendramini@unibocconi.it

G. Festa (✉)
Department of Economic and Statistical Sciences, University of Salerno, via Govanni Paolo II, 132, 84084 Fisciano (SA), Italy
e-mail: gfesta@unisa.it

E. Coscioni
Department of Ascending Aorta and Thoracic Surgery, University Hospital "San Giovanni e Ruggi d'Aragona", Salerno, Italy

P. Adinolfi and E. Borgonovi (eds.), *The Myths of Health Care*,
https://doi.org/10.1007/978-3-319-53600-2_7

has further contributed to this discourse in the context of public healthcare organization, with emphasis put on privatization, on commissioning to private providers rather than providing through public ones, and on the introduction of quasi-market configuration for health systems (Degeling et al. 2003; Ham 2012; Ackroyd et al. 2007). The new rhetoric-viewed business-like approaches as the panacea for the enduring problems of health systems, especially with regards to the cost escalation and the sustainability challenge. Yet, there is no evidence of these benefits. While we have clear signs that business-driven health systems cost more and have greater problems in equity in access to healthcare delivery, variation in outcomes, adverse selection and opportunistic behaviors, such as disease mongering and more (Blank and Bureau 2013). Further, and more important, even if it is arguable the fact that a business approach could be beneficial for some aspects, to develop a constructive debate we first have to agree on what is meant by "treating health care as a business."

In the following of this article, I will argue how we need to look beyond rhetoric. Igniting a serious debate about when and how business-driven approaches are useful to support the quest of health organizations for improvement of their performance. The work will proceed as follow, with the aim of illustrating why treating health care as a business is not the right thing to do, but could be helpful to do things right:

- first, I will recollect the aims of health systems and health organizations and their implications for management practice. This is to provide a broad but more bounded definition of what we can consider "treating health care like a business";
- second, I will demonstrate why health systems and organizations have specific features and dynamics which, although they can certainly benefit from business techniques and logics, do require different management practices;
- third, and finally, I will argue about what health care can positively learn and import from business, and vice versa why we should avoid treating health care as a mere business.

7.1.2 *What Is Treating Health Care Like a Business?*

With regards to the aims of health systems and health organizations, there are thousands of publications that investigate and discuss in detail the scopes and goals, better than I could ever do here. However, in short, it would be difficult to disagree that the end point is taking care of and curing patients, providing access to education, prevention, expertise, technology, and everything else that is necessary to perform and deliver health services. In recent times, most of the debate has focused on how to provide all this while securing the sustainability of health systems and health organizations. Universalism and sustainability have become popular issues (Value in Health 2013). Quite often, sustainability has become the dominant issue.

No surprise, as the Romans taught "primum vivere, deinde philosophare." Though, the cultural dominance of the economic field has caused a cultural shift, an inversion among ends and means, where cost management became "the one and only issue." Consequently, health systems and health organizations have been too often reconfigured, transformed, downsized, merged, redesigned, streamlined, etc. for the purpose of improving their capacity to manage cost. To reduce cost. A large part of the discussion on value-based health care was reduced to the point of the ratio of volume of health services delivered per dollar/euro paid. Efficiency (if not rationing) ruled over appropriateness (Value in Health 2013). Eventually, the quality of patient experience went into the picture. Very few voices highlighted the risks of such economic-driven framing of issues in the agenda of health systems and organizations. Very few advocated for cultural shift towards "less is more," "more/big is not better," or "focus rather than size" approaches, such as choosing wisely and similar movements (Brody 2010).

In this respect, treating health care with a business-like approach was seen as the "one best way" to enhance capacity of health organizations for effective cost management. This one best way was in effect twofold.

On one side, health organizations were expected to take a new strategic posture, acting as businesses. And eventually they were to be transformed from a legal viewpoint into businesses, as health systems were progressively transformed and reconfigured in markets and health organizations and professionals were subject to a corporatization process. For instance, in Mintzberg's own words, "This is a particularly popular prescription in the United States. Perhaps no country on earth treats health care more as a business, or is more encouraging of competition in this field…. In the name of competition, American health care in fact suffers from individualization: every professional and every institution for his, her, or itself." Business-like approach to management here meant great emphasis on bottom-line results, share of market, revenue growth, competition. Competitive and economic success is the driver. This would grant better care because patients would select only the best, and the poor performers would exit the market. All clear and easy, certainly … if patients knew which were the best providers, if information asymmetry, disease mongering and failures of markets were just a theoretical issue. They are not. As we have known for decades. Competition without control, without appropriate steering, will bring health organizations and systems to row in the wrong direction.

On the other side, becoming competitive required a specific "business" toolbox: strategic planning, performance management, operations management, lean management systems, human resources strategic management, etc. Tools are by nature neutral, as they serve the scope of those who use them. They could be more or less appropriate, more or less effective, in relation to the context in which they are implemented. They can support the quest of healthcare organizations for improving their capacity to operate in a sustainable equilibrium within a complex (if not hostile) environment of growing demand and expectations by patients, skyrocketing costs connected to technology advances, financial pressures posed by third party payers.

So, "treating health care like a business" could refer to two different meanings. First, the emergence of competition, marketization, corporatization, profit-driven rather than mission-driven health organizations, etc. Second, the introduction of business tools and practices. Support the corporate and marketing processes will also improve efficiency, efficacy, robustness and quality of the delivery of health services within any organizational and cultural context. The latter may require further analysis and exploration, for the benefits it promises and the challenges it encompasses with the introduction of such tools and practices in the context of health organizations.

7.1.3 What Makes Alike Health Organizations from Businesses

There is one simple sentence that sums up the distinctiveness of health organizations: "they are certainly more than just the sum of their professionals, as they require resources, technology, logistics, etc., but they'll never be better than what their professionals want them to become."

This remark underlines a huge difference. In businesses the human side is important, but not as much as in health organizations (Freidson 1994; Fitzgerald and Ferlie 2000; Borgonovi and Landau 2008). Businesses need leaders, but then the job of the leaders is to make the people (employees) fit the system. The employees are selected, trained and "indoctrinated" to support the system (organization). The system is the independent variable. In healthcare organizations, it is rather the opposite: the system is mainly engineered to support the practices of healthcare professionals. The practices are the independent variable. They are introduced and changed by professionals. Not by the system. Obviously, we do not have to build health organizations around all professionals' wants or needs, otherwise we will be back to the old days when they were idiocrasies or professional bureaucracies (Lega and De Pietro 2005), but a degree of customization is required. This characteristic brings consequences and managerial implications. Such as the fundamental role that the processes of alignment of interests play, the so-called sharing of minds among the professionals and the management (Lega 2012; Lega and Cuccurullo 2001). Which is even more vital when professionals play the hybrid role of doctor–manager (Lega et al. 2014, 2015; Lega and Sartirana 2015; Drife and Johnston 1995; Davies and Harrison 2003).

We do have evidence that management matters in health care. We do have evidence that the introduction of managerial practices makes the difference in performance of healthcare organizations (Lega et al. 2013). But we also know that this introduction and development does not mean we can treat healthcare organizations as mere businesses.

First, decision-making in health organizations cannot be driven exclusively by market opportunities. Their focus is the mission, its definition and operation are not just a problem of top management. Rather, it is a collective process (Lega and Cuccurullo 2001) which involves the alignment of interests and priorities between managers, doctors, and other health professionals. Even if it could be based on a strategic posture that is close to a business-like approach to decision-making, yet it involves a collective agreement and endorsement (Lega and Cuccurullo 2001; The King's Fund 2011). Strategy and decision-making are defined at the intersection among different cultures (professional, bureaucratic, and managerial), values (political, social, entrepreneurial, individual) and interests (different professional families, groups, and individuals). Decision-making is becoming increasingly more difficult as every health organization faces four inexorable trends: a demographic shift toward the elderly, the skyrocketing pace of technological innovation, the rising consumer expectations, and rising costs. Many decisions are wicked problems, with not one single best solution, increasingly complicated by ethical concerns (Lega et al. 2013; Borgonovi 2008). Furthermore, many health organizations are public or operate and are embedded in a highly regulated public environment. Therefore, they are subject to specific dynamics. Complexity. Public health organizations generally have a variety of stakeholders who place demands and constraints on the managers. Permeability. Public health organizations are "open systems" that are easily influenced by external events. Instability. Political constraints result in frequent policy changes and the imposition of short time horizons on health managers. Greater bureaucracy. Public health organizations are subject to more formal procedures for decision-making and are less flexible and more risk-averse than their counterparts in the private sector (Lega 2012; Borgonovi 2008; Allison 1993; Boyne 2002). Decreased managerial autonomy. Managers in public organizations have less freedom to act and react according to personal views to the circumstances that they face (Boyne 2002). The level of organizational commitment is believed to be lower in the public sector largely because of inflexibility in personnel procedures and weak links between performance and rewards (Borgonovi 2008; Allison 1993; Boyne 2002).

Second, because the introduction of management tools is not straightforward as in business contexts. In the last 15 years, much of what has been written applauds the notion that the core issue for health organizations has centered on providing better tools to achieve better performance. This view has been strongly influenced and supported by the rationalism of NPM reforms, particularly strong in countries where public involvement in healthcare delivery is pervasive. Unfortunately, NPM theorists appear more concerned with doing things the right way, such as adopting strategic planning, performance management, quality systems, than with doing the right things, such as developing a strategic management approach to identifying priorities and lead changes in complex contexts (Berry 1994). In this respect, the introduction of management techniques, such strategic planning, performance management, operations management, quality systems, and other, requires customization and higher degree of institutional legitimacy. That is, normative, political or social steering that back up managers' efforts to introduce and consolidate such managerial tools. For instance, strategy-making is a collective process, strongly affected by emergent strategy, characterized by a strategy-as-practice approach (Lega and Cuccurullo 2001). Performance targets are often not imposed, but are built and "shared" with professionals (Lega et al 2013; Spurgeon et al. 2011). Quality is often defined by external professional bodies (Freidson 1994).

7.1.4 The Business Suit that Fits Healthcare Organizations

Mintzberg stated: "So again, let's try it differently: Healthcare functions best as a calling, not a business; as such, it needs greater cooperation, not competition, among its many players and institutions. Physicians may be well paid, but these are smart people capable of earning large incomes elsewhere. What keeps many, if not most, of them in healthcare is the sense of service. This applies equally, if not more so, to the nurses, who don't earn that kind of money, and many of the managers too." The whole discussion of the previous paragraphs supports this view.

Yet, we also alluded to the fact that some business-like approaches can be positive. Specifically, the management side of business. Health systems and health organizations face tremendous challenges, and they struggle to answer the fundamental question: what makes them valuable. Prioritization, decision-making, resource allocation, reconfiguration of services are difficult and complex tasks, but at the same time essential as ever. Though it requires specific customization, the introduction of business-like techniques and practices seems to be the way to go (Lega et al. 2013; Bohmer 2009). To support health systems and health organizations in selecting the right things to do, and then do them right.

In the end, in these turbulent times—a new normality—health systems and health organizations require a greater "discipline" to manage their specific organizational dynamics. Business tools—such as performance management, quality systems, lean techniques, operations management, business planning, humans resource strategic management, etc.—would allow health organizations—public as well as private—to manage more effectively and efficiently the "black box" of healthcare delivery (Lega et al. 2013; Vissers et al. 2001; McCarthy 2006; Davies and Walley 2000; Lega and Calciolari 2012). Where it is clearly understood that if it is true that no margin = no mission, it is also even more important to remember that margin is not the mission.

This is the business suit that can help them. A customized business suit dressed in a context dense of healthcare values.

Not a business context with healthcare suits dressed by doctors–business men longing for market success.

7.2 Business Versus Nonbusiness Model in Health care

Emanuele Vendramini

7.2.1 Introduction

Henry Mintzberg (2012) in his article "Managing the Myths of Health care" takes into consideration the different Myths related to the healthcare sector; specifically Myth #4 states that: "The healthcare system can be fixed by treating it more as a business" and highlights the reasons why this assumption is not true:

- Health care functions best as a calling, not a business
- Physicians are motivated by the sense of service and not, just, by large incomes
- Cooperation and not competition.

Most of the aforementioned points are related to the dichotomy "business versus nonbusiness" and precisely: if an organization is business it means it has to be market driven while a nonbusiness should be related to cooperation, motivation, a call, and not a business.

The paradigm "business versus non business" could be elaborated and discussed taking into consideration the specificities of healthcare organizations; in fact Myth #4 could be analyzed and discussed using three words:

1. Ambidexterity (Duncan 1976)
2. Professionalism (Bartol 1979; Noordegraaf 2015)
3. Accountability (Kaplan and Norton 1996; Scally and Donaldson 1998).

7.2.2 Ambidexterity

Ambidexterity is linked to the fact that healthcare organizations are expected to deliver care (and innovate in technology and in clinical pathways) and at the same time be financially sound. So they are asked to maximize these two dimensions at the same time. Some authors (Masini 1979; Porter and Kramer 2011) suggested that even private for profit companies are analyzed under the shared value perspective and business is not, just, considered as a market driven entity that has to maximize profits at the expense of society (Masini 1979) and, considering a hospital, there should not be something wrong or bad if a unit of medicine, dermatology or some other medical specialties, produces a loss as long as there is another unit that for different reasons (volumes, fees, economies of scale) produces a profit, and that the profitability is analyzed at a corporate level not as a single unit. It has also to be taken into consideration that, often, the most profitable unit in a given hospital is not necessarily the best unit.

So Healthcare organizations should consider cost control and contribution margin as tools and not the aim.

Ambidexterity is the ability to maximize the different aims: provide valuable health care and be profitable. So it is not just an aim nor pure business. It is management or, better, healthcare management. H. Mintzberg's assumption is very robust health care is not just business as usual, it is more sophisticated, it is healthcare management and it is different from producing standardized goods.

7.2.3 Professionalism

The second word is strictly linked to one of Mintzberg's points and specifically "Physicians are motivated by the sense of service and not, just, by large incomes." That is true but it is important to highlight that physicians have to be recognized as professionals in terms of knowledge, in terms of autonomy, in terms of freedom of deciding what is best for their patient. So the concept of sense of service has to be elaborated taking into consideration different dimensions such as the following:

- Competences development
- Career path development
- External perceptions.

The main purpose of a healthcare organization is to provide care, so for the physician it is important to have the right number of cases (and case mix) to be able to tackle all the different situations and be able to offer a state of the art service. This point is strictly linked to how the hospital is organized; maybe too many small units focused on a never-ending turf war is not the most effective and desirable working environment.

Career path and career development are other important elements of professionalism mainly because in a professional environment the organizational structure is more fluid and less hierarchical so having common values, clear rules, incentives, produce the right motivations. In a professional environment, the most powerful incentives are nonfinancial not only because the marginal benefit of an incentive decreases but also because physicians consider them relevant for internal recognition. Being recognized, as a valuable professional by a colleague is the most powerful and relevant incentive.

Healthcare organizations provide a specific product: health, so the impact of their performance on external stakeholders is massive (e.g., effects on the media about malpractice cases) and the main implication is that it is important for physicians to work in a well-recognized/reputed organization.

These three dimensions are strictly linked, the best physicians work in the best organizations (and vice versa) where competences, development, and professional upgrades are structured in a meritocratic system with shared values.

Even taking into consideration this second element (professionalism) H. Mintzberg's approach is very intriguing specifically when he highlights that the complexity of the healthcare organizations cannot be simply defined as business management approaches. Health care is not "just" business and it is not fixed when it is considered as a business.

7.2.4 Accountability

Accountability is somehow the most powerful element to understand the reasons why a healthcare organization is not "just" business as usual. Measuring the performance of a private for profit company is "quite" simple; historically the most relevant questions were: Is it profitable? Is it enlarging its market share? Since the 90s scholars agreed these arguments were not enough; in fact profit companies were requested to have a balanced approach (Kaplan and Norton 1996) otherwise they would have risked going out of business (because of inefficient processes, unsatisfied customers, brain drain, etc.). Now, if this multidimensional approach is appropriate for these types of companies (private and for profit) what would the implications be if applied to healthcare organizations? There would be quite some unexpected outcomes. In fact, applying the traditional Balanced scorecard process perspective to a hospital would imply the introduction of:

- Clinical pathways, the lean clinical governance (business process dimension)
- Continuous upgrade of clinical guidelines and the organizational capacity (learning and grow dimension)
- Implementation of a stakeholder approach (stakeholder dimension).

This multidimensional approach will lead to a major issue: how could we check if a cardiology unit is doing things right? And when is it doing the right things too?

There is a need for a very sophisticated performance measurement system, and specifically Scally and Donaldson (1998) have highlighted that "A commitment to deliver high quality care should be at the heart of everyday clinical practice. In the past many health professionals have watched as board agendas and management meetings have become dominated by financial issues and activity targets. The government's white paper on the NHS outlines a new style of NHS that will redress this imbalance. For the first time, all health organisations will have a statutory duty to seek quality improvement through clinical governance. In the future, well managed organisations will be those in which financial control, service performance, and clinical quality are fully integrated at every level."

So, again, H. Mintzberg's contribution confirms that health care does not need a "business as usual" approach. The Healthcare system needs to make physicians (and nurses too) accountable and their performances measured using financial and nonfinancial indicators. The complexity of making physicians accountable is given by the fact that no one can argue about the way they treat "their" patients because they are the Doctors and they work in a professional environment where professional autonomy is guaranteed. This point is also linked to the previous parts and specifically to the implications of professionalism and the ambidexterity of healthcare organizations. But if the aim is making physicians accountable as to which are their first choice drugs that have to be prescribed and make them understand that a non-necessary MRI has financial implications on the unit's budget, it is clear why health care is not business as usual and the uniqueness of healthcare management.

The third point addressed by H. Mintzberg is related to the need for more cooperation and less competition in the healthcare system. Many publications were produced on this point mainly in the 80s and many approaches were provided but in the 90s, 2000s, and 2010s literature produced many more publications highlighting how a "more cooperation less competition" perspective of analysis should be considered from a different point of view and the debate in the healthcare sector has been shifted to the effectiveness of quasi markets (Le Grand and Bartlett 1993; Le Grand et al. 1998; Mays et al. 2000; Porter and Teisberg 2005; Propper et al. 2008; Mays et al. 2011) and on the governance mechanism that better fits the system and its effectiveness (Shortell et al. 1996). So the third point of Mintzberg's approach is very valid mainly taking into consideration the variety of solutions that are in between the two extremes: cooperation versus competition.

The possible analysis of the three points provided by H. Mintzberg to support that "The healthcare system can NOT be fixed by treating it more as a business" is very robust and supported by many other contributions and publications and add value to the actual debate within the healthcare system.

7.3 The Corporatization/Humanization Binomial

Giuseppe Festa and Enrico Coscioni

7.3.1 Introduction, Objective, and Methodology

The strongest feature that we can ascribe to the health sector concerns the nature of the asset in question, namely the health service. Historically distinct from health, defined by WHO as "… a state of complete physical, mental and social well-being and not merely the absence of disease or infirmity," then to be understood as a condition, health care is characterized by the nature of performance (service).

While not specifically "health," health care is the set of activities that allow producing health and therefore the two are naturally commingled. In this synthesis is the main torment of health: how is it possible to combine health care and economics in the same reasoning, i.e., forcing a human condition to be treated in a way that must take into account money?

It seems appropriate that this dilemma is solved immediately, because when considering health and the economy together there is no oxymoron. Indeed, tackling the analysis of the health sector with a solid economic culture is very appropriate if, simplifying a lot the scientific rationale, we want to think about not only today's health care for one, but also today's health care for many if not for everyone, and especially about tomorrow's health care (again for many if not all).

Even today, however, many professionals, and specifically health professionals in the strict sense, complain vigorously about this combination, seen as a kind of unnatural condition in the world of health, as it is also true that economy professionals in the broad sense have turned to the health sector using purely and simply methodologies, techniques and tools of economics tout court, without an essential work of contextualization, which remains a crucial conceptual operation (Golinelli 2011; Russo 2012; Lega 2013). What remains indisputable, however, are the economic implications of health, which normally bestow upon the organizations responsible for the pursuit, achievement and maintenance of health their "business" nature, if for no other reason than the company is the economic order of the organization of human institutions (Antoldi 2012).

How is it then possible that one of the leading management scholars in the world, Professor Henry Mintzberg, can come to view as a myth to be dispelled the implied accuracy of a better model of health care if managed in the business perspective? The question, really, is wide and delicate: it was no accident that we previously spoke about a real "torment."

It is essential to approach from a methodological point of view these only apparent ambiguities, which some indeed consider as conflicts, thus developing a conceptual analysis based not on a specious "logomachy," but on the shared indications and peculiarities typical of business culture. More specifically, the objective of this contribution, of course theoretical, is to represent the cost effectiveness in health as a justifying rationality of the combination between humanization and corporatization, just moving from the critical analysis of the myth of health care as a business.

7.3.2 The Economic and Business Perspective in the Governance and Management of Health care

In the elaboration/provocation of "Myth #4 The Healthcare System Can Be Fixed By Treating It More As A Business," Mintzberg focuses his criticism in particular on the United States, which he accuses of administrative, professional and competitive hypertrophy, also considerably inefficient when compared to the best outcomes generally recorded in many other countries, whose health systems are often based on less private and fairer mechanisms. In short, it is not true that managing health care as a business is the best way to secure an overall improvement in health care and health: the United States, for example, which have made the economic vision of health care a cornerstone, complain of a blatant contradiction.

At the same time, there seems to be a widespread awareness of the necessity and not only the opportunity to address the problems related to the financing of health care costs, especially in times of crisis such as those recently experienced by the more developed countries (and in some ways still strongly ongoing). Not surprisingly, some healthcare systems, such as the Italian one, only fairly recently, but with clear determination, have given a purely corporate rank to health facilities (see especially Legislative Decrees no. 502/92, no. 517/93 and no. 229/99).

Cooperation and not competition, vocation and not entrepreneurship, humanity and not market: Mintzberg's words seem more like those of a physician that of a business economist. For the careful reader, however, there can be no surprise in these statements, which, in hindsight, support a heartfelt accusation to a business-like but, as said, hypertrophic and inefficient management of health care: in other words, they prompt addressing a nontrivial application of managerial skills to health care.

A more careful analysis of Mintzberg's words suggests the real problem that persists at the core of the myth of the healthcare corporatization: the individualization of the economic perspective of the health service, the economic perspective of the physician-patient relationship and the economic perspective of health as an institutional service (of society for society). "In the name of competition, American health care in fact suffers from individualization: every professional and every institution for his, her, or itself" (Mintzberg 2012, p. 5).

Therefore, it is not a matter of managing or not, it is not about corporatizing or not, it is not about business or not. This is instead about addressing the dramatic problems that prevent better organization of the overall available resources to provide the best possible health services to those who really need them: it is clear to everyone that an individualistic (and not social) vision is born inherently lame in walking that line, because the union of forces, if well governed and managed, can only bring benefits.

Moreover, health professionals should have identified, in the above words, concepts and tools by now wellknown to clinical practice: appropriateness, clinical governance, healthcare networking, and so on. The lesson that we can draw from the "demythologizing" of the myth of health as a business is therefore very clear: we must reject the vision of corporate health care led not by the sustainability of the system, but that remains trapped in merely addressing the cost of each individual case, perhaps to be handled in a standard manner to honor a false economic inspiration.

Of course, this rejection of individualization weighs on Mintzberg's own reflections specifically in the economic perspective, it not being at odds, but taking instead justification, from clinical and health individualization. "It is more important to know what person the disease has than what disease the person has" is the aphorism traditionally attributed to Hippocrates, in whose work "… the lack of anatomical, pathophysiologic, pharmacologic knowledge is compensated by an extraordinary attention, rather than to a single disease, to the patient as a whole person (Epidemics)" (Treccani Online 2016, translation).

An enlightened corporate vision is well aware of this fundamental truth: the health professional must be left independent judgment in choosing the overall health service to be performed in clinical terms, assessing the possibility/opportunity/obligation to vary, case by case, its technical aspect. In this regard there are guidelines, protocols and procedures (in which in any case the "clinical discernment" is essential), but these address health issues, not economic matters (or so should be in a nondistorted view of economy in health care).

The economic aspect may influence these choices, in compliance with the requirements for sustainability, but always with an ancillary role to medicine or healthcare disciplines in general. It is equally true that the clinical discernment is consistently associated with a relative responsibility (in each case, professional, organizational, civil or even criminal, or combinations of these), but in hindsight it has always been, still is and will always be so, because the healthcare professional, precisely in the sense of vocation recalled by Mintzberg, knows that he/she must respond to the patient, to the structure and finally to society.

If this is the moral, conceptual and theoretical scope in which to suitably fit the corporate vision of health care, we may at this point wonder what might happen if the economic mechanisms became overwhelming, as for example during a severe financial crisis, as happened recently. We must not forget that corporatization definitely concerns revenues, but in any case costs, even when health organizations were not (formally) managed as companies.

Firstly, the primary economic interest cannot be in the intention of the corporatization, which, as mentioned above, plays a supporting role (ancillary, if necessary) to the clinical and healthcare part. Secondly, the primary economic interest cannot be in the intention of the physician, who should rightly be paid for his/her professionalism, but not at the expense of patients' health, however such a distortion may show up. Thirdly, the primary economic interest cannot burden the conduct of the physician, as this may trigger the transition from defensive medicine to defensive healthcare economy.

All this is not unlikely: indeed, according to some, this is already happening. Some physicians do not prescribe tests, visits, surgery, treatments or medications because their costs are or would go beyond a certain budget, thus essentially devaluing the clinical choice because of economic reasons. This also happens in other circumstances, such as with triage in war zones or in greatly depressed areas of the world, but these circumstances are too uncommon to justify a common situation.

When it happens "normally," it is rather a neglected situation, when the economic motivation intervenes improperly in clinical-healthcare practice, applying slavishly an outright linear-cut policy. If we really want to put at the center of health care the person, the sick man mentioned by Hippocrates, while at the same time appropriately aiming for an ancillary role of economy, we must instead cut out the deadwood, thus offering the possibility and the opportunity to govern and manage entrepreneurially, i.e., with committing aims addressing development (Cuomo and Metallo 2013), what already works or could or should work better.

Therefore, it should not be surprising that economics and management should actually be assigned an ancillary role in the overall organization of healthcare systems, because the economic facet is in fact required to be impeccable, but not a substitute for medicine. Mutatis mutandis, this was, for example, the purpose of economics as envisioned by Federico Caffè, who advocated an economy at the service of man.

7.3.3 An Attempt to Synthesize Corporatization and Humanization in Health care

The ever-increasing spread of new technologies in society has obviously occurred also in the healthcare sector, which in fact has always been targeted by multi-disciplinary developments of knowledge, due to interdisciplinarity of medicine in the broad sense (chemistry, biology, computer science, etc.). Economics and management are part of these new technologies too, to be understood not as in the hard technical sense, but in the softer sense of competence.

In the case of health, however, we have even witnessed the birth of a new discipline, halfway between economics and healthcare disciplines, named HTA (Health Technology Assessment). HTA basically uses concepts, techniques and tools from pharmaco-economics, of which, in a kind of chronological short circuit, HTA is the "mother" competence, considering the drug as a technology (as it actually is).

The considerable exposure of medicine to new technologies has led over the years to the birth of a new need in health care, i.e., the humanization of the physician-patient relationship. This is actually a fundamental feature in the healthcare context, which, however, seems to have weakened over time precisely because of the excessive "technicalization" of medical science.

An economic vision and even more a corporate vision of health care, legitimate and necessary in a proper perspective of business culture, as has been discussed so far, to be constantly marked by a solid business ethics (Werhane 2000; Weber 2001; Winkler et al. 2005; Russo 2014), has prompted many operators (in all fairness, mainly, if not exclusively, health care operators) to put forth another version of the dilemma in question, namely between corporatization and humanization, with an obvious bias in favor of the second concept. An interpretation of this latest aspect of the problem of the present study may perhaps provide an additional small contribution to the development and maybe to the solution of the myth of health care as a business as formulated by Mintzberg, as proposed in synoptic form in the following figure.

What shown in Fig. 7.1 seems fairly easy to understand. The patient will approach the health professional for a health problem (which, in Hippocrates'

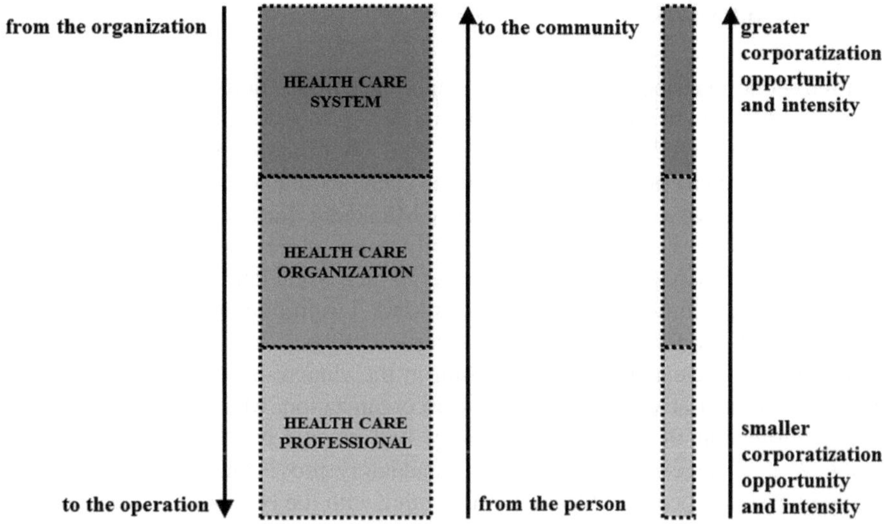

Fig. 7.1 A synoptic view of corporatization and humanization. *Source* developed by the authors

vision, can be generalized but is however always personal), a problem that requires some operational action by the health professional, who works in a healthcare organization, which is integrated in a healthcare system, hopefully organized for the community.

It is therefore clear that corporatization and humanization are not antithetical dimensions, but rather complement each other. In the more personal relationship with the patient, humanization scores better than corporatization, especially because of that healthy, mainly clinical individuality (and far less economic) which was mentioned earlier, while in the broader relationship with society, corporatization scores better than humanization, trivially by virtue of a planning intended to organize and ensure a priori the potential satisfying of the right of all to health care.

Rightfully, some might not (personally) be satisfied with this dynamic, but on one essential point there seems to be no compromise. Health organizations, which are acknowledged as such even formally (as today in Italy) or not (as in the past in Italy), are always businesses, each with its own specific economic purpose (for profit or nonprofit) (Festa 2003).

The theoretical investigation on the economic justification (cost effectiveness) of the governance and management of health care can undoubtedly serve to better streamline, organize and implement healthcare activities to serve the community (Marinò 2008). However, to imagine having health organizations, up to the functioning of health systems, not addressed as businesses not only is impossible because of the times, strongly characterized by the need for economic sustainability and not only (Borgonovi and Compagni 2013), but it is deeply wrong in cultural terms, obviously in the view of a healthy business culture.

7.3.4 Discussion and Conclusion

That the economic aspect is of decisive importance in health care is an institutional, strategic and operational truth for scholars and professionals, which is by now largely acknowledged, apart from those who on principle refuse, in form and substance, the concept of "corporatization." One should wonder, however, in the provocative and wise way Professor Henry Mintzberg does, if a vision exclusively or even excessively economic may actually cause more harm than good to the governance and management of health care: in fact, when talking about excess, one cannot but agree immediately, because, as Mark Twain pointed out, even water, if not drunk with moderation, is harmful (Digilio 2005).

It is therefore clear that a professional, in the clinical-healthcare area or in the technical-administrative area of a healthcare organization, who places the economic aspect before that of human individuality will always be "conceptually" in the wrong, even if forced or legitimized by mandatory provisions. Thus, how does it become possible to combine this essential value with the economic requirements of health organizations, whose operators under normal conditions work with great effort and in abnormal situations work in sometimes unthinkable conditions?

Mintzberg actually even takes it a step further, to the point of wanting to dispel the myth of health care that will "always" function best when run as a business. As pointed out, though, what Mintzberg actually condemns is the economic individualization of healthcare service, i.e., health care governed and managed in a view exclusively or mainly economic, and in this case too it is easy to agree.

With this contribution we have tried to provide a possible key to this dreaded dilemma: how to combine health and economics in health care? Specifically, we have tried to propose a conceptual framework summarizing the need and not only the opportunity of combining corporatization and humanization: the usefulness of this vision is clearly more practical than theoretical, aiming to provide professionals working in the healthcare structure a kind of framework of values.

However, to say it with Kurt Lewin, "there is nothing as practical as a good theory" (Lewin 1951, p. 169): Professor Mintzberg's studies and a critical analysis of Myth #4 allow us to understand that the myth of health care (only) as a business is clearly a myth to overcome with theoretical and practical courage (Adinolfi 2010) or at the most to be used, as Plato did, with exegetical, educational and informational purposes (e.g., as in the myth of the cave). Completely different, however, is to lean towards a wise economic management of health care, which in the theoretical contribution offered here becomes the conceptual glue of the synthesis of corporatization and humanization.

References

Ackroyd S, Kirkpatrick I, Walker R (2007) Public management reform and its consequences for professional organisation: a comparative analysis. Public Admin 85:9–26

Adinolfi P (2010) Oltre i miti del management. Sviluppo & Organizzazione 237:81–85

Allison GT (1993) Public and private management—are they fundamentally alike in all unimportant respects? In Perry JL and Kraemer KL (eds) Public management. Public and private perspectives. Mayfield Publishing, Palo Alto

Antoldi F (ed) (2012) Economia e organizzazione aziendale. McGraw-Hill, Milan

Bartol KM (1979) Professionalism as a predictor of organizational commitment, role stress, and turnover: a multidimensional approach. Acad Manag J 22(4):815–821

Berry FS (1994) Innovation in public management: the adoption of strategic planning. Public Adm Rev 54(4):322–330

Blank R, Bureau V (2013) Comparative health policy. Palgrave Macmillan, Basingstoke

Bohmer R (2009) Designing care: aligning the nature and management of health care. Harvard Business Press, Boston

Borgonovi E (2008) La tutela della salute è il fine, il funzionamento dei sistemi e delle aziende è il mezzo. Egea, Milano

Borgonovi E, Compagni A (2013) Sustaining universal health coverage: the interaction of social, political, and economic sustainability. Value Health 16(s1):s34–s38

Borgonovi E, Landau J (2008) Relationship competence for health care management. Peer to peer. Palgrave, Basingstoke

Boyne G (2002) Public and private management: what's the difference? J Manage Stud 39(1):97–122

Brody H (2010) Medicine's ethical responsibility for health care reform—the top five list. N Engl J Med 362:283–285

Cuomo MT, Metallo G (2013) Sviluppo manageriale per le imprese. Giappichelli, Torino

Davies H, Harrison S (2003) Trends in doctor-manager relationships. Brit Med J 326:646–649

Davies C, Walley P (2000) Clinical governance and operations management methodologies. Int J Health Care Qual Assur 13:21–26

Degeling P, Maxwell S, Kennedy J et al (2003) Medicine, management and modernisation: a "danse macabre"? Brit Med J 326:649–652

Digilio G (ed) (2005) Pratiche e politiche per la salute mentale. Armando, Roma

Drife J, Johnston I (1995) Management for doctors: handling the conflicting cultures in the NHS. Brit Med J 310:1054–1056

Duncan R (1976) The ambidextrous organization: designing dual structures for innovation. In: Killman RH (eds) The Management of Organization. North Holland, New York, pp 167–188

European Observatory on Health System and Policies (EOHSP) (2009) Financing the Health Care in European Union. Available from: http://www.euro.who.int/__data/assets/pdf_file/0009/98307/E92469.pdf. Accessed 1 July 2012

European Observatory on Health System and Policies (EOHSP) (2011) Health systems, health, wealth and societal well-being. Assessing the case for investing in health systems. Available from: http://www.euro.who.int/__data/assets/pdf_file/0007/164383/e96159.pdf. Accessed 1 July 2012

Festa G (2003) Evoluzioni del marketing management nelle aziende sanitarie. Scenari e soluzioni ICT. Giappichelli, Torino

Fitzgerald L, Ferlie E (2000) Professionals: back to the future? Hum Relat 53:713–739

Freidson E (1994) Professionalism reborn: theory, prophecy, and policy. Polity Press, Cambridge

Golinelli GM (2011) L'Approccio Sistemico Vitale (ASV) al governo dell'impresa, vol II. Verso la scientificazione dell'azione di governo. Cedam, Padova

Ham C (2012) The management of the NHS in England. Brit Med J 344:e928

Kaplan RS, Norton DP (1996) Using the balanced scorecard as a strategic management system. Harvard Bus Rev 74(1):75–85

Le Grand J, Bartlett W (eds) (1993) Quasi-markets and social policy. Macmillan, Basingstoke
Le Grand J et al (eds) (1998) Learning from the NHS internal market: a review of the evidence. King's Fund, London
Lega F (2012) Beyond rhetoric: inquiry on the essence of strategic management in public health care organisations. Int J Clin Leadersh 17(3):176–184
Lega F (2013) Management della sanità. Lineamenti essenziali e sviluppi recenti del settore e dell'azienda sanitaria. Egea, Milano
Lega F, Calciolari S (2012) Coevolution of patients and hospitals: how changing epidemiology and technological advances create challenges and drive organizational innovation. J Healthc Manag 57:17–33
Lega F, Cuccurullo C (2001) Effective strategizing practices in pluralistic settings: the case of academic medical centers. J Manage Governance 17(3):606–629
Lega F, De Pietro C (2005) Converging patterns in hospital organization: beyond the professional bureaucracy. Health Policy 74(3):261–281
Lega F, Sartirana M (2015) An international perspective on medical leadership. Future Hosp J 2 (3):218–220
Lega F, Prenestini A, Spurgeon P (2013) Is management essential to improving the performance and sustainability of health care systems and organizations? Value Health 16(s1):s46–s51
Lega F, Sartirana M, Prenestini A (2014) Medical management: hostage to its own history? The case of Italian clinical directors. Int J Public Sector Manag 27(5):417–429
Lega F, Prenestini A, Calciolari S, Grilli R (2015) The relationship between senior management team culture and clinical governance: empirical investigation and managerial implication. Healthc Manage Rev 40(4):313–323
Lewin K (1951) Field theory in social science: selected theoretical papers. In: Cartwright D (ed) Harper & Row, New York
Marinò L (2008) La ricerca dell'economicità nelle aziende sanitarie locali. Concetti, modelli, decisioni. Giappichelli, Torino
Masini C (1979) Lavoro e Risparmio. UTET, Torino
Mays N, Mullugan JA, Goodwin N (2000) The British quasi market in health care: a balance sheet of the service. J Health Serv Res Policy 5(1):49–58
Mays N et al (2011) Understanding new labour's market reforms of the English NHS. King's Fund, London
McCarthy M (2006) Can car manufacturing techniques reform health care? Lancet 367:290–332
Mintzberg H (2012) Managing the myths of health care. World Hosp Health Serv 48(3):4–7
Mladovsky P, Srivastava D, Cylus J et al (2012) Health policy in the financial crisis. Eurohealth 18:3–6
Noordegraaf M (2015) Hybrid professionalism and beyond: (new) forms of public professionalism in changing organizational and societal contexts. J Prof Organ 2(2):187–206. doi:10.1093/jpo/jov002
O'Reilly CA III, Tushman ML (2004) The ambidextrous organization. Harvard Bus Rev 82(4):74–81
Porter M, Kramer MR (2011) Creating shared value. Harvard Bus Rev 89(1–2):62–77
Porter ME, Teisberg EO (2005) Redefining health care. Harvard Business School Press, Boston
Propper C et al (2004) Does competition between hospitals improve the quality of care. J Public Econ 88:1247–1272
Propper C et al (2008) Competition and quality: evidence from the NHS internal market 1991-9. Econ J 118(525):38–170
Russo S (2012) Economia e management delle aziende sanitarie pubbliche. Profili evolutivi, assetto istituzionale e performance. Cedam, Padova
Russo F (2014) What is the CSR's focus in health care? J Bus Ethics 134(2):323–334
Scally G, Donaldson LJ (1998) Clinical governance and the drive for quality improvement in the new NHS in England. BMJ 317(7150):61–65
Shortell SM, Gillies RR, Anderson DA, Erickson KM, Mitchell JB (1996) Remaking health care in America. Hosp Health Netw AHA 70(6): 43–4, 46, 48

Spurgeon P, Clark J, Ham C (2011) Medical leadership: from the dark side to centre stage. Radcliffe Publishing, London

The King's Fund (2011) The future of leadership and management in the NHS. The King's Fund, London

Thomson S, Mossialos E (2004) Funding health care from private sources: what are the implications for equity, efficiency, cost containment and choice in Western European health systems? In: den Exter A (ed) World Health Organization Regional Office for Europe, Copenhagen

Value in Health (2013) Sustainability of universal health coverage: five continents, four perspectives. Value Health 16(s1):s4–s51

Vissers JMH, Bertrand JWM, De Vries G (2001) A framework for production control in health care organizations. Prod Plan Control 12:591–604

Weber LJ (2001) Business ethics in health care: beyond compliance. Indiana University Press, Bloomington

Werhane PH (2000) Business ethics, stakeholder theory, and the ethics of health care organizations. Camb Q Healthc Ethics 9(2):169–181

Winkler EC, Gruen RL, Sussman A (2005) First principles: substantive ethics for health care organizations. J Healthc Manage 50(2):109–119 (discussion 119–20)

Chapter 8
Myth #5: Health Care Is Rightly Left to the Private Sector, for the Sake of Efficiency

Oriana Ciani, Aleksandra Torbica, Francesca Lecci, Marco Morelli, Michael Drummond, Rosanna Tarricone, Maurizio de Cicco, Salvatore Russo and Luca Del Bene

8.1 Public Versus Private Provision of Healthcare Services

Oriana Ciani and Aleksandra Torbica

8.1.1 Introduction

The Henry Mintzberg's myth #5 has been inspired by "conventional wisdom" according to which ownership of healthcare providers plays an important role in the efficiency in producing services. Moreover, Henry Mintzberg argues that health care is rightly controlled by the public sector, for the sake of equality (Mintzeberg 2012). Based on these two apparently contrasting arguments one can conclude that

---

O. Ciani (✉) · R. Tarricone
Centre for Research in Health and Social Care Management (CERGAS), Università Bocconi, Via Rontgen, 1, 20136 Milan, MI, Italy
e-mail: oriana.ciani@unibocconi.it

A. Torbica
Department of Policy Analysis and Public Management, and Senior Researcher, Centre for Research in Health and Social Care Management (CERGAS), Bocconi University, Via Rontgen, 1, 20136 Milan, MI, Italy

F. Lecci · R. Tarricone
Department of Policy Analysis and Public Management, Bocconi University, Via Rontgen 1, 20136 Milan, Italy
e-mail: francesca.lecci@unibocconi.it

M. Morelli
Corporate and Real Estate Finance Department, SDA Bocconi School of Management, Milan, Italy

P. Adinolfi and E. Borgonovi (eds.), *The Myths of Health Care*,
https://doi.org/10.1007/978-3-319-53600-2_8

in the system where most of provision is public, there should be some trade-offs between equality and efficiency.

Whether privatization of healthcare provision actually leads to the improvement in efficiency has been the subject of what appears to be a considerable amount of research, both theoretical and empirical (Shen et al. 2007). According to standard economic theory private hospitals are predicted to outperform public hospitals in terms of efficiency. However, the existing theoretical literature as well as empirical studies, offer conflicting and inconclusive evidence on this issue (Burgess and Wilson 1996; Eggleston et al. 2008; Tiemann et al. 2012). In this short commentary on Henry Mintzberg's myth #5, we briefly outline the most common theoretical frameworks and provide a short summary of empirical studies conducted to investigate whether ownership matters for hospital performance in terms of efficiency. The final aim is to illustrate and provide arguments that could support or contrast the commonplace of private primacy in healthcare provision expressed by Henry Mintzberg.

8.1.2 Theoretical Framework

In a nutshell, there are three fundamental theories that can be drawn upon when comparing public and private provision of healthcare services: (1) agency/property-rights theory; (2) public choice; and (3) organization theories. (Villalonga 2000)

According to agency/property-rights theory, since private providers have well defined control rights they have a strong incentive to invest in innovation, maximize their profits through a high degree of technical efficiency. The property rights model predicts that private owners achieve lower costs in service provision than their

M. Drummond
Centre for Health Economics, University of York, Alcuin a Block, York, North Yorks YO1 5DD, UK
e-mail: mike.drummond@york.ac.uk

R. Tarricone
SDA Bocconi School of Management, Milan, Italy

M. de Cicco
Viale G.B.Stucchi, no. 110, 20900 Monza, Italy
e-mail: maurizio.de_cicco@roche.com

S. Russo
Department of Management, University of Venice, Dorsoduro 3246, 30123 Venice, Italy
e-mail: salvus@unive.it

L. Del Bene
Department of Management, Polytechnic University of Marche, Ancona, Italy

government counterpart that have less control to implement changes. Furthermore, the income of individual decision makers is more frequently tied to a hospital's performance in private settings. Consequently, it is assumed that the monitoring of a hospital's performance will be automatic and self-imposed by the manager leading to greater efficiency. The public choice school's central argument is that politicians pursue their own utility rather than the public interest. Accordingly, they impose on public organizations goals that can lead them to gain votes but can conflict with efficiency. Public choice theory argues that rationale for privatization is that the resulting changes in hospital's incentives lead to improved performance. Consequently, private hospitals are expected to improve technical efficiency by suppressing politically motivated resource allocation and expanding their output at least to the point where total cost equals total revenue. Finally, organizational theories focus on the organizational characteristics of private hospitals that are different from state-owned providers firms, such as incentives and control mechanisms, objectives, organizational structures and, most importantly, the culture.

Based on these strongly embedded and fairly convergent theoretical predictions regarding the performance effects of hospital privatization, a "conventional wisdom" solution to inefficiencies in the healthcare sector was that of opening the doors to private forces (Shen et al. 2007). Consequently, numerous empirical studies have been conducted to test these theoretical predictions in different contexts and by adopting different methodological approaches. A typical study that estimates the impact of ownership on efficiency uses ownership type (private vs. public) as independent variable and some measure of efficiency as the dependent variable in the empirical model. Thus, in order to shed light on the inconsistencies and make further sense of the results obtained across the studies, it is important to define clearly these two cardinal concepts.

Defining the ownership type of providers is not as straightforward as one may think, especially in the healthcare market where different forms of ownership co-exist: public, private for profit and private not-for-profit (Barbetta et al. 2007). Within the same ownership structure (i.e. private), differences in their mission (for-profit or not-for-profit) may have direct consequences on the incentives and strive for efficiency. Understanding whether profit status or public/private control affects efficiency is essential for many policy issues.

Efficiency measures whether healthcare resources are being used to get the best value for money. Most empirical studies focus on one or more of the following forms of efficiency in healthcare organizations: technical efficiency, productive (cost) efficiency and profit efficiency. Technical efficiency refers to the physical relation between resources (capital and labour) and health outcome. The concept of productive (or cost) efficiency refers to the maximization of health outcome for a given cost, or the minimization of cost for a given outcome. Finally, profit efficiency refers to maximization of profits which does not necessarily derive from more efficient use of resources.

8.1.3 Empirical Evidence on the Relationship Between Ownership and Hospital Performance

An increasing number of studies investigating efficiency—variously defined—in the healthcare systems has been published in recent years, the first dating back to 1984 (Sherman 1984). Across Europe and the US, the healthcare system is perceived to be hospital-centred, with hospitals acting as one of the major cost drivers of the total healthcare budget. It is not surprising then that the literature on the technical or allocative efficiency in health care mainly deals with hospitals and their performance. Due to the diffusion of private non-profit hospitals in Western countries, scholars have been able to test theories that deem non-profit organizations as more efficient than public providers in markets characterized by asymmetric information and uncertainty.

According to the theoretical background introduced above, one major factor determining the efficiency of hospitals is the ownership type, whether public (federal, state or regional) or private (for profit or not-for-profit). This topic has been extensively researched, however, with mixed conclusions. For instance, Wilson and Jadlow (1982), using a linear programming technique, found that for-profit hospitals were more efficient than others, whereas Zuckerman et al. (1994) and Puig-Junoy (1998) found public and non-profit hospital more efficient than for-profit ones. On the contrary, Vitaliano and Toren (1996), by means of stochastic frontier regressions (SFR), could not find any significant difference in efficiency between hospitals with different ownership structures. In general, previous attempts to pool the empirical evidence on this topic have demonstrated no systematic differences in efficiency between for-profit and not-for-profit hospitals (Sloan 2000). Moreover, studies using different techniques to estimate efficiency scores or exploring different forms of efficiency reached very different conclusions. Indeed, one study investigated all three forms of efficiency with a single data set and found that private hospitals are not significantly less cost- or technical-efficient than public institutions but have significantly higher profit efficiency compared to public hospitals (Herr et al. 2011).

A recent study by Czypionka and colleagues (Czypionka et al. 2014) on Austrian hospitals indicates that private non-profit hospitals outperform public hospitals in terms of technical efficiency irrespective of the breadth of medical services provided. In their analyses both diagnosis related groups (DRG) points or DRG points in addition to outpatient visits were considered as outputs, leading to similar findings. This conclusion contrasts that of a comparable study performed in Germany (Tiemann and Schreyogg 2009), whose healthcare system stands in the Bismarckian tradition as the Austrian counterpart. In this publication, the authors found public hospitals to be more efficient than private for-profit and non-profit hospitals.

This apparently contradictory evidence highlights the importance of the national hospital financing system and incentive structures when interpreting efficiency data. While a DRG-system to fund hospital care is in place in both countries, the system is ex-ante cost covering in Germany and covers only 50% of hospital costs in Austria. Here, a federal law establishes every year how much of the extra costs have to be covered ex-post by the government or its municipalities. The remaining costs have to be borne by the respective owner, whether an investor or the federal state. In this sense, in Germany public cost coverage for private and public hospitals is more equally distributed within a tough competitive environment, whereas in Austria financial risk is considerably higher for private not-for-profit hospitals, thus spurring more efficient behaviours. For the sake of completeness, one should also acknowledge a more recent publication by the same German authors where the impact of privatization on hospital efficiency was estimated (Tiemann and Schreyogg 2012). By applying an innovative difference-in-difference regression model to matched longitudinal data with bootstrapped data envelopment analysis (DEA) efficiency scores as dependent variables, they showed that conversion from public to private for-profit status in Germany was associated with a significant improvement in efficiency than a comparable sample of hospitals that remained instead public. However, this efficiency gains were negatively associated with the introduction of the DRG-payment system meaning that it became more challenging for hospitals that were converted to private status to realize their performance improvement in the post-DRG era.

On a similar note, Barbetta and colleagues (Barbetta et al. 2007) investigated the impact of different proprietary forms (public vs. private non-profit) and reimbursement systems on hospitals efficiency in Italy between 1995 and 2000. Within this time frame, the funding system of Italian hospitals moved from ex-post cost coverage or bed-day rate, for public or private organizations, respectively, to a prospective payment system based on DRG that applied to all types of hospitals. Using both nonparametric (i.e. data envelopment analysis) and parametric (i.e. corrected ordinary least squares and stochastic frontiers) approaches, the authors test the hypothesis that differences in public or private non-profit hospitals technical efficiency disappear after the introduction of a common DRG-based payment system. They found some evidence of convergence in efficiency scores of the different ownership structures, thus supporting the claim that differences in economic performances are more the results of institutional settings rather than the consequence of incentives systems embedded in the different proprietary forms.

Any meaningful discussion around hospital performance should also take quality of care into consideration. There are different ways of measuring quality in health care, e.g. waiting lists, patient satisfaction, innovation or adherence to guidelines, however, these have been rarely included in empirical evaluation of hospital efficiency and proprietary forms. In most quality-adjusted efficiency scores, (inpatient) mortality rates are used. In 2005, Milcent (2005) analyzed the effect of hospital ownership and reimbursement systems on mortality rates in France. Here hospital care can be provided by the public or the private sector. The former is funded under a global budget system, whereas the latter is paid on a fee-for-service mechanism. A crude comparison of mortality rates across hospitals reveal an 8% reduction in mortality rates in for-profit hospitals compared to public ones. However, rankings of hospital quality are easy to misinterpret if patient characteristics are not factored into the analysis. After implementing a duration model applied to panel data that allows controlling for the fact that disease severity of patients admitted to private or public sector may be different, she found no significant differences in outcomes, although heterogeneity was greater in for-profit hospitals. Indeed, a meta-analysis of 31 studies examining findings regarding hospital ownership and quality of care, as measured by mortality or adverse events rate, yield a pooled effect size statistically equivalent to zero, suggesting no difference between for-profit and not-for-profit hospitals (Eggleston et al. 2008). In a subset of studies representative of the US, private for-profit hospitals tend to show lower quality than non-profit counterparts, thus highlighting the importance of data source selection, timing and regional context in this type of empirical assessments.

8.1.4 Discussion

In summary, we can say that empirical literature on hospital performance generally recognizes that ownership and profit status affect hospital operations. However, as we highlighted in the short review above, the positive effects of privatization on efficiency predicted by the different theories are not always supported by the existing empirical evidence. There are several arguments that have been put forward to explain this mismatch between theory and empirics.

The first line of arguments concerns the methodology employed. It has been highlighted that study design (cross-sectional vs. longitudinal) and data analysis methods (DEA vs. SFR) significantly impact the results and consecutive conclusions (Shen et al. 2007).

The second line of arguments underlines the fact that public–private distinction is only one part of a broader and more complex link. Political, institutional and organizational factors, independent of the private–public distinction, also intervene in the relationship between privatization and efficiency and are likely to affect hospital efficiency, either positively or negatively, and therefore, reinforce or counteract the effect of the change in ownership per se. For example, incentives created by the prospective payment system (DRGs) for hospitals in many countries have significant impact on efficiency of all hospitals, regardless of their ownership type (Villalonga 2000).

Further research is needed to understand in depth the institutional context in which ownership matters for provider performance. Only when we have understood in depth organizational decision-making and market-level dynamics across a range of economies we can firmly state that privatization of healthcare provision leads to better efficiency. Until then, the statement "if left to the private sector it (health care) would be more efficient" will continue to be a myth.

8.2 Managing Efficiency in Health care: A Matter of Private and Public Processes

Francesca Lecci and Marco Morelli

8.2.1 Trends in Health care and Impacts on Efficiency Management

In the last few years, healthcare systems of developed countries have been characterized by the attempt to manage the tension between two apparently opposite pressures: the increase in the demand of healthcare services, due to the ageing of populations and the development of new treatments, and the reduction of resources available for funding healthcare systems, as a consequence of the economic crisis.

Both these dynamics have required healthcare organizations to improve their efficiency in order to survive. Efficiency measures if healthcare resources are being used to get the best value for money and are concerned with the relation between resource inputs (costs, in the form of labour, capital, or equipment) and outputs (numbers treated, waiting time, etc.). As suggested by Palmer and Torgerson (1999), "inefficiency exists when resources could be reallocated in a way which would increase the health outcomes produced". The authors identify three different forms of efficiency: technical efficiency addresses the issue of using given resources to maximum advantage; productive efficiency, of choosing different combinations of resources to achieve the maximum health benefit for a given cost; and allocative efficiency, of achieving the right mixture of healthcare programmes to maximize the health of society.

The main trends experienced by healthcare systems in the last ten years can be explained as an attempt to reach the three different categories of efficiency.

The first trend observed within many healthcare systems (especially Beveridge-like) has been the reduction of inappropriate treatments. For example, in the Italian NHS, hospital discharges have been reduced by approximately 20% in the last ten years. This result was reached not only by eliminating inappropriate inpatient services but also by converting them into outpatient activities. This is an example of allocative efficiency and it has equally impacted private and public providers.

However, outputs cannot be endlessly contained without affecting universal coverage, if any, and leaving unmet healthcare needs. In that respect, a second observed trend refers to the attempt to reduce the amount of inputs used. In fact, in many countries initiatives of spending review have been developed in order to contain costs incurred for the acquisition of all relevant healthcare inputs: personnel (in Italy, many regional governments have cut personnel costs by even 20% in the last five years), drugs (ceilings on the overall drugs consumption has been defined in many countries), services. At the same time, in an attempt to gain scale benefits, both public and private healthcare providers have experimented initiatives of mergers and acquisitions: in the last ten years, 50% of Italian public hospitals owned by local healthcare authorities have been merged, while 35% of Italian private hospitals have been acquired by big healthcare groups. The two examples provided may be interpreted as actions aimed at gaining technical efficiency and, as described, they have almost equally impacted private and public providers.

As far as productive efficiency is concerned, one of the most important trends in health care is for sure technological innovation. New therapeutic technologies, either pharmaceutical, medical devices or of other types, are an important and pressing issue for both developed and emerging economies. With the convergence of many scientific and technology breakthroughs, the pace of medical innovation is accelerating, generating better clinical outcomes with less invasive procedures and shorter recovery times, all in lower cost settings (in the last five years public healthcare expenditure in Italy has increased by 0.7% per year on average, while in the previous five years the growth rate was nearly 6% per year). The phenomenon described equally has affected private and public providers.

The three above-mentioned categories of efficiency have an impact on the way organizations design and run operating processes. In the last few years, the scientific literature and evidence provided by practitioners both highlight how processes are the key object of analysis when trying to measure and manage efficiency (Kaplan and Porter 2011). Given this evidence, in the next two sections of the chapter we will analyze the main innovations implemented by public and private healthcare services providers in terms of process measurement and management.

8.2.2 Measuring Process Efficiency

It is a well-known management axiom that what is not measured is generally difficult to be managed and, more importantly, improved. Traditionally, healthcare providers have implemented measurement systems aimed at controlling the costs incurred by organizational units. As highlighted by Kaplan and Porter (2011), value (and efficiency) in health care is measured in terms of patient outcomes achieved per input used. In that respect, it is necessary to measure both items of the efficiency formula, inputs and outputs: while the literature has provided in the last few years new methodologies to measure outputs in health care, existing costing systems seem still weak in measuring inputs. More specifically, traditional costing systems, by focusing on individual departments, services or support activities, often encourage what the two authors call "micromanagement of costs", namely the optimization of input–output at the individual organizational unit level, without adopting an end-to-end perspective on the whole process of care. This is a relevant limit, since a highly fragmented delivery process characterizes the path of care, where numerous distinct and independent organizational units are involved in treating a patient. In order to properly represent and analyze this complexity, a good accounting system should be able to account for all the resources used by a patient as she or he traverses the system.

Given this evidence, many healthcare organizations have developed systems that are able to measure the costs incurred in delivering healthcare processes.

If we look at the Italian NHS, Florence Local Health Authority no. 10 provides one of the first cases analyzed by healthcare scholars of process-oriented costing systems (Vannozzi and Fedeli 2011). More specifically, this organization has implemented a bill of material, namely a sort of matrix mapping the association between resources and activities along surgery processes. The project started with a detailed analysis aimed at describing and codifying the phases of each process; then, for each phase, a standard full cost has been computed. One of the key success factors of this project was the cooperation between the management control team and physicians/nurses, traditionally represented as two conflicting roles. The main objectives of the implemented innovation were to support some key decision processes:

- internal benchmarking, by giving the opportunity to physicians to codify and compare their surgery practices in order to identify best practices;
- external benchmarking, since the system now allows a comparison between costs incurred for surgical procedures (inputs) and the official rates provided by the DRG system (value given to the output);
- planning and control, a process that can be now linked to a different object of analysis. While traditionally the budget is prepared with a departmental perspective, the new system allows a process-oriented planning procedure;
- business process reengineering, as a result of the evidence provided by internal and external benchmarking.

A similar innovation was implemented by the IEO—European Institute of Oncology (Dallocchio et al. 2016), an Italian private hospital awarded with the accreditation from the Italian NHS. In order to analyze day surgery procedures, IEO has developed a process-oriented costing system. More specifically, also in this case a bill of material for each surgery process has been created, supported by the implementation of a new information system allowing the monitoring of materials consumption on a single patient basis. In IEO too, the implementation of the bill of material required a close cooperation between the controlling department and physicians. The adoption of the new system was one of the key drivers of the company turnaround: IEO registered a €18 million loss in 2011, while in 2014 the net profit was €6.5 million. The information provided by the new costing system fostered attention on resource consumption not only in the control department, but also among physicians. More specifically, after one year of adopting this innovation, all the day surgery procedures experienced a significant reduction in resource consumption, without affecting quality. Thanks to these results, all the procedures analyzed had a positive margin net of full cost. This can be considered as a real cost management (and not cost-cutting) initiative, since apart from generating cost savings, it allowed the optimization in the use of the two most important capacity resources: operating theatres and beds.

Many other healthcare providers have adopted analogous measurement systems. As the two above-mentioned cases demonstrate, innovation in management accounting systems is not a peculiarity of private hospitals, since it often arises in public organizations.

The two cases also show how measurement systems can create value and, more specifically, efficiency only when the information produced is linked to managerial decisions.

8.2.3 Managing Process Efficiency

In the last twenty years, the scientific debate highlighted the need to move from a pure efficiency and cost measurement perspective to an efficiency and cost management approach. This change of paradigm is consistent with the above-mentioned link between economic information and managerial decision; in fact, cost management can be defined as the deliberate decision-making aimed at aligning the cost structure of organizations with the strategy and optimizing of the use of resources (Lord 1996). In a broad sense, cost management can be defined as "a proactive process of identifying causes of costs, with the objectives of managing and minimizing the total costs associated with the provision of products and services to customers" (Chivaka 2007, p. 38). This means that cost management starts with the identification of cost drivers within the organization's value chain, with the aim of taking a proactive stance in reaching efficiency.

If we look again at the Italian NHS, we can find many examples of cost and efficiency management initiatives. One of them refers to the Giovanni XXIII Independent Hospital, a public hospital, operating in the North of Italy. The Giovanni XXIII implemented one of the first projects of intensity-of-care operating model. Traditionally, the operating units were the main cost object for the hospital, however, this system was not consistent with a business model by intensity-of-care, hence the collection and segmentation of data had to be turned around cross-functionally (across the operating units). A cost analysis suggested that drugs had a high incidence in the cost structure of many healthcare processes. The Giovanni XXIII, then, launched a project aimed at reengineering logistics and distribution of drugs, pharmaceuticals and medical products (Morelli and Lecci 2014). The project can be broken down into two phases: (i) the implementation of a new stock management policy for medical devices; (ii) the digitalization of drugs prescription. As a result, the implementation of the first initiative has allowed decreasing the ratio Average Inventory/Purchases for high value items from 25.6 to 2.5% over seven years; while the digitalization of drugs prescription decreased average inventory levels (−30%), wrong prescriptions and related legal arguments (−30%) and insurance costs (−4.5%).

Not so far from the Giovanni XXIII, another relevant innovation was experimented by Humanitas, a highly specialized, privately owned teaching and research hospital. Accredited by the National Health Service, Humanitas has been granted by the Ministry of Health the status of "Research Hospital" (IRCCS) with a focus on diseases of the immune system, ranging from cancer to rheumatoid arthritis. Since its foundation, in 1996, Humanitas has combined lean factory and total quality management approaches in order to maximize efficiency and effectiveness. More specifically, the Humanitas management model is based on ensuring demand, ensuring that patient move rapidly through the system and that the system is never blocked, therefore reducing paths variation. This allowed the hospital to experience a 300% growth in sales in the period from 2000 to 2013 and to increase its operating margin from 7 to 12% (Lecci and Longo 2015). Other healthcare providers, both public and private, have implemented lean management and other efficiency management approaches (Francesconi and Lecci 2014). Such models may apply to the organization as a whole (e.g. the AOU Senese Independent Hospital, a public provider) or to specific segments. The Lodi Local Health Authority, a public organization, implemented a business process reengineering for redesigning the diabetes diagnosis and treatment plan. The Ospedale Pediatrico Bambin Gesù (a private IRCCS) applied lean management to the transplant department. The AOU Riuniti di Trieste Independent Hospital (a public provider) implemented a kaizen costing project for the laboratory.

8.2.4 Discussion and Conclusions

Is health care rightly left to the private sector for the sake of efficiency? The cases presented in this chapter show how measuring and managing efficiency is not a peculiarity only of the private or of the public sector. Additionally, the analyzed cases both refer to service providers (hospitals) and regulators (Local Health Authorities). Thus, efficiency is not driven by the governance structure (public or private), but it is the result of the ability to manage input–output relationships within delivery processes. In this sense, at the moment, public organizations have a great opportunity: since in many countries they are both regulators and providers, they may have an end-to-end perspective of healthcare delivery processes. In fact, managing efficiency at individual department, service, support activity, or even provider (company) level often encourage the shifting of costs from one type of service or provider to another, or to the payor or consumer: gaining efficiency on a specific phase of the value chain does not necessarily imply increasing the efficiency of the healthcare system as a whole. This is the reason why the processual end-to-end perspective is so important to manage efficiency.

The difficulty often experienced in health care in implementing efficiency measurement and management initiatives is not linked to ownership (public or private), but to characteristics embedded in all healthcare organizations (Lega 2009): the clash between professionals and administrators; coordination problems generated by internal borders among different specializations; innovation itself, since professional organizations tend to bureaucratise their functioning as professionals are keen to "capitalize" on their know-how; triangulation problems, deriving from leading professionals (especially physicians), that have strong ties with external networks (political bodies, scientific societies, etc.) that can be activated to impose their will over the hospital management. Thus, not only it is important to generate innovation in processes, but it is also critical to adopt a processual approach in innovation management in order to manage all the above-mentioned tensions.

8.3 Public Versus Private Financing

Michael Drummond and Rosanna Tarricone

8.3.1 Introduction

The debate about public versus private health care has two components: the choice of public or private financing and the choice of public versus private provision. In this paper we address the financing question. Torbica and Ciani (2016) address the issue of public versus private provision. In his discussion on this myth, Henry Mintzberg (2012) rightly states that, for many individuals, the choice between a public or private sector healthcare system is driven by a desire to have equity in access to health care. The equity arguments are discussed later in the chapter dealing with Myth #6 below, but it should be acknowledged that the desire for equity of access is not universal and depends on the culture and values in the country concerned (Torbica et al. 2016). Therefore, it is important to address the efficiency arguments, since if publicly financed healthcare systems were more equitable but less efficient, we would still have to consider the trade-offs between these two laudable, but different, objectives.

8.3.2 Pros and Cons of Private Financing

The main argument for private funding stems from the notion that a perfectly functioning market should lead to both technical and allocative efficiency. However, two major characteristics of health care, uncertainty and asymmetry (of information), potentially leads to market imperfections (Folland and Rocco 2014). The existence of uncertainty (i.e. the consumer does not know if and when they are likely to become ill) means that some form of insurance is required. Insurance mechanisms are a sensible institutional response to the problem of uncertainty, but healthcare insurance markets often fail because of moral hazard. The term "moral hazard" refers to the change in the attitudes of consumers of health care, resulting from them becoming insured against the full costs of such care. Since the consumer faces no cost at the point of use, the levels of demand are greater than would be the case in a perfect market with fully informed consumers paying the full costs of their care.

The existence of asymmetry of information (i.e. consumers cannot easily assess the likely benefits of receiving health care) means that they need to rely on the provider (i.e. a health professional) to act as their agent. The consumer becomes reliant upon the doctor/supplier because (1) the search costs associated with the acquisition of information (e.g. a second medical opinion) may be very high and (2) also because the search costs are generally coupled with what can be called "anxiety costs" arising from the fact that the consumer is ill. The patient and the doctor are therefore in an "agency-relationship". However, the agency relationship in health care is quite different from the usual agency relationship, in which the two actors—the "principal" and the "agent"—seek to maximize their interdependent, but separate, objectives and utility functions. Conversely, in health care the doctor's ethical obligation is to act in the patient's interest. The doctor is expected to take the patient's place and to maximize his or her utility function. This suggests that the doctor has full knowledge about his patient's needs, utility function, tastes, preferences and so on. This is unlikely to be the case and it is therefore unlikely that a perfect agency relationship will exist. Since a perfect agency relationship is unlikely to exist, healthcare providers can manipulate patients' choices, to the extent that they might exploit consumers' willingness to pay for their own personal benefit. Although codes of ethics and compliance to internationally agreed clinical guidelines can effectively limit supplier inducement, it is not in doubt that the supplier of health care has the potential to exploit consumers' willingness to pay. This is sufficient to affect efficiency in the healthcare market, usually manifested through supplier-induced demand and escalating healthcare costs. Providers and hospitals may also face other incentives to provide more care, depending on the fee payment system, especially under fee-for-service.

Another potential source of inefficiency in private markets for health care is the existence of externalities. Externalities are spill-overs from people's production or consumption of commodities, which affect other individuals in either a negative or a positive way. The costs and benefits of such spill-overs cannot be accounted for in market transactions, because consumers and suppliers consider only costs and benefits to themselves. Health care creates external benefits. These benefits may arise from knowing that others can consume a public health intervention, such as vaccination, which has direct effects on risks to one's own health (selfish externality) or may arise from knowing that someone is receiving needed health care which does not necessarily affect one's own health status (a caring externality). As unregulated markets do not account for individuals' willingness to pay for external benefits, such markets will lead to underproduction of health care (Donaldson and Gerard 1993). The clearest manifestation of this is the failure to achieve herd immunity levels in some vaccination programmes if individuals only consider the costs and benefits to themselves and not the benefits that the protection that their vaccination confers to others.

8.3.3 Public Financing in Health care

So what are the main arguments for or against, the public financing of health care? The first argument is that, under public financing, it may be easier to prevent escalating costs. As mentioned above, since the consumers of health care often do not know the value of the services on offer, they have to rely on the providers of those services (i.e. their physicians) to make the choices for them. This leaves open the possibility of "over-selling" the benefits of health care, leading to a continual escalation of expenditure.

Of course, there are many actions that can be taken, within a privately financed healthcare system, to counteract these forces. Patients could be required to make co-payments at the time of receiving care, physicians and hospitals could be given appropriate incentives to provide care efficiently and utilization reviews could be conducted to ensure that appropriate care was delivered. However, it may still be more difficult to control the growth of expenditure than it is in a publicly financed system with a single paper, mainly because there are multiple sources of funding that need to be controlled. Reinhardt (2003) points out that, in comparing the Canadian and US healthcare systems, the existence of public financing (through national health insurance) in Canada has helped to reduce cost escalation, with no apparent reduction in the outcomes, in terms of improved health, produced.

The second argument is that the administrative costs associated with the private financing may be higher than those for public financing. It was mentioned above that many policies may be required to ensure that the private market functions efficiently. In addition, with private health insurance the costs of marketing, writing insurance contracts and processing claims are substantial. Comparisons of administrative costs show that these tend to be higher, as a percentage of total expenditure in privately financed systems. For example, Woolhandler et al. (2003) reported that, in looking at the insurance element, the Canadian single payer insurance system operated with overheads of 1.3%, comparing favourably with Canadian private insurance overheads of 13.2%, US private insurance overheads of 11.7% and US Medicare and Medicaid overheads of 3.6 and 6.8%, respectively. Of course, these types of comparisons are fraught with definitional judgments and the administrative costs of publicly financed systems are often regarded as a cause for concern. Nevertheless, it is likely that the administrative costs of operating a privately financed system are high. In addition, it is often cheaper to raise the funds for publicly financed systems, since raising funds through taxation is relatively inexpensive and the costs of borrowing are usually lower for governments than for private industry.

The third argument relates to the level of control over how the funds are allocated within the healthcare system. Even when the funding has been raised and the overall level of expenditure controlled, it is still important to ensure that those funds are allocated efficiently, since the signals provided by a perfectly functioning market are absent. In the last 30 years, one of the major forces to increase the efficiency of health care has been the increased use of health technology assessment. Here, the benefits and costs of treatment alternatives are compared in order to assess which treatment strategy will deliver the greatest value for money. Henry

Mintzberg (2012) was somewhat skeptical of the use of measurement and "evidence-based medicine" as a way of improving health care. However, while he is right that measurement should not be exclusively pursued at the expense of judgment, it is undeniable that assessment of the outcomes of healthcare treatments and programmes is critical, owing the information asymmetry mentioned above and the fact that many common practices in health care have not been adequately evaluated.

While in principle health technology assessment could be used in all healthcare systems, it has thrived to a much larger extent in publically financed healthcare systems, such as Australia, Canada, Sweden and the United Kingdom. The reasons for this are complex, but are in part related to the explicit nature of the budgetary constraint in publicly financed systems and the relative ease of concentrating resources to conduct studies to satisfy the needs of a single public payer. Health Technology Assessment is not totally absent in privately funded healthcare systems like the US, but as Sullivan et al. (2009) point out, it is "fragmented and uncoordinated, and includes both the public and private sector". They note that a number of US health technology programmes predate those in countries with well-known efforts such as Australia, Canada, Sweden and the UK, but that "regrettably, a number of these early efforts have been discontinued or have been substantially altered in large part because of political, financial and commercial pressures."

A key component of health technology assessment is the use of economic evaluation, where the costs of alternative healthcare treatments and programmes are compared with their costs. A major area for the application of economic evaluation has been in decisions on the pricing and reimbursement of pharmaceuticals. In reviewing worldwide experience with the use of economic evaluation over the last 20 years, Drummond (2013) argues that it has been effective in helping to target expensive therapies to the patients who would benefit most and in securing price reductions. In addition, in comparing the United Kingdom, a heavy user of HTA, with the US, Mason et al. (2010) note that cancer drugs licensed since 2004 were all reimbursed by payers in the US, often without restrictions, but that they received considerably more scrutiny in the UK.

In conclusion, there are few compelling reasons to believe that leaving the financing of health care to the private sector would automatically lead to greater efficiency. In fact there are some reasons to believe that the opposite might be true.

8.4 The Future of Complementary Health care

Maurizio de Cicco

8.4.1 The Context

Moving from the considerations related to the evolution of health management models—from the biomedical one (totally linear and impervious to the external environment) to the industrial-fordist one which introduces measurement parameters, such as the duration of visits, rigid division of operators' work and economic performance evaluations, this chapter aims to be a reflection about the myth #5, which emphasizes pros and cons of the growing involvement of the private sector in the organization and management of the health service.

When talking about health care in Italy, two important premises must be considered.

Firstly, the Italian health system has been ranked second best in the world by the World Health Organization, with only the French system ranked higher.

Secondly, the Italian National Healthcare Service (SSN) has deep roots. Created in 1978 to replace a previous system based on a multitude of insurance schemes, the NHS was inspired by the British National Health Service and has two underlying principles: every Italian citizen and foreign resident has the right to health care and the system covers all necessary services and treatments.

The starting point of any reflection is, therefore, that in Italy the management approach toward health is fundamentally paternalistic, providing the right for all, under article 32 of the Italian Constitution for universality, equality and equity. The best universalistic experiment developed worldwide.

Nevertheless, even if Italy is the European country with the lowest healthcare expenditure, we have been unfortunately experiencing a growing unsustainability of the public system to guarantee adequate levels of assistance, services and accessible innovation. Unacceptable discrepancies have emerged over time between the Northern and Southern Regions.

Moreover, the declining conditions of public finances have emphasized the need for further spending restraint policies and new rules have been defined to control Regional Governments: not only they are now required to break-even but they are also subjected to sanctions in case of failure, ranging from a general loss of autonomy, to a financial recovery plan or repayment plan supervised by the Central Government.

While searching for pragmatic solutions to save the universalistic concept of health care, the Italian situation has been rapidly worsening—as demonstrated by the latest Research lead by Fondazione Censis and RBM Salute ("Building the complementary health care")—with immediate and direct effects on the population, who has to face endless waiting lists, even for services of primary importance.

Italian citizens are now finding themselves at a crossroad; those who can afford private healthcare insurance, deciding to pay for what the NHS should guarantee, and those who cannot afford it, having to deal with the System's inefficiencies, giving up prevention exams, tests, check-ups and therapies.

Today health care is mainly funded by public funds. In 2014, 77% of expenditure was covered by the NHS, whilst the remaining 23% was paid by citizens (a considerable share and on the increase in recent years.).

In 2015, about 11 million Italians had to give up health benefits. Private health expenditure has grown to 34.5 billion euro (+3.2% over the past two years): double the increase in overall spending on household consumption in the same period

(+1.7%). A sum that, divided by every citizen, amounts to 570 euro per year, or 2000 euro per household.

This result becomes even more significant if we consider the deflationary dynamic, relevant in the case of some health products and services.

10 million Italians resort more to the private sector and 7 million to Intramoenia because they cannot wait. It is not by chance that one citizen out of two—26 million—affirms he is likely to accede to integrative health solutions.

More than half of the population believes that those who can afford a health insurance policy or who work in a company where integrative health care is available should take out a policy and stick to it. On one side, this would bring public benefits because many people would use private facilities therefore freeing up space in the public sector, and on the other side this would introduce more resources in the health system.

The need for concrete and sustainable solutions will surely increase. In June 2016 the Lancet published a study of the Institute for Health Metrics and Evaluation, funded by the Bill & Melinda Gates Foundation. The researchers carried out the forecasts for 184 countries. The global healthcare spending, both public and private, will increase from 7.83 trillion dollars in 2013 to 18.28 trillion dollars in 2040. During this period, health spending per capita will increase by 2.7% per year in high-income countries, by 3.4% per year for those with upper middle income, by 3% for those with low and middle-incomes and finally 2.4% in low-income countries.

In Italy an annual growth rate of 2.6% is estimated which would lead in 2040 to a total (public and private) health spending per capita of $5968 (with a range between $5013 and $6804), compared to $3077 in 2013 with almost 80% covered by public health spending and the rest as private spending.

The conclusions of the study do not sound positive for many countries, including Italy. Despite the many advances made in the field of health, the low and middle-income countries will not be able to effectively meet health expenditure objectives at a global level by 2040. Even the health expenditure gap between the poorest and the richest countries will not significantly shrink in the coming years unless action is taken today, with important policy interventions and concerted actions.

Italy is currently ranked fourth among the G7 countries with a share of private spending higher than Japan, the UK and France, not much less than Germany and Canada and well below the United States, where private health expenditure is always more than 50% of the total expenditure and health insurance represents a substantial proportion of this share.

What differentiates Italy from other countries is the high incidence of out-of-pocket spending rather than the overall private spending, with consequences less and less equitable from the viewpoint of distribution and with some concerns for the future stability of the overall health system.

Our National Health Service recognizes the opportunity for citizens to supplement the benefits provided by the public service by resorting to private insurances or forms of voluntary mutual aid. The health funds are included in supplementary mutuality and thus in the non-profit sector being directed to provide additional benefits to those provided by the NHS according to a logic based on the principle of solidarity between occupational categories and groups of citizens. The regulatory framework distinguishes between the matching funds into two categories: so-called funds "Doc" and "non Doc." The former are traditionally defined matching funds of the National Health Service, while the latter are corporations, welfares and mutual aid societies which have exclusively charitable purposes. These not only integrate the performance of the NHS, but also offer support measures related to performance which fall within the essential levels of care guaranteed by the NHS. Along with these types of funds there are private insurances.

8.4.2 Present and Future Role of Complementary Health care

Currently integrative health plays a marginal role, the prerogative of a "few privileged people", even if someone believes today it is considered a way to obtain additional benefits (avoiding queues, shortening time, improving the hospital stay, etc.) and not really used in case of particularly complex situations, where the NHS remains the first choice.

In the last couple of years private expenditure has increased by 6.5% and since 2010 beneficiaries have nearly doubled, amounting to 88%.

Nevertheless, the percentage of private health expenditure negotiated by insurance fell from 14 to 13% of the total, although more and more Italians think they can one day join some form of supplementary assistance.

Moreover if we consider supplemental health insurance policy costs, on average, about 70% of what each citizen spends on visits and examinations in a year, the opportunity coming from this form of funding becomes more evident, also because big funds can provide much more affordable prices than those a single person or patient could ever obtain.

According to politicians, policy makers and technicians, private health care should be extended to the entire population as far as possible, with a general objective of safeguarding public health.

Some technical commission representatives believe the role of collective policies could be a good opportunity for risk-pooling, thus enabling those people with a higher risk to obtain insurance coverage.

Certainly, opportunities from integrative health care have not yet been fully grasped and it could become a synergic element of the System. Like collective health funds, to which from the past subscriptions have been encouraged and in a near future they could substitute lots of services of the NHS, promoting a better efficiency and a deeper transparency for future development.

According to Censis—RBM Salute research, massive adherence to these systems would free up about 15 billion euro of additional resources in health care.

The perspective changes if we consider the position of Citizens Associations, such as Active Citizenship. They worryingly underline how Italians pay twice for a service: they pay for health care through public taxes on the one hand and pay for healthcare insurance on the other. While arguing, however, that innovation is not insurable and that no health insurance can offer the patient the opportunity to be treated with innovative drugs, the Association proposes forms of experimentation where the supplementary health can raise the standards of NHS structures, thus engaging a positive circle with better services for everyone, both for those who use private health care and for those who remain exclusively within the scope of public health.

What is lacking in the Italian scenario is a centralized political choice on the role that the private health sector should have in the overall system. Alongside the undeniable défaillances of the public mechanism, it appears to be in fact a fragmented and largely unregulated sector.

Just consider that Italy is the only Organization for Economic Cooperation and Development (OECD) country in which there coexists an integrative health service (providing, for example, dentistry or social assistance services), a complementary health service (for example in case of complex radiological examinations difficult to access) and a replacement or substitute health service (which mainly covers hospitalizations and operations/interventions).

The image represents a peculiarity which is completely local, that comes up again when you look at those who buy insurance policies; ranging from Public Administration/Government categories, to social security institutions of professionals, from individual companies to national categories contracts, passing for funds subscribed on a territorial basis in some regions and individual citizens.

From this picture the need to proceed to a rationalization of the landscape is evident. In order to gain improved efficiency in a sector, like the private one for health services, Institutions cannot continue pretending it does not exist.

How can this be achieved? Censis—RBM Salute research suggests Italy should take into consideration a new system of deductions and detractions that today penalize the policies individually subscribed, and which aims to reward the ability to mediate the expense of citizens. In many cases in particular, health insurance policies are not considered as a luxurious asset, but as a need.

The current social security model needs to be urgently reformed to take on more flexible dynamics, in order to better adapt to the evolving needs. We can aspire to integrate the first and foremost public pillar with the private and complementary one, through the synergy among different dimensions and mechanisms (company and community category funds).

8.4.3 Insurance Scheme for Innovative Drugs

And what about drugs?

In the last 10–20 years the health revolution has started. Firstly, a new approach in Government policies and in people's mindset: moving beyond the notion of merely treating disease towards prevention and wellness, with several pioneering programmes leading the way. Secondly, pharmaceutical companies have altered their Research and Development focus from primary care—where the medical need has been reduced and the most common diseases can be adequately treated with established and mostly generic treatments (i.e. cardiovascular, pain, GI, anti-inflammatory/infections, etc.)—to speciality care, where there is the highest medical need, in disease areas with currently no or inadequate treatment options. New treatment options (i.e. for certain cancers, HCV, hospital infections) offer significant additional clinical and economical value, compared with the standard of care, or offer, often for the first time, treatment options for orphan/rare diseases (i.e. IPF) which result in higher costs per treatment/patient. The more therapeutic solutions become available, the more budget pressure will increase with access issues for all eligible patients.

At the same time these are the areas where it has become increasingly difficult for Pharma to demonstrate incremental value and cost-effectiveness versus new options brought by effective generics and achieving adequate pricing rewarding the investments made in R&D.

One thing is clear: a healthy storm of innovative drugs is here to come, and it will require to be driven, guided and controlled.

If on one side, Italian political and technical healthcare institutions have been putting in place really praiseworthy efforts, such as the creation of a dedicated fund for innovative drugs or the reconsideration of pricing mechanisms, on the other side we should admit they certainly move in the right direction, but this will not be enough in the medium term.

Our National Health Service alone can no longer cope with the new health needs of citizens, with the care needs of people that have changed considerably since the end of the 70s when the NHS started to rule health care in Italy.

Beside the demographic development with ageing societies in the whole of Europe—the need for, or the consumption of, medical care and treatment (in particular for specialty care products such as in oncology, in CNS or in immunology) is strictly correlated with the ageing phenomenon and strongly contributes to budget constraints. Immigration into the EU has significantly increased and considering how many immigrants cannot immediately find employment and are therefore not contributing to financing health care, this has further strained existing healthcare budgets.

The result of this mix of factors—increasing costs (due to the increasing number of patients) for primary, secondary care and rehab—leads to growing budget pressure and in parallel reduces saving potential in these healthcare areas.

Consequently payers, that have to secure the financial sustainability of the health system without undermining the values shared by the universal coverage, solidarity in financing, equity of access and the provision of high-quality health care, are looking for increasing resources progressively driven by cost-minimization rather than value based decisions. As a direct result they keep on drawing from the pharma sector.

On the contrary, today we need to fund research, prevention, new drugs and face the challenge of longevity.

There is no one to blame but, if the NHS, like that of the rest of the major OECD countries, is definitely shaky and at risk of sustainability, we do need to take stock of things and act to identify the necessary countermeasures. We need to firmly focus on a health system reform in our country, with the contribution of all the healthcare stakeholders, including insurance companies, supplementary health funds but also pharmaceutical companies, to identify additional sources of financing to enable citizens to maintain adequate levels of assistance.

Some argue that it might be useful to start this process at national level for the definition of healthcare priorities with the active participation of citizens. The process has been running for over 20 years in many European countries such as Sweden and Norway, where there are still national health services that certainly have not been "dismantled". The answer to the growing needs of the population on the basis of ethical criteria of solidarity could therefore make it possible to identify priority classes, by which to allocate the available financial resources. The lowest priority classes may be included in the supplementary forms of assistance in a perspective of cooperation and "take care" of the patient in shared assistance pathways.

Our country is called upon to make choices.

We are certainly proud to have a model that is universalistic but with all its differences of which we are perfectly aware. At least 50% of the out-of-pocket expenditure is due to the fact that the universalistic health often does not work.

Considering the actual situation and the future scenario, one of the points under discussion is related to the possible benefit coming from a specific treatment and on the role a pharmaceutical company could play in the identification of new paths.

From my perspective, if on one side pharmaceuticals should take part in this evolution, on the other side insurance companies should identify and present a business model which can be applied to drugs, and in particular to innovative treatments.

What is to come, are really revolutionary medicines, able to treat or control not only diseases with a high social effect, like Alzheimer Disease or Parkinson, but also many types of tumours which can now be considered chronic.

For all these reasons it is crucial to find a new model to sustain our Healthcare System, and certainly the solution is not to increase the healthcare fund defined year per year.

"The" decision maker—which is the institutional role that is predominantly called to manage this matter—has to take the opportunity coming from this historical moment, when different players are debating about possible solutions, analyzing models and benchmarking other countries' systems, finally admitting it is no longer possible for the actual universalism to go on.

Taking stock of all above positions and considerations, I would like to offer some final food for thought. A few years ago we started talking about "health consumptions", that is to say we started measuring health care through the parameters of service consumption. Eventually, this new trend led to the creation of "local healthcare companies" (ASL).

What has been going on in the last 20–30 years—perhaps without even really realizing it—is the transformation of health, which has become more and more subordinate to market imperatives and economic criteria. Thus, citizens have become customers, rights have become needs, and welfare has become a social market.

If on one side, avoiding waste and rationalizing expenditure must be the starting point, on the other side it should be done without reducing it, but making it more efficient. This growing corporatization of health (and social), sacrifices quality, the human dimension and the efficiency and performance of care in the end. But health is not a commodity.

In conclusion, if we take a final look at the starting point of this dissertation —"health care is rightly left to the private sector for the sake of efficiency"— probably the only way out of this whirlpool is to choose a mixed system, admitting that a co-participation of citizens is needed, guaranteeing the most vulnerable, while asking those who can economically afford to pay for health services to contribute. This option could bring a double benefit: firstly it gives access to free health resources (making more funds available for the growing lower and middle class) and secondly it could contribute to the recovery of that humanity of Health that in recent years has been put on the back burner to the detriment of the quality of care, in a holistic sense.

As often happens in life not everything is either black or white: the countless shades in the middle may represent viable solutions.

8.5 The Challenge of Public–Private Partnerships in Health care

Salvatore Russo and Luca Del Bene

8.5.1 Introduction

As many experiences across the world demonstrate, Public–Private Partnerships (PPPs) in health care have been considered for a long time a pursuable way for building and renovating hospitals (Froud 2003; Broadbent et al. 2003; Grimsey and Lewis 2004).

In the light of the current literature debate, in this paper we analyze the main features of PPPs, keeping into account outcome, policy and practice according to the latest perspectives of analysis tending to observe approaches to this subject (Roehrich et al. 2014).

The enduring dilemma concerns whether the confidence in PPPs is still acceptable, according to an optimistic bias and what precautions should be taken so that the PPP model can be virtuous enough to create effective advantages and social benefits. The PPPs provide a kind of complementarity and integration of the private myth, all over the world even if in the first phase of their application in health care, in the case of the construction of hospitals and subsequent management by private operators, have shown some criticalities. PPPs may therefore be some kind of mediation of Henry Mintzberg's myth (2012) between efficiency (private sector) and equity (public sector).

The achievement of value for money, the testing of a long-term affordability and the risk transfer continue to be the cause of the serious apprehensions that have so far accompanied PPP contracts (Broadbent et al. 2008; Demirag and Khadaroo 2008; English et al. 2010).

Nevertheless, as observed in the experiences carried out in other countries (essentially Australia and UK), the frequently-asked question is whether such investment strategies are the result of an opportunistic approach rather than of a rational choice. This has unavoidably pushed academics and scholars to explore "the underlying nature and rationale for PPPs; processes and procedures aiding decisions to undertake PPPs; processes and procedures for ex-post evaluations of PPPs; the merit and worth of PPPs; PPPs regulation and guidance" (Andon 2012, p. 878).

8.5.2 A PPP for Any Season

The long wave of PPPs is rooted in the changing context of the New Public Management (NPM). Consequent reforms, through a redefinition of the boundaries between State and market, have encouraged the acceptance of a contractual approach to public service delivery (Hood 1991; Lane 2000; Osborne 2000). Despite the different labels by which public agencies decide to provide a public service with a private business support, the political meaning is the same. PPPs have been coherently considered an "extension" of the NPM agenda for change (Broadbent and Laughlin 2003) and their introduction "has largely been evaluated through conceptual lenses that emphasize either the administrative, managerial, financial or technical dimensions of this reform strategy" (Flinders 2005, p. 215).

Originally, the Private Finance Initiative (PFI) was launched in the UK in 1992 as part of the Conservative government's initiative to increase the level of private sector involvement in the delivery of public services and tap the funding capacity of private financial institutions, and followed a series of popular privatizations of publicly owned utilities. This policy was introduced to increase the involvement of the private sector in the provision of public services (Spackman 2002; Pollock et al. 2001; Broadbent and Laughlin 2003). In 1997, with the advent of the Labour Party, the same formula was proposed under the label of PPP and was still used more than before. The objective was "to accelerate the process by which PPP contracts are agreed, in part by taking equity stakes in projects and in part by providing loans to public bodies" (Parker and Hartley 2003). In the UK in fact the PPPs have been abundantly used, despite all the criticism and obvious weaknesses. The echo of the PPPs had a diffusion in other countries across Europe, including Italy and after a first phase of experimentation, in 2004, the European Commission issued the Green Paper on PPPs and Community Law on Public Contracts and Concessions to launch "a debate on the application of Community law on public contracts and concessions to the PPP phenomenon". More recently, many countries have started a review of the procedures, keeping in consideration limits and criticalities emerged in the previous experiences. For instance UK has been promoting a series of reforms and adjustments in the transition from PF1 (the old PPP model) to PF2 (the new PPP model) with the most radical changes relating to the provision of equity finance (Buisson 2013).

8.5.3 Less Idealization, More Concretism

Among the advantages of a PPP, the opportunity of mixing public and private skills is one of the most relevant, being a contract where partners, public and private, act for distinctive purposes but for mutual benefit. So, they have to find a composition in organizational and managerial terms.

A PPP is usually a long-term contract between a public party and a consortium of private companies—referred to as a Special Purpose Vehicle (SPV)—under which the private company is required to Design, Build, Finance and Operate (DBFO) an infrastructure in return for payment for both the cost of construction and operation of the related services (Grimsey and Lewis 2004; Yescombe 2007). The facility remains under public-sector ownership, or reverts from private partner to public-sector ownership at the end of the PPP contract. Its economic relevance depends on the fact that:

- cash flows generated by the operating process are the main guarantee and the source for covering the debt service;
- implementation of the private initiative should be accompanied by an adequate level of project certainty and reliability deriving from a rigorous analysis and an indispensable risk adjustment;
- sustainability of the initiative does not depend on the reliability of a company but concerns the quality of the single project (including the capacity to generate the cash flows with reference to a given level of risk);
- the initiative takes advantage of a project autonomy—due to the constitution of an ad hoc company to safeguard the stakeholders' interests;

- the operational phase represents the critical success factor as only a management based on a high level of performance can contribute to generate the cash flows that are indispensable to satisfy shareholder expectations;
- the most significant guarantees connected with the initiative have a contractual nature rather than a real one (this is the so-called "without recourse operation");
- all the phases of the operation converge in a negotiation process, which has a variable duration and is considered to be a decisive factor in the risk allocation between public and private partners.

This partnership procedure cannot be explained just by the concession of both the construction and the management of an infrastructure to a private partner because of the lack of financial resources, but it must be based on an effective assessment of both value for money, through the appraisal of the public sector comparator and risk transfer (Gaffney and Pollock 1999; Edwards and Shaoul 2003).

A reflection on PPP leads us to consider some sort of hybrid problem. The public entity remains the owner of the function. The private body intervenes in order to financially support and to provide support to the production process. PPP is a broad term that can be applied to anything from a simple, short term management contract (with or without investment requirements) to a long-term contract including funding, planning, building, operation, maintenance and divestiture. PPP arrangements are useful for large projects that require highly-skilled workers and a significant cash outlay to get started.

The public sector should benefit from the presence of the private party, above all in terms of reduction of the total financial commitment, investment promptness and, consequently, the timeline of service use. This implies that the convenience of the operation must be analyzed under two different profiles. On the one hand, it would be advisable to verify the advantage for the Public Administration by taking into account value for money and, on the other hand, risk transfer. Value for money is the key rationalizing motive for partnership. As Edward and Shaoul (2003) assert, "its meaning in the context of PFI is no more precise and is similarly based upon the economy as reflected in the use of discounted cash flows over the lifetime of the project". Valuc for money depends on the "estimate of future costs and operates only at the point of procurement". Many studies and reports have been carried out in the UK on this topic given that accountability depends on the detailed recognition of value for money, by discharging accountability to the stakeholders, the lack of which in PPP has been persistently criticized (Demirag et al. 2005; Demirag and Khadaroo 2008). Risk transfer and uncertainty seem to be the crucial elements under discussion since under PFI private sector borrowing, transaction costs and the requirements for profits necessarily generate higher costs than conventional public procurement (Broadbent et al. 2008).

8.5.4 Rise and Fall of PPPs for Hospitals in Italy

Italy is a country where healthcare services are largely public. In the last decade some actions have been undertaken with the purpose of making rules more flexible in the context of public procurement and facilitating private participation in the realization of public infrastructures (most frequently by the DBFO formula). In particular, at the local level, where the requirements for investment increased because of the partial introduction of the fiscal federalism rules, PPP has shown itself as an innovative instrument. According to data collected by Finlombarda (2012), in 2011 there was a decline in PPP use, although the government has repeatedly encouraged the use of the procedure. However, several obstacles seem to stand between the launch of initiatives and financial close, mainly due to the shortage of liquidity together with lengthy procedures and unpredictable times. The awards amounted to approximately EUR 6.6 billion a year, but in the last four years, the financial close has stopped at EUR 1.8 billion.

The normative point of reference is the model of the "concession" with or without private initiative. The PPP is, in fact, regulated by law as in other countries (Belgium, Poland, Spain, Portugal) even if it is widely known that a specific PPP law is not a necessary condition for PPP development. The legal framework can also be provided by changing existing legal provisions which may have an impact on the PPP project (EPEC 2011). Even if an explicit program has not been launched, the Italian Government created a centralized office, the Technical Unit for Project Financing (in Italian: Unità Tecnica Finanza di Progetto, UTFP) to facilitate privately financed infrastructures. This organization as a taskforce of the Ministry of Economy and Finance has the aim of promoting the use of PPPs, also supporting the public administration at the regional and local level, for its implementation. After the uncertain debut of the implementation procedures and an unclear meaning attributed to the PPP, the UTFP (2002) outlined a stable framework tending to identify PPPs in three main subcategories: (1) the granting of construction and operation; (2) the granting of services; (3) other residual formulas.

The typical features of PPP concur therefore to make some observation about its advantageous application in the Italian National Healthcare Service, by considering an increasingly higher need for buildings and hospital modernization (Amatucci and Vecchi 2009). By taking into account the continuous technology evolution and the strategies implemented for a rationalization of the health expenditure, hospital sector has appeared particularly interested in a PPP utilization. Health policy and guidelines have aimed to reorganize the hospitals. So they are no longer considered the only source of healthcare services delivery, and currently new typologies influenced by the technological progress seem to succeed in a renewed vision of the primary care, in a position to absorb a considerable quota of services that traditionally were of hospital care type.

The main factors behind the need for modernization are attributable to the following:

- the gradual increase in the average age of the population (involving an increase in per capita expenditure);
- innovation and advanced technologies;
- the scientific and cultural progress of the population catalyzing the demand for services in health care in terms of quality and quantity.

In addition, there has been a gradual reduction in the number of ordinary admissions (acute patients) and a greater development of day hospital and day surgery care.

Moreover, a certain importance is given to the long-stay structures, where health care needs are to be considered together with the request for comfort of the accommodation and the quality of the service.

Between 2002 and 2005 there was a 30.6% rise in the number of projects (27) and a 56.7% increase in spending (EUR 1298 million). In value terms, 93% of the initiatives promoted involved the building or refurbishment of healthcare facilities, with nonmedical support services (non-core) entrusted to the concessionaire. This proportion has remained unvaried over time (Finlombarda 2005, 2012). The use of PPPs can therefore be defined as swinging for several difficulties in implementation. The main obstacles are derived from the complexity of the procedure and a not always convenient financial solution. According to the experience observed in the first enthusiastic wave (2000–2006) of PPPs, the method focused on a cost-benefit evaluation for both the public health care institutions and users/patients, although this appraisal has led to large uncertainties.

In this kind of PPPs, the private partner (frequently financing not more than half of the total amount) typically takes on the responsibility for the management of the services mix regarding the functioning and maintenance of the structure and part of the core and non-core services. In particular, the system of services includes the following categories:

- the facility management for buildings and supporting systems such as the thermic heating system, refrigerator system, air conditioning, electrical equipment and plumbing, medical gas supply systems;
- hotel services (catering for in-patients and staff, cleaning, disposal of waste material, reception, reservation centre, parking);
- other services (stock management, hospital information systems, supply management, chemist, set-up of operating theatres, etc.).

Another criticality derives from the composition of an annual fee and a tariff. The annual fee is paid by the healthcare institution when a new hospital starts running (from the service availability date). This consists of two components, fixed and/or variable, and has to cover the services management, the facility management and the assistance to the medical structure. The private partner is thus allowed to have a return on investment. The fee is determined and paid according to different criteria. The tariff relates to the operating costs of both commercial spaces and services. The payment consists of revenues deriving from the lease or direct management of the adjacent commercial areas.

Such a payment concerns the volume and typology of activities regarding the structure itself and is a function of the management system defined and/or contracted, from time to time, between the SPV and the healthcare institution. For this revenue, the commercial risk is borne by the SPV. It is, however, clear that the main risk concerns demand. This means that any compensation arising from the operations of additional services partially affects the risk simulations contained in the business plan. These two heterogeneous components justified the potential application of the PPP in the specific case of the hospitals making it possible even in the presence of a public payment (subsidies). Hospitals appeared initially as belonging to a not-self-financing category because of the lack of correspondence between utilization and payment of tariffs by users reimbursed by the healthcare institution on behalf of the patients (Amatucci 2002).

Through hospital activity development and a clear identification of its components, it has been possible to postulate the application of PPP for hospital construction. On one hand, the fee is like a shadow toll, paid by the healthcare institution for supporting services; on the other hand there are the prices paid by users for commercial services. This mechanism does not rule out placing the instrument of the public contribution side by side with the two mentioned above (Amatucci and Biondi 2002). In fact, the application of shadow tolls is commonly considered inappropriate because it implies such a low risk transfer as to put the project back on the public sector balance sheet (Yescombe 2007, p. 235).

Last but not least, the structure of the fee. It consists of a fixed part corresponding to the equivalent amount in order to cover building availability; and a variable part, representing the equivalent sum in order to reimburse the services delivered by the SPV, according to volume and quality parameters (payment for usage, volume or demand). The fixed part is now under revision in many PPP contracts because of its excessive way of protecting the private partner from demand risk.

8.5.5 Conclusions

This contribution is to highlight the specificities of the PPPs in their connection to Henry Mintzberg's myth about the role of private organizations in health care. PPPs are alternative/integrative to the common belief that "private is more efficient than public".

PPPs are the hybrid expression of this myth, and they have yet to meet a better convenience in this second "generation". In the case of PPPs, the myth that "private is better than public" is hindered by the inability to overcome organizational issues concerning the same contract of partnership. Private operators take advantages in providing a public service without market risks, and on the other hand, do not give up extra-profits, by imposing excessively high fees.

Insufficient public–private collaboration, excessive gains by equity providers, lack of transparency and accountability, and inefficient risk transfer make PPPs unsustainable (these criticalities have been emerging in the UK too). Therefore, at this stage, only revisionism may guarantee the continuity in use. PPPs in health care are under review about the role of both public and private, and especially the way in which public hospitals pay no core services provided by private partners. The lesson learned is that the myth of the superiority of private operators regarding efficiency and quality may resist and recommend PPPs as an institutional formula where equal roles and tasks still meet the value for money.

References

Amatucci F (2002) Il Project Finance nelle Aziende Pubbliche. Egea, Milano

Amatucci F, Biondi Y (2002) Project Finance nel Settore Sanitario Italiano: Esperienze e Modalità di Applicazione. In: Anessi Pessina E, Cantù E (eds) L'aziendalizzazione della Sanità in Italia, Rapporto OASI 2001. Egea, Milano, pp 371–391

Amatucci F, Vecchi V (eds) (2009) Le Operazioni di Project Finance: stato dell'arte e indicazioni per il futuro. Egea, Milano

Andon P (2012) Accounting-related research in PPPs/PFIs: present contributions and future opportunities. Account Auditing Accountability J 25(5):876–924

Ball R, Heafey M, King D (2000) Private finance initiative—a good deal for the public purse or a drain on future generations? Policy Politics 29(1):95–108

Barbetta GP, Turati G, Zago AM (2007) Behavioral differences between public and private not-for-profit hospitals in the Italian National Health Service. Health Econ 16(1):75–96. doi:10.1002/hec.1143

Broadbent J, Laughlin R (2003) Public private partnerships: an introduction. Account Auditing Accountability J 16(3):332–341

Broadbent J, Gill J, Laughlin R (2003) Evaluating the private finance initiative in the National Health Service in the UK. Account Auditing Accountability J 16(3):422–445

Broadbent J, Gill J, Laughlin R (2008) Identifying and controlling risk: the problem of uncertainty in the private finance initiative in the UK's National Health Service. Critical Perspect Accounting 19:40–78

Buisson A (2013) From PF1 to PF2: the reform of the public private partnership, Norton Rose Fulbright LLP model in the UK, www.nortonrosefulbright.com

Burger P, Tyson J, Karpowicz I, Coelho M (2009) The effects of the financial crisis on public-private partnerships. International Monetary Fund, WP/ 09/144, http://papers.ssrn.com/sol3/papers.cfm?abstract_id=1442246. Accessed 15 Jan 2013

Burgess JF, Wilson PW (1996) Hospital ownership and technical inefficiency. Manage Sci 42 (1):110–123. doi:10.1287/mnsc.42.1.110

Chivaka R (2007) Strategic cost management: context and philosophy—part 1, Accountancy SA, June

Cori R, Giorgiantoni C, Paradisi I (2010) Risk allocation and incentives for private contractors: an analysis of Italian project financing contracts. Bank of Italy Occasional Paper, http://papers.ssrn.com/sol3/papers.cfm?abstract_id=1825983. Accessed 20 Feb 2013

Czypionka T, Kraus M, Mayer S, Röhrling G (2014) Efficiency, ownership, and financing of hospitals: the case of Austria. Health Care Manag Sci 17(4):331–347. doi:10.1007/s10729-013-9256-9

Dallocchio M, Lecci F, Morelli M (2016) L'Istituto Europeo di Oncologia: evidenze empiriche. In: Dallocchio M et al (eds) Valore e misurazione delle performance. EGEA, Milano, pp 111–153

Demirag I, Khadaroo I (2008) Accountability and value for money in private finance initiative contracts. Financ Accountability Manage 24(4):455–478

Demirag I, Khadaroo I (2011) Accountability and value for money: a theoretical framework for the relationship in public–private partnerships. J Manage Gov 15(2):271–296

Demirag I, Dubnick M, Khadaroo I (2005) A framework for examining accountability and value for money (VFM) in the UK's private finance initiative (PFI). In: Demirag I (ed) Corporate social responsibility, accountability and governance: global perspectives. Greenleaf Publishing, Sheffield

Demirag I, Khadaroo I, Stapleton P, Stevenson C (2011) Risks and the financing of PPP: perspectives from the financiers. Br Accounting Rev 43(4):294–310

Donaldson C, Gerard K (1993) Market failure in health care. In: Donaldson C, Gerard K (eds) Economics of health care financing: the visible hand. MacMillan, Basingstoke

Drummond MF (2013) Twenty years of using economic evaluations for drug reimbursement decisions. What has been achieved? J Health Polit Policy Law 38(6):1081–1102

Dunnigan M, Pollock A (2003) Downsizing of acute inpatient beds associated with private finance initiative: Scotland's case study. Br Med J 326(7395):905

Economic Commission for Europe (ECE) (2002) A review of public-private partnerships for infrastructure development in Europe. Working party on international legal and commercial practice fiftieth session 11–13 March 2002

Edwards P, Shaoul J (2003) Partnerships: for better, for worse? Account Auditing Accountability J 16(3):397–421

Eggleston K, Shen YC, Lau J, Schmid CH, Chan J (2008) Hospital ownership and quality of care: what explains the different results in the literature? Health Econ 17(12):1345–1362. doi:10.1002/hec.1333

English L, Guthrie J (2003) Driving privately financed projects in Australia: what makes them tick? Account Auditing Accountability J 16(3):493–511

English L, Skellern M (2005) Public–private partnerships and public sector management reform: a comparative perspective. Int J Public Policy 1(1):1–21

English L, Guthrie J, Broadbent J, Laughlin R (2010) Performance audit of the operational stage of long-term partnerships for the private sector provision of public services. Australian Accounting Rev 20(1):64–75

European PPP Expertise Centre (EPEC) (2011) The guide to guidance how to prepare, procure and deliver PPP projects, www.eib.org/epec/g2g/index.htm. Accessed 20 June 2012

Finlombarda (2005) Finlombarda survey of project finance in healthcare sector. IV Report http://www.finlombarda.it/. Accessed 20 June 2012

Finlombarda (2012) Finlombarda survey of project finance in health care sector. X Report. Maggioli, Rimini

Flinders M (2005) The politics of public-private partnerships. Br J Polit Int Relat 7(2):215–239

Folland S, Rocco L (2014) The economics of social capital and health a conceptual and empirical roadmap. World Scientific, Washington, DC

Francesconi A, Lecci F (2014) Innovazioni nei sistemi di controllo e governo dei costi: le risposte delle aziende sanitarie alla crisi economica. In: CERGAS Bocconi (eds) L'aziendalizzazione della sanità in Italia. Rapporto OASI 2014, EGEA, Milan, pp 555–580

Froud J (2003) The private finance initiative: risk, uncertainty and the state. Acc Organ Soc 28 (6):567–589

Gaffney D, Pollock AM (1999) Pump priming the PFI: why are privately financed hospital schemes being subsidised? Public Money Manage 17(3):11–16

Gaffney D, Pollock A, Price D, Shaoul J (1999) NHS capital expenditure and the private finance initiative—expansion or contraction? Br Med J 319:48–51

Greve C, Graeme H (eds) (2013) Rethinking public-private partnerships. Routledge, London

Grimsey D, Lewis MK (2004) Public private partnerships. The worldwide revolution in infrastructure provision and project finance. Edward Elgar, Cheltenham, UK

Grimshaw D, Vincent S, Willmott H (2002) Going privately: partnership and outsourcing in UK public services. Public Adm 80(3):475–502

Hellowell M, Vecchi V (2012) An evaluation of the projected returns to investors on 10 PFI projects commissioned by the National Health Service. Financ Accountability Manage 28 (1):77–100

Herr A, Schmitz H, Augurzky B (2011) Profit efficiency and ownership of German hospitals. Health Econ 20(6):660–674. doi:10.1002/hec.1622

Hood C (1991) A public management for all seasons? Public Adm 69:3–19

Jackson A, Lapsley I (2003) The diffusion of accounting practices in the new "managerial" public sector. Int J Public Sector Manag 16(5):359–372

Kakabadse NK, Kakabadse AP, Summers N (2007) Effectiveness of private finance initiatives (PFI): study of private financing for the provision of capital assets for schools. Public Adm Dev 27(1):49–61

Kaplan R, Porter M (2011) How to solve the cost crisis in health care. Harvard Business Rev 89 (9):6–52, 54, 56–61 passim

Khadaroo I (2008) The actual evaluation of school PFI bids for value for money in the UK public sector. Criti Perspect Account 19(8):1321–1345

Kouzmin A, Leivesley R, Kakabadse N (1997) From managerialism and economic rationalism: towards reinventing economic ideology and administrative diversity. Admin Theory Praxis 19 (1):19–43

Lane JE (2000) New public management. Routledge, London

Lecci F, Longo F (2015) Humanitas research hospital. In: Minoja M (ed) Bene comune e comportamenti responsabili. EGEA, Milano, pp 175–195

Lega F (2009) Strategic, organisational and managerial issues related to innovation, entrepreneurship and intrapreneurship in the hospital context: remarks from the Italian experience. J Manage Mark Healthc 2(1):77–93

Lord BR (1996) Strategic management accounting: the emperor's new clothes? Manage Account Res 7(3):347–366

MacDonald M (2002) Review of large public procurement in the UK. www.hmtreasury.gov.uk/mediastore/otherfiles/greenbook_mott.pdf. Accessed 15 June 2008

Martiniello L, Zaino A (2009) Analisi delle tecniche di valutazione per la scelta del modello di realizzazione dell'intervento: il metodo del Public Sector Comparator e l'analisi del valore. Settembre, Unità Tecnica Finanza di Progetto. http://www.utfp.it/doc_eco.htm. Accessed 20 Oct 2012

Mason A, Drummond MF, Ramsey S, Campbell J, Raisch D (2010) Comparison of anticancer drug coverage decisions in the United States and the United Kingdom: does the evidence support the rhetoric? J Clin Oncol 28(20):3234–3238

Milcent C (2005) Hospital ownership, reimbursement systems and mortality rates. Health Econ 4 (11):1151–1168

Mintzeberg H (2012) Managing the myths of health care. World Hosp Health Serv 48(3):4–7

Morelli M, Lecci F (2014) Management control systems (MCS) change and the impact of top management characteristics. The case of healthcare organisations. J Manag Control 24(3):267–298

Osborne S (ed) (2000) Public-private partnerships: theory and practice in international perspective. Routledge, London

Palmer S, Torgerson DJ (1999) Definitions of efficiency. BMJ 318(7191):1136

Parker D, Hartley K (2003) Transaction costs, relational contracting and public-private partnerships: a case study of UK defence. J Purchasing Supply Manag 9(3):97–108

Pollitt C, van Thiel S, Homburg V (eds) (2007) New public management in Europe: adaptations and alternatives. Palgrave MacMillan, Basingstoke

Pollock AM, Shaoul J, Rowland D, Player S (2001) Public services and the private sector: a response to the IPPR. A Catalyst Working Paper, London

Puig-Junoy J (1998) Technical efficiency in the clinical management of critically ill patients. Health Econ 7:263–277

Reinhardt UE (2003) Costs of healthcare administration in the United States and Canada. N Engl J Med 349(25):2461–2464

Roehrich JK, Lewis MA, George G (2014) Are public–private partnerships a healthy option? A systematic literature review. Soc Sci Med 113:110–119

Shen YC, Eggleston K, Lau J, Schmid CH (2007) Hospital ownership and financial performance: what explains the different findings in the empirical literature? Inquiry 44(1):41–68. Retrieved from http://www.ncbi.nlm.nih.gov/pubmed/17583261

Sherman D (1984) Data envelopment analysis as a new managerial audit methodology—test and evaluation. Audit J Pract Theory 4:35–53

Sloan FA (2000) Not-for-profit ownership and hospital behavior. In: Culyer AJ, Newhouse JP (eds) Handbook of health economics, vol 1B. Elsevier, Amsterdam, pp 1141–1174

Spackman M (2002) Public-private partnership: lessons from the British approach. Econ Syst 26:283–301

Sullivan SD, Watkins J, Sweet B, Ramsey SD (2009) Health technology assessment in health-care decisions in the United States. Value in Health 12(Suppl 2):S39–S44

Tiemann O, Schreyogg J (2009) Effects of ownership on hospital efficiency in Germany. BuR Bus Res 2(2):115–145

Tiemann O, Schreyogg J (2012) Changes in hospital efficiency after privatization. Health Care Manag Sci 15(4):310–326

Tiemann O, Schreyogg J, Busse R (2012) Hospital ownership and efficiency: a review of studies with particular focus on Germany. Health Policy 104(2):163–171. doi:10.1016/j.healthpol.2011.11.010

Torbica A, Ciani O (2016) Myth #6 If left to the private sector it would be more efficient. Public vs. private provision of healthcare services. In: Adinolfi P, Borgonovi E (eds) What is right and what is wrong in healthcare management? Commenting on Henry Mintzberg's myths. Springer, Berlin

Torbica A, Tarricone R, Drummond MF (2016) The impact of culture, values and institutional context on the methods and use of economic evaluation. Value Health 19(3):A292

Vannozzi D, Fedeli G (2011) La distinta base applicata all'azienda. Mecosan 20(77):105–129

Villalonga B (2000) Privatization and efficiency: differentiating ownership effects from political, organizational, and dynamic effects. J Econ Behav Organ 42(1):43–74. doi:10.1016/S0167-2681(00)00074-3

Vitaliano DF, Toren M (1996) Hospital cost and efficiency in a regime of stringent regulation. Eastern Econ J 22(2):161–175

Wilson GW, Jadlow JM (1982) Competition, profit incentives, and technical efficiency in the provision of nuclear medicine services. Bell J Econ 13(2):472–482

Woolhandler S, Campbell T, Himmelstein DU (2003) Costs of healthcare administration in the United States and Canada. N Engl J Med 349:768–775

Yescombe ER (2007) Public-private partnerships. Principles of policy and finance. Butterworth-Heinemann, Oxford, UK

Zuckerman S, Hadley J, Iezzoni L (1994) Measuring hospital efficiency with frontier cost functions. J Health Econ 13:255–280

Chapter 9
Myth #6: Health Care Is Rightly Controlled by the Public Sector, for the Sake of Equality

Andrea Silenzi, Alessio Santoro, Walter Ricciardi, Anna Prenestini, Stefano Calciolari, Silvio Garattini, Vittorio Bertelè, Riccardo Mercurio, Stefano Consiglio and Mariavittoria Cicellin

9.1 Future for Publicly Funded Health care Is a Matter of Systematization and Leadership

Andrea Silenzi, Alessio Santoro and Walter Ricciardi

9.1.1 Introduction

The healthcare sector has all the characteristics to be considered a complex system. Indeed, its extrinsic complexity is related to its openness, since the health system is affected by the political, social, and financial context where it operates. Moreover,

A. Silenzi (✉) · W. Ricciardi
WHO Collaborating Centre for Health Policy, Governance and Leadership in Europe, Institute of Public Health, Catholic University of the Sacred Heart, Rome, Largo Francesco Vito, 1, 00168 Rome, Italy
e-mail: andrea.silenzi@unicatt.it

W. Ricciardi
e-mail: walter.ricciardi@unicatt.it

A. Prenestini (✉)
CeRGAS, SDA Bocconi - School of Management, Bocconi University, Via Roentgen 1, 20135 Milan, Italy
e-mail: anna.prenestini@unibocconi.it

V. Bertelè
Laboratory of Drug Regulatory Policies, IRCCS Istituto di Ricerche Farmacologiche Mario Negri, Via Giuseppe La Masa, 19, 20156 Milan, Italy
e-mail: vittorio.bertele@marionegri.it

P. Adinolfi and E. Borgonovi (eds.), *The Myths of Health Care*,
https://doi.org/10.1007/978-3-319-53600-2_9

health systems are intrinsically complex, since many components should be in place in order to ensure their proper functioning (De Toni and Comello 2007). A healthy workforce is a prerequisite for the delivery of qualitative services. Adequate funding, drugs, and technologies should be guaranteed. Moreover, policy-makers should govern health systems appropriately and inform their decisions according to reliable and timely health information (WHO 2007).

9.1.2 A Health System Thinking Approach

The overall aim of health systems is to ensure that everyone, everywhere, can access quality health services without facing financial hardship as a result. This principle is widely known as Universal Health Coverage (UHC). UHC entails that all people must have access to needed promotive, preventive, curative, and rehabilitative health services, of sufficient quality to be effective, while also ensuring that people do not suffer financial hardship when paying for these services. Therefore, UHC is profoundly intertwined with the dimension of equity, since achieving UHC means crafting health systems around the inspiring principle of equity. But what is equity and how is equity embedded in health systems? It is crucial to shed light on the concepts of equity and equality. Equality means "the same." No one would presume that the use of healthcare services should be equal among individuals. Conversely, equity is related to the concept of social justice. Sick people should have higher access to healthcare services than healthy individuals. The same applies to financial contributions. The wealthier should pay

R. Mercurio · M. Cicellin (✉)
Economia, Management, Istituzioni, University of Napoli Federico II, C.U. Monte Sant'Angelo—Via Cinthia, 80126 Naples (NA), Italy
e-mail: mariavittoria.cicellin@unina.it

S. Consiglio
Department of Social Sciences, University of Napoli Federico II, Vico Monte della Pietà, 1, 80138 Naples (NA), Italy

S. Calciolari
Institute of Economics (IdEP), Università della Svizzera Italiana, Via G. Buffi 13, Lugano, Switzerland
e-mail: calciolari.stefano@gmail.com

S. Garattini (✉)
Directorate, IRCCS Istituto di Ricerche Farmacologiche Mario Negri, Via Giuseppe La Masa, 19, 20156 Milan, Italy
e-mail: silvio.garattini@marionegri.it

A. Santoro
Department of Public Health and Infectious Diseases, University of Rome La Sapienza, Piazzale Aldo Moro 5, 00185 Rome, Italy
e-mail: alessio.santoro@live.it

more. Inequities in health are defined as the "differences in health that are not only unnecessary and avoidable, but in addition unfair and unjust" (Whitehead 1992). UHC fosters the establishment of a health system shaped around the principle of equity. Equity in health systems means that people should get the health services they need and fund the health system according to their ability to pay. Access should be granted according to needs, funding according to ability to pay.

Achieving equity in health care is a challenging exercise. The Final Opinion of the European Commission "Expert Panel on Effective Ways of Investing in Health" recently acknowledged that both financial and access equity in the European Union is massively changing and advocated change (EXPH 2015). Despite past achievements, the Panel concluded that the financial crisis reversed the positive trends and inequities are on the rise. Budgetary cuts have shrunk the provision of health services and reduced their quality. The growing dissatisfaction has made privatization appealing and undermined "social justice." In an editorial published in the British Medical Journal, Martin Mckee and David Stuckler reaffirmed the crucial role played by universalism in supporting social justice. Indeed, the authors argued: "who would benefit from a privatization of the healthcare system? Obviously not the lower classes who could not afford private care. And not even the middle-classes, since an individualized system is more expensive than what existed previously, often of poorer quality. The real beneficiaries of such policies would be the highest social classes, who no longer have to pay for services they never used anyway" (McKee and Stuckler 2011).

Interestingly, the calls for privatization are profoundly misleading. Robust evidence clearly highlights that privately funded health care systems are not equal. A thorough assessment of equity conducted across different countries highlighted that the US health care system is the least equitable, compared to France, Canada, and Great Britain. Indeed, it is the only health system where a significant portion of the population is uninsured and where access to healthcare access is based on the ability to pay. In the US, systematic inequities exist in the health services received by the insured compared to the uninsured (Università Cattolica del Sacro Cuore and Abbvie 2015).

The conclusion is that publicly funded health systems are critical for equity.

Unfortunately, it would be unrealistic to craft tomorrow's health systems only around the principle of equity. Indeed, health systems cannot be isolated from the external context, where financial resources are constantly shrinking. Moreover, patients' expectations are on the rise and the epidemiological transition to chronic disease will place an additional burden on health systems resources. By 2050, 37% of the European population is expected to be over the age of 60, overstretching the capacity of the health systems to respond (WHO 2000). European health systems are being required to deliver more and better services, with reduced financial resources. Whether they want it or not, policy-makers will have to shape and tailor the upcoming health systems according to these givens. In such a scenario, the opponents of a publicly funded system might argue that privatization should be encouraged as it boosts efficiency in health care. However, are privately funded health systems more efficient? Robust evidence highlights that such a preconceived idea is misleading. The World Health Report 2000 unequivocally highlighted that public health systems are or could be extremely efficient. Seventeen publicly funded European health systems populated the top-twenty list. The privately funded US health system ranked 37th (Bloomberg 2015). Bloomberg recently confirmed these findings. By analyzing data from the World Bank, IMF, and WHO, it concluded that the US health system is the 44th health system in the world, in terms of efficiency (Koh and Nowinski 2010). Health systems do not need to be private to perform well. They could be rightly left to the public sector.

Publicly funded health systems could foster equity while working efficiently. However, the legacy of the financial crisis will not be mitigated anytime soon and there is an urgent need to transform the threat of budget cuts into an opportunity to scale-up performance. Moreover, inequities are widespread both across and within countries. Reforms are urgently needed. Italy represents a perfect case study to explore in order to advocate for reforms. It has a long-established publicly funded health system, accounting for more than 70% of the total national health care expenditure. Ensuring equal access to uniform levels of health services, while controlling health expenditure, is one of the inspiring principles of the health system. Therefore, the Italian Ministry of Health defined a package of essential health services to be provided to all its citizens nationwide. Furthermore, internal market mechanisms as well as managerial elements were introduced in order to control health expenditure. However, over the past years, inequities have increased and are nowadays clearly manifested. A striking example is provided by the adoption of cancer screening policies across the regions. Such policies were not uniformly activated nationwide, leading to massive internal inequities. The result being that Italy has one of the best public healthcare systems in the world, which only applies to a minority of Italians. Unfortunately, the problems faced by the Italian health system are shared by several publicly funded health systems.

9.1.3 The Myth of Equality

Therefore, how to protect the universalistic model? How to drive changes in public health systems in order to ensure equity while operating efficiently? Several recipes should be adopted.

First, governance for health is the driver for change in health care and the core energy that makes change happen. It has to be performed by all actors of the system regardless of formal management or leadership position. The new leadership that is required of managers and formal leaders in health care is to lead a widespread leadership. Tackling disparities and achieving true health equity will only come through a leadership—collective and individual—that embraces the powerful integration of science, practice, and policy to create lasting change (Koh and Nowinski 2010).

Second, a greater sense of responsibility by health professionals and civil servants should be promoted alongside citizens. Within the healthcare system, the main challenge for leaders is to link actions aimed at transforming structure, systems, and culture. These actions are often inconsistent with each other because of the time needed to influence each issue: it is relatively short for structure changes, longer for organizational system transformations, and much longer for culture transformations (Muir Gray 2011). This requires that societies invest in future leadership and that governments strengthen and modernize education for health care professionals, overcoming formal education and moving forward to a transcultural education focused on how to tackle inequities and address social determinants of health, while operating within limited resources (Institute of Medicine 2016).

Third, designing appropriate policies, establishing monitoring platforms, and evaluating achievements is critical for every healthcare system. Policies should be informed by reliable and timely health data, and monitoring their implementation should be an integral part of each health plan since this would allow addressing corrective actions, and evaluating the achievements should inform the design of forthcoming strategies. For publicly funded healthcare systems, performance measurement is an extremely challenging task, which should be conducted across all the dimensions of health care, including the equity-related aspects at local, regional, and national levels.

Fourth, reforms need to be informed by strong evidence and by cost-effectiveness. Bridging the gaps between implementers and research is crucial. Health system research evidence is not always communicated effectively or in a timely manner, and health system managers, policies, and decision-makers do not always have the skills, tools, and capacity to find and use research evidence. Policies should be designed carefully and monitored closely. Research should be operational and target real-life health-service delivery questions. A growing body of the literature is addressing inequities in health care. Such findings should extensively feed and promptly inform policy-making.

To conclude, it is critical to reaffirm that policies should not be driven by financial constraints and interests, but rather by Rawls' "theory of justice." Rawls argued that a fair society is one designed as if from behind a "veil of ignorance," meaning that class and social forces are to be removed from policy-making. As he put it, behind the veil "no one knows his place in society, his class position or social status, nor does anyone know his fortune in the distribution of natural assets and abilities, his intelligence, strength, and the like." Rawls argued that in such circumstances decision-makers would create a society that does not privilege one group over another, as no one can know where they will end up. Universalism is critical in maintaining equity in health care. Undermining the welfare state that European countries have struggled to implement would have a massive repercussion on Rawls' "theory of justice." Public systems should be protected since they ensure universalism. However, several challenges should be overcome in order to prevent the rise of the misleading calls of private interests. Health systems have to reframe its management as distributed, its strategy as venturing, its organizing as collaboration and as a system beyond its single parts.

9.2 Is Good Health care a Matter of Competition or Collaboration?

Anna Prenestini and Stefano Calciolari

9.2.1 *Introduction*

In the last half century, legislation in several countries has converged to establish a relevant role of the public subject in several sectors (e.g., railways, local transportation, education). Currently, the prescription of fixing major problems by treating such sectors in a more business-like manner is quite popular (Mendoza 2015). As far as health care is concerned, it is rare to find a Western country where the policy maker does not significantly limit this business with a heavy regulation and direct interventions in the financing and provision of services. Therefore, the recipe of fostering business-like dynamics has many champions in health care.

At this point, any physician could assimilate such a recipe to a drug prescription and legitimately ask: if this is the cure, what is the diagnosis? Anybody less knowledgeable about medicine may recall the answer of the Cheshire Cat to Alice's request: "Would you tell me, please, which way I ought to go from here?," "That depends a good deal on where you want to get to." If the "where" is not much of a problem, then uncertainty only concerns how long it will take to get somewhere. However, can patients wait until a reform will get the system somewhere?

The uncertainty around (and the burden of) any reform is sustainable if its changes, at the very least, are designed to address specific problems. Therefore, we suggest starting by summarizing the main challenges of advanced health systems and then providing recommendations about appropriate changes aimed to enable health systems to deal with such challenges.

9.2.2 *A Brief Diagnosis: What Are the Priorities?*

The uncertainty around health reforms orientation is partly due to a rapidly changing context in terms of both social pressures (Guidotti 2015; Resnik 2007) and financial constraints (Anessi Pessina and Cantù 2006; Lega and Calciolari 2012). This tends to generate a sense of urgency for major interventions but without suggesting priorities to shape a coherent vision.

Health systems are facing complex challenges largely driven by two main sector-specific catalysts: technological development (Anessi Pessina and Cantù 2006; Glendinning 2003), epidemiologic, and demographic trends (Lega and Calciolari 2012).

The first driver, together with the rapid expansion of medical knowledge, is responsible for the major advances in medicine but it is also associated with the growth of clinical specialization and the consequential fragmentation of patient care in advanced health systems (Calciolari and Ilinca 2016; Lega and Calciolari 2012).

As far as the second driver is concerned, population aging is a pervasive and enduring phenomenon with profound implications for health care—not to mention the social and political spheres (United Nations 2001). In 2015, over 16% of the population was 65 years or older in developed countries, a proportion which will exceed 22% by 2030 and approach 26% by 2050 (World Bank 2016). Aging is closely linked to the prevalence of chronic conditions, which account for an overwhelming share of the total burden of diseases (WHO 2008). This epidemiologic trend is associated with emerging clusters of patients characterized by complex needs that cut across disease categories and medical specialties. Addressing such needs—belonging not only to a disease, but also to associated conditions, complications, and circumstances—calls for organizing care around the patient. This requires coordinated processes that might involve professionals from different disciplines, organizations, and sectors to integrate all the resources (from simple information to concrete services) necessary for a single patient (Goodwin et al. 2014; Porter and Lee 2013).

9.2.3 *Is More Business the Appropriate Cure?*

On the one hand, technologic advances and medical knowledge expansion tend to orient health professionals toward pigeonholing and care fragmentation; on the other hand, patients need more and more cooperation among health providers and institutions.

In this situation, increasing competition between players does not help health care to accommodate the present growing needs. One might use the classic argument that competition contains costs. However, competition does not address the challenges of population aging and its associated argument is questionable. Actually, in 2007 Bernasek (2007) pointed at the higher share of U.S. health costs dedicated to administration compared with the Canadian single-payer (i.e., much less business-like) health system; in 2015 the first evaluation of the introduction of a prospective payment system to finance Swiss hospitals—a competition-oriented reform with cost containment as one of its main goals (Consiglio Federale Svizzero 2004)—did not show evidence of improved efficiency after three years of implementation (OFSP 2015).

If we consider the previously depicted health care scenario, providing appropriate care (in terms of quality, patient satisfaction, effectiveness, and cost-effectiveness) is a matter of collaboration between healthcare professionals and organizations. The cooperation between healthcare professionals takes different paths: multidisciplinary teamwork and collaboration between specialists of same discipline and/or different professions (e.g., between doctors and nurses).

As far as multidisciplinary teamwork is concerned, scientific literature shows important advantages associated with multidisciplinary cooperation in oncology. The systematic review made by Prades et al. (2015) found that teamwork communication and cooperation improve patient outcomes in terms of diagnosis and/or treatment planning, survival, patient satisfaction, and clinicians' satisfaction. This because team members work together toward a common goal: obtaining the patient's best outcomes as efficiently as possible (Porter and Lee 2013). They have specialized expertise, trust one another, and meet or communicate frequently to review data on their own performance. Based on those data, they work to improve care quality and outcomes, by establishing new protocols, devising better ways to empower patients (e.g., change behaviors, improve medication adherence) and their caregivers, change practices, reach out to other professionals, etc.

The cooperation between specialists of the same discipline and/or different professions can modify clinical practices and procedures, raise clinical standards, and improve performance in terms of quality for patients. For instance, in 2001 two Italian healthcare organizations in the Emilia Romagna region (Santa Maria Nuova Hospital Trust and Local Health Authority of Reggio Emilia) observed a variability in the way that endoscopies were performed and in terms of completeness, accuracy, sedation, and comfort for patients. In 2004, the top managers of the two organizations asked their clinicians to collaborate together to develop an integrated and standardized approach to perform colonoscopies (Formisano et al. 2007). Moreover, a mass screening for colorectal cancer was to commence. A working group including 16 physicians, 8 nurses, and one biostatistician (who were working in the two healthcare organizations and in five different hospitals) was trained in clinical audit. Both physicians and nurses actively participated to the pre-audit (run-in period), as well as in the audit, with the aim to establish common clinical standards and a single procedure for colonoscopies. After the implementation of the new procedure, important clinical targets were achieved by the professionals of each hospital (Formisano et al. 2007): for example, the crude rate of completeness moved from 87.7% (appraisal in 2003) to 95.7% (appraisal in 2006); adequate sedation was also more frequently used, from 51.1% (2003) to 94% (2006). The experience is a good example of how cooperation between healthcare professionals can deeply modify practice and improve performances. Nowadays the cooperation between the two health care organizations has extended to other specialties, involving many different professionals. Similar approaches are applied in many cases of conversion of small hospitals, located in rural and/or remote areas, into health centers (Calciolari et al. 2015), where efficiency and effectiveness of care are of paramount importance. Here the cooperation involves the personnel of the new center, the primary care local actors, and the closest hospitals.

A more extensive form of collaboration consists of the development of networks involving health professionals, healthcare organizations, national and regional health departments. An interesting example is represented by the cancer networks created in several countries. These collaborative structures improve patterns of cancer care and outcomes for patients by: (a) the promotion of efficient and effective data collection; (b) the creation of common wide cancer repositories; (c) the implementation of supporting clinical audit (i.e., techniques of retrieval and appraisal of the evidence, identification of indicators and standards, etc.); and (d) the development of complex research programs.

Important conditions for the benefits associated with the described forms of collaboration are professional education, training toward cultural change, and investment in technological solutions enabling effective communication (especially when co-location of professionals is not possible or too expensive).

In general, providing appropriate care by reorienting services toward coordination and cooperation (or "integration") calls less for structural solutions and more for "soft" aspects. In the past years, different business-like approaches were used to direct professional behavior towards better quality and appropriateness of care (Adler and Kwon 2009): ranging from hierarchical control, to economic incentives for achieving defined targets, to public disclosure of information on the quality of services provided by healthcare organizations and/or professionals, etc. However, managing such aspects through hierarchical control or performance-based accountability systems proved to be complex and did not completely solve problems, due to the pervasiveness of care quality and appropriateness issues (Marshall and Davies 2000). Clinical behavior can be changed and oriented toward desired goals by means of working on clinicians' attitudes, cultures, and the way they perceive their position and responsibility in their organizations.

As a consequence, academics and decision-makers have increasingly focused on clinical engagement: a change management approach leveraging on health professionals' willingness to actively participate and take direct responsibility in the decision-making processes of their organizations. Such an approach allows for working on aligning clinicians' interests with those of the organization to foster performance and quality of care (Spurgeon et al. 2011; Grilli et al. 2016; Guthrie 2005; Lega et al. 2013).

Finally, organizational culture—the apparatus of symbols, values, attitudes, and beliefs shared by the members of an organization (Davies et al. 2007)—is one of the most important factors that promotes clinical practices fostering quality and contrasting issues of under- or oversupply, turf wars, and errors plaguing modern medicine (Roehr 2011; Prenestini et al. 2015). Therefore, healthcare organizations should focus on appointing top managers with the leadership style most apt to facilitate the growth of collaborative cultures and include cooperation among the learning objectives of their training programs.

9.2.4 Conclusions

Sometimes doctors may not have a clear diagnosis for their patients. In such circumstances, one may argue that integrating knowledge with experience and intuition—always keeping in mind the best interest of the patient—is reasonable and can help. Likewise, in the policy or management field, a rational approach to change consists of assessing the diagnoses, experience, intuitions (and interests) of reform champions. In particular, comparing and challenging the different diagnoses —and the evidence on which they are based—and distinguishing them from conjectures is a good premise to avoid reforms built on myths and mystifications.

In health care, the mere presence of (more) business-like models/practices is no guarantee to foster better performances. Further, if they are not coupled with change management approaches enhancing clinical engagement, multidisciplinary and multi-professional cooperation, and integrated service delivery, any reform runs the risk of dismantling the good of health systems and hampering the best developments.

9.3 Equality in Health Care: A Mirage or a Reality

Silvio Garattini and Vittorio Bertele'

9.3.1 Introduction

Equality is a general aim but in the field of health it is a must. Equality in health care is met when everybody has access to the services and benefits they need, which should be the best available, and sustainable. Only a publicly driven health sector can ensure impartial distribution of resources and provision of benefits ideally, but in reality this is not always achieved.

9.3.2 Public Health Authorities Do not Set Priorities

Public health authorities should first identify the unmet needs of the population and set priorities according to criteria not only of equality but also of solidarity. This means, for instance, looking at emergencies arising in society, such as diabetes or senile dementia in Western countries. But they must also consider neglected diseases, such as the 6–7000 rare diseases that affect more than 30–40 million people in the European Union, though each one affects no more than 1 in 2000 inhabitants. Instead, it is the private sector which establishes what people mostly need. Privately owned businesses follow commercial criteria together with marketing opportunities which satisfy their stockholders' wishes, not necessarily people's health priorities.

Private hospitals often select remunerative pathologies and interventions (obesity, plastic surgery, etc.) but pay little attention to multiple chronic diseases in the elderly or expensive and risky emergency interventions. Industry prefers to invest in R&D on products (diagnostics, medical devices, and medicines) that people want or attract professionals' interest, though most often meeting secondary needs. It is surprising that among the pharmaceutical blockbusters of the last decade there are drugs addressing erectile dysfunction, which may be a cure for a minority but are a plaything for the majority. It is the latter that ensures a return on investments.

When a no profitable pathology such as the one mentioned can be identified, the industry invents diseases and leads people to believe that they need interventions. This strategy is called "disease-mongering," which essentially involves trying to convince healthy people that they are sick, and mildly sick people that they are very ill (Moynihan et al. 2002). Examples include the so-called chronic fatigue syndrome, restless leg syndrome, fibromyalgia, motivational deficiency disorders, and so on. This strategy also involves lowering the thresholds that define disease status or risk factors (blood pressure, hyperglycemia, or hypercholesterolemia, etc.). All of a sudden, many previously healthy people become sick and need intervention.

All this is a consequence of a lack of strategy in the public sector, which ceases to drive the process. Identification and selection of health priorities would educate the public, and at the same time would satisfy its real needs. People would not be abandoned to a marketing pressure that tries to convince them they have needs in addition to or in place of the ones they actually have, as happens with any commercial goods.

9.3.3 Public Health Authorities Do not Promote Innovation

Of course, the industry also develops innovative technologies for real diseases. Its efforts have produced a great deal of innovation and improvements over the last century, substantially contributing to longer survival and improving people's quality of life, at least in developed countries. Huge progress in the prevention and treatment of infections, cardiovascular diseases, and cancer stems from the research carried out by the industry. Moreover, industrial production scale-up could make the costs of innovative diagnostics, medicines, and medical devices sustainable for the most part, which is becoming rarer and rarer.

The pharmaceutical industry's innovative attitude, however, has gradually lost impetus with the realization that promotion yields more than research, and me-too products for widespread conditions, such as hypertension, guarantee greater profits than innovative orphan drugs for rare diseases (Joppi et al. 2013).

An impartial public sector, instead, should ensure that any medicines brought into the market not only provide a benefit, but are also better than those already available in terms of effectiveness and/or safety and/or cost. This goal is rarely achieved, since pharmaceutical legislation does not require it.

The regulatory bodies themselves state that "the most common primary objectives for pivotal clinical trials [those backing the marketing authorisation applications] are to demonstrate superiority to placebo control, or to demonstrate non-inferiority [...] to an active control." (Committee for Medicinal Products for Human Use 2011). Besides being unethical (Garattini and Bertele' 2007a, b), placebo-controlled and non-inferiority trials may allow products into the market that are less effective or less safe than those already in use, and do not help patients or the health authorities establish the respective places-in-therapy of newer and older medicines (Bertele' et al. 2012).

In line with these regulatory requirements, the industry-driven approach aims at producing copies and me-too drugs, leaving to their marketing departments the promotion of virtually identical products to health professionals or even patients. This in turn leads to scant innovation that damages patients' and public health. In the last decade, only a little more than 1% of the over 1000 approved medicines have offered a real advantage for patients. Even when they are only copies, newer medicines are sold at progressively higher prices, because of alleged secondary properties, e.g., a slightly different mechanism of action, greater ease of use, better compliance, etc., which do not necessarily result in better health for patients.

Public health authorities should require for any product seeking marketing authorization, a demonstration of its added value compared to those available, rather than only its good quality, efficacy and safety, as required by the current legislation, (Garattini and Bertele' 2007a, b). Needless to say, the public sector should also require that, in order to obtain marketing authorization, other health technologies undergo the same evaluation process as drugs. This is not the case with diagnostics and medical devices so far.

9.3.4 Public Health Authorities Do not Rely on Independent Research

Other deficiencies in drug development contribute to the unclear value of medicines. These include the surrogate outcome measures adopted in clinical trials involving new drugs. Endpoints such as lower glycaemia or reduced tumor volume are offered as possible benefits but do not address—and even less so prove—what most matters to patients, i.e., a longer and/or better life. Small clinical trials make it difficult to distinguish the effect of chance from that of the experimental intervention, thus betraying the trust of trial participants and the overall patient community—and so do the unpublished results from negative studies and the unreported evidence of post-marketing risks.

This situation would require public health authorities to promote and rely on independent clinical research to enable it to take sound decisions based on unbiased evidence. In the premarketing phase, regulatory authorities should be able to rely on at least one pivotal phase III trial conducted by independent nonprofit scientific organizations, in addition to those conducted and promoted by the pharmaceutical companies (Garattini and Bertele' 2007a, b).

After marketing authorisation has been granted, the authorities should promote, commission, and fund independent research on critical safety issues (Garattini and Bertele' 2011), since spontaneous reporting of adverse events by health professionals and their collection by the companies concerned have proved neither reliable nor effective (Garattini and Bertele' 2010).

9.3.5 Public Health Authorities Do not Select Innovative Cost-Effective Products

Since public health leaves it to industry to select targets and how to address them, in the end it has to deal with products whose clinical value is questionable and place-in-therapy uncertain. Lacking this information, how can health authorities approve a product, establish its economic value, and negotiate appropriate conditions for its reimbursement with public funds? Nevertheless, products like these are allowed onto the market and even into national reimbursement schemes by the public authorities. We are facing a situation in which the industry can produce whatever it reckons it can sell, useful or not, innovative or me-too. The regulatory bodies (the EMA, European Medicine Agency, in the EU) assess medicinal products only on the basis of their quality, safety and efficacy, with no cross-comparison with other available therapies and therefore no (verifiable) added value. Thereafter the political level (the European Commission) allows them onto the market. In the meantime, the pharmaceutical companies promote the alleged secondary advantages of their products to patients and physicians and eventually set prices. At this point national public payers have no margin for negotiation as, responding to the marketing effort, patients and doctors demand the supposedly innovative products, whose real clinical value is unknown; the industry argues that prices cannot differ much across countries in order to avoid parallel import–export. As a result there is no way health authorities can assess whether the alleged benefits are worth paying for, rather than using public resources to adopt other health technologies or satisfy other public health needs (Bertele' and Garattini 2015).

9.3.6 Public Health Authorities Do not Protect the Poor

To ensure equality, health authorities should mostly protect the poor. This does not always happen. Even a system like the Italian one, which in theory aims at universality, equality, and solidarity, suffers from several drawbacks. As an example, the distribution of skills and facilities is not even throughout the country. Most people and their relatives have to travel, usually from southern to northern Italy, to receive adequate care.

In addition, there is a co-payment system to obtain services or diagnostic tests or medications. The so-called “tickets” which patients have to pay vary among the different regions, not necessarily according to local financial ability. Some people are exempted from paying tickets, but exemptions are granted based on disease rather than income. This may meet the solidarity aim of the National Health Service, not equality, which should really base exemption on individual purchasing power.

Another distortion of the system is the so-called intramoenia (i.e., “within the walls”) activity. This term covers physicians/clinicians who usually serve as public employees being allowed to work as private professionals within the hospital where they work. As a result, wealthy people who can afford private visits have privileged access not only to hospital physicians/clinicians but also to the diagnostic and therapeutic interventions they prescribe. All the others have to put themselves on waiting lists that may be weeks or months long. This looks more like the inequality expected in a private-driven health system.

9.3.7 Conclusions

Equality in health is an elusive goal that is hard to achieve. Public institutions are the only ones that can aim for this goal as they could and should devote themselves exclusively to it, while private institutions have to set other goals first or at least take them into account. However, the public sector often gives up its role, and appoints the private sector not only to provide services and goods but even set policies, rules, and the means to follow them. This implies an uneven and inefficient distribution of professional and economic resources and, in the end, of health.

9.4 Beyond Public and Private. Social Innovation in Healthcare System

Riccardo Mercurio, Stefano Consiglio, Mariavittoria Cicellin

9.4.1 Introduction, Aim and Scope

In recent years, both the "myth" of public control over health care and the "myth" of the dynamism and high quality of health services managed by private sector have shown their weakness. As it is known, the creation and consolidation of these "myths" concern country-specific peculiarities of the different healthcare systems. In particular, the "myths" refer to the dominance of a professional institutional logic typical of the public intervention or that one led by market forces and the intervention of private business in the health management and social issue. Henry Mintzberg and other scholars such as Porter and Teisberg (2006) have analyzed weaknesses and strengths of these myths in the health systems of several countries, highlighting inefficiency of both entirely "government-controlled" and "market-controlled" solutions.

There are many studies that have shown both government and market failure in the management and financing of social economy (e.g., Cheng and Mohamed 2010; Murray et al. 2010; Noya 2010; Phills et al. 2008).

In Italy, the need to overcome these approaches and to explore new organizational models is related to two main reasons. On the one hand, in the last decade, we were looking at an astonishing growth in the demand for health care; on the other hand, market dynamics are having a strong impact on healthcare services (Chauvin et al. 2015). We are witnessing a steady increase in private health expenditure, €32,971 bn in 2014 with a 2% increase compared to 2001 (22.4% on the operating health expenditure of NHS that in 2014 was €114,057 bn) (Armeni and Costa 2015) which inevitably is having a negative impact on a large part of the population. Regarding the latter aspect, in 2014 the percentage of out of pocket (private expenditure not covered by any insurance type) on total expenditure is one of the highest in Europe, at about 22%, with €33 bn (Del Vecchio et al. 2015). In addition to these two reasons, we should add the radical change of public policy patterns, in order to respond to the crisis of welfare (e.g., Cicellin and Galdiero 2009).

In this context, new paths are increasingly arising referring back to the concept of low cost, low profit, and light health care. Such experiences have been created to meet the social demand of health that cannot be completely satisfied by either public or private health. They are based on the bottom-up complex world of services and needs and can be labeled as social innovation models (Leadbeater 2007). In the healthcare field, all the European countries are giving relevance to the social innovation issue. The European Parliament published a series of documents underlying the strict need to create a new welfare system built on the model of the Civil Economy, in order to recognize the crucial role of actors involved in the social economy sector, and to take steps to ensure their development (see the Report on the Social Economy 2008/2250 of the Commission on Employment and Social Affairs).

The aim of this chapter is to analyze the concept of social innovation in health care as an alternative path to the two "myths." From our point of view, the paradigm of social innovation is the main key to understand the phenomenon of low-cost services in health care. We are interested to shed light on the current experiences of low cost for health care in Italy, in order to understand organizational paradigms, motivations, services offered and arrangement, compared to the established "myths." This work represents a very first attempt to link these concepts in health care field.

The recent evolution of the low-cost services in health care is likely to be a very interesting opportunity for the development of social initiatives beyond public and private sectors. Henry Mintzberg talks about "plural sector," that is the social sector which includes associations, NGOs, cooperatives, etc. (Mintzberg and Azevedo 2012). The low-cost services try to reread the interconnections between public and private sectors, profit and non-profit, efficiency and equity, and appropriateness of care models. The main goal of low cost in health care is to overcome a context where the public segment operates in a totally separate manner from the private one, in order to create an interconnected healthcare industry, both in terms of goals to be pursued (the best of health care involving both the public and private resources available) and of operational activities (what happens in a segment positively impacts on the other). This phenomenon goes through and beyond the debate on mutualism for integrative health. Actually, low-cost services projects arise mainly for health specialists and are based on the ability to connect economic (in terms of efficiency), social (in terms of relationships), cultural (linked to values), and institutional aspects (in terms of social capital that is generated) (Rago 2012; Donati 2011).

9.4.2 The Paradigm of Social Innovation in Healthcare Systems

Social innovation in the healthcare sector is still under study, and in Italy is closely related to the change sweeping the welfare system. The (re)definition of welfare policies appears today as one of the main goals in the field of health care. Alongside the increased demand for health, there is a deep change affecting types and quality of needs, referring to a renewed emphasis of aspects such as patient identity and its relational dimension (Rago 2012).

Social innovation, while having as its main goal the creation and maximizing of common good, pays great attention to the issue of economic sustainability, and aims at developing the sense of civil society (Phills et al. 2008). Profitability, pursuit of efficiency, and ability to boost employment are some of the key words of social innovation, which seeks to overcome the antagonism state versus market and the cage of the "tout court" associations. Moreover, this model is based on bottom-up participation and the concept of "extended enterprise," where the boundaries between internal and external resources are no longer so clear and defined (Murray et al. 2010).

Social innovation in health care can be viewed in the development of new networks of cooperation between public healthcare organizations, private and non-profit organizations, changing the relationship between patients and physicians. The incorporation of a social innovation view leads to an increase in knowledge bases and the information provided to patients also thanks to the ICT and the Health 2.0 (Eysenbach 2008).

Therefore, innovation is the emergent result of a collective action of society, rather than an action promoted by an individual or a small group of innovators. This leads to new roles played by managers, professionals, local administrators and communities, volunteers, workers, and patients. Therefore, social innovation not only aims at increasing life quality standards, but plays a crucial role in terms of competitive improvement, efficiency of the resources employed, sustainability, and scalability (Hulgård 2011). It is noteworthy that this aspect is an opportunity for the development of new products and processes, in line with the criteria of appropriateness in healthcare delivery. In this view, Henry Mintzberg's thinking (2012) about "The Sector Issue" fits well, because of the understanding of the social sector in health care, halfway between public and private ones.

The features of participation and originality of contents, the application of new ideas for services, processes, and organizational forms to better well-being and social value, let us to claim that social innovation is a pivotal key for an emerging reality in health care: the low cost. In particular, as we will consider in the next paragraph, in the low-cost services logic, we find many organizational characteristics referring to social innovation, as it allows linking health services demand and supply in a faster and more flexible manner.

9.4.3 Low-Cost Services for Health

In health care, the low-cost service business model represents a breakthrough that is increasingly gaining success, showing great potentiality. Low-cost concerning health care is a true model of social innovation because it is a real response to the call for health, overcoming the income issue. From the demand point of view, the low-cost model puts the patient back in the center, focusing on the "customization" of the relationship between individuals and health (Castelli et al. 2010). The model has as its main strengths: specialization, attention to price and combination of quality, continuous upgrading and fast access to health services. These are elements that the Italian NHS is not always able to offer due to the constraints imposed by the semi-free access conditions and because, at the same time, those are the strengths of the private sector, for which patients often have to pay very dearly. The low-cost services approach is therefore created to provide citizens with an affordable alternative to conventional private health care, in terms of price but not quality. Moreover, this alternative can also be an answer to citizens demotivated by the low quality of public health care (e.g., poorly welcoming environment, long waiting lists, lack of supply individualization, etc.).

The low-cost health care is a new economy path already well established in other countries, such as Great Britain. It is important to emphasize that Italy is achieving good results, as shown by the first experiences started in the North and which are now spreading to the South too, thanks to specific areas in which different new actors can enter and offer services with competitive pricing and quality.

The low-cost service logic identifies the process of change occurring in the Italian welfare system, allowing the coexistence of the everlasting State intervention and the customization of the needs that drives its orientation. Price is not the only distinctive element. Another one refers to a new concept of care and self-care, which in some way, reopens the debate on modern mutualism for integrative health. In fact, low-cost services projects mainly arise for specialist healthcare programs and for specific fields. In this sense, the model aims to reduce waste and duplication, focusing on the core of health services, according to the principle of appropriateness of care provided.

From the supply point of view, low-cost services are expanding into areas of intervention where SSR (Regional Health Services) do not provide full coverage, such as dental care, blood tests, ophthalmology, psychology, and psychotherapy, but also in some more specific areas. The annual Assolowcost Report (the association of companies and service organizations that aim at reducing costs while maintaining high quality) argues that people who choose these structures supporting the low-cost code of ethics, can save up to 30% on health services (Del Vecchio and Rappini 2011). In this regard, Assolowcost coined the "low cost high value" formula. Behind this concept, there is a strong motivation of many health specialist centers, clinics, and day hospitals to decrease the recent national (from one Region to another) and international health tourism trend (Castelli et al. 2010).

Low-cost service organizations in health care have a strong focus on the idea of service standards. Apart from low cost, there is a high attention on communication and marketing aspects to better reach out to patients, highlighting physicians' professionalism and employing advanced 2.0 technologies. In all the low-cost cases and apart from the specific and different projects implemented, the aim is to offer a qualitatively higher service than those currently available on the healthcare market. For this reason, there is no doubt that low-cost services projects cannot be ascribed to a mere logic of affordability, but they set up a radically new model, especially if compared to the standard offered by private health care (Del Vecchio and Rappini 2011).

The great potentialities and the peculiarity that can facilitate the implementation in the Italian healthcare sector have been proven by several studies. Among the more detailed ones, we emphasize the one conducted by scholars of the CERGAS (Bocconi University, Milan) research center, which analyzed the main Italian low-cost services experiences in the OASI Report of 2011. The most significant cases studied were based on the following criteria: attention to quality, long-term continuity, economic sustainability, location, and mapping of specializations. The cases studied are three organizations of the Assolowcost Association: "Centro Medico Sant'Agostino" in Milan, the dental project "Amico dentista" in Apollonia, "Welfare Italia Servizi," that started a project to develop medical group practices involving public and private partners, together with the CGM cooperative group (the National Consortium for social cooperation "Gino Mattarelli"); "Città di Nuova Capurso" near Bari, the first low-cost outpatient clinic in Southern Italy; and the case of "Medical Division" (MD).

These low-cost service cases unavoidably focus on the idea of price as an expression of social commitment.

We assert that the idea of opportunity and sustainability and the relational dimension are the most definite elements of social innovation spread in the low-cost service model. The study by CERGAS is geared toward a consolidated definition of low cost for the Italian health care, emphasizing the elements of originality, and the pervasiveness of social value that cannot be underestimated by the welfare system, in changing its policies and role.

9.4.4 Final Considerations

Health for everyone, against any fiction and according to the principles of appropriateness of care, is no longer a real and indisputable fact. Private health care is nowadays very widespread among the Italian population for two main reasons: attempting to overcome the waiting time list of the public service; avoiding the inconvenience of health trips for those people in areas less covered by the NHS. This situation certainly entails a cost that many people are no longer able to afford and that makes health care a luxury service and no longer a right.

As a result, low-cost service has been analyzed as a "no-waste" option instead of a low-quality one. Although the model still displays a limited diffusion and application, also because it is little known and acknowledged by citizens, it is an alternative and a valid process worth being employed. In this view, the low-cost service paradigm does not merely consist in the slogan "low prices for high-consumption" as a competition strategy. On the contrary, it focuses on the idea that the social sector can offer something more than "all public" or "all private" models do. Therefore, as already stated, low-cost services provide a primary service, making it available and open to everyone, generating participation and new social inclusion and cohesion. Innovation is the key word of each low-cost service project, and this aspect fully strengthens its pivotal role in the healthcare sector, thanks to the promotion of patient centrality, (re)starting from their needs and wishes. These aspects represent a positive mark to be enhanced.

Although it is early to draw final conclusions, our work needs to shed light on the link between the social innovation paradigm and health care, analyzing the low-cost service model as one of the clearest and best answers to this link.

It is important to highlight a few considerations recently drawn. Del Vecchio et al. (2015) state that the whole low-cost sector does not seem to be overall sufficiently responsive. At the moment, the actors of low cost appear unable to establish themselves in the "private-private" track (out of pocket) and to intercept the demand migrating from the public health.

We wish to contribute to the debate on low cost in Italian health care taking into account different aspects. First, we will highlight some critical issues relating to the most profound changes that are still ongoing in the world of health care and welfare and that in our opinion should be better explored, for example in terms of public versus private, of roles and responsibilities of actors involved, especially referring to the relations between NHS organizations and low-cost service providers. Second, the specific purposes of low-cost service projects are yet to be defined: in fact, some of these refer to the so-called "light" health, where the boundary between health and well-being is still not well defined. We also stress the potential "free riding" issue of operators and patients who, however, have to deal with the Italian dominant public logic. Finally, another aspect is the price flexibility of demand. This could lead to the risk of a value judgment biased more towards price and less according to the real services offered. It should not be forgotten that price is the much-criticized starting point for the transformation of patients into customers. In our opinion, this shift, as well as the nature of low-profit that characterizes low-cost service projects, could weaken the role of the State as guarantor of the collective public health as constitutionally established, transforming health care in a market not distorted by the profit maximization logic.

Finally, some questions will drive our future steps. Does it really make any sense to "demystify" and "demyth" the State in the management of public health care? Could the low-cost service model be a partner of public organizations in the support of specific projects, for example in disease prevention campaigns.

References

Adler PS, Kwon SW (2009) Community, market, and hierarchy in the evolving organization of professional work: the case of medicine. In: Ackroyd S, Muzio D, Chanlat JF (eds) Redirection in the study of expert labour. Palgrave Macmillan, New York

Anessi-Pessina E, Cantu E (2006) Whither managerialism in the Italian National Health Service? Int J Health Plann Manage 21(4):327–355

Armeni P, Costa F (2015) La spesa sanitaria: composizione ed evoluzione. In: Cantù E (eds) L'aziendalizzazione della sanità in Italia. Rapporto OASI 2015. Egea, Milan, Italy

Bernasek (2007) U.S. health care debate burdened by ideology: suspicion stalls single-payer insurance. Int Herald Tribune, 11

Bertele' V, Garattini S (2015) Health Care: make pharma justify the price of drugs. Nature 523:290

Bertele' V, Banzi R, Gluud C, Garattini S (2012) EMA's reflection on placebo does not reflect patients' interests. Eur J Clin Pharmacol 68:877–879

Bloomberg (2015) Most efficient health care 2014. Available from: http://www.bloomberg.com/visual-data/best-and-worst//most-efficient-health-care-2014-countries

Calciolari S, Ilinca S (2016) Unraveling care integration: assessing its dimensions and antecedents in the Italian Health System. Health Policy 120:129–138

Calciolari S, Ferrari D, González Ortiz LG, Meneguzzo M (2015) Organizing health care in remote rural areas: comparing experiences of service delivery re-design. Int J Healthc Manage. doi:10.1080/20479700.2015.1101939

Castelli M, Cerutti E, Giuliani R, Insalata V, Marinelli M, Sirressi V (2010) Dalla sanità tradizionale a percorsi di nuova economia: la sanità low cost, Rapporto Fondazione ISTUD, Fondazione ISTUD, Milano

Chauvin P, Simonnot N et al (2015) Access to health care for people facing multiple vulnerabilities in health in 26 cities across 11 countries. Report on the social and medical data gathered in 2014 in nine European countries, Turkey and Canada. In: Doctors of the world—Médecins du monde international network, Paris, May 2015

Cheng W, Mohamed S (2010) The world that changes the world: how philanthropy, innovation and entrepreneurship are transforming the social ecosystem. Jossey-Bass, San Francisco, CA, USA

Cicellin M, Galdiero C (2009) L'evoluzione dei modelli di governance nel sistema sanitario italiano. In: Mercurio R, Martinez M (eds) Modelli di governance e processi di cambiamento nelle public utilities, FrancoAngeli, Milano

Committee for Medicinal Products for Human Use (2011) Reflection paper on the need for active control in therapeutic areas where use of placebo is deemed ethical and one or more established medicines are available. EMA/759784/2010. Available on the web: http://www.ema.europa.eu/docs/en_GB/document_library/Scientific_guideline/2011/01/WC500100710.pdf

Consiglio Federale Svizzero (2004) Messaggio concernente la modifica della legge federale sull'assicurazione malattie (Finanziamento ospedaliero). Messaggio 04.061, 15 Sept 2004

Davies HTO, Mannion R, Jacobs R, Powell AE, Marshall MN (2007) Exploring the relationship between senior management team culture and hospital performance. Med Care Res Rev 64:46–65

De Toni AF, Comello L (2007) Journey into complexity. Marsilio Editori, Venezia

Del Vecchio M, Rappini V (2011) Low cost in sanità. In: Cantù E (ed) L'aziendalizzazione della sanità in Italia. Rapporto OASI 2011. Egea, Milano, Italy, pp 331–368

Del Vecchio M, Fenech L, Rappini V (2015) I Consumi Privati in Sanità. In: Cantù E (ed) L'aziendalizzazione della sanità in Italia. Rapporto OASI 2015. Egea, Milano, Italy

Donati P (2011) Il valore aggiunto delle relazioni sociali. Sociologia e Politiche Sociali 14(1):9–22

Expert Panel on Effective Ways of Investing in Health (EXPH) (2015) Preliminary report on access to health services in the European Union, 25 Sept 2015. Available from: http://ec.europa.eu/health/expert_panel/opinions/docs/010_access_healthcare_en.pdf

Eysenbach G (2008) Medicine 2.0: social networking, collaboration, participation, apomediation and openness. J Med Internet Res 10(3):e22. doi:10.2196/jmir.1030

Formisano D, Sassatelli R, Gigliobianco A, Nicolini F, Mazzi G, Bedogni G, Riccò D, Manghi I and The Colonoscopy Audit Group of Reggio Emilia (2007) Clinical audit for quality improvement in digestive endoscopy: an Italian experience. International Forum on Quality and Safety in Health Care, Barcelona, 18–20 Apr 2007

Garattini S, Bertele' V (2007a) Non-inferiority trials are unethical because they disregard patients' interests. Lancet 370:1875–1877

Garattini S, Bertele' V (2007b) How can we regulate medicines better? BMJ 335:803–805

Garattini S, Bertele' V (2010) Rosiglitazone and the need for a new drug safety agency. BMJ 341: c5506

Garattini S, Bertele' V (2011) Anything new in EU pharmacovigilance? Eur J Clin Pharmacol 67:1199–1200

Glendinning C (2003) Breaking down barriers: integrating health and care services for older people in England. Health Policy 65(2):139–151

Goodwin N, Dixon A, Anderson G, Wodchis W (2014) Providing integrated care for older people with complex needs. Lessons from seven international case studies. The King's Fund, London

Grilli R, Agati R, Ferro S, Finelli C, Fusconi M, Gaggioli A, Gubellini M, Merighi A, Nicastro O, Perrone A, Pianori D, Prenestini A (2016) Aspetti rilevanti per la partecipazione dei professionisti alla governance. Una preliminare analisi empirica delle opinioni dei medici. Politiche Sanitarie 17(1):21–33

Guidotti TL (2015) Health and sustainability. Oxford University Press, New York

Guthrie M (2005) Engaging physicians in performance improvement. Am J Med Qual 20:235–238

Hulgård L (2011) Social economy and social enterprise: an emerging alternative to mainstream market economy. China J Soc Work 4(3):201–215

Institute of Medicine (2016) A framework for educating health professionals to address the social determinants of health. Available from: http://www.nationalacademies.org/hmd/reports/2016/Framework-for-Educating-Health-Professionals-to-Address-the-Social-Determinants-of-Health

Joppi R, Bertele' V, Garattini S (2013) Orphan drugs, orphan diseases. The first decade of orphan drug legislation in the EU. Eur J Clin Pharmacol 69:1009–1024

Koh HK, Nowinski JM (2010) Health equity and public health leadership. Am J Public Health 100 (Suppl 1):S9–S11

Leadbeater C (2007) Social enterprise and social innovation: strategies for the next ten years. Office of the Third Sector, London

Lega F, Calciolari S (2012) Coevolution of patients and hospitals: how changing epidemiology and technological advances create challenges and drive organizational innovation. J Healthc Manag 57:17–33

Lega F, Prenestini A, Spurgeon P (2013) Is management essential to improving the performance and sustainability of health care systems and organizations? A systematic review and a roadmap for future studies. Value Health 16:S46–S51

Marshall MN, Davies HTO (2000) Performance measurement and management of health care professionals: some topical issues. Dis Manage Health Outcomes 7(6):305–314

McKee M, Stuckler D (2011) The assault on universalism: how to destroy the welfare state. BMJ 343:d7973
Mendoza K-A (2015) Austerity. The demolition of the welfare state and the rise of the Zombie economy. New Internationalist, Oxford
Mintzberg H (2012) Managing the myths of health care. World Hosp Health Serv 48(3):4–7
Mintzberg H, Azevedo G (2012) Fostering "Why not?" social initiatives—beyond business and governments. Dev Pract 22(7):895–908
Moynihan R, Heath I, Henry D (2002) Selling sickness: the pharmaceutical industry and disease mongering. BMJ 324:886–891
Muir Gray JA (2011) How to build health care systems. Offox Press, Oxford
Murray R, Caulier G, Mulgan J, Mulgan G (2010) The open book of social innovation. http://www.youngfoundation.org/files/images/Open_Book_of_Social_Innovation.pdf
Noya A (2010) Social entrepreneurship and social innovation. In: OECD (ed) SMESs entrepreneurship and innovation. OECD Publishing, Paris
OFSP (2015) Evaluation de la révision de la LAMal dans le domaine du financement hospitalier. Résultats intermédiaires. Rapport de l'OFSP au Conseil fédéral, 13 May 2015
Phills JA, Deiglmeier K Jr, Miller DT (2008) Rediscovering social innovation. Stanford Soc Innov Rev 6(4):34–43
Porter ME, Lee TH (2013) The strategy that will fix health care. Harvard Bus Rev 91(10):50–70
Porter ME, Teisberg EO (2006) Reforming health care. Harvard Business School, Boston
Prades J, Remue E, Van Hoof E, Borras JM (2015) Is it worth reorganising cancer services on the basis of multidisciplinary teams (MDTs)? A systematic review of the objectives and organisation of MDTs and their impact on patient outcomes. Health Policy 119:464–474
Prenestini A, Calciolari S, Lega F, Grilli R (2015) The relationship between senior management team culture and clinical governance: empirical investigation and managerial implications. Health Care Manage Rev 4(4):313–323
Rago S (2012) Italian mutual benefit societies: an organizational social innovation in health and health care system. Working paper AICCON Ricerca, Bologna
Resnik DB (2007) Responsibility for health: personal, social, and environmental. J Med Ethics 33 (8):444–445
Roehr B (2011) Defensive medical practices consume 35% of orthopaedic imaging costs, study finds. Br Med J 342:d1037
Spurgeon P, Mazelan P, Barwell F (2011) Medical engagement: a crucial underpinning to organizational performance. Health Serv Manage Res 24:114–120
United Nations (2001) World population ageing: 1950–2050. Department of Economic and Social Affairs, Population Division, New York
Università Cattolica del Sacro Cuore, Abbvie (2015) Acting together: a roadmap for sustainable health care. Available at: http://www.eu-ems.com/summary.asp?event_id=254&page_id=2247
Whitehead M (1992) The concepts and principles of equity and health. Int J Health Serv 22 (3):429–445
World Bank (2016) Health, nutrition and population data and statistics. Accessed at: http://data.worldbank.org/data-catalog/health-nutrition-and-population-statistics. July 2016
World Health Organization (2000) The world health report 2000. The health systems, improving performance. Available on: http://www.who.int/whr/2000/en/whr00_en.pdf
World Health Organization (2007) Everybody's business. Strengthening health systems to improve health outcomes. World Health Organization, Geneva
World Health Organization (2008) The global burden of disease: 2004 update. WHO Press, Geneva, Switzerland

Chapter 10
Myth #7: The Myth of Measurement

Matteo Motterlini, Carlo Canepa, Sabina Nuti, Marina Davoli, Chiara Marinacci, Renato Botti, Giuseppe Iuliano, Gaetano Matonti, Paolo Tartaglia Polcini, Ettore Cinque, Francesco Bevere and Paola Adinolfi

10.1 Behavioural Sciences and Evidence-Based Health care: What Do We Really Need to Measure?

Matteo Motterlini and Carlo Canepa

10.1.1 Measuring Models or Changing Behaviours?

The mantra that inspires healthcare systems is: "If you can't measure it, you can't manage it." The measuring process is closely related to the epistemological ideal of modern science. This has been developed through a world simplification, which is considered useful to disclose principles that work under surrounding reality.

The original version of this chapter was revised: Affiliation were updated for E. Cinque. The erratum to this chapter is available at https://doi.org/10.1007/978-3-319-53600-2_15

M. Motterlini (✉)
Philosophy Department, Center for Experimental and Applied Epistemology, University Vita-Salute San Raffaele, Milan, Italy
e-mail: matteo.motterlini@unisr.it; matteo.motte@gmail.com

C. Canepa
Center for Research in Experimental and Applied Epistemology, University Vita-Salute San Raffaele, Milan, Italy

S. Nuti (✉)
Management and Healthcare Laboratory, Sant'Anna School of Advanced Studies, Pisa, Italy
e-mail: sabina.nuti@sssup.it

M. Davoli
Department of Epidemiology, Lazio Regional Health System, Rome, Italy

P. Adinolfi and E. Borgonovi (eds.), *The Myths of Health Care*,
https://doi.org/10.1007/978-3-319-53600-2_10

The search for natural laws carries a distinctive component: phenomena are not accepted as they are, but they are instead transformed through abstraction and experimentation. What is considered as real is the result of abstraction and experimentation. This attitude, however, entails that some reality aspects are sacrificed in their variety and entirety. In economics, especially in the rational choice theory, the world, where we make decisions and judgments, is not real, but outward and accidental. In its stead, we find abstract constructions of expected utility maximization and pursuit of self-interest.

Here we claim that, in order to improve decision-makings about health and the administrative environment, we need to understand if we are really measuring what we want to manage. In this sense, we accept Henry Mintzberg's challenge ("Managing the myths of healthcare"), which has pointed out the "measuring process" as one of the "myths" associated with the traditional biomedical model. The measurement problem as a healthcare myth carries the "rational agents" assumption. It depends on the price we have to pay in terms of abstraction from the real world, concrete decisional contexts and decision-makers' cognitive faculties, in order to measure exactly. The point is: What do we really need to measure and consequently manage?

(a) Are we aiming at measuring and managing the idealistic behaviour of omniscient and hyper-rational agents which act in the vacuum of abstract economics models? Or, rather,
(b) Are we aiming at measuring and managing the decisions of human beings made of flesh and bones with their cognitive and emotional boundaries, greatly influenced by specific "choice environments"?

We shall argue that the latter is the relevant question. In light of experiments and case studies from the behavioural applied sciences, we claim that in order to improve the quality of a sustainable healthcare system, the systematic nature of human irrationality has to be taken into account. This sort of evidence is crucially needed for efficient and focused interventions.

C. Marinacci (✉)
Italian Ministry of Health, Rome, Italy
e-mail: c.marinacci@sanita.it

R. Botti
School of Management, Italian Ministry of Health, Rome, Italy

G. Iuliano · G. Matonti (✉) · P. Tartaglia Polcini · P. Adinolfi
CIRPA (Interdepartmental Centre for Research in Economics, Law and Management of Public Administrations), University of Salerno, Fisciano, Salerno, Italy
e-mail: gmatonti@unisa.it

E. Cinque
Department of Economics and Management,
Università degli Studi della Campania "Luigi Vanvitelli", Caserta, Italy

F. Bevere (✉)
AGENAS—National Agency for Health Services, Italian Ministry of Health, Rome, Italy
e-mail: bevere@agenas.it

10.1.2 Choice Architecture and Evidence-Based Nudges

Why do people continue to behave in a manner detrimental to their good health, in spite of awareness campaigns and education? Why do patients often follow wrongly the medical treatments and the intake of drugs in spite of detailed care information? Why do doctors often overestimate their own capabilities, prescribe useless tests and not use simple checklists, which could avoid many deaths? These are some of the practical challenges faced by the behavioural approach to improve specific choice environments and consider how human beings really make decisions.

The concept of choice architecture is crucial here. It refers to the way in which choice options are presented during a decision procedure. In the same way as a building structure fixes physical restrictions on how we can move inside it, the way in which choice space is structured affects decision-making results. Every detail counts and conditioning capacity is omnipresent and never neutral. We never make decisions in a vacuum, but in a specific context. Structuring the context is the chosen aim of the architect. In policy making procedures, institutions can exert leverage on citizens' cognitive mechanisms to lead them towards virtuous behaviours—in favour of themselves and collectivity—using a "gentle nudge." According to R. Thaler and C. Sunstein, a nudge is an architectural element choice, which systematically (and predictably) modifies human behaviours, without limiting freedom of choice, or significantly changing economic incentives.

In a healthcare system, a nudge, which has proved its efficiency, concerns organ donations. In many western countries, declared donation percentages stay low—around 20%—in spite of the great majority of citizens asserting that they agree with donating their organs. How is it possible? A comparison between two culturally similar countries can answer this question. Germany and Austria show considerably different donors percentages. The first does not reach 18%, the latter touches 99%. The explanation of such a difference has to be tracked down to the different default options that regulate the enrollment in the national donors register in these two countries. In Germany there is an opt-in system; a citizen is a default non-donor, and if someone wants to become a donor, they need to actively enrol in a specific register. In Austria, instead, there is an opt-out system: an Austrian is a default donor, but if they want, they can opt out. The way in which choice options are structured should not modify a rational agent's preferences, but that is not so. Small, low-cost, well-devised and transparent "architectural elements" can point towards virtuous decisions, which are better for society.

Furthermore, the potentials of behavioural approaches are evident, thanks to the evaluation experimental methods, like randomized controlled trials. Generally, a nudge is applied to a group of people—called the treatment group—which is compared with a second group—the control group—to whom the treatment is not applied. Precisely like testing drug's effectiveness, the experimental method can evaluate which nudge works, without making ordinary selection and attribution biases thanks to randomization. That way, policy makers can overtake traditional models that interpret social sciences in quantitative and idealized terms. How is this achieved? By evidence-based designed interventions to promote prevention behaviours and to simplify doctors and patients' architectural choices.

10.1.2.1 The Case of the Behavioural Insights Team

Behavioural Insights Team (BIT) is an association of behavioural scientists which has been the first to apply the nudging approach. Since 2010, the BIT has collaborated with many British governmental departments, like the National Health Service (NHS). The "Nudge Unit" works applying a framework contained in the MINDSPACE acronym, in which every letter represents factors that influence citizens' behaviours. People are strongly affected by who conveys information (Messenger); peoples' responses to economic incentives (Incentives) are regulated by various cognitive mechanisms; citizens are influenced by what others do (Norms); they tend to choose habitual and default options (Default); their attention is directed by new and salient surrounding elements (Salience); their actions are guided by cues that work at a subconscious and automatic level of cognitive elaboration (Priming) and by emotional states (Affect); people tend to be consistent with their public promises and reciprocal actions (Commitment); they act to improve their self-esteem and wealth (Ego).

The BIT is guided by the principle that if promoting behaviours is necessary we have to make them easy. Since 2011, the BIT has introduced prompted choices in the regulations for organ donations. When a citizen renews their driver's license or identity card, they have to choose whether or not to enrol in the organ donor register. The choice is easily modifiable online.

The NHS has exerted leverage on social comparison to reduce the "Did Not Attends" (DNAs) by 31%, which are scheduled appointments that patients miss. DNAs have an enormous impact on the healthcare system in terms of cost and waiting time, significantly adding to delays along the patient's pathway. So the real percentage of fellow citizens who respect appointments is communicated to patients who book a visit. This message carries the social norm of respecting appointments. In addition, an active commitment is requested, i.e. a patient has to fill out a form by hand, where they insert the day and hour of the visit. Research data shows that adherence to social norms, with active behaviour, works both as a reminder and as a support to self-control and willpower.

10.1.2.2 Fight Against Smoking

The World Health Organization data shows that more than half of all years of healthy life lost are as a result of behavioural factors—including smoking, diet, alcohol and unsafe sex—which are entirely avoidable. How can behavioural approaches help, for example, in the fight against tobacco smoking? Cigarette packages with strongly emotive images are more effective than written information warnings, like olive green standardized packages, whose aim is to reduce both social effects (which commercial brands use especially on young people) and perceived quality of the tobacco. Captivating design packaging propels purchases, while anonymous packaging influences negatively on the perception, taste and associated consumption of tobacco by smokers. Another introduced intervention consists in reducing the visibility of smoking products inside stores, which are often purposely displayed to catch the consumer's attention.

Using economic incentives is part of traditional models utilized in changing behaviours. The novelty of the behavioural approach consists in taking advantage of incentives in a behaviourally informed way, i.e. taking into account how citizens really react to incentive modifications and not how citizens ought to react according to classical economic models. In the fight against tobacco, this method has shown encouraging results. A study by Kevin Volpp and colleagues has found that it is possible to obtain an increase of 15% of subjects who stop smoking in a 12-month period, thanks to an economic incentive—in this case a $100 bonus offered to employees of an American multinational. The same results have been found using incentives to reduce tobacco abuse by pregnant women in lower middle class families.

10.1.2.3 Obesity: The Power of Context

Small contextual changes in the choice environment can guide citizens towards healthier eating habits, reducing the incidence of phenomena like obesity and being overweight on the costs of the healthcare system. In this domain, research focuses on the disposition of items in canteens and supermarkets, and how it affects the consumers' choices. The way in which food is unveiled and the significance of plates and glasses, influence what people will eat and in which quantities. In a study, Paul Rozin and colleagues manipulated two factors in a self-service canteen: the proximity of high calorie dishes, which were distanced 25 cm from the consumer's usual location; and a spoon which was replaced by tongs as a serving tool. Both modifications, which work on the location and accessibility of dishes (and not directly on their quantity), have led to a decrease of unhealthy consumptions from 16 to 8%. Similar research has shown how the order of the names in a menu affects the choice of dishes. Those located at the top and at the bottom of the list tend to be chosen twice as often as those located at the center.

10.1.2.4 Increasing Prevention

With regard to vaccinations and screenings controls, Katherine Millikan and colleagues have shown that active commitments, which oblige employees to write the date and hour of an influenza vaccine, have increased the percentage of vaccinations by 4.3%. With regard to colonoscopy screenings, the same method has obtained an increase by 15%.

Greg Chapman and colleagues have shown how default options can enhance vaccinations inside a university. Two different messages via email were compared. One group was informed that flu shots were free, with the possibility of booking a vaccination online. Another group was informed that every member had been included in an anti-influenza vaccination, with the possibility of deleting the default visit online. The second group, with the opt-out system, has showed a 45% vaccination rate, against the 33% of the first group, in which an opt-in system was applied.

10.1.2.5 Simplifying Doctors' Choices

Not only citizens, but also doctors can benefit from better choice architectures. How can we help physicians to make more precise decisions and to avoid errors? At first it is possible to simplify the complexity of the environment where decisions are made. An effective tool is by using control lists. Checklists, with orderly steps to be applied, can have a huge impact on surgical operations. Many post-operative complications are due to human avoidable errors. In 2009, The World Health Organization published a report to subsidize the diffusion of checklists for security in the operating room. It contains 19 items as a guide for supporting surgeons (which instruments to be used, which anaesthetic, etc.), systematically favouring adherence to security standards recommended to prevent mortality. The report, based on a study sample of 3955 patients, showed post-operative mortality dropping from 11 to 7% after the implementation of checklists.

10.1.3 Concluding Remarks and Next Steps Forward

The nudge approach provides policy makers with the capacity to face present and future challenges inside health policies, without intending to substitute traditional tools. The newness is twofold: (i) evidence-based behavioural policies help citizens fill the intention-action gap, which characterizes the majority of health-related behaviours. (ii) it fuels the culture of experimentation inside institutions, which enables the efficient allocation of resources and award interventions that work and which are based on: evidence of effectiveness. Future research should focus on: (i) long-term duration of changes in choice architectures; (ii) understanding how people interact with them in a social network, and not only how they individually make decisions; (iii) the importance of the replication of applied interventions.

In their ultimate complementary relationship, cognitive psychology and economics provide the opportunity to construct decision-making models able to mediate between abstract principles of rational behaviour and real human behaviour in action. These particular and integrated models are the best chance we have for future success in mapping out efficient and targeted interventions for the world we live in rather than the abstract world of abstract theories. When the moment of economic policy decisions comes—quoting the Nobel Herbert Simon "better to be roughly right than precisely wrong." Public policy choices are too often affected by purely abstract models and reasoning, which are distant from the study of a particular context in which concrete problems are located. The evidence-based policy theoretical framework, linked with applied behavioural sciences, shows how to correctly rebalance the connection between theory and evidence, without levelling traditional healthcare and managerial models on the false measurement myth.

10.2 Performance Measurement at Work: How Can It Be an Effective Management Tool

Sabina Nuti

10.2.1 Premises

"The Myths of Measurement and of Scale Measurement is a fine idea, as long as it does not mesmerize the user. Unfortunately, it so often does: both managers who rely on it for control and physicians who believe that being 'evidence-based' always has to be better than 'experienced-based.' Management and medicine alike have to balance these two in order to be effective. Unfortunately, too much health care at both the administrative and clinical levels has been thrown out of balance by their obsessions with measurement." (Henry Mintzberg 2012a, b).

The view of Henry Mintzberg is very stimulating and provocative for experts of measuring systems in health care. Of course, regarding this issue, not all cultural settings are the same. In some countries measures such as outcomes, quality of care, timeliness, access, financial sustainability or patient satisfaction are available and widespread, also in terms of public disclosure. In Italy the propensity to measure is quite recent.

Indeed research on comparative content analyses of the Italian regional acts, concerning the performance evaluation system adopted in the regional healthcare sector carried out some years ago, showed that only 18% of the regions based their objectives mainly on quantitative indicators. The study analyzed the acts of 14 out of 21 regions between 2008 and 2011 and pointed out that past performance was not taken into consideration because of the large use of qualitative targets (Vainieri and Nuti 2015).

In recent years the situation also in Italy has changed a lot: at a national level the National Agency for Healthcare Services on behalf of the Ministry of Health has developed The Italian National Outcome Evaluation Programme (NOEP) that measures outcomes nationwide (http://95.110.213.190/PNEed15/index.php). Moreover, the Ministry uses the "LEA" grid (i.e. the essential levels of care) that includes a set of 30 indicators to measure the capacity of the regions to ensure access and adequate care. Most Italian regions, on their side, in collaboration with the Laboratory of Management and Health of the Scuola Superiore Sant'Anna of Pisa (MeS-Lab), have adopted—on a voluntary basis—the Inter-Regional Performance Evaluation System (IRPES) http://performance.sssup.it/netval. This system provides a multidimensional evaluation of performance including efficiency, appropriateness, integration and quality of care.

Therefore now, the main actors of the healthcare system have much more measures to lean on, but this does not mean that these data are actually used to support decision-making and improvement processes. The risk that administrators and clinicians are obsessed by measurement appears to be still very weak.

Indeed measurement should be the starting point for promoting a changing process able to have an impact on the value produced for patients, i.e. on quality of care and cost sustained. But how can this be done? Indeed, as Henry Mintzberg states "the Myths of Measurement and of Scale Measurement is a fine idea, as long as it does not mesmerize the user. Unfortunately, it so often does: both managers who rely on it for control and physicians who believe that being "evidence-based" always has to out-do being "experienced-based." Management and medicine alike have to balance these two in order to be effective." Which elements therefore can assure that the measures now available can become really useful and have a role in improving the healthcare system performance? To answer the previous questions it is necessary to keep account of various critical issues.

10.2.2 *From Measurement to Action: Which Critical Issues Should Be Considered?*

Many authors have underlined that governance of any complex system has to rely on planning and control systems with performance indicators (PIs) and targets based on a set of measures are able to represent social complex phenomena. This translation process—from social phenomena to quantitative measures—requires careful design.

First, only a part of the phenomena can be represented by quantitative figures, because indicators portray the "measurable" part of the observed object.

Second, the measurement process can have different degrees of accuracy. Inaccuracies in the measurement process may bring about false positives and false negatives.

The process of governance by PIs and targets relies on the assumption that available indicators are both representative and accurate.

The so-called "synecdoche" principle assumes that the measurable part is able to satisfy both conditions (representativeness and accuracy) by representing the whole object. However, measurement systems almost never comply with the "synecdoche" principle, because the set of selected indicators is rarely able to portray the complexity of the evaluated processes (Bevan and Hood 2006).

The failure to design a panoptic performance measurement system may cause some potential distortions. The choice of a limited set of indicators to evaluate and manage an organization can actually stimulate undesired behaviours on the agents who are controlled by the system. These may react to measurement processes and to management objectives by adapting their behaviour merely to achieve single targets, with scarce attention to the quality of the service as a whole.

Studies on the potentially distorting effects of control systems are extensive (Briers and Hirst 1990; Le Grand and Bartlett 1993). The key point is that, in order to make the planning and control scheme meaningful, the measures used should be consistent with the performance targets—which should, in turn, be the representation of organizational objectives—so that the behavioural responses of the agents are likely to be matched to the requirements of the principal (Smith 1995). The selection of the indicators and the consequent target-setting phase are therefore crucial, since they can potentially generate incoherent behaviours in the system and lead the organizations towards undesired goals (Ferreira and Otley 2009).

Since 1950s, scholars have been studying dysfunctional consequences of measurement; in particular, many of them have inquired the so-called "output distortions," i.e. the attempts to achieve single targets at the cost of significant but unmeasured aspects of performance (Hood 2002; Propper and Wilson 2003a, b; Bevan and Hood 2006).

In Bouckaert and Balk (1991) wrote about "13 diseases" of public productivity measurement. Similarly, Smith wrote about eight potential and unintended behavioural consequences of performance data use. Indeed, they are all the result of some violations of the "synecdoche" principle by the performance evaluation system, which causes an inconsistency between the goals of the agents and the ones of the principal: "tunnel vision," "sub optimization," "myopia," "measure fixation," "misrepresentation," "misinterpretation," "gaming," "ossification" (Goddard et al. 2002; Hopwood 1973). In particular, "tunnel vision" happens when management emphasizes phenomena quantified in the performance measurement scheme, at the expense of unquantifiable or unconsidered aspects of the performance. "Sub optimization" occurs when key organizational objectives are compromised by the lack of congruence with targets for individual benefit offices (Ridgway 1956). "Measure fixation" occurs when the pursuit of success as measured, rather than as intended, becomes the main focus (Kerr 1975). "Misrepresentation" occurs when managers deliberately manipulate data under their control to show their organization's performance in the most advantageous light. This risk is more common when indicators are not measured in benchmarking and the outputs are self-referred (Flynn 1986).

Since the 2000s, many scholars have also started investigating the reasons behind the potential failures of measure results-based management, with a particular focus on the public sector (Eden and Hyndman 1999). They have confirmed the hypothesis that reliance on quantitative measures to monitor social phenomena can lead to several unintended consequences that may not only invalidate conclusions on public sector performance, but also negatively influence performance. Smith highlights that the problem of objectives that cannot be quantified is particularly acute in the public sector for three reasons:

(a) Stakeholders usually hold a large number of diverse objectives with respect to a public sector organization;
(b) Many important objectives in the public sector simply defy adequate quantification;
(c) It is a common feature of public sector services that the ramifications of their activities extend well beyond the immediate target of service delivery.

All these elements are also relevant to the healthcare sector, but with an additional specificity thanks to the role that clinicians play in the system. These professionals have a key role in creating value for patients by containing costs and improving quality, since they are responsible for about 75% of the costs incurred by healthcare organizations (Tjosvold and MacPherson 1996). Indeed healthcare organizations traditionally present a reverse hierarchy conceptual structure, in which key decisions are made by the employees (as physicians) in direct contact with patients, while senior management positions support and control their activities and try to orient their actions (Mosley 2014). Physicians are at the basis of the clinical service delivery and their performance is the primary determinant of the service value (quality/cost) delivered to the patient. In this perspective, the physicians' engagement becomes the keystone of improvement processes in the healthcare system.

10.2.3 Measures and Clinicians Engagement Process

To drive consistent improvement, the method to be adopted includes bottom-up strategies where the clinician's engagement process faces data analysis first: a structured platform to compare data should be then available. A transparent Performance Evaluation System comparing data in benchmarking and the use of effective tools to represent performance (dartboard and geographic maps) pointing out geographic variation and best practices are essential. Moreover public disclosure of data indeed raises concerns about outcomes and geographic variation (Hibbard et al. 2003) and this yields to a sort of "reputational competition" among professionals that captures their attention.

This evaluation process is occurring in most of the regions that have adopted IRPES, where governance systems and improvement targets are set considering the performance results monitored (Nuti et al. 2016).

Through this process all healthcare professionals and managers can be aware of their own results in benchmarking. However, this public comparison of results and the "naming and shaming" process are not enough to ensure change (Berwick 2003). A permanent community of practice should also be created to assure a trustworthy environment where professionals can systematically discuss their experience and the related data, receiving constructive feedback thanks to peer pressure. In addition, this approach actually enhances best practices and builds reputation among peers, sharing what good care looks like and what should be done to improve it (Nuti et al. 2016). Moreover, management staff should play a strategic role in shifting the focus of clinicians towards reducing unwarranted variation fostering a Population Medicine approach. Gray proposes this approach as a means of encouraging clinicians to focus on the entire pathway and not only on the clinical phases of which they are in charge. Clinicians are asked to share responsibility "to the population they serve, to the patients they never see, as well as to the patients they have treated or referred" (Gray 2013) as "public health professionals." This approach stops clinicians being responsible for a specific phase or ward and instead makes them jointly responsible for the network of services, the outcomes and the resources linked to a specific pathway.

In conclusion, in a Public Healthcare System, which pursues universal coverage and equity, health professionals, managers and policy makers should be engaged in a cultural change driven by performance measures. These should be presented in benchmarking with public disclosure pointing out geographic unwarranted variation. Moreover, these measures should be fully analyzed by a stable community of practitioners in order to identify and tackle barriers to reducing unwarranted variation, improvement and equity. This allows professionals and managers to share a joint accountability for both the outcomes and the costs of the care paths in which they are involved and not just for the patients they directly care for, the phases for which they are responsible, or the productive factors they manage.

10.3 The Myths of Measurement and Scale in Planning of Health Services

Marina Davoli, Chiara Marinacci and Renato Botti

10.3.1 Introduction

This paper focuses on Henry Mintzberg's considerations about the correlated myths of measurement and scale. According to Henry Mintzberg, measurement is mythologized by managers and policy makers, as well as by clinical professionals under the guidance of evidence-based medicine. Henry Mintzberg is challenging us by claiming that "too much of healthcare at both the administrative and clinical levels has been thrown out of balance by their obsessions with measurement." Recently, Greenhalgh et al. (2014) have identified five possible reasons for the crisis of the evidence-based movement:

1. The evidence-based "quality mark" has been misappropriated by vested interests;
2. The volume of evidence, especially clinical guidelines, has become unmanageable;
3. Statistically significant benefits may be marginal in clinical practice;
4. Inflexible rules and technology driven prompts may produce care that is management driven rather than patient centred;
5. Evidence-based guidelines often map poorly to complex multimorbidity.

It is clear, from the different contributions to the debate, that the weaknesses are not in the concept of evidence base itself, but rather in its application; Greenhalgh et al. highlight possible solutions in order to reduce the gap between evidence and practice. These solutions range from informed shared decision-making processes on the patient and clinical side to a less automatic approach in moving from measurement to judgment at the health policy level. Indeed, the right balance between measurement and judgment in managing resources for health service planning is the key issue on which we are focusing here.

10.3.2 Why Should We Measure?

Several international organizations have invested in the development of quality measurements, and comparative results have been used to enhance accountability, showing an improvement in levels of quality (Chassin et al. 2010).

In Italy too, we are witnessing a phase of increasing investments in measurement systems. Such investments are closely linked to the most recent challenges faced by our National Health Service (demographic and epidemiological transition, progress and introduction of new costly technologies, increasing health expectation of the population), which are also occurring in other contexts at the international level. This is causing pressure requiring mechanisms to ensure NHS sustainability, while maintaining its constitutive principles of equity and universality in the healthcare provision throughout the country. In the specific Italian case, the strategic option to address the challenge of sustainability was to carry out an in-depth review of health spending, initially leading to a generic reduction of resources aimed at achieving a balance between costs and revenues. In recent years, governmental authorities have been making an effort to review the organizational structure of health services in order to improve quality, appropriateness, efficiency and equity, in order to combine expenditure control with the optimization of its healthcare value for the population. Within this framework, the Italian Health Service is evolving towards a growing importance of measurement systems, both process and result-oriented, specifically to identify areas of inefficiency, inappropriateness and ineffectiveness of services and facilities, while monitoring equity in healthcare access and promoting continuous improvement of the healthcare organization. Consequently and by the same token, measurement systems are becoming a central instrument in the evaluation of health service management. Although quality measures and quality monitoring are a relatively recent exercise in Italy, there is already considerable evidence of its impact in improving healthcare quality (Pinnarelli et al. 2012; Nuti et al. 2012, 2013; Colais et al. 2013; Renzi et al. 2014).

10.3.3 What We Do Measure

The Italian National Health Service is based on the principles of universal coverage, social financing by general taxation and aims at creating an effective and uniform health system covering the entire population, irrespective of income or contributions, employment status or pre-existing health conditions.

Italian regions are responsible for providing healthcare to their residents, through local health units, while the central level is responsible for defining the essential levels of Healthcare (LEA) and monitoring their application to all citizens by the Regional Health Services.

The Ministry of Health is responsible for monitoring the provision of LEA at regional level, and the healthcare outcome at hospital and local health unit level, through the National Outcome Programme, developed by the National Agency for Regional Health Services. The regions adopt their own monitoring systems in order to measure compliance with LEA at local level. The different monitoring systems are described in a recent EU publication (Expert Group on Health Systems Performance Assessment 2016).

10.3.3.1 Monitoring the Provision of the Essential Levels of Health Care at Regional Level

The Permanent Committee for Monitoring the Provision of Essential Levels of Healthcare (LEA Committee) has been established within the Ministry of Health to assess homogenous LEA provision under appropriateness and efficiency conditions. It performs its mission through a system aimed at verifying LEA implementation and regional compliance with national regulations and State-Regions agreements related to LEA provision; the outcomes of this monitoring system enable regions (with the exception of the autonomous regions of Valle d'Aosta, Friuli Venezia Giulia and Sardegna, and the autonomous provinces of Trento and Bolzano) to fully receive their health fund. Among the tools specifically designed for assessment, the "LEA Grid" is a set of quantitative indicators, implemented for all Italian regions, designed to monitor the actual uniform provision of LEA within the Italian territory. The "LEA Grid" currently consists of a system of 32 indicators, calculated at regional level, monitoring regional performance in providing LEA and focusing on four levels of health care: prevention, outpatient and community care, hospital care and emergency care.

Among the main challenges related to LEA provision assessment is the capacity to translate the defined essential levels of care into measurable indicators. Moreover, some methodology limitations particularly affect the "LEA grid," resulting in a recent ongoing review of the evaluation system focusing on: (1) the need to describe analytically at each level of care, the individual qualifying attributes of the process through which it is provided; (2) the fact that, relying on regional syntheses, each LEA grid indicator does not take into account sources of geographical heterogeneity within the regions in the targeted service provision, which might result from the concurrent presence of sub-regional populations adequately cared for—or high performing providers—with groups or providers where LEA are not guaranteed. Nevertheless, it is worth mentioning the significant value of measurement in monitoring the performance of Regional Health Services according to LEA provision, as an objective way to evaluate system equity and promote its continuous improvement (Expert Group on Health Systems Performance Assessment 2016; Ministero della Salute 2015).

10.3.3.2 Measuring Outcome of Care at Hospital and Local Health Units Level

The main objectives of the National Outcome Programme (PNE) are benchmarking among health providers, useful in identifying potential critical organizational or clinical factors, and benchmarking among areas, for the evaluation of residents' health protection and equity in access to effective health care (Agenas 2015). PNE investigates the heterogeneity of access to health care across both geographical areas and hospitals, focusing on those healthcare interventions for which evidence of effectiveness is available. The outcome indicators measure the result of a healthcare process in terms of clinical outcomes (e.g. mortality, morbidity, hospitalizations). The process indicators measure the healthcare process adherence to the standards of evidence-based best clinical practice. For this reason, they are considered proxies for health outcomes and their predictability of clinical outcomes depends on the strength of recommendations and level of clinical evidence on which they were based.

10.3.4 Are Measurements Used for Management Purposes?

Progress in national measurement instruments was recently joined by their use as quality standards for important healthcare planning acts at the national level, aimed at optimizing both quality and efficiency of the system.

In this regard, it is worth mentioning the recent Regulation on Hospital Standards (Decree of the Minister of Health April 2, 2015, n. 70). It provides quantitative parameters for reorganizing hospital care into an integrated network system, aimed at reducing an extreme supply fragmentation, and improving safety and quality of the health care provided by public and private structures. A very limited minimum set of outcome indicators has been included among the required quality standards of each hospital in Italy. The standards have been chosen because of a sound evidence base and validity of the measures. Minimization of adverse outcomes of some surgical processes (30 days mortality after CABG surgery), or the maximization of outcomes affecting survival and quality of life of patients (PCI within 90 min in patients with AMI, and timely surgery for hip fractures) have been included.

Another recent example of measurement-based regulation has been included in the Law 28 December 2015, n. 208. All public hospitals, teaching hospitals, national trusts, and research hospitals are called upon to address critical points in both efficiency and effectiveness. The former is measured as the unbalance between revenues and expenses, while the latter is measured on the basis of a set of healthcare quality indicators included within the National Outcome Programme.

Finally, at regional level, more and more regions have introduced measurable quality standards to set up specific goals for the CEOs of their hospitals and healthcare units, linked to mechanisms for the evaluation of the management activity carried out, leading to possible resolution of contracts.

10.3.5 The Myth of Scale: Just a Matter of Cost Efficiency?

Henry Mintzberg challenges the myth of scale by saying that "Too much of the management of health care has come to be about using scale to reduce measurable costs at the expense of difficult-to-measure benefits, leading to economies of scale, rather that effectiveness of scale."

Indeed much of the discussion is strongly connected to the controversial issue of closing hospitals with low volume of activity. Besides efficiency and scale economy issues, in many clinical areas volume represents a process measure that proved to be significantly affecting effectiveness of interventions. The association between volume of activity and outcome was documented in several systematic reviews. A recent review of systematic reviews and empirical analysis of Italian data (Amato et al. 2013) showed a strong improvement in outcomes in the first part of the curve (from very low volumes to higher volumes) for the majority of the studied conditions. In some cases, the outcome improvement remains gradual or constant with the increasing volume of care, in others the analysis could identify the level of threshold values beyond which the outcome does not improve. However, we cannot identify a volume threshold on the basis of scientific evidence alone. A good knowledge of the relationship between treatment effectiveness and costs, the geographical distribution and the accessibility of healthcare services are necessary to choose the minimum volumes of care, under which specific health procedures in the NHS should not be provided.

10.3.6 Discussion

The number of quality measures has increased exponentially in the last decade and there is an open debate on balance and parsimony in measuring quality (Meyer et al. 2012).

We are aware that investing in measurement systems cannot be the only way to achieve performance improvement targets; in its recent editorial in JAMA, Berenson (2016) points to the emphasis on measurement given by health policy experts, as summarized by the popular quotation "if something cannot be measured, it cannot be improved," to share some reflections on the sole use of statistics to help improving performance. In this regard, he resumes Deming's cautioning arguments on measurement requirements to guide management decisions, observing that the most important data needed to manage are often unknown and unknowable. According to Berenson, the measurement requirement as being essential to management and improvement is a fallacy. Surely public reporting of performance has changed medical culture, leading to a growing acceptance that the quality of clinical practice does not depend on the unmeasurable "art of medicine." Comparative public performance using meaningful and accurate measures has led to quality improvements, as clinicians and hospitals reflect on their own comparative performance and seek to improve their public standing. In most clinical areas, however, we lack readily available measures to use as valid benchmarks to assess performance. Another major problem with the current concern with measurement, as the central route to improvement, is the assumption that if a quality problem is not being measured, it basically does not exist: an important example is diagnosis errors.

Related arguments are synthesized by Carroll (2015), on the specific issue of the increasing push to pay for quality and not quantity. Paying hospitals differently according to their performance relies on the mandatory capacity to validly differentiate between those who deserve higher payments and those who do not. Carroll discusses the adequacy of these capabilities and the bias of quality metrics, as related to things that clinicians and hospitals could not control. For instance, poor patients may be more likely to be readmitted to the hospital than wealthier patients, as might patients with substandard housing or low education, leading to the worry that safety net hospitals which care for low-income patients might appear, through no fault of their own, to be delivering lower quality care than those which do not. Some have argued that factors like individual patient race and socioeconomic status, insurance, education and home environment, play significant roles in readmission risk and that we might still be able to use these metrics to measure performance accurately, by adjusting for these factors. Much of this has been theoretically and empirically documented in the USA context where patient characteristics, outside of hospital's control, account for a large amount of the variation seen in readmissions, above and beyond the quality of the hospital's performance. Quality assessment systems often use the available data, mainly administrative information, instead of the data properly needed to measure quality, and consequently tend to penalize those hospitals already caring for the most disadvantaged patients. Trying to get more comprehensive information might make measurements more accurate, but could be too expensive. We then need a balance within the field of measurement, from a less accurate but systematic measure to a more "ad hoc" investigation to measure determinants of variation and change.

In conclusion, we argue that it is not just a question of measurement overload but it is mainly a question of selecting proper quality measures, differentiating the level of measurement (national, regional, local, organizational, etc.), and identifying the proper use of measurements. We suggest here some possible recommendations for a better balance between measurement and judgment:

- Choose quality standard measures assessing the quality and safety of the process of care delivery, based on critical evidence-based practices strongly related to health outcomes.
- Clearly separate external, independent quality measurement from internal measurement, within each organization, the former focused on outcome and value and the second focused on process analysis.
- Select measures taking into account the cost of data collection and reporting, relative to the measure's impact on quality, outcomes and costs.
- Establish a systematic process of data quality control and a systematic update of measures used, involving different stakeholders.
- Ensure transparency of methods and operational definitions, giving the possibility, for all the assessed administrations and/or providers, to replicate measures, and to define their own targets according to measures and clinical and/or organizational processes required to achieve them.
- Use measurement for different purposes, avoiding automatic applications:
  - Medical education and professional training.
  - Performance management.
  - Budget management.
  - Provider payment mechanisms including case-based payment.
  - Communication of entitlement to patients and their families.
  - Clinical audit and provider benchmarking.
  - Provider regulation and accreditation.

As far as the myth of scale is concerned, it is again a question of balance between measurement and judgment. Closing or reconverting hospitals require the appropriate consideration of numerous factors ("judgment"), including epidemiological context, geographical constraints and organization of outpatient and community services. The issue here is to ensure an adequate organization of the whole social health and proximity supply system; too often hospitals have been used inappropriately on behalf of other type of services for community care. In the inner areas of some Italian regions (Piemonte, Lombardia, Marche, Abruzzo), the process of reorganizing the hospital care system presented an opportunity to accelerate processes towards the ongoing improvement of outpatient and community care through a new healthcare organization, as, for example, improving proactive care models for patients (Agenzia per la Coesione Territoriale 2016). Empowering citizens, adopting telemedicine services and increasing home care might facilitate the humanization of the care process and bring services to the patients, rather than the opposite. Actually, we could falsify the myth of the economy of scale by saying that closing small hospitals, by itself, does not automatically reduce healthcare costs, but often requires more investment in better community care.

Eventually, reducing the gap between evidence and practice is a desirable aim for both patients and payers. Healthcare providers should offer their patients the highest possible quality, using the latest knowledge and most efficient technology, and healthcare funders should get the best possible value for their money.

The systematic measurement of selected quality standards and wise use of measurement for healthcare planning, rather than an automatic use of measurement, should be promoted in order to facilitate improvement of healthcare quality, efficiency and safety.

10.4 Performance Measurement in Health Care: What Should and What Shouldn't Be Measured

Giuseppe Iuliano, Gaetano Matonti, Paolo Tartaglia Polcini and Ettore Cinque

10.4.1 Introduction

Henry Mintzberg (2012a, b) highlights the difficulties in measuring performance in healthcare organizations because of the nature of their role in saving public health. "The problem with measurement is that, while the treatments exist in standard categories … their outcomes are often not standard, and therefore can be tricky to pin down by measurement. That is because we, as individual patients, are not standardized, and so our treatments have to be tailored to our individual needs and conditions" (Henry Mintzberg 2012a, b, p. 5). The myth of measurement is not totally convincing, but only the overly enthusiastic use in healthcare organizations.

The aim of this contribution is twofold. First (this section), taking into account the criticism of Henry Mintzberg about the measurement in health care, through the analysis of the main literature, this contribution will discuss the relevance and the usefulness of a measurement system in a healthcare organization. Second (next section), taking into account the need for a measurement system this contribution will discuss what should be measured and what should not in order to reduce the criticism highlighted by Henry Mintzberg.

Healthcare organizations are among the most complex in society, and they provide services to the general public and ensure that these services are provided in the best manner, in an efficient and effective way with regards to financial sustainability. Moreover, healthcare expenditure represents a major use of a nation's financial resources and has been growing rapidly over time. Factors such as the ageing population, the increased personal use of health care, and medical advances that have opened the way for more treatment options and diagnostics have contributed to a rise in the demand for health care. Increased pressures on healthcare resources have led policy makers, administrators and physicians to search for more efficient ways to deliver health services (Peacock et al. 2001). Efficiency improvements in the health sector, even in small amounts, can yield considerable savings of resources or expansion of services for the community.

Managing with patients is a collective and cooperative effort that requires continuous communication of performance data and is subject to emerging contingencies that require specific actions. Since patient responses to care can never be fully anticipated, treatment is never really routine. The healthcare system is further characterized by distributed decision-making by people with different perspectives. In performing these purposes, healthcare organizations manage with several human, technical and financial resources (Stahr et al. 2000), which are used in a series of processes aiming to improve the medical condition of the patient and contribute to healthier communities (Rivers and Boe 1999). Value for the patient is created by healthcare providers' combined efforts over the full cycle of care, and the benefits of any intervention for ultimate outcomes are related to the effectiveness of other interventions throughout the care cycle (Porter 2010). Finally, the National Health System of some countries (e.g. Italy, UK) is mostly tax-funded and financial resources attributed to healthcare organizations are related to their performances and results (Jommi et al. 2001).

To deal with the complexity of healthcare organizations, New Public Management (NPM) policies have been introduced into public health care across most OECD countries since the 1980s (Malmmose 2012).

Theory (e.g. Andrews 2013; Alonso et al. 2015) suggests that policies based on NPM may enhance the efficiency of public service delivery, such as healthcare provision. According to the NPM philosophy, performance measurement becomes a central concept for audit and overseeing bodies (Lapsley 2008; Gasper and Mkasiwa 2013) in doing their job.

With regard to the usefulness of a measurement system in a healthcare organization, in the literature, two points of view compete with each other.

The first one criticizes the measurement system because it distracts physicians from their mission. In more specific terms, some literature criticizes performance measurement in healthcare organizations because the overuse of the measurement systems may stress physicians. In fact, in adopting NPM philosophy, physicians become administrators (Jones 1999), and their jobs and results (performances) are stressed by the limited financial resources available for the healthcare system. Several researches have shown that physicians would like and need more stability, less administration and closer contact with patients and colleagues (Brorström and Nilsson 2008) which are in conflict with implementing new organization models and performance measurements (e.g. Mannion et al. 2007). Moreover, chief executives and directors in the health care in the UK are not motivated by financial rewards and personal reputation, but by more responsive service to patients, opportunity to increase staff moral and increased quality of results (Mannion et al. 2007). This approach is not consistent with the NPM that focuses on financial sustainability and effectiveness of healthcare organizations.

Vakkuri and Meklin (2006) highlight that methodologies, techniques, standards and indicators (Brown et al. 1993) were implemented in healthcare organizations by transposing them from private organizations, without considering the nature of these non-profit organizations. Probably, these methodologies are less suitable for healthcare organizations (Lapsley and Mitchell 1996) because of their organizational learning capacities, the specificity of their output, and/or the incomplete data systems (Vakkuri 2003).

Propper and Wilson (2003a, b) highlight that the risk of a measurement system is the misinterpretation and the misrepresentation of performances. In the U.S. healthcare system, performance measures and measurement have resulted in inappropriate care and have decreased the focus of hospitals on patient concerns and services (Powell et al. 2012). In the UK, performance measurement has caused long waiting lists (Propper and Wilson 2003a, b). Moreover, performance measures have resulted in manipulation of evidence (Gasper and Mkasiwa 2013).

Healthcare performance measurement systems are focused on the costs of care and limit the degree of freedom a physician has as a way to cut costs. In particular, Porter (ICHOM 2015, p. 32) highlights that physicians have to pay great attention to costs, to comply with the hospital budget. Spigelman (2006, p. 3) in discussing about the measurement of court performances (public sector), points out that not everything that counts can be counted and measured. Some matters can only be judged, in the sense that they can only be assessed in a qualitative way.

The second point of view, instead, supports the measurement systems in healthcarc organizations because it helps management in controlling efficiency, effectiveness and financial sustainability of these organizations.

Healthcare providers share a common goal: providing high-quality care to their patients. Measuring performance can help in understanding how well a healthcare organization is accomplishing this goal. A measurement system allows management for an analysis of where and what changes need to be made in order to improve performance and the quality of care provided (the focus is the patient, taking into account the financing system). Moreover, measuring performance also allows providers to understand what is working well and this information can be shared with other providers who can learn from these successes.

According to this point of view, explicit formal measures of performance are promoted all over the world as an important tool to improve organizational efficiency and effectiveness (Hood 1995; Halachmi 2012), because they encourage productivity, contribute to the legitimacy of the organization, stimulate learning processes and generate information that may enhance an organization's intelligence (de Bruijn and Van Helden 2007). In other words, a major part of the NPM purpose to implement management accounting and managerial performance measurements systems in these organizations in order to control costs and become market-oriented to meet patients' needs. At the same time, these systems make the healthcare organizations accountable for their measured performance and increasingly base resource allocation on performance. Thus, one of the core issues of NPM is the health system performance (and outcomes) measurement (Dunleavy et al. 2006) in order to increase value for patients and the public in general. Information (the output of a measurement system) plays a central role in the ability of a health system to secure improved health for its population. It can be used in many diverse ways, such as tracking public health, monitoring healthcare safety, determining appropriate treatment paths for patients, promoting professional improvement, ensuring managerial control and promoting the accountability of the health system to the public. Underlying all of these efforts performance measurement drives the decisions of different stakeholders (e.g. patients, clinicians, managers, governments and the public) (Smith et al. 2008). The fundamental role of a performance measurement system is to help stakeholders to make informed decisions (Smith et al. 2008, p. 1).

Based on the above, taking into account the organizational complexity, the particular output (outcome) and the financial sustainability of healthcare organizations, a performance measurement system should be needed in order to monitor their efficiency, effectiveness and financial sustainability. Probably, these healthcare organizations need specific measurement systems, taking into account the nature of the outcome and the specificity of the health services.

Measurement is an important part of any effort to improve the quality of healthcare systems, because measurement helps in understanding the change in organization and in management in order to improve the patient experience. Hibbard et al. (2005) state that most proponents of the public release of healthcare performance information believe that making this information public will increase healthcare providers' motivation to improve. The identification of reliable and scientifically valid performance measurement strategies would be of benefit to the policy makers and stakeholders (Hollingsworth and Street 2006). Inefficiency measures could be also incorporated into schemes designed to improve the performance of the healthcare system (Peacock et al. 2001).

Performance measurement also offers policy makers a major opportunity to secure health system improvement and accountability, enabling national priorities for health reform to be translated into organizational and individual objectives (Smith et al. 2008). Therefore, its role is to improve the quality of decisions made by all actors within the health system, including patients, practitioners, managers, governments at all levels, insurers and other payers, politicians, and citizens as financial supporters. According to this point of view, measurement of performance is vital for healthcare organizations and for the distinct nature of the financing system.

To conclude, performance measurement should measure performance and outcomes, enabling innovations in care and generating value for patients and society. Nevertheless, a measurement system should not exceed some limits as regards what is measured (scope of measurement) and how it is measured (level of measurement), because if the measurement is excessively stressed it can produce much more damage than benefit.

According to this point of view, the next section highlights what should and should not be measured.

10.4.2 What Should and What Should Not Be Measured

It is very important to measure the quality of healthcare systems. We can develop and use different types of measures, using data to evaluate the performance of health plans and healthcare providers.

Measures can take many forms. They assess care along the full continuum starting from the moment at which the patient enters the treatment to the time he/she leaves. Different measures are used in health care, generally they fall into four categories: (a) structure, (b) process, (c) outcome and (d) patient experience.

10.4.2.1 Structure Measures

There are three basic areas to consider: (1) Health Plan, when we assess the overall performance of providers in the network of a plan; (2) provider, when we assess the quality of a provider's facilities and/or his/her overall quality of care; (3) Healthcare Professional, when we assess the quality of care provided by an individual healthcare professional. Structure measures evaluate healthcare infrastructures, such as hospitals or doctor offices. These measures assess the structural characteristics, including facilities, personnel and organizational models (for example, we can ask if an intensive care unit has a critical care specialist on staff at all times).

Structural measures should be considered a key part of a suite of quality measures, but they should never be relied on as the exclusive measure of quality. Although structure measures provide essential information, it is important to note the limitations of these measures. For example, the fact that a hospital has the ability to perform certain functions does not capture whether or not these functions actually occur, nor does it capture whether those functions improve patient health.

Structure measures are necessary to provide essential information about a provider's ability and/or capacity to provide high-quality care, but they cannot measure the actual quality of the care.

10.4.2.2 Process Measures

Process measures are used to determine to what extent healthcare providers give patients specific high-quality services. They appreciate the ability of services provided to patients to be consistent with routine clinical care and with procedures or treatments that are known to improve health status or prevent future complications or health conditions.

Process measures, more than structural measures, have an immediate impact on healthcare providers, because they can provide actionable feedback to improve their actions and performance.

Even in this case, as in the previous one, however, over-reliance on process measures to track performance and to manage provider incentives can be problematic, for one main reason: process measures are not available for many key areas. For example, quality process measures for the cure of mental illness may not capture the true quality of the care provided.

10.4.2.3 Outcome Measures

Outcome measures evaluate patients' health as a result of the care they have received. More specifically, these measures look at the effects, either intended or unintended, that care has had on patients' health. For example, measures can answer the following question: what is the survival rate for patients who experience a heart attack? In fact, outcome measures frequently include traditional measures of survival (mortality), incidence of disease (morbidity), and health-related quality of life issues. The problem of these measures is that they do not assess the full extent of the patient's experience because they often do not incorporate patient-reported information about how satisfied they are with the healthcare services received. Another critical consideration is related to developing, evaluating and using outcome measures, because outcome parameters are often influenced also by social determinants, as well as critical differences in patient populations. In other words, outcomes are often the result of factors outside the control of the health system and for this reason using these types of indicators represents a critical activity. These problems are noticed, as we shall see later, not when we choose these measurement systems but in the operating mode and when we attribute meaning to them.

10.4.2.4 Patient Experience Measures

Patient experience measures provide feedback on patients' experiences of their care, including the social aspects of care. These measures assess many other aspects of care, ranging from the clarity and accessibility of information that doctors provide, to whether doctors tell patients about test results, to how quickly patients are able to get appointments for urgently needed care.

Administrative data are easy and cheap to collect, but they often cannot provide the appropriate level of detail to assess patient experience measures.

Electronic medical records are a useful key source of data for reporting patient experience measures. However, a lack of standardization across record systems can make it difficult to get these kinds of measures. Finally, while qualitative data such as patient surveys are important for measuring patient experience, they can be time-consuming and expensive to collect.

10.4.3 Concluding Remarks

Conclusively, it should be noted that every healthcare measurement process has to be based on some evidence. Measurement begins with clinical research that links a particular process, structure or outcome with health results of care or cure. Once an organization establishes what needs to be measured, related key indicators have to be identified and data must be collected to support that measure. This data comes from a variety of sources. Often, complex measures require data from more than one source. Some common sources of the data that are currently used to track quality measures include: administrative data, disease registries, medical records and qualitative data. The expanding use of system management medical records has the potential to transform the way data is collected, assessed and reported; as a result information about healthcare and health outcomes become more accurate, timely and useful.

Using measurement methods and techniques to improve health care is a new challenge. While the medical information system has made great strides in the development and application of a good measuring system over the last two decades, nevertheless there is still a lot of work to do. Quality measurement can be used to improve health care by preventing the overuse, underuse and misuse of healthcare services. It identifies what works properly in health care—and what does not—and drives improvement.

It is important to note that no single type of measure can give a complete representation of the quality of care that is provided or received. Rather, each type of measure addresses a key component of care. Furthermore, their usefulness is limited by the fact that measures are really significant only if joined with detailed information available solely in medical records, and this information is difficult and expensive to obtain.

In assessing the performance, measures will also have to consider that indicators which are not adequately composed could have the opposite effect than the one desired. This principle, known as Hawthorne effect (that descends directly from the Heisenberg uncertainty principle, where the observer/measurer can influence the observed/measured object), generates some intrinsic weaknesses in the performance measurement system. In addition, it should be noted that the main goal of measuring is to compare the performance by using the space-time coordinates. In fact, organizations compare performance over time with their own, or with similar organizations. From this point of view, it must be well known that the healthcare production systems can be standardized only to some extent: no two patients are identical and a therapeutic path can be assessed only in conjunction with the specific characteristics of the person being cured. So, measures have to be interpreted in the context of the specific circumstances in which the healthcare process is included.

The efficiency of the health system refers to the efficiency, effectiveness and financial sustainability, and from the economic perspective looks at the relationship between effects and expenditures. Performance measurement also offers policy makers a major opportunity to secure health system improvements and accountability, enabling national priorities for health reform to be translated into organizational and individual objectives. Therefore, its role is to improve the quality of decisions made by all actors within the health system, including patients, practitioners, managers, governments at all levels, insurers and other payers, politicians and citizens as financial supporters. According to this point of view, measurement of performance is vital for healthcare organizations also for the nature of the financing system. The case-based hospital reimbursement system, that paid healthcare providers with a fixed and centrally determined price for every procedure that they carried out (the Diagnosis-related Group), could lead to quality competition between hospitals and improve patient outcomes. Healthcare providers, in fact, were paid by the number of patients they were able to attract, in a market that only allowed healthcare providers to differentiate themselves on quality rather than price. Given that, the healthcare providers (in Italy the Hospitals and the "Aziende Sanitarie Locali") were rewarded for increasing their volume (in order to increase financing), taking into account the quality of the healthcare services. Patients were attracted by high-quality health services and by good outcomes. To provide high-quality services, healthcare providers should assess their healthcare processes (what they do), identifying the resources used to deliver their output, in the light of efficiency, effectiveness and financial sustainability goals. According to this point of view, considering the limited financing resources available for healthcare providers, the quality of the healthcare system may be assessed by a performance measurement system which may provide governments, users and everyone else involved in this system with appropriate information about the state of their healthcare system.

As a consequence, an adequate measurement system (without obsessions on measurement) is a precondition of an effective healthcare system. Measures (especially accounting measures of financial sustainability) are an essential tool to ensure that a healthcare system can monitor its own ability to survive on time and to continue to provide patients with cure and care.

Finally, as strictly related to measurement aspects, a quick look at new developments which may come from activity-based costing methods in the healthcare field is needed. New methods are in a phase of experimentation within a Harvard University research project which widens the observation of the whole healthcare processes and more specifically identifies their related costs, to be compared with related benefits. The patient care cycle starts from the first pre-operation appointment and ends one year after the day of surgery (Kaplan and Porter 2011). Extending the analysis to one year from the care allows to measure all aspects, even the social outcome and patient experience measures. It is believed that this longer period is adequate to assess any surgical complications that may arise in the short term so this creates more meaningful performance measures.

10.5 A Complex Approach to Measurement in Health Care

Francesco Bevere and Paola Adinolfi

10.5.1 Introduction

Over the years, the myth of measurement has characterized the development of the healthcare system. At least two phenomena stand out in this regard. On the one hand, the worsening financial sustainability of health systems, which has resulted in a greater focus on the ability of health organizations to manage the resource available more effectively and efficiently (Birch et al. 2015), and on the other hand, the control-obsessed approach promoted by the legislator in the aftermath of the business-oriented reforms addressing the health system (Verbeeten and Speklé 2015). Some empirical studies have pointed out how the marked measurement-oriented approach, not integrated by an assessment-oriented approach, has prevented meaningful and tangible improvements in the outcome of healthcare organizations. Measuring systems have been interpreted as superstructures that, instead of subsidizing managerial decisions, introduce additional rigidity and organizational inertia and, therefore, they often have proved to be a source of resistance to change (Aryankhesal et al. 2015). In this perspective, the myth of measurement has resulted in a "management-by-objectives" unable to reflect and embrace the complexity typical of healthcare organizations.

Common practice shows that measurement has rarely been combined with staff assessment, as indicated in the "performance plans." "Performance plans," imposed by law, have been usually introduced top-down by the strategic apex of organizations, without involving middle managers. Due to the lack of synergy between measurements and human resource evaluation (and, more broadly, human resource management), measuring systems have not been able to provide substance to the "performance plans," which are mostly incapable of stimulating the implementation of strategies and the improvement of effectiveness and sustainability over time. The measurements have been used for feeding the information needs of a bureaucracy unable to identify and reward the contribution of individuals to organizational performance, thus being relegated to an aseptic and sterile exercise. Typically a fragmented approach has been followed, focused on the measurement of single departments or sectors: administrative, managerial, organizational, clinical, all separated from each other and independently of the strategic mission of the reference organization. This approach has not favoured the identification of indicators able to mediate and create a link among the various areas of the health care and the different components of the performance, determining, for example, a separation between the often negative assessment of the economic and financial performance of hospital sectors characterized by high levels of clinical complexity and the results achieved, most of the times brilliantly, in terms of effectiveness of diagnostic and therapeutic intervention. This approach has also prevented an appropriate evaluation of university hospitals, able to adapt the measuring mechanisms to the complex missions carried out by these important scientific communities.

Further consequences of the myth of measurement in decision-making and performance relate to the problems of "measurement fixation," "tunnelling," "myopia" and "quantification privileging" (Mannion and Braithwaite 2012). In other words, the obsession with control determines the presence of prejudices and bias, which in turn translate into significant constraints to management activities, influencing the decision-making of health managers.

10.5.2 The Myth of Measurement and the Spending Review

Most of the problems above mentioned stem from an acritical and simplistic approach to measurement. This is particularly evident when looking at the effects of measuring without assessing as regards the implementation of spending review policies.

Normally, one of the first cost items to be addressed by the axe of cost-cutting policies in the health sector is the staff. Taking into consideration that staff accounts for about 2/3 of the budget of healthcare organizations, and that in the public sector there is a natural trend to increase staff, in most developed countries restrictive manpower policies have been implemented, affecting both medical and support staff. It is interesting to note that this type of linear intervention affects situations in which there is either staff surplus or staff shortage, on the one hand cutting costs but, on the other, creating irreparable imbalances in the operating processes.

If there is a staff surplus, cost-cutting actions, because linear, may still result in a surplus. Normally, such residual staff surplus is not offset by investing in space and equipment, which would offer the possibility of boosting the productivity of clinicians and technicians. In fact, in the absence of a culture of evaluation rather than measurement, organizations usually do not assess the costs of idle space, unused equipment and staff, not recognizing that unused capacity costs much less than unused staff. The obvious consequence is their inability to manage excess capacity and to optimize the productivity of the most valuable assets of the healthcare system, i.e. staff.

If, conversely, there is a situation of under-staffing, simplistically linear cost-cutting promotes excessive and harmful staff exploiting, in an attempt to compensate for lower productivity. Shortening patient visit time will inevitably affect service quality, with negative consequences on patient safety. As an example, Kaplan and Haas (2014), in an article published in the Harvard Business Review titled "How Not to Cut Health Costs," estimated that, in the case of chronic kidney disease, the reduction of the standard visit duration by 15 min produces savings which are only 1% of the additional costs incurred because of the inappropriateness of the service provided: in fact, if the time for medical front-end counselling is reduced, dialysis is usually started sub-optimally (with a catheter rather than with a fistula or a graft), resulting in a negative impact on life expectancy and complications which the patient is not able to co-manage.

If healthcare providers are not able to meet healthcare needs by stressing clinician/technician productivity, they tend to resort to alternative solutions, such as temporary work agencies, HS-covered external specialist centres, and internal subcontracting. We are talking, in any case, of solutions that have higher costs than directly employing staff. In particular, internal subcontracting, in addition to costing much more than employing ordinary staff, has negative effects on safety, because of the excess of stress placed on healthcare staff.

The myth of measurement has also affected management decisions, addressing the purchase of goods and services. While some interventions, such as reducing the number of contracting authorities and centralizing purchases, may be reasonable, a linear approach is not beneficial in this case either, because of a narrow focus on the cost of single items that does not take into account their use over a patient's complete cycle of care. As an example, the price paid for the purchase of bone cement varies greatly across hospitals, but the type of more expensive bone cement may be premixed antibiotic cement or hand-mixed cement, linked to reduction in the need for antibiotics or in the amount of cement used, with a positive impact on the overall costs of the process (Kaplan and Haas 2014).

These examples provide evidence of an exaggerated and simplistic approach to measurement in the management of health care, which is unrelated to the organization of resources and the quality of outcomes. It is necessary to acknowledge that to reinvigorate the sustainability of the health system, the only effective approach involves in-depth analysis of the processes involved in treating each medical condition, and identifying (also through benchmarking) best practices including the best combination of resources for each complete cycle of care.

Organizations or individual professionals often tend to take care paths for granted, without questioning them (although these will differ greatly among various organizations and even within the same organization). This precludes the identification, through experimental evidence-based studies, of what works best in specific contexts, of innovative connections between unconnected resources that would appear under-utilized in the light of a new cultural framework, a frame that goes beyond the traditional idea of the typical industrial economy value chain, adopting instead a more complex approach, according to which all the parties involved form a value-generating system, and, ultimately, a health-generating system.

10.5.3 An Integrative Approach to Health Measurement and Management

In addition to the points so far discussed, the myth of measurement has produced a further negative effect in the health system. In their obsessive focusing on costs based on the financial measurement of clinical performance, healthcare providers have typically neglected to focus on quality and security of healthcare, thus neglecting the risk of medical mistakes, which is a very significant issue. Referring just to Italy, an analysis of the history of accidents and reports published by insurance companies and regional bodies, based on data collected by health providers that have adopted "risk management" strategies, shows that, in the face of a slow decrease in medical malpractice, albeit with differences between North and South, there has been a steady increase in medical error-related costs and an increasingly widespread practice of the so-called defensive medicine.

It seems quite urgent to tackle the problem of defensive medicine and medical error in a radical and thorough manner. To this end, beyond the actions recommended by the law (including the introduction of clinical risk units as enforced by the latest Italian Stability Law), it is essential that risk assessment becomes an integral part of financial evaluations carried out within the management control cycle.

Despite the growing sensitivity on the issue of expenditure control and health risk, solutions addressing the problem in an integrated manner are yet to be found. Currently, the available supply is mainly advisory and is confined to: staff training on costs, risk and quality issues; financial analysis aimed at a better recognition of the benefits produced by the diagnostic-related groups; process certifications based on IT modelling; document management procedures aimed at better legal protection.

When going beyond mere document management protocols, inspired by a defensive administrative approach—which adds to the defensive medicine one—the typical approach is aimed at identifying the "best practice" for specific procedures, or related to specific risk management aspects. In most cases, there is acceptable compliance with one or more "best practice" models, but also a dramatic drop in reliability and consistency when evaluating the process on the whole. Even when managing to achieve full application of the entire treatment process developed in the literature with the input of the relevant national and international scientific associations, there is hardly a context-specific scope of application, involving ICT-based tools able to create the necessary interconnections across the various clinical and health information systems involved, and promote the analysis of critical areas and possible innovative connections that include all the assets and the subjects involved in the value chain. To allow for an integrated evaluation of costs, risks and outcomes.

In order to take a positive new path pursuing effectively and sustainably the problem of healthcare expenditure in the regional health systems, it is necessary to adopt an integrated approach that, overcoming the myth of measurement, would lead to the achievement of key goals in the rethinking of health management. This first entails attaining the development of innovative tools for the analysis and formal modelling of social healthcare processes, in order to produce integrated (and even inter-organizational) paths featuring a flexibility capable of accommodating, on the one hand, the established scientific references and, on the other, the local and structural variables related to individual patients, in a complex perspective in which all actors (including the patient and his/her family, as well as suppliers) are part of a process of creation of health as a value. These tools need to adopt standardized and easy to use/adapt protocols consistent with national and European guidelines regarding interoperability. To reach such a goal, it is essential to adopt patient-based cost evaluation models, i.e. based on process, activity-based methods capable of replacing the traditional top-down measurement techniques.

All this would not lead to significant results without the presence of risk assessment models taking into account the various steps of the healthcare processes. Such models could be derived from algorithms used in other fields, according to the principles of reliability science, but specifically adapted to the healthcare setting. Obviously, it is essential to ensure a validation of the algorithms, through a comparison with the data available referring to past management (i.e. accident timeline), in order to define a risk score for the processes. Moreover, it is necessary to develop tools to help in choosing the optimal path, based on measurable indicators of cost, risk and outcome; similarly, the implementation of monitoring tools of diagnostic and care paths is essential, in order to track protocol adherence and provide real-time feedback on deviations and possible alternatives, giving immediate indications on costs/risks/outcomes. It might also be useful to create a national database of risks, costs and outcomes of clinical processes, interconnected with international databases, with indications on general technical–legal–regulatory aspects and on update and access procedures for healthcare staff.

These innovations can only be developed and designed involving the whole organizations and, therefore, involving the main actors of each organization and citizens as users of the services.

When the culture of measurement reaches this level of maturity, we will be able to have a dynamic dashboard of indicators truly reflecting the levels of complexity that the health system has reached over the years. To be used with judgment.

References

Agenas (2015) Programma Nazionale Esiti http://95.110.213.190/PNEed15/index.php. ultimo accesso 1 luglio 2016

Agenzia per la coesione territoriale (2016) http://www.agenziacoesione.gov.it/it/arint/. ultimo accesso 1 luglio 2016

Alonso JM, Clifton J, Díaz-Fuentes D (2015) The impact of new public management on efficiency: an analysis of Madrid's hospitals. Health Policy 119(3):333–340

Amato L, Colais P, Davoli M, Ferroni E, Fusco D, Minozzi S, Moirano F, Sciattella P, Vecchi S, Ventura M, Perucci CA (2013) Volume and health outcomes: evidence from systematic reviews and from evaluation of Italian hospital data. Epidemiol Prev 37(2-3 Suppl 2):1–100

Andrews R (2011) NPM and the search for efficiency. In: Christensen T, Lægreid P (eds) The Ashgate research companion to new public management. Ashgate, Farnham, pp 281–294

Aryankhesal A, Sheldon TA, Mannion R, Mahdipour S (2015) The dysfunctional consequences of a performance measurement system: the case of the Iranian national hospital grading programme. J Health Serv Res Policy 20(3):138–145

Berenson RA (2016) If you can't measure performance, can you improve it? JAMA 315(7):645–646

Berwick DM (2003) Improvement, trust, and the health care workforce. Qual Saf Health Care 12 (6):448–452

Bevan G, Hood C (2006) What's measured is what matters: targets and gaming in the English public health care system. Publ Adm 84(3):517–538

Birch S, Murphy GT, MacKenzie A, Cumming J (2015) In place of fear: aligning health care planning with system objectives to achieve financial sustainability. J Health Serv Res Policy 20 (2):109–114

Bouckaert G, Balk W (1991) Public productivity measurement: Diseases and cures. Public Prod Manage Rev 15(2):229–235

Briers M, Hirst M (1990) The role of budgetary information in performance evaluation. Account Organ Soc 15(4):373–398

Brorström B, Nilsson V (2008) Does organization matter? A study of physicians' ideal organization. Financ Acc Manag 24(2):193–206

Brown GA, Collins R, Thornton DB (1993) Professional judgment and accounting standards. Acc Organ Soc 18(4):275–289

Carroll A (2015) We need to use better data to measure quality. Accessible in https://newsatjama.jama.com/2015/10/07/jama-forum-we-need-to-use-better-data-to-measure-quality. ultimo accesso 1 luglio 2016

Chassin MR, Loeb JM, Schmaltz SP, Wachter RM (2010) Accountability measures–using measurement to promote quality improvement. N Engl J Med 363(7):683–688. doi:10.1056/NEJMsb1002320

Colais P, Pinnarelli L, Fusco D et al (2013) The impact of a pay-for-performance system on timing to hip fracture surgery: experience from the Lazio Region (Italy). BMC Health Serv Res 7 (13):393

Cooper Z, Gibbons S, Jones S, McGuire A (2011) Does hospital competition save lives? Evidence from the English NHS patient choice reforms. Econ J 121:F228–F260. doi:10.1111/j.1468-0297.2011.02449.x

Crivellini M, Galli M (2016) Sanità e salute: due storie diverse. Sistemi sanitari e salute nei paesi industrializzati. Franco Angeli, Milano

de Bruijn H, Van Helden GJ (2007) A plea for dialogue driven performance based management systems: evidence from the Dutch public sector. Financ Acc Manag 22(4):405–423

Dunleavy P, Margetts H, Bastow S, Tinkler J (2006) New public management is dead: long live digital-era governance. J Public Adm Res Theory 16(3):467–494

Eden R, Hyndman N (1999) Performance measurement in the Uk public sector: poisoned chalice or Holy Grail? optimum. J Public Sector Manage 29(1):9–15

Expert Group on Health Systems Performance Assessment (eds) (2016) SO WHAT? Strategies across Europe to assess quality of care. Luxembourg Publication Office of the EU, 2016. Accessibile in http://ec.europa.eu/health/systems_performance_assessment/docs/sowhat_en.pdf. ultimo accesso 1 luglio 2016

Ferreira A, Otley D (2009) The design and use of performance management systems: an extended framework for analysis. Manage Acc Res 20(4):263–282

Flynn N (1986) Performance measurement in public sector services. Policy Polit 14(3):389–404

Gasper F, Mkasiwa T (2013) Managing performance or legitimacy? The case of Tanzanian local government authorities. J Acc Emerg Econ 5(4):424–456

Goddard M, Davies HTO, Dawson D, Mannion R, McInnes F (2002) Clinical performance measurement: Part 2—avoiding the pitfalls. J R Soc Med 95(11):549–551

Gopal K, Patrícia Moura e Sá P (2003) Sustaining health care excellence through performance measurement. Total Qual Manage Bus Excellence 14(3):269–289. doi:10.1080/1478336032000046607

Gray M (2013) Perspectives. The Lancet 382:200–201

Greenhalgh T, Howick J, Maskrey N (2014) Evidence Based Medicine Renaissance Group. Evidence based medicine: a movement in crisis? BMJ 348:g3725. doi:10.1136/bmj.g3725

Halachmi A (2012) Mandated performance measurement: a help or a hindrance? Nat Prod Rev 18 (2):59–67

Hibbard JH, Stockard J, Tusler M (2003) Does publicizing hospital performance stimulate quality improvement efforts? Health Aff 22:84–94

Hibbard JH, Stockard J, Tusler M (2005) Hospital performance reports: impact on quality, market share, and reputation. Health Aff 24(4):1150–1160

Hollingswort B, Street A (2006) The market for efficiency analysis of health care organizations. Health Econ 15:1055–1059

Hood C (1995) The "new public management" in the 1980s: variations on a theme. Acc Organ Soc 20(2):93–109

Hood C (2002) Control, bargains, and cheating: the politics of public-service reform. J-PART 12 (3):309–332

Hopwood AG (1973) An accounting system and managerial behaviour. Saxon House, Lexington, Mass

ICHOM, International Consortium of Health Outcomes Measurement (2015) What matters most: patient outcomes and the transformation of health care. Available at www.ichom.org/file-library/. Accessed 12 May 2016

Jommi C, Cantù E, Anessi-Pessina E (2001) New funding arrangements in the Italian National Health Service. Int J Health Plann Manage 16:347–368. doi:10.1002/hpm.641

Jones SC (1999) Developing financial accountability in British acute hospitals. Financ Acc Manag 15(1):1–20

Kaplan RS, Cooper R (1988) Make cost right: make the right decisions. Harvard Bus Rev 66 (5):96–103

Kaplan RS, Haas DA (2014) How not to cut health care costs. Harvard Bus Rev 92(11):116–122

Kaplan RS, Porter ME (2011) The big idea: how to solve the cost crisis in health care. Harward Bus Rev 89(9):46–52, 54, 56–61 passim

Kerr S (1975) On the folly of rewarding A, while hoping for B. Acad Manage J 18(4):769–783

Lapsley I (2008) The NPM agenda: back to the future. Financ Acc Manag 24(1):77–96

Lapsley I, Mitchell F (1996) The accounting challenge: performance measurement in the private and public sectors. In: Lapsley I, Mitchell F (eds) Accounting and performance measurement. Issues in the private and public sectors. Paul Chapman, London

Le Grand J, Bartlett W (eds) (1993) Quasi-markets and social policy. Macmillan, London

Malmmose M (2012) The role of management accounting in new public management reforms: implications in a socio-political HEALTH Care context. PhD Dissertation: Submitted to Business and Social Sciences, Aarhus University in Partial Fulfillment of the PhD Degree in Economics and Business. Available on the internet at https://www.google.it/url?sa=t&rct=j&q=&esrc=s&source=web&cd=29&ved=0ahUKEwiXh6vOwq3NAhXHkywKHd7-B204FBAWCGQwCA&url=http%3A%2F%2Fpure.au.dk%2Fportal%2Ffiles%2F51069575%2FMargit_Malmmose_PhD_Thesis.pdf&usg=AFQjCNEJCoUxjeddJq64-RbGe_4QfkZ2lA&sig2=Sz6CSDXbKKRTjHtJ6t-Wqw&bvm=bv.124272578,d.d24. Accessed 16 June 2016

Mannion R, Braithwaite J (2012) Unintended consequences of performance measurement in health care: 20 salutary lessons from the English National Health Service. Int Med J 42(5):569–574

Mannion R, Goddard M, Bate A (2007) Aligning incentives and motivations in health care: the case of earned automomy. Financ Acc Manag 23(4):401–420

Meyer GS, Nelson EC, Pryor DB, James B, Swensen SJ et al (2012) More quality measures versus measuring what matters: a call for balance and parsimony. BMJ Qual Saf 21:964–968. doi:10.1136/bmjqs-2012-001081

Ministero della Salute (2015) Rapporto annuale sull'attività di ricovero ospedaliero (Dati SDO 2014). http://www.salute.gov.it/portale/documentazione/p6_2_2_1.jsp?lingua=italiano&id=2397. ultimo accesso 1 luglio 2016

Mintzberg H (2012a) Managing the Myths of health care. World Hospital Health Service 48(3):4–7

Mintzberg H (2012b) Managing the myths of health care. Word Hosp Health Serv 48(3):4–7

Mkasiwa TA, Gasper AF (2014) Complexities in performance measurement and the reaction of actors: the case of Tanzania. J Financ Acc 2(3):41–50

Mosley D (2014) Supervisory management. Cengage Learning, Hampshire

Normann R (2001) Reframing business: when the map changes the landscape. Wiley, Chichester

Nuti S, Seghieri C, Vainieri M, Zett S (2012) Assessment and improvement of the Italian health care system: first evidence from a pilot national performance evaluation system. J Healthc Manage 57(3):182–198

Nuti S, Seghieri C, Vainieri M (2013) Assessing the effectiveness of a performance evaluation system in the public health care sector: some novel evidence from the Tuscany region experience. J Manage Gov 17:59–69. doi:10.1007/s10997-012-9218-5

Nuti S, Vola F, Bonini A, Vainieri M (2016) Making governance work in the health care sector: evidence from a "natural experiment" in Italy. Health Econ Policy Law 11(1):17–38

Peacock S, Chan C, Mangolini M, Johansen D (2001) Techniques for measuring efficiency in health services. Productivity commission staff working paper, July. Available on the internet at https://www.google.it/url?sa=t&rct=j&q=&esrc=s&source=web&cd=2&cad=rja&uact=8&ved=0ahUKEwjdyszknq_NAhWJ3CwKHfjsAkgQFggxMAE&url=http%3A%2F%2Fwww.pc.gov.au%2Fresearch%2Fsupporting%2Fmeasuring-health-services%2Ftmeihs.pdf&usg=AFQjCNEC-zsZ5Vy_59p1_GVY542eAV5YKQ&sig2=qP1MdElarAR618SpsL6s8A. Accessed 16 June 2016

Pinnarelli L, Nuti S, Sorge C et al (2012) What drives hospital performance? The impact of comparative outcome evaluation of patients admitted for hip fracture in two Italian regions. BMJ Qual Saf 21(2):127–134

Porter ME (2010) What is value in health care? New Engl J Med 363(23):2477–2481

Powell AA, White KM, Partin MR, Halek K, Christianson JB, Neil B, Hysong SJ, Zarling EJ, Bloomfield HE (2012) Unintended consequences of implementing a national performance measurement system into local practice. J Gen Intern Med 27(4):405–412

Propper C, Wilson D (2003a) The use and usefulness of performance measures in the public sector. Oxf Rev Econ Pol 19(2):250–267

Propper C, Wilson D (2003b) The use and usefulness of performance measures in the public sector. Oxford Rev Econ Policy 19(2):250–267

Renzi C, Asta F, Fusco D, Agabiti N, Davoli M, Perucci CA (2014) Does public reporting improve the quality of hospital care for acute myocardial infarction? Results from a regional outcome evaluation program in Italy. Int J Qual Health Care 26(3):223–230

Ridgway VF (1956) Dysfunctional consequences of performance measurements. Adm Sci Q 1 (2):240–247

Rivers P, Boe S (1999) Aligning information systems for effective total quality management implementation in health care organisations. Total Qual Manage 10(2):281–289

Shaw C (2003) How can hospital performance be measured and monitored? World Health Organization Office. Available on the internet at http://www.euro.who.int/document/e82975.pdf. Accessed on 16 May 2016

Smith P (1995) On the unintended consequences of publishing performance data in the public sector. Int J Public Admin 18(2):277–310

Smith PC, Mossialos E, Papanicolas I (2008) World Health Organization (eds) Performance measurement for health system improvement: experiences, challenges and prospects. Available on the internet at https://www.google.it/url?sa=t&rct=j&q=&esrc=s&source=web&cd=

1&ved=0ahUKEwjc4aWm3KTNAhWBvBQKHZlwBaQQFgghMAA&url=http%3A%2F%2Fwww.who.int%2Fmanagement%2Fdistrict%2Fperformance%2FPerformanceMeasurementHealthSystemImprovement2.pdf&usg=AFQjCNGwnV8YSGpsjDIX0lsxzZJO9E28uQ&sig2=SPZdORQ-06HZXmNzc1Beug&bvm=bv.124272578,d.d24. Accessed 13 June, 2016

Spigelman J (2006) Measuring court performance. J Judicial Adm 16(2):69. Available at SSRN: http://ssrn.com/abstract=1806782, pp 1–41

Stahr H, Bulman B, Stead M (2000) The excellence model in the health sector: sharing good practice. Kingsham Press, Chichester

Tjosvold D, MacPherson RC (1996) Joint hospital management by physicians and nursing administrators. Health Care Manage Rev 21(3):43–54

Vainieri M, Nuti S (eds) (2015) Governance e meccanismi di incentivazione nei sistemi sanitari regionali, IInd edn. Mulino, Bologna

Vakkuri J (2003) Research techniques and their use in managing non profit organizations. An Illustration of DEA analysis in NPO environments. Financ Acc Manag 19(3):243–264

Vakkuri J, Meklin P (2006) Ambiguity in performance measurement: a theoretical approach to organisational uses of performance measurement. Financ Acc Manag 22:235–250. doi:10.1111/j.0267-4424.2006.00401

Verbeeten FH, Speklé RF (2015) Management control, results-oriented culture and public sector performance: empirical evidence on new public Management. Organ Stud 36(7):953–978

WHO (2010) Report on the burden of endemic health care-associated infection worldwide. WHO Document Production Services, Geneva

Chapter 11
Myth #8: The Myth of Scale

Rocco Palumbo, Gabriella Piscopo, Maria Grazia Sampietro, Marcello Martinez, Luigi Moschera, Gianluigi Mangia, Daniela Scaramuccia and Alberto Calvo

11.1 Reframing Scale: From Reductionism to Complexity

Rocco Palumbo, Gabriella Piscopo and Maria Grazia Sampietro

11.1.1 Introduction

Elephants have bigger brains than humans, but less interconnected and, consequently, less developed ones (adapted from Morgan 1986).

The quest for measurement in health care paved the way for the myth of scale, which ultimately assumes that higher dimensions are associated with better organizational performance. Moreover, it pretends that organizational design is a simple issue, which could be dealt with through reductionism (Gharajedaghi 1999). Organizations are conceived as engines (Morgan 2016): human resources are easily replaceable and performance is predictable (Thiétart and Forgues 1997). This

---

The original version of this chapter was revised: Affiliations and email ID were updated. The erratum to this chapter is available at https://doi.org/10.1007/978-3-319-53600-2_15

R. Palumbo (✉) · G. Piscopo
Department of Management and Innovation Systems, University of Salerno,
Via Giovanni Paolo II, no. 132, Fisciano, Salerno 84084, Italy
e-mail: rpalumbo@unisa.it

L. Moschera
Department of Business and Economics, University of Naples Parthenope, Naples, Italy

D. Scaramuccia · A. Calvo (✉)
Value Partners Management Consulting S.P.a, Via Vespri Siciliani, 9, Milan 20146, Italy
e-mail: alberto.calvo@valuepartners.com

P. Adinolfi and E. Borgonovi (eds.), *The Myths of Health Care*,
https://doi.org/10.1007/978-3-319-53600-2_11

approach produces a veil of ignorance, which diminishes the meaningfulness of organizational science. Sticking to this, several scholars have found that organizational dimensions are able to affect organizational performance in terms of efficiency (Chadwick et al. 2004), effectiveness (Sahin and Ozcan 2000), and adoption of innovative technologies (Irwin et al. 1998). However, this reductionist reasoning does not capture the real nature of healthcare organizations.

In fact, three sources of complexity affect the design and functioning of healthcare organizations: (1) macro (scenario) sources: changes of social, demographic, and epidemiologic determinants generate momentous drawbacks on health needs, which inspire the work of healthcare organizations (Borgonovi 2008); (2) meso (context) sources: healthcare organizations show deep interdependence with other entities operating in social care and public health, sharing responsibilities and liabilities with them (Borgonovi 2007); (3) micro (organizational) sources: healthcare professionals are connected with each other by weak ties when cooperating to achieve an increased ability to meet the health needs of the population served (responsiveness); at the same time, they strive to maintain their own distinctiveness (Orton and Weick 1990).

The complexity perspective encourages us to reconceptualize the idea of performance in the health sector. Anderson's article More is Different (1972) is the manifesto of the complexity revolution against reductionism. "A complex system is not merely constituted by the sum of its components, but by the intricate relationships between these components. In 'cutting up' a system, the analytical method destroys what it seeks to understand" (Cilliers 1998, p. 2). From this point of view, healthcare organizations should be considered as brains rather than engines. This metaphor suggests that healthcare organizations should be dealt with as organic, dynamic, living, and social systems (Capra 2002), where the human and the technological dimensions interact.

11.1.2 Moving Beyond the Myth of Scale: Exploratory Insights

In line with these arguments, some empirical evidence invites us to go beyond the myth of scale, and to support the role of complexity in health care. The case of caesarean sections (C-sections) in Italy helps in making the point. The incidence of C-sections is a widely accepted performance measure to assess the quality of

M. G. Sampietro
National Social Security Institute, Rome, Italy

G. Mangia
Department of Economics, University of Naples "Federico II", Naples, Italy

M. Martinez (✉)
Department of Economics, Università degli Studi della Campania "Luigi Vanvitelli", Caserta, Italy
e-mail: marcello.martinez@unicampania.it

healthcare systems all over the world. In fact, the rate of C-sections is assumed to imply poorer quality of care and higher inappropriateness in the access to health services (Agenas 2008). Among other things, Italy shows a high risk of inappropriateness, disclosing an average rate of C-sections of 25.69%, which significantly exceeds the 15% threshold suggested by the WHO (1994).

A recent assessment (PNE 2015) pointed out that negative performance was more common in small healthcare facilities, which performed less than 1000 births per year. On the other hand, higher performances were consistently achieved by larger facilities, which performed more than 1500 births per year. This data—at first sight—seems to confirm that scale played a significant role in affecting organizational performance. However, a more insightful analysis of the national assessment suggests that three small healthcare facilities performing less than 800 births per year were found to report a C-section rate ranging from 6.06 to 7.7%, in line with international standards.

There is a possible explanation for these diverging findings concerning the relationship between organizational dimensions and performance: a more complex reality lies behind the rising number of C-sections, which could not be affected by the myth of scale.

Indeed, the adoption of a complex framework allows us to shed light on the dynamics and the variables which compound the risk factors and the socio-demographic determinants which are contemplated by traditional assessment tools. In fact, health outcomes are deeply affected by contingency issues, as well as by non-linear relationships between patients, carers and providers, both within and outside the healthcare facilities, which pave the way for unexpected and unpredictable effects. In specific social contexts the dominant thinking incites to perceive the C-section as an elective choice for patients, due to either the clinical approach of the childbirth process as promoted by providers or the insufficient information affecting users, who are usually unaware of alternative options. At the moment, medical dominance and patient psychological weakness are two important determinants which affect the appropriate access to care and decrease health outcomes.

Non-conventional organizational models which encourage revisiting the traditional myth of scale in health care are desperately needed to enhance the sustainability of the healthcare service system. Even though scale could produce positive effects in terms of managerial and economic results, it neglects the role played by several determinants of organizational performance, producing only a limited and partial interpretation of the complex reality of healthcare organizations.

11.1.3 New Perspectives: Complex Models in Health care

Complex Adaptive Models (CAMs) and Self-Organizing approaches (SOs) are generally presented as the main solutions to increasingly turbulent environments which improve the ability of healthcare organizations to enhance their viability. On the one hand, CAMs allow the achievement of enhanced organizational resilience and flexibility. On the other hand, SOs improve the organization's abilities to deal with the growing competitive challenges of an unpredictable and complex environment, emphasizing the role played by temporary and emergent solutions in meeting the evolving needs of external stakeholders. The establishment of loosely coupled relationships is considered especially effective in dealing with complexity, since it produces enhanced organizational knowledge and learning.

Drawing from the prevailing literature, CAMs seem to be common in health care (see, among the other, Rouse 2008; Rangachari 2009; Plsek and Wilson 2001). In particular, the healthcare organizations which adopt CAMs are likely to show the following attributes: (1) Many different, but interconnected agents, who are able to learn from their relationships; (2) Self-organization; (3) Emergency; and (4) Co-evolution.

The Mayo Clinic has been discussed by Mintzberg (2012) himself as an illustrative example of complex and adaptive organization. Actually, the Mayo Clinic was successful in reframing the traditional myths of healthcare management—including the myth of scale—by fostering collaboration beyond control and encouraging community beyond leadership.

The Mayo Clinic could be described as a healthcare network, rather than as a specific healthcare facility. Both the institutional and the structural features of the Mayo Clinic are consistent with a complex approach to healthcare management. In particular, the Mayo Clinic adopts a multi-disciplinary approach to health care provision, aimed to promote a patient-centred approach and enhancing clinical excellence by virtue of a physician-led governance structure which puts the needs of the patients first. The Mayo Clinic model shows all the features that distinguish an effective CAS, including diversity and interdependence of relevant agents, non-linearity of interconnections, a structural configuration inspired by self-organization, the emergence of innovative organizational practices and the pursuit of a co-evolutionary approach to organizational development.

Human resources are known to be the most important source of the Mayo Clinic's competitive advantage. Indeed, the provider-led approach to governance is understood to be crucial to improve the flexibility, creativity and adaptability of the organization, as well as to enhance the ability of the latter to anticipate external changes and to react to environmental unpredictability. Healthcare professionals are encouraged to work with complexity rather than to dilute it through the adoption of rigid managerial approaches. From this point of view, the establishment of multi-disciplinary teams, which are continuously encouraged to increase their internal diversity in order to match external diversity, is assumed to be the most effective solution to face the growth of complex environmental challenges. As reported in Table 11.1, the healthcare professionals of the Mayo Clinic are included in flexible and fluid departments and centres, which are aimed at valuing the contributions of all the members and blending individual skills in deep collaborations. In particular, fluidity does not imply the absence of organizational patterns; rather, it involves a flexible structural approach, which relies on adaptability in dealing with environmental uncertainty.

The agents operating within the Mayo Clinic are encouraged to establish local, but non-linear interpersonal relationships. Non-linear and local interconnection

Table 11.1 Mayo Clinic as a CAS

CAS attributes	Illustrative examples drawn from the Mayo Clinic case study
Diverse and interdependent agents	Healthcare professionals are involved in flexible and fluid teams, which are aimed at blending the individual skills in unsurpassed collaboration
Non-linear relationships	Departments and centres are organized in light of both the bio-medical specialization and the emerging issues raising from environmental challenges
Emergence	Organizational models are the results of emergent patterns, which derive from the mutual interaction of different sub-units
Self-organization	Mayo Clinic sticks to a fluid and versatile organizational model, which is not top-down, but is co-designed and co-implemented bottom-up
Co-evolution	Healthcare delivery, research, and education are blended in a homogeneous organizational efforts. Open structures are endorsed

Source authors' Elaboration

paves the way for the arrangement of innovative and effective answers to unpredictable pressures, preserving a focus on everyday organizational practices. Collaborative and co-participating task forces are established to deal with the managerial issues which affect the different parts of the organization. Knowledge sharing and continuous innovation are also steadily stimulated, with the eventual purpose of enhancing the dynamic capabilities and the resilience of the organization. ICT-mediated inter-professional relationships are encouraged to enhance the weak collaborative ties between the healthcare professionals who participate in the same project. As an illustrative example, both blogs and social networks are used as catalysts for interpersonal relationships and information exchange, thus paving the way for the establishment of a learning organization.

The role played by healthcare professionals in managing operational issues and, at the same time, in participating in the organizational governance of the Mayo Clinic in light of a patient-centred approach to care is an essential ingredient of the recipe for the arrangement of a structural configuration which relies on self-organization. In fact, the patterns which inspire the governance of the Mayo Clinic are assumed to be the result of local interactions between smaller elementary parts of a supposedly disordered system, that is to say the different teams operating within the organization. These teams are designed as communities of practice, where dynamic personal relationships and established ways of interacting between the members allow knowledge creation, organizational commitment and value co-creation. In other words, the Mayo Clinic sticks to a fluid and versatile organizational model, which is not top-down arranged, but is co-designed and co-implemented by the different members of the organization. A horizontal structural pattern prevails on a vertical and hierarchical one: healthcare professionals are encouraged to ask one another for advice and counselling in providing health services, thus performing as actual team members in any organizational circumstance.

Organizational models and managerial practices are the results of emergent practices, which in turn derive from the mutual interaction of different agents who do not have to accept macro-level patterns. Order emerges from the everyday activities performed by healthcare providers to deal with the health-related needs of their patients. That is to say, operations inspire organizational design, paving the way for a structure which is arranged according to the demands of the users, rather than to the competences of healthcare providers.

Both self-organization and emergence are the outcome of a strategic approach which endorses co-evolution. The environment and the organization are assumed to co-evolve and develop together, in a strictly interdependent way. On the one hand, the environment influences the organization, shaping its structural features in light of the evolving needs of the population served. On the other hand, the organization affects the evolution of the environment through the institutionalization of structural configurations and managerial practices. Continuous information exchange and knowledge sharing are two key tools to go through co-evolutionary paths. In particular, the Mayo Clinic fosters the exchange of information and the contamination of knowledge by merging education and research in everyday healthcare practices. Education and research are carried out through five specialized bio-medical schools (the Mayo Graduate School, the Mayo Medical school, the Mayo School of Continuous Professional Development, the Mayo School of Graduate Medical Education, the Mayo School of Health Sciences), which provide formal educational programmes and encourage knowledge dissemination sticking to a conceptual framework inspired by the complexity theory. These schools perform as boundary spanners of the Mayo health system, allowing the establishment of a dynamic and vivid relationship with the external environment.

In summary, the Mayo Clinic is designed as a full-fledged complex adaptive system, which relies on both organizational agents' diversity and non-linear interconnections to achieve emergent structural configuration and self-organization. The success of the business model adopted by the Mayo Clinic is aimed to establish co-evolutionary paths between the organization and its environment, thus leading to sustainable growth. The merge between healthcare provision, research, and education is ultimately intended to establish a living and learning organization, which is able to continuously adapt to the stimuli of the external environment.

11.1.4 Conclusions

Until recently, the quest for control pervaded the healthcare service system, in an attempt to destroy uncertainty through reductionism. The ambition to control healthcare organizations was merged with the attempt to increase their dimensions, to realize the full potential of scale. The scientific literature has emphasized that health care organizations are complex entities. Far away from stability, they operate at the edge of chaos, where instability prevails and innovation emerges (Russ 1999). To deal with complexity, healthcare organizations should not rely on norms and procedures. Rather, they should behave as brains and operate as living organisms. From this point of view, control and scale turn out to be a myth rather than a reality.

The complexity perspective incites to critically re-examine scale in the health-care arena. On the one hand, economies of scale are valid strategies in the short period, since they allow to meet the financial constraints of healthcare systems. On the other hand, they prevent the differentiation of services and produce less flexible ways of working, which are not suitable to take care of sick people that have different and not standardized needs.

The complexity of coordination activities curtails the benefit of greater specialization. In general, the coordination and management of large units is more complex as compared with small organizations. Moreover, it is likely that large units are not able to reach the maximum of efficiency, due to problems related to the management of relationships among people, greater supervision costs, waste of resources and low employees' motivation.

In other words, the myth of scale overlooks organizational interdependences, which are emergent and non-linear. Interdependences make healthcare organizations cognitively developed. From this point of view, they improve the organizational ability to change and adapt. Small dimensions, even though sacrificing efficiency, are able to absorb variety and to enhance sensemaking. Flexible mode of operation allows organizations to adapt to the external environment and make them working as a brain, developing the interdependencies among the different and strongly connected components. In this way, the employees develop competences that are polyvalent, making the system agile, not rigid and dependent on hierarchical management. Flexible healthcare organizations concentrate more on actions that need to be avoided than on what they are supposed to do. Defining only what the organizations need to avoid makes the working environment agile, dynamic and capable of adapting within pre-established limits. Clearly, this is a radical structural change, which would require the acceptance by the management of a lack of influence and power in favour of a spread empowerment across the organization.

This study has also shown that quantitative variables provide a reductive snapshot of the health care system, which overlooks its complexity. A more realistic view should emphasize the natural co-evolution between healthcare organizations and the external environment, leading to a managerial approach which is consistent with a patient-centred philosophy and acknowledge the non-linearity of organizational relationships. A greater insight into the role of human resources, especially healthcare professionals, the enhancement of organizational interdependencies and the improvement of self-organization are critical to achieve greater efficiency and effectiveness in health care. From this standpoint, ramification and boundarylessness—rather than scale—should be the ideas inspiring the future shapes of healthcare systems.

11.2 Beyond Scale: The Quest for Quality

Marcello Martinez, Luigi Moschera and Gianluigi Mangia

11.2.1 Economies of Scale and not Effectiveness of Scale

"Small is beautiful" because it is flexible, and even "giants can dance". As size grows so too does complexity, but equally the reduction in complexity—for example the processes of extreme division of work and the related segmentation—helps to increase the corporate size. Research and development and innovation are facilitated in large companies, so how can the proliferation of incredibly innovative small start-ups be explained?

These are just some of the contradictions which can be found in scientific literature with regard to the concept of size and they are intensified by the process of the development of the actual scientific knowledge of organizational thinking. Henry Mintzberg himself has underlined these difficulties: "Notice the term: economies of scale. Not effectiveness of scale but economies of scale. Too much of the management of health care has come about through using scale to reduce measurable costs at the expense of difficult-to-measure benefits".

Myth, used as the key to interpret reality, can assist the process of critically re-assessing the subject of importance of size in the success of healthcare organizations.

The first consideration refers to the fact that large sizes can lead to dangerous illusions of superiority. Organizational literature, which has focused on the issue of the importance of size as a factor in competitive advantage, has highlighted that, in themselves, large volumes and a large share of the market do not always result in competitive advantage, nor do they guarantee success in survival. Revisiting the ancient legend of David's battle against Goliath, as described in the Old Testament book of Samuel, leads in a mythical way, to such considerations. Goliath, the dreadful champion of the Philistines, is a big man, but his large size is not enough for him to prevail and, in actual fact, it creates a dangerous air of superiority in Goliath's mind that persuades the giant to misjudge his adversary. The tiny David, armed only with a simple sling, is victorious. The most interesting aspect is that David's victory, supported obviously by God, comes as a surprise and wrong foots all those present, because it overturns the deep-rooted but erroneous conviction that being big guarantees success.

The second consideration refers to the fact that, in certain circumstances, size does not play a crucial role in competition, but rather that it is an additional factor compared to others which are far more important: strategic vision; the ability to predict the opponents' moves; believable products; efficient and effective organization and so on. In this case too another legend, this time of Greek origin, might be of help. In the war for the control of Olympus the giants, whose strong point is their "gigantic" size, succumb to the craftiness and unexpected blows of Zeus as well as to his ability to form alliances. When Zeus is in trouble, his greatest help comes from Cadmus who, as a mere mortal, lets Typhon fall asleep and then robs him, surreptitiously, of the tendons of which Zeus had been deprived. As soon as Zeus regained his strength he annihilates Typhon with his own bolts of lightning and crushes him under the weight of an enormous boulder which was then to be transformed into Mount Etna. Here too, therefore, the larger size is not a decisive factor and does not determine the final outcome.

The third consideration refers to the possible seduction exerted by the growth in size. Modern-day society is fiercely permeated by a capitalist style vision, in which scientific and technical know-how is geared in every way towards the creation of value. In this process of creating value and accumulation, size takes on a very powerful meaning, because it symbolically represents an obvious element for success and achievement, with respect to competition. In this case the seductions of size, just like the song of the Sirens for Ulysses in the Odyssey, can represent a dangerous distraction for healthcare organizations. In other words, pursuing the path of growth in size as an element of achievement can lead to a collapse that is all the more painful and unforeseen, as was the overpowering illusion of achieving success through pursuing a strategy of growth in size.

11.2.2 Size in the Organizational Theories

The absence of certain absolute truths, which are now constant in the development of organizational thinking, becomes apparent, even when one is confronted by or comes face to face with the issue of "scale" and the optimum size.

The reasons for this loss of role, of these difficulties associated with size, can be seen again on the one hand in the development of epistemological models and organizational thinking in general and on the other, in the change in the level of analysis and in the disappearance of organizational boundaries.

From the first point of view the issue of size has usually been tackled through organizational studies primarily in the functionalist contributions and/or in those which, with an "objective" and objectivizing approach, reify the organization itself. Size and measurement in general are at the heart of rational logic, be it absolute or limited. The first crisis of size, as an explicative element or one that conditions organizational dynamics, comes with the change viewed through the lens of organizational analysis: with the criticisms of the functionalism of the 1970s or the more recent ones of economic organizational models (for example, the one for transaction costs), with the subjective approach or interaction with cognitivism, with postmodernism and the "fragmentation" of the organizational problem, with the same symbolism that exaggerates the aspects of size in the analysis of the "physical" aspect of the organizational artefacts. In all of these studies these size-related aspects and their associated problems of quantification lose their centrality.

In this sense it is also possible to perceive a reduced effect from the size element in the individual approaches to the theory of organization. The reassuring and prescriptive formulations of the traditional approaches (that would, for example, impose limits of scale to the span of control in a hierarchy, the ideal level of production in order to guarantee the most efficient use of resources, the generic reference to economies of scale to increase the company's efficiency and so on) fade in the contingency approaches (that examine, even if less prescriptively, the fit between size levels and structures) and disappear altogether in more modern-day approaches.

From a second perspective the problem of an organization's size is directly linked to a basic assumption that perhaps no longer applies in the current competitive arena: the presence of clear and precise organizational boundaries. The problem of the object being analysed and its boundaries has, on the other hand, been intrinsically bound to the development of the company since the beginning of the last century to the present day. In the classical studies of the first half of the twentieth century the size and quantification of the same were not a problem: the object of the analysis by scholars always or often corresponded with the physical boundary of the individual unit: department, plant and factory. The individual company corresponded to a clearly identifiable legal entity. But what sense is there today in speaking of corporate size for businesses that have short-lived and unsteady boundaries that change over time? From the vertically integrated and impressively sized businesses to the hollow corporations that with a relatively small nucleus have control over inter-organizational networks and size circumstances that are even more impressive. What is the size of a business that manages a social network with relatively few employees but that has hundreds of millions of clients (take Facebook for example, that has around a billion or Tencent's Qzone with its 620 million)? Is Apple, which is capable of influencing the technological perspectives of companies, larger than one of its major suppliers, Foxconn, with its one million employees (more than 200,000 in one establishment alone)? Looked at in these terms the wearing away of the clear and immovable organizational boundaries have certainly prompted the discussion on the opportunity of continuing to use size as a discriminatory variable and on its measurement.

11.2.3 The Search for a Balance Between Quality and Management

11.2.3.1 The Traditional View of the Myth About Size

Henry Mintzberg identifies the prevailing organizational models of healthcare systems (hospitals) as the result, be it good or bad, of managerial choices aimed at applying control systems suitable for mechanical bureaucracies over professional bureaucracies. What follows is a gap between administration and operation.

From this point of view what emerges is tension between a management intent on pursuing economies of scale that are useful for managing the activities of administration and the quality of the delivery of healthcare services, namely attention to the patient, innovation and the customizing of care. In fact, according to the traditional Tayloristic vision, economies of scale are achieved by pursuing a "larger sizing" of healthcare and hospital structures, with the supposition that, by combining, rationalizing and reducing fixed costs, and merging procedures, activities and skills, it is possible to achieve greater efficiency.

On the contrary, quality is instead understood to mean the attention to the patient and the search for innovative solutions from the point of view of health and therapeutic care and is pursued precisely by eliminating the mechanistic perspective that is founded on inflexible, predetermined standards (such as healthcare protocols, procedures, management control systems), which traditionally are the only way to manage a "large size" and therefore pursue economies of scale and efficiency.

11.2.3.2 New Organizational Models: Beyond the Myth of the Large Size as a Condition for the Pursuit of Efficiency

The conceptual categories of mechanical and professional bureaucracies probably make it possible to observe one part of the multiplicity of organizational models that are emerging from healthcare systems.

At the heart of the new organizational models there are different dynamics founded, in the main, on the adopting of new ICT technologies relative to the myth of the large size as a condition for the search for economies of scale in as much as they remove the supposition that efficiency can be achieved by "concentrating" many activities into one physical, administrative, technical and organizational structure. The search for efficiency shifts from running costs to those of control and coordination, which is why the reduction in coordination and control costs is pursued by means of ICT systems.

More specifically it is possible to identify the following major dynamics that are currently to be found in healthcare systems:

- The introduction of transaction processing system-type ICT systems that allow the hyper-automation of many of the supporting admin activities (management of stores and pharmaceutical logistics; accountancy and HR management systems; public/patient communication systems for A&E operations; appointments; managing test results; electronic medical records, etc.). This allows the centralized management of the same for a multitude of healthcare and hospital structures across one single territorial area.

- The introduction of knowledge level ICT systems (electronic archives; electronic medical records; shared databases; group decision support systems; social networks; virtual teams and videoconferencing; etc.) that allow the smooth distribution, sharing and combination between healthcare operatives of the areas of professional knowledge which are at the heart of the choices they make as part of their operational activities; this is done in such a way that the access to databases and storage areas is not conditional on exclusive investments in one single health care and hospital structure and are available, irrespective of size.
- The adoption of Management Level type ICT systems (electronic auctions, performance monitoring systems) that allow the allocation, management and control of outsourcing contracts for managing the facilities. These activities include cleaning, maintenance, building construction, systems and technologies, etc., nursing assistance, or the assignment of entire hospital structures for specific periods of time to third parties, even though the private–public method of partnering. This transfers the focus of the research on efficiency using possible economies of scale of non-internal specializations, from one single health care or hospital structure onto each individual involved. This presupposes that he or she has been chosen because of their greater skills in undertaking the work with which they have been entrusted.

11.2.3.3 ICT Organizational Models

Obviously, the methods used for adopting the different ICT technologies influences the setup of the organizational models adopted, in as much as it is possible to achieve different types of effects in terms of centralisation and development of the organizational size.

Panopticon models: the standardization of the traditional mechanistic model is reinforced, allowing greater efficiencies through a reduction of the organizational structures responsible for internal coordination and control, but the concentration of activities in individual structures of greater size with greater capacity and fewer costs are maintained.

Joystick models: the responsibility for carrying out the activities is decentralized, whereas the ex-ante and ex-post coordination and control of the execution of the same is centralized and standardized (accreditation systems; quality; control based on standard costs set by the regions or the ministry).

Hub & Spoke models: the responsibility for carrying out the activities as well as their ex-ante operational coordination and control is decentralized, but the coordination and control over the results (ex-post) remain centralized through flexible and variable contractual systems (electronic auctions for procurement; centralized pharmacy stores; specialist centres connected on the network but spread across the territory).

11.2.3.4 ICT and CMS

To round off the line of reasoning about the impact of ICT, it is considered appropriate to present some of the major features that qualify the approach of the critical management studies on the point.

In the light of the need for technology to be all pervasive, it is incorrect to interpret this as an isolated topic of study with limited interconnections with management research and management training. The ICT and IS tools are in fact used within organizational contexts to rationalize and reorganize organizations, starting from the supposition that IT systems come about and are planned in such a way as to introduce best practice and to facilitate cost-cutting policies and increase the level of profitability efficiency to help organizations operate on a global scale.

This assumption, based on a rationality of an instrumental nature, that, on the other hand, legitimizes managerial ideology, is rarely discussed and challenged in research on IS of a mainstream nature. The major outcome to which the critical-based studies have attempted to respond is that some consequences coming out of the introduction of the technological artefacts in organizations are by and large overlooked and not closely scrutinized.

The focus on the development and implementation of IT systems in terms of functions and processes brings with it the risk of totally losing sight of the issue of fragmentation, of routine, the absence of discretion, the rise in the levels of control and supervision. In contrast with the predominantly theoretical approach that is conditioned by a technologically determinist vision, the scholars of IT systems of a critical nature have pitted themselves against the idea that technological development means a tout-court progress and that it can be achieved through an "objective" science.

In conclusion, the adoption of a pluralist perspective to the study of IS makes it possible to integrate the positive vision with those of an interpretive and critical nature. One of the most promising lines of study on IS from a critical perspective in particular implies their contextualisation within the wider organizational problem. In actual fact, those phenomena of the adoption and institutionalization of the ICTs cannot be understood in the absence of clear organizational and policy perspective. In other words, the introduction of ICTs is not neutral compared to the internal organizational dynamics both with respect to the structure and the organizational size and the functioning of the control mechanisms. The empirical experience confirms the assumption for which the introduction of ICT systems for sharing information (for example an Intranet network) can generate fierce resistance. Moreover, it produces an effect on the levels of organizational control. In fact, the sharing of information does not represent a neutral element for the purposes of the dynamics of control. One final aspect, necessary to emphasize, refers to the dimension of the organizational macro-structure; in actual fact, the development of ICT systems, and in this case too it is possible to obtain numerous confirmations of the experience, can bring about a reduction of an intermediate hierarchical level.

11.3 The Myth of Scale: True or False?

Daniela Scaramuccia and Alberto Calvo

11.3.1 Scale Still Is a Valid Toolkit for Many Businesses

Over the last 70 years, and growing rapidly after the second World War, the concept of scale as a primary competitive factor across any economic sector has hardly been debated. Scholars, academics and management consultants have been quite busy in reaffirming the idea that those who had the ambition of "ruling the world" in their specific activities, necessarily had to pay tribute to scale in its various forms, which might in turn take the name of size, extension, coverage, etc.

This flurry of studies was pivoting around a definitely strong point. In most western countries, where modern industrial economies have been developing after 1950, scale was a simple and effective recipe for success. Managers and entrepreneurs quickly realized that the bigger their estates, the easier it was to gain and sustain a competitive advantage, typically in the form of lower per-unit production costs, higher overall productivity and access to large R&D budgets.

Most industries which drove economic growth over the last century were clearly proving this simple logic true. Think of businesses where competition is not possible unless very high entry barriers in technology or cost-effectiveness can be overcome (Automotive, Chemicals, Oil & Gas) or where there is basically no room for more than a fairly limited number of players, much less for the destruction of the overall industry value (Telecoms, Aerospace & Defence).

11.3.2 Technology Innovation Confirms the Scale Paradigm, Too

More recently, the unprecedented development of new technologies has forced management thinking to challenge this concept once again, and to stress test it in order to see whether it could still work in specific industry dynamics. Many have in fact questioned its validity, and instead proposed a paradigm by which "technology substitutes (or even, destroys) the notion of scale".

Typically, this statement is based on the simplistic acknowledgement that the pervasive diffusion and low-cost access to technologies such as the Internet and connectivity have permanently broken down the barriers to access any business sector, "democratizing" the participation of all kinds of entrepreneurs to them.

Surprisingly, in many of those cases where disruptive innovation has taken place because of the "Internet revolution", traditional competitive patterns were ultimately replicated. Think for example of the "winner takes it all" paradigm typically associated with the champions of our digital age: in online advertising, Google has managed to build a dominant position, which is constantly reinforced by the hefty resources devoted to the optimization and improvement of its search engine, leaving everyone else far behind; in e-commerce, the relentless ride of Amazon in multiple product categories, which is based on a superior technology platform and customer service (deliveries, returns, feedbacks, matching/suggestions), has left little to share with its global competitors; also across social networks a new version of scale has been introduced, where the "crowding in" to a few, more attractive sites (Facebook + Instagram, Linkedin, etc.) has hollowed out subscriptions to all other community websites.

Rather than invalidating the importance of scale as a key success factor, technological innovation has changed the understanding of its meaning. Whereas in the past gaining scale translated into the effort of piling up "hard stuff" like plants, equipment, real estate and so on, in these new markets it is very likely that assets such as competence, systems and knowledge would have a much bigger impact.

In this respect, when looking at some of the most remarkable tech-stories of the recent years, it is easy to identify their secret sauce in a smart way to build soft-infrastructures enabling innovative services, often deployed globally through scale (and most times, not really denting or cannibalizing existing markets, but rather creating new value pools). Airbnb, Uber, Stripe, Blablacar, Spotify, Zalando and Thumbtack have grown out of unique service ideas combined with vision and speed into greatly designed software packages, which indeed required huge investments to be completed, again confirming that the notion of scale is still in good shape, alive and kicking. Technological innovation will progressively make old asset categories obsolete and capital will then be redeployed to consolidate new sources of competitive advantage, which—again, there is no evidence to the contrary yet—will still have to abide by the rules of Scale.

11.3.3 *Yet, Scale Is Almost Irrelevant Where Businesses Stay Away from the Commodity Trap*

The validity of "scale" as a strategic management tool remains undisputed in all those businesses that eventually fall prey to commodity production. By contrast, there are a few sectors that have demonstrated over time a significant resilience to the arguments of scale. Typically, public interest services like education, health care, elderly care, professional training and many other similar in nature are barely sensitive to the so-called economies of scale.

Over time, though, management theory has further developed the notion and applicability of scale, to account for several phenomena not quite well explained by a rigid definition of it. Clearly, the greater the importance of factors like creativity, personalization, local touch and uniqueness, the less relevant the concept of scale becomes: anyone can witness the plethora of small, vibrant companies thriving everywhere in fashion, design and furniture that can survive despite their small size; or the fact that very successful restaurants would not benefit much from tripling their capacity, as well as it would happen to a cosy hotel-de-charme in Tuscany.

The main reason why many of these local businesses can comfortably prosper without enjoying massive scale is that, given the unique nature of the products or services offered, they can provide a premium value to customers, which is large enough to compensate for the lack of scale advantage. In food, for example, large brands have conquered the planet in many grocery categories, but there is always room in your shopping basket for a tastier bar of chocolate crafted by a small manufacturer, a vitamin-rich range of drinks produced out of fresh fruits gathered locally, and special cookies with organically cultivated raisins and chestnuts.

11.3.4 A Case in Point: Health care Is a Complex and Peculiar Environment

Take for instance healthcare management, with its huge complexity, evident across whichever dimension the reader might want to consider. In fact, healthcare organizations have to ensure access to care to extremely diversified groups of people, each with their own lifestyles, habits, culture, education and expectations, and to deal with a wide array of stakeholders, like policymakers, regulators, providers of goods and services as well as payers, insurers, creditors, doctors and physicians. These organizations have to deal with constant innovation and cutting-edge technology deployment (think of robot-based surgical procedures) but also to acknowledge that they operate in a constrained budget environment; they need to design management systems that work well both for very specialized competence areas (rare diseases, cardio and neurosurgeries, transplants, etc.) applied to tailor-made, target therapies as well as to mass, chronic diseases (diabetics, hypertension, …), which need to be effective both when applied to large therapeutic centres, home-based assistance or standard GP practices. Can scale be practically applied in this context? Does it make any sense, for example, to merge GP practices into larger, more standardized organizations? Would this have any impact on the fairness and equality of access to care, and its quality?

To secure universal access to healthcare treatment, cost containment has always been a major challenge for policymakers, and "scale" is often being regarded as a viable solution to grant sustainability. Managers and healthcare systems' experts have been debating these issues for a long time, aware of being confronted with a unique market characterized by, de facto, a never-ending demand to be served "mandatorily", and a profile which has worsened in the last decades due to an ageing population. Moreover, new therapies have in some cases managed to obtain extremely high reimbursement rates whose burden on the system was clearly not sustainable (take for instance the Sofosbuvir case, where the cost of treating the whole patient pool is higher than the yearly Italian drug budget).

In healthcare management, a clear distinction needs to be made. Experience has demonstrated that scale is a key success factor in reducing costs and improving efficiency when considering back-office processes (such as administration, procurement, logistics, etc.) or achieving better clinical outcomes (e.g. breast units, obstetricians units, etc.). Yet, scale is almost irrelevant if applied to other aspects (such as prevention, chronic care management, PA stroke or poly-traumas intervention), where excellence in performance is clearly dependent either on time to treatment, or the individual knowledge of patients, or again on the definition of custom protocols for patient in-treatment, while taking into consideration cultural and environmental peculiarities.

11.3.5 Scale in Health care: Where it Works…

As in many other industrial sectors, scale can also be a practical method to reduce costs in hospitals, and centralized procurement processes can definitely help in this respect. For instance, the introduction of National and Regional procurement offices in Italy increased transparency and competitiveness in a very fragmented market, with the price index dropping by 20% in 5 years (2007–2012). Similar results were achieved in facility management costs (energy, cleaning, laundry), and across cost categories such as purchasing basic drugs or catering expenditures. However, more important results are to be achieved only when a more structured, disciplined sourcing approach is also extended to core expenditures such as high-preference clinical supplies (like cardiac stents, surgical packs, orthopaedic implants, and other items physicians typically hold strong opinions about). Clearly, this is not an easy task for healthcare managers, as it requires dealing with physicians' expectations while ensuring at the same time that quality of care is not affected. The quest for economies of scale cannot really help here; solid, modern management techniques need to be applied to encompass sourcing excellence, ranging from organizational solutions (deploying for example cross-functional working teams including procurement experts, but also clinicians, pharmacists, to balance the pros and cons of each alternative option), to a systematic demand management, progressive vendor consolidation and adoption of generic equivalents.

Scale can be a success factor also to guarantee quality of treatment; more specifically, for some clinical procedures a minimum critical mass to ensure quality can be defined. It is well known for instance that obstetric units with less than 500 deliveries per year should no longer exist, as they cannot ensure proper clinician competences and technologies and register worst clinical outcomes, the same holding true for cardio surgery units with less than 500 procedures per year, or breast units with less than 150 surgeries per year.

11.3.6 … And Where It Doesn't

Nonetheless, in the modern healthcare management time to treatment has turned out to be the key success factor for many procedures. Let us think for example of the door-to-balloon 90 min golden standard for the effective treatment of acute ST-segment-elevation myocardial infarction (STEMI), or the "golden hour" for poly-traumas, and the three hours for the tPA stroke intervention. Scale is almost irrelevant here, while it is critical to guarantee a proper design of the healthcare network, so as to ensure the proper time to treatment.

For other therapeutic areas, instead, individual knowledge makes the difference. A clear example is the management of chronic patients, which constitutes the major burden for modern healthcare systems. Data from the early 2000s in the United States indicate that about 40% of all visits to physicians were for chronic diseases; about 80% of these were scheduled for routine follow-ups. When considering primary care physicians only, 46% of visits of previously known patients were aimed at solving chronic illnesses, and 91% of these were for routine follow-ups (Wolff et al. 2002). Chronic patients are often affected by multiple disease (in the United States, about 80% of Medicare spending is devoted to patients with four or more chronic conditions), with costs increasing exponentially as the number of chronic conditions increases.

Policymakers and clinicians have been debating for years and, in the end, results and reviews showed that the Chronic Care Model (or the Extended Chronic Care Model) can indeed improve the management of chronic conditions and reduce healthcare costs (Bodenheimer et al. 2002). At the basis of the CCM there is a strong paradigm shift from a disease-based approach to a patient-focused one, which envisages an informed patient interacting with an integrated, proactive practice team. In all these cases, proactivity and personalization are the key tools, again not scale.

Finally, being able to positively influence a specific cultural environment can make a huge difference. Let us take for instance primary prevention. It is well demonstrated that behaviour plays an important role in people's health (for example, smoking, poor diet, lack of exercise and sexual risk-taking can cause a large number of diseases). Typically, however, different behavioural patterns are deeply rooted into people's social and material circumstances, and their cultural context. Devising smart and effective ways to change people's behaviour has an enormous potential to alter current patterns of disease propagation, but this is notoriously very hard to achieve. As a pioneer in this area, the Nice (National Institute for health and Care Excellence, UK) developed a set of specific guidelines and recognized that a combination of interventions addressing population, community and individual-level factors are needed to help people change their behaviour in the longer term. Again, scale is not a success factor.

So, we can say economy of scale is a key success factor for some back-office processes like procurement, facility management, information system and for standardized and consolidated healthcare procedures, while scale is irrelevant for procedures and healthcare treatments that are or should be innovative and personalized. Economy of scale and greater dimensions should be pursued whenever organization complexity has no negative impact on health professionals (doctors, nurses, other healthcare supplier) and patient relationships.

References

Agenas (2008) La governance della sanità. Monitor 39:1–50

Anderson PW (1972) More is different. Broken symmetry and the nature of the hierarchical structure of science. Science, New Series, 177(4047): 393–396

Bodenheimer T, Wagner EH, Grumbach K (2002) Improving primary care for patients with chronic illness. JAMA 288:1909–1914

Borgonovi E (2007) Considerazioni per una teoria degli stakeholder nelle Amministrazioni Pubbliche. In: Freeman RE, Rusconi G, Dorigatti M (eds) teoria degli stakeholder. FrancoAngeli, Milano

Borgonovi E (2008) La tutela della salute è il fine, il funzionamento dei sistemi e delle aziende è il mezzo. Egea, Milano

Capra F (2002) The hidden connections. Doubleday, New York

Chadwick C, Hunter LW, Walston SL (2004) Effects of downsizing practice on the performance of hospitals. Strateg Manag J 25(5):405–427

Cilliers P (1998) Complexity and postmodernism. Routledge, London

Gharajedaghi J (1999) Systems Thinking: Managing chaos and complexity: a platform for designing, 1st edn. Butterworth-Heinemann, Woburn

Irwin JG, Hoffman JJ, Geiger SW (1998) The effect of technological adoption on organizational performance: organizational size and environmental munificence as moderators. Int J Organ Anal 6(1):50–64

Ministero della Salute (2015) Programma Nazionale Valutazione Esiti. Agenas, Roma

Mintzberg H (2012) Managing the Myths of Health Care. World Hospitals and Health Services 48 (3):4–7

Morgan G (2016) Images of organization: 30th, Anniversary edn. Sage, New York

Orton JD, Weick KE (1990) Loosely coupled systems: a reconceptualization. Acad Manag Rev 15:203–223

Plsek PE, Wilson T (2001) Complexity, leadership, and management in healthcare organisations. Br Med J 323(7315):746–749

Rangachari P (2009) Knowledge sharing networks in professional complex systems. J Knowl Manag 13(3):132–145

Rouse WB (2008) Healthcare as a complex adaptive system: implications for design and management. Bridge 38(1):17–25

Sahin I, Ozcan YA (2000) Public sector hospital efficiency for provincial markets in Turkey. J Med Syst 24(6):307–320

Thiétart RA, Forgues B (1997) Action, structure and chaos. Organ Stud 18(1):119–143

Wolff JL, Starfield B, Anderson G (2002) Prevalence, expenditures, and complications of multiple chronic conditions in the elderly. Arch Intern Med 162(20):2269–2276

Chapter 12
Health Myths and Service-Dominant Logic

Evert Gummesson, Gerardine Doyle, Alessandra Storlazzi, Carmela Annarumma, Giuseppe Favretto, Aurelio Tommasetti and Massimiliano Vesci

12.1 Some Insights on the Future of Health care

Evert Gummesson

12.1.1 Introduction

It has always been an inspiration for me to be exposed to Henry Mintzberg's innovative and pragmatic ways of addressing a specific field. First it was organi-

E. Gummesson (✉)
School of Business, Stockolm University, Stockolm, Sweden
e-mail: eg@sbs.su.se

G. Doyle (✉)
College of Business, University College Dublin, Belfield, Dublin 4, Ireland
e-mail: gerardine.doyle@ucd.ie

C. Annarumma · A. Tommasetti · M. Vesci (✉)
Dipartimento di Scienze Aziendali – Management & Innovation Systems, Università degli Studi di Salerno, Via Giovanni Paolo II, 132, 84084 Salerno, Italy
e-mail: mvesci@unisa.it

C. Annarumma
e-mail: cannarumma@unisa.it

G. Favretto
Dipartimento Di Economia Aziendale, Università Degli Studi Di Verona, Via Cantarane 24, 37129 Verona, Italy
e-mail: giuseppe.favretto@univr.it

A. Storlazzi
Università degli Studi Suor Orsola Benincasa - Facoltà di Scienze della Formazione, Corso Vittorio Emanuele 292, Naples, Italy
e-mail: alessandra.storlazzi@unisob.na.it

P. Adinolfi and E. Borgonovi (eds.), *The Myths of Health Care*,
https://doi.org/10.1007/978-3-319-53600-2_12

zation theory, then strategy and now it is health care. I listened to him at the University of Salerno and read his article Managing the Myths of Health care (Henry Mintzberg 2012) finding that I agree with almost everything. I totally agree with him that the solutions of the past rarely solved anything but despite this, they are the same "panaceas," such as reorganization, which are still suggested today.

However, his expose raised some questions in my mind and touched on some of my own experiences and research. I have followed the healthcare sector since the 1970s. It started with my own health. For a period, my energy had been low and I felt it a strain to keep up. I went to the local general practitioner who sent me for some routine x-rays and prescribed a combination of vitamins. I did not feel any commitment from him and after two months, there still were no improvements.

In the meantime, I had read about a doctor who had started a health spa based on fasting with vegetarian drinks free from chemicals and pesticides. It was specifically for people who did not find that their hospital had helped them. Not surprisingly, the majority were elderly, but not all. Apparently, there was nothing wrong with me, although in my 30s I felt like an elderly person and began to fear that my low energy might be chronic. The fasting week together with lectures, exercise and a relaxed atmosphere completely changed my perception of health and illness. Fasting is not a cure-all but, together with other therapies and gradual change of lifestyle, it can do wonders. It also led to an integration of the study of disorders and health cases with my knowledge of management and scientific methodology. It was a changing point in my life, and it was a point-of-no-return.

12.1.2 My Scientific Credo

In my research, I start with personal observations about something being good or bad. Not to be prejudiced, I always begin inductively and never deductively with received, mainstream theory. This complies with grounded theory, a research methodology introduced by Glaser and Strauss (1967) and still followed by numerous books and articles. Initially it was used in health care, especially in nursing research. Today it is used in all types of social sciences. In my research, extant theory may come in later but it is never forced on reality. Data may come to me as observations in my private and everyday life, in my research projects, or in society and politics.

That is also how I started to study service. After graduation, I was employed as product manager in a consumer goods company and three years later I was recruited by a major international management consulting company. I went from a business-to-consumer (B2C) goods company to a business-to-business (B2B) service company. I found that the consulting firm was successful despite in its marketing they did nothing of what was recommended in the American textbooks. This suggested following one of two possible strategies: (1) the consulting firm lacked knowledge about modern marketing and should have started changing this; (2) as they were successful anyway, one should find out why. I followed the second strategy and found that they were right in almost everything and the majority of US textbook recommendations were irrelevant to them. The consulting firm did not sell packaged and standardized consumer goods in supermarkets; they sold a complex and costly service customized to the individual needs of their clients.

There is a direct analog in health care. Patients are not standardized "goods" but their health is individual and formed by a complex combination of numerous factors. The patient needs customized treatment, which means that there may be a series of medical modules which can be combined to fit the individual, although sometimes this is not enough. The therapy can only be defined when doctor and patient meet and interact and the doctor adds his/her experience and insights.

This commentary is dedicated to Henry Mintzberg's Myth #2 that the healthcare system can be fixed by clever social engineering. The myth will be put into the context of my own research and reflections.

12.1.3 Building Health Factories

I totally agree that doctors and nurses alone cannot solve the healthcare dilemma. But who can? In the 1960s, it had become trendy among politicians, bureaucrats and administrators in Sweden to claim that hospitals would be much more efficient and economical if they were large. They were probably persuaded by accountants who only looked at cost and not revenue and contribution to value.

But getting the whole solution defined by precise numbers seemed so "scientific" to them. Too many courses in management, business, and economics pay homage to mathematical and statistical research as the ultimate truth and science.

Steel mills became their role model. A steel mill can grow to any size and still lower its cost per unit without reducing quality. Same with people, they concluded. With the allegedly fast progress of medical research, anything can be cured by a trained doctor.

Hence, get patients into the health factory, set a diagnosis and match it with the proper therapy, and let a specialist implement it. Big hospitals can have specialists in everything. The problem is that with almost 200 specialties in Western medicine, all with sub-specialties, the diagnosed disorder is treated out of context. A doctor rarely has enough general knowledge of the human being and the complex interaction between the patient's physiological and mental state, different organs, bacteria, the patient's food and drink intake, life style and other living conditions. A special disorder is basically dealt with as a stand-alone.

This also thrived on the naive idea that health disorders are clearly defined—and most still act as if this were the case. To use mathematical set theory, diseases are sometimes crisp sets but health as such is a complex amalgamation of fuzzy sets. A crisp set is an unambiguously defined box in which the disease is contained; a fuzzy set has a core but then fades away gradually and overlaps with several other sets. For example, if you cut your leg and it is not very deep, the cut can be treated as a box using a standardized therapy, and it will heal quickly. I could actually do it myself. But if you contract a complex disease such as cancer, even the diagnosis can be hard to establish. The standard cancer therapies of hospitals—radiation, surgery, and medication—require judgment calls based on explicit knowledge as well as the tacit knowledge of a doctor: experience, feeling, common sense, and so on. In Western medicine, the cause of cancer is not well understood and therapies may only remove symptoms. After a year or more, the cause of the cancer—which was not removed—will catch up and cancer establishes itself in other parts of the body (metastasis).

12.1.4 How Scientific Is Western Medical Science?

Today, the ruling hype is evidence-based medicine and in its extension evidence-based doctors who only practice what has been found in randomized experiments, meta-analyses of several experiments and published in so-called "top" international medical journals. This is now promoted as the gold standard of science (see further Gummesson 2017).

Investigating simplistic correlation between allegedly independent variables and dependent variables is positivism from the classic scientific revolution 400 years ago. It is not good enough today. In practice, evidenced-based medicine is just an incomplete way to test medication, "pills," on a "standard" person. An old person may easily have ten pills prescribed by his/her doctor and the synergy effect of these is not known. Elvis Presley died a sick man at the age of 42 and Michael Jackson at 53. They were musical geniuses and performers and led a hectic life, "supported" by doctors who prescribed a large number of medicines but had little or no idea of how these interacted with each other and with eating habits, sleeping habits, etc., of their patients. They were turned into prescribed-drug "junkies."

The observations of clinicians are given less and less credibility; the "experience" of a doctor and his/her continuous observations are referred to as "anecdotal evidence" of no scientific value. There is no space to go further into this here. I can only conclude that a published article by a Western medical "top" journal is not the "real truth;" it is just an operational definition and therefore its validity is low (Gummesson 2017).

There is a long tradition of elaborate testing of a drug before general approval for use in human beings. But this is increasingly circumvented by the live testing of new drugs in patients when there is no approved drug available and there is a chance that the new drug may slow down the progress of a disease. Persuading patients to do this offers two advantages for doctors: they are paid for it by the manufacturer and they get data to publish new articles which is essential for their career.

I asked a friend of mine who is an MD but has knowledge beyond mainstream Western medicine to take a good look at the drugs sold in pharmacies in Sweden and their recommended use, content, side-effects, etc. There is an official book listing some 2000 drugs approved by the medical authorities in Sweden and allowed to call themselves "läkemedel" ("means for cure"). My question was: How many of these actually cure a disease as the term promises, and how many just temporarily alleviate symptoms, such as pain or fever? Of the medicines in the book, his estimate was that only 15–20% cured a disease. Hence, the designation "means for cure" is false advertising. Having worked all my life with marketing, I doubt there is any profession or sector that spends so much money on promotion and advertising, and even more on covert ways of influencing the market and society in general. It is advanced lobbying, press releases, and media reports on fast progress and breakthroughs in cancer and other diseases, research grants to university hospitals, branding and image-building, including fancy designations of their products and science ("läkemedel," evidence-based medicine, life science).

12.1.5 Stakeholders in Health care

There are numerous groups of healthcare stakeholders and which group exerts the highest influence may vary or is hard to establish. I have led numerous seminars on healthcare quality with doctors, hospital managers, politicians, and other stakeholders and they rarely, if ever, mentioned the patient who is of course the No. 1 stakeholder. Unless the patient is cured or becomes better, the other stakeholders are redundant.

Medical staff should of course have a high position in the stakeholder hierarchy, but Henry Mintzberg finds them at the low end. They include doctors, nurses, lab analysts, rehabilitation specialists, pharmacists, paramedics, and ambulance drivers. Supportive stakeholders include the hospital CEO, hospital management, accounting and financial staff, the maintenance of buildings, cleaning personnel, food suppliers, computer and software specialists, receptionists, and others. On a macro-level, we have governments, special government agencies, politicians, bureaucrats and financiers. Especially in the US, insurance companies and lawyers have considerable power with questionable added value to the mission of health care. For the macro-groups, the focus is increasingly focused no more than on reduced cost and maximum short-term shareholder profit.

A highly influential stakeholder group that is often not mentioned consists of suppliers of drugs, medical equipment and disposable products. These are focused on profit maximization. They direct medical research through funding and consulting assignments to medical scientists and practicing doctors. University hospitals around the world are highly dependent on them.

12.1.6 Health care as Every Citizens' Right

The whole network of stakeholders is extremely complex and partially conflicting, meaning that the patient, instead of being the No. 1 stakeholder, in practice risks becoming no more than a residual. A politician needs to stay popular and get votes, please the media to get publicity, and pursue his party's ideological advocacy such as "equality." Every citizen should have access to health care; it should not be just for the rich. This is a sound principle because if people stay healthy they also handle their lives better and contribute more to the whole of a nation and its wealth.

However, there are also irrational political and ideological influences. For instance, in Sweden it meant that if you got some irritant in your eye that prevented you from working, you should wait with everybody else at an emergency clinic even if all the doctors were doing trauma surgery on victims of a car crash, an operation that could take 5 or 10 h. The eye problem could be cured very quickly by a doctor or a nurse removing the irritant.

But is it "democratic" to wait for your turn without considering the circumstances? When two doctors in Stockholm wanted to open an emergency clinic for the most frequent but light disorders that could be quickly fixed so that patients could get back to normal, the Social-Democratic party and the Communists started to shout about inequality. The reaction was not true socialism but a Soviet Bolshevik application introduced by Lenin right after the 1917 communist revolution and followed up by Stalin and others, and since then proven inefficient and inhuman in practice. Strangely enough, it still lives on in Europe today.

As luck would have it, the two doctors were smart and entrepreneurial and negotiated a temporary permission to open the clinic. It was an immediate success among patients and still is after 35 years—despite the fact that authorities kept harassing them, fortunately with limited success. In the "light" clinic, the patient should wait a maximum of 20 min. I have been there a couple of times and learnt that if for some reason—a doctor had suddenly become sick or more patients than normal came—the waiting time could not be kept, they informed me that they were sorry that it will take, say, 1 h and 30 min. I could wait or come back at that time still keeping my place in the waiting line.

Health care in Sweden is a huge problem in many ways, but during the past 20 years the Social-Democrats have become less dogmatic. Communists have changed their name for public relations reasons and now call themselves The Left Party but are still as dogmatic as before. The liberal government we had from 2006 to 2014 speeded up the process toward practical solutions based on the mixed economy ideology: some things have to be run by the government but there should also be alternatives for patients. These can be managed by private clinics in competition. It has opened up a combination of government-run hospitals and private hospitals. The government has outsourced certain types of health service to private clinics, meaning that patients can use tax-paid health insurance even at the private clinic, which is reimbursed by the state or the region. This is common in Europe and in Canada.

Still, it is absolutely necessary to keep the power over health care within the public sector. Health care is not the same as selling soda drinks. In service management, patients have been called customers to stress that they are there to be served. Stretched too far, this concept will go wrong; health is in the interest of a nation. Being a citizen is more than being a consumer.

Like Henry Mintzberg says, initiatives and solutions do not come from the top but from the ground. Nevertheless, traditional Western-trained doctors can be very conservative and their knowledge limited. For example, in the 1980s the waiting-time for hernia operations was 6 years in Stockholm! On average, the operation takes 45 min. Why then such waiting times? Because the hospitals used the same system as when my father had hernia surgery in the 1950s: diagnose hernia, hospitalize the patient on a Friday, let him (it is almost exclusively a male) stay in bed until a surgeon checks him on Monday, schedule an operation for Wednesday and then let him stay in the hospital bed for another week. A new procedure, day surgery, has been designed internationally to speed up the process and lower the costs, at the same time as the quality of the operation has improved. The new process too has its weaknesses, but they are less than before and can be prevented—if the doctors are knowledgeable enough and the patient does his part.

Younger doctors learnt about it and when they were finally allowed (with opposition from the Social-Democrats, the Communists and conservative doctors) to do day surgery, a couple of doctors were allocated to get rid of the waiting times in Stockholm. They did so in one year. When I had my hernia operation about 10 years ago, I only waited a few days. I arrived in the morning at 8:30 and left at 2:00 pm. Two days after the operation I was back at work after resting at home for one day and with the instruction not to carry heavy objects for the next two months.

12.1.7 A Note on Theory of Service

In my presentation at the Salerno conference I brought up similar issues as are stressed in Henry Mintzberg's article but I added the new developments in service theory, what I refer to as Paradigm 3: The new theory of service. My recommendation is that Henry Mintzberg includes this in his agenda; it is partly similar to his but it adds some critical dimensions (Gummesson 2012).

We have to recognize that the societies of today are extremely complex and understanding the complexity is a condition for transforming service into simple and efficient systems. To address the complexity, network theory and systems theory are helpful (Mele and Polese 2011). They let us sort out details, link them and create more coherent ecosystems. It is demanding but in service we have lacked grand theory helping us to see both the parts and the whole and the final outcome.

There are especially two promising contributions that are developing continuously and are highly relevant to health care. How it is applied depends on the context as health care has to handle a multitude of diverse disorders.

One is Service-Dominant (S-D) Logic, suggested by two professors as a theoretical contribution to previous ways of addressing service (Lusch and Vargo 2014). In S-D logic customers are cocreators of service. Cocreation is a step further than cooperation; the patient is a resource not just a person to whom the expert does something but one who the expert does something with. Patients know a lot about themselves that the doctors do not, but they know different things. These days more and more people read up on symptoms and illnesses on Google and are better prepared to meet the doctor than before. This makes some doctors insecure; they still like to demonstrate superiority. Instead they should see it as productive resource integration. The doctor offers a value proposition. The traditional idea of doctor's orders—the sick person comes, the doctor sets a diagnosis, prescribes a remedy and the patient becomes healthy—exists but is the exception rather than the rule.

On the practitioner side, IBM, today the world's largest management consulting firm with 360,000 employees globally, has set the 20 year Service Science Program is in progress (Maglio and Spohrer 2008). The program is half way and IBM is collaborating with 500 universities around the world. Its purpose is to transfer IBM's business mission from computer science, which is product- and supplier-centric, to service science, which is centered on creating smarter service systems for users, striving to improve the understanding of service systems that create value for its users and contributors.

This is highly relevant in medicine. A patient confronted with a hospital easily gets lost in its fragmented activities and does not understand where to turn and what to get out of it. The service science program has adopted S-D logic as its grand theory helping them to see the overriding principles for successful value cocreation in a complex world of numerous stakeholders. Through these insights, the service system can become better and we can leave the pile of fragmented and non-coherent activities behind.

12.1.8 Social Engineering in Health care

Social engineering is what the word says: manipulation of people, rules, and regulations to exert bureaucratic control of their thinking and behavior, and standardization. It is useful but only up to a degree; it is doing things to people. In new service theory, the emphasis is on doing things with people through cocreation and resource integration. This applies very well to health care.

It is now 40 years since I began to see that the overriding aspect of service was relationships, networks, and interaction. I have stayed with it ever since and the new service theory corroborates my conclusions. I will continue to work on the rejuvenation of health care but will also bring in thoughts that are beyond Henry Mintzberg's current agenda and the new service theory.

12.2 Health Literacy and Service-Dominant Logic

Gerardine Doyle, Alessandra Storlazzi, and Carmela Annarumma

12.2.1 Introduction

Could rejecting a managerial paradigm seem hazardous to managers?

We will explore Henry Mintzberg's (2012) vision and Gummesson's (2014) new logic of service in order to challenge some of the traditional assumptions of management thought as applied to the provision of healthcare services.

Our reflections aim at offering a way forward for such reframing, which could "come largely out of the operations, and diffuse across them" (Henry Mintzberg 2012, p. 4), to be activated by both a renewed interpretation of the operational levels of the organization alongside a collaborative and inclusive logic towards patients and other stakeholders.

Healthcare organizations are "complex adaptive systems" (Glouberman et al. 2006): strong interactions among different groups (i.e., policy makers, top and middle managers, physicians, nurses, team members, patients, and their informal caregivers) are fundamental for their functioning. We suggest that focusing on the quality of interactions and communication with the patient becomes particularly crucial within the special and complex context of care and well-being. Such an approach can lead to an enhanced ability to navigate the healthcare services and improved health outcomes for patients.

In the same vein, Gummesson (2014) likewise reflects on the management of healthcare systems. He identifies the framework of a new logic of service including the Service-Dominant Logic (S-D logic) based on relationships, networks and interactions. S-D logic uses the concept of cocreation, it acknowledges the patient as an active resource, not a person to whom the professional does something, but one who the professional does something with.

For Gummesson (2014), healthcare value proposition consists of many parts within a complex network, such as medical examinations, diagnosis, medication, surgery and the allied services. Health care is much more than medication. At the heart of Gummesson's proposition is the creation of value for improved health. Everything that is produced and sold should have the potential to create value and render service. Hospitals must learn to better cocreate service with patients (Gummesson 2014). The patient is the most important stakeholder followed by medical staff, administrators and politicians. Gummesson argues that "preventing an illness to get a foothold in your body is always the best "therapy" and that has to do with the patient's lifestyle like eating habits and can be better supported by health care in a co-creative mode" (Gummesson 2014, p. 6). According to him, the new logic of service with service science, S-D logic, network theory and systems theory offer new possibilities.

Gummesson's approach enables us to focus on the possible links between the S-D logic and the health literacy paradigm, which is receiving growing attention by academics and policy makers.

12.2.2 The Concept of Health Literacy

Numerous attempts have been made to define the term "health literacy" (Sørensen et al. 2012). The continued and global expansion of the field suggests that both academics and practitioners consider health literacy a concept worth pursuing (Fullam 2014, p. 4). In the first instance, health literacy focused on "reading" and "numeracy" skills (Simonds 1974; Baker et al. 1998; Parker et al. 1999) and took into account level of education, communication, information, and health skills (Simonds 1974). Even considering the fundamental importance of health education (Yost et al. 2009; Adams et al. 2009), the academic debate around "health literacy" has been enriched by the inclusion of other factors such as cognitive, social, and behavioral factors that affect the level of health literacy (Nutbeam 1998) and influence an individual's ability to collect and process health information (Nielson-Bohlman et al. 2004).

Consensus among scholars and practitioners has emerged in a way such that health literacy is a strategic determinant of an individual's health empowerment to interact with the social environment offering an innovative approach in promoting health (Kickbusch and Maag 2008). Appropriate health choices affect the healthcare system, fostering outcomes (Baker et al. 2007; DeWalt et al. 2004), influencing the costs of health service provision (Eichler et al. 2009; Vernon et al. 2007) and limiting inequity of access to health care (von Vagner et al. 2007; Volandes and Paasche-Orlow 2007; Nutbeam and Kickbusch 2000). As a consequence, an irreversible virtuous cycle emerges. It is moved by the individual level of empowerment, and produces improved public health (Koh et al. 2012; Levy and Royne 2009).

From this standpoint, health literacy arises as a tool for health promotion, to be managed by policy makers (Parker et al. 2003), which can produce both health and social outcomes (Nutbeam 2001). Recent literature views health literacy as a dynamic and variable process which affects the life course of each individual (Rootman and Gordon-El-Bihbety 2008; Mancuso 2008) and his/her quality of life (HLS-EU Project 2008; U.S. Department of Health and Human Services 2010), in addition to overall levels of well-being (Freedman et al. 2009). The interaction of both the environment and the people who produce health care feeds this process (Ishikawa et al. 2008). Health literacy may also play a strategic role in pursuing fair and appropriate health policies, centered on patient's needs (European Patients' Forum Spring Conference 2008).

Following these evolving trajectories, the concept of health literacy goes beyond the scope of education and involves the community, through a continuous and dynamic interaction with the social environment, paving the way for a strong guarantee of quality of life and ultimately acting as a decisive strategic determinant for public health.

12.2.3 Patient Cocreation

Since the 1970s, research on service marketing has shown that a service context enables companies to approach customers in fundamentally different ways compared with conventional marketing models that reflect a goods logic and stem from a manufacturing context (Grönroos and Gummerus 2014). A different model has emerged in the service-dominant (S-D) logic. In S-D logic (Vargo and Lusch 2004, 2008), value cocreation is accomplished through resource integration. Building on the emerging model of cocreation of value (Lusch et al. 2007; Schau et al. 2009; Vargo and Lusch 2008), in which value is determined "in use" through activities and interactions of customers "with" the service provider, customer value cocreation can be defined as the "benefit realized from integration of resources through activities and interactions with collaborators in the customer's service network" (McColl-Kennedy et al. 2012, p. 1). "This new definition breaks free from the previous two party (firm-customer) conceptualization of value creation, extending it to the customer's service network" (McColl-Kennedy et al. 2012, p. 2).

This new understanding views customers as active, rather than passive (McColl-Kennedy et al. 2012). "While it is recognized that some styles of value cocreation are important from an organization's perspective, insofar as they increase 'productivity' (Chase 1978), little empirical research has addressed the customer's role in value cocreation and its subsequent effect on important customer outcomes, such as quality of life" (McColl-Kennedy et al. 2012, p. 6). "There is a link between customer value cocreation practice styles (CVCPS) and quality of life" (McColl-Kennedy et al. 2012, p. 1).

Focusing on health care as stated by Gummesson (2014) "S-D logic uses the concept of co-creation which recognizes the patient as an active resource." "Furthermore, there is growing acknowledgment within health care that treatment plans and related activities can extend beyond interactions with doctors to include broader aspects of the individual's life such as lifestyle and beliefs" (Michie et al. 2003). For example, "customers may co-create value with others outside the traditional health care setting, such as complementary therapies, and/or with the customer's private sources such as peers, family, friends. Furthermore, customers may cocreate value through self-activities. These activities may be self-generated (such as activities engaged in by the self that ultimately contribute to the cocreation of value, such as cerebral activities—positive thinking, reframing and sense-making, emotional labor, and 'psyching oneself up'")" (McColl-Kennedy et al. 2012, p. 2). Within health care there is now recognition that the "successful management of chronic diseases, such as cancer, is related to the collaborative interactions between the individual and the health provider and the active involvement of the individual (Holman and Lorig 2000) (McColl-Kennedy et al. 2012, p. 7). The healthcare customer value cocreation approach includes a range of activities, behavioral and cognitive, and interactions (McColl-Kennedy et al. 2012). Patients cocreate health with the medical staff and administrators. The patient is the primary resource integrator in the cocreation of his/her own healthcare management, but as argued by McColl-Kennedy et al. (2012), he/she integrates other sources including private sources (friends/family), market-facing sources (firms, clinics, hospitals, various healthcare professionals including doctors, nurses, dieticians, physical therapists, alternative medicine practitioners, acupuncturists, meditation, and yoga teachers) and public sources (community self-help groups, associations, governmental health departments) through activities and interactions with a range of others in the patient's service network (Vargo 2011).

12.2.4 Conclusions

Health literacy combines personal, social, and environmental factors which affect the individual level of health literacy, together with the determinants which affect population level of health literacy. In such a context, skills related to accessing, understanding, appraising, and applying health information are crucial. These skills require not only cognitive effort, but also behavioral effort. Simultaneously, as stated by Gummesson (2014) "S-D logic uses the concept of cocreation which permits the recognition of the patient as an active resource." Within this perspective, patients are called upon to play an active role in the care process. They cocreate health with the medical staff and administrators.

For both S-D logic and health literacy perspectives, patient empowerment in the production of health is essential to generate better outcomes in care services and to reduce the risk of inappropriate access to care. Furthermore, fostering the process of patient empowerment becomes a crucial action to gain more "engaged clinicians" in the design of the organizational strategy (Henry Mintzberg 2012, p. 4).

Indeed, with the eventual purpose of effectively reframing the strategy of healthcare organizations, the higher the level of patient empowerment, the greater the ability of professionals in activating strategic initiatives. Involving the patient in the provision of care undoubtedly favors professionals in making effective "hospital decisions" (Henry Mintzberg 2012, p. 6).

Going beyond its entailments in improving logical participation and fostering individual ability to handle health-related issues, the development of a new theory of society coherent with S-D logic and health literacy promotes new management trajectories. As stated before, S-D logic and health literacy turn out to be crucial in enhancing the involvement of the patient in the provision of care. In this way, patients may cocreate partnerships and healthcare value with the professional staff. The latter could have a more appropriate perception of the need for care, and their "venturing activities" (Henry Mintzberg 2012, p. 6) would be strongly facilitated.

Hence, a managerial approach which pays attention to both health literacy and S-D logic ultimately performs as a strategy aimed at closing that "administrative gap" mentioned by Henry Mintzberg (2012, p. 6) which divides "those who administer and those who deliver the basic services" (Henry Mintzberg 2009, p. 171).

It could be argued that the confusion and frustration of people (namely, the professionals) who are below such a "gaping hole" (Henry Mintzberg 2009, p. 171) are intensified by the efforts to cope with patients who are not health-literate and are not empowered.

Consequently, the integration of health literacy and S-D logic approaches within the functioning of healthcare organizations could be considered also as a means to overcome professionals' distress, paving the way for their fully fledged participation in the process of reframing the organizational strategy.

12.3 Health Care Management: An Integrated Perspective

Giuseppe Favretto, Aurelio Tommasetti, and Massimiliano Vesci

12.3.1 Introduction

Some of the most interesting cues deriving from Gummesson's (2010) and Henry Mintzberg's (2012) contributions seem to be particularly appropriate to describe the Italian context. Furthermore, the views of these two authors mark a breaking point in the literature and represent a first step in building a new theoretical and interdisciplinary framework allowing us to analyze the issue of healthcare management.

In particular, Gummesson introduces three frameworks: Network and System Thinking (ST), Service-Dominant Logic (SDL), and Service Science (SS). These perspectives seem to be very helpful in approaching the issues of health, being at the same time perfectly complementary to each other and above all completely integrated with the overcoming of the healthcare management myths mentioned by Henry Mintzberg. Moreover, the Gummesson and Henry Mintzberg indications appear to represent altogether a perfect theoretical framework for a new approach to health care in general and to Italian health care in particular.

12.3.2 Three Theoretical Pillars for Overcoming the Myths of Italian Healthcare Management

Actually, exactly in the same way as Henry Mintzberg, in the aforementioned work, Butera et al. (2004) highlighted some of the limitations involved in the traditional studies on management, namely in the so-called mainstream of management studies. In particular, the authors notice that the process of privatization characterizing Italian healthcare systems determines substantial alterations, not only in the modalities of individuals' health management but also in system operators' conduct. The most important aspect is that these effects are not always positive, especially with reference to subjects' behaviors and perceptions of their role.

A critical interpretation of Henry Mintzberg's and Gummesson's viewpoints allows us to underline the theoretical pillars supporting their arguments. Even if both the authors propose a departure from mainstream logic, the first identifies the elements to overcome and the modalities of this process, whereas the second stresses the necessity of adopting a new approach possibly based on the combination of three theories: Network and ST, SDL, and SS.

Although being introduced in different ways, the two views show remarkable points of convergence, simultaneously leading to the proposal of an innovative pathway for the abandonment of classical managerial principles.

The aim of Gummesson's contribution is to reinterpret the concept of relationships: in fact, the author explores management adopting a point of view focused on notions such as network and interactions. In this perspective, reality is a set of relations, nodes, links, and interactions connecting the previously mentioned elements.

Specifically, Gummesson's view is founded on the shift from one-to-one relationships to many-to-many relationships (Gummesson 2008). If one-to-one relationships emphasize dyadic connections between single individuals, many-to-many relationships take into account all the active stakeholders involved in marketing contexts. The author emphasizes the reticular nature of the healthcare system, interpreted as a relationship network based on the centrality of patients both as supervisors of the whole service network and value cocreators. With regard to this network-based approach, the fundamental contribution (in such a theoretical construction) of system thinking and in particular of Viable System Approach (VSA) should be remarked in this context. In fact, VSA (Barile 2009; Barile and Polese 2011) represents "general reference schemes that are useful in interpreting the concept of complexity, highlighting its systemic nature, and that can support the investigation of the general implications of complexity for decision making in service systems" (Wieland et al. 2012, p. 19). At the same time, it is a governance methodology according to which "all entities (individuals, consumers, organizations, or communities) should be perceived as systems that are made up of interlinked subcomponents that strive towards a common goal" (Wieland et al. 2012, p. 19).

The remaining two theoretical pillars identified by Gummesson are SDL (Vargo and Lusch 2004, 2008; Lusch and Vargo 2006) and SS (Maglio and Spohrer 2008) which are strictly related, deriving the first from theory and the latter from practice.

SDL represents a services marketing paradigm symbolizing the new service era, marked by the centrality of the immaterial aspects of consumption, and counterpoising Good-Dominant Logic (GDL). Moreover SDL has been effectively employed to analyze a wide range of consumer behaviors in the field of marketing and recently in health care also (Joiner and Lusch 2016). One of the main differences between SDL and GDL concerns the definition of value exchange. In fact, according to the first approach, value is interpreted as value-in-exchange, while for the second value refers to value-in-use or better to value-in-context (Vargo et al. 2008). This notion implies that there is "no value until an offering is used—experience and perception are essential to value determination" (Vargo and Lusch 2006, p. 44).

Another important dissimilarity between the two viewpoints relates to customer role in value creation. In fact, in GDL consumers are destroyers of the value provided by organizations. Instead, in SDL, users actively participate in value cocreation, being viewed as integrators of the resources provided by organizations, by others subjects (such as public or private companies) and even by other clients. In this way, users are no longer viewed as mere receivers of goods, services, experience and then value, but on the contrary organizations "must seek to engage people as active cocreators of value (Botti et al. 2017) everywhere in the system" (Ramaswamy 2009, p. 11). This assumption reaffirms the urge to reframe management beyond its myths.

As debated above, Gummesson and Henry Mintzberg address a total reconsideration of mainstream management logics. In fact, the first author pinpoints the three theoretical pillars, whereas the second proposes, from an operational point of view, the detachment from managerial myths (Fig. 12.1).

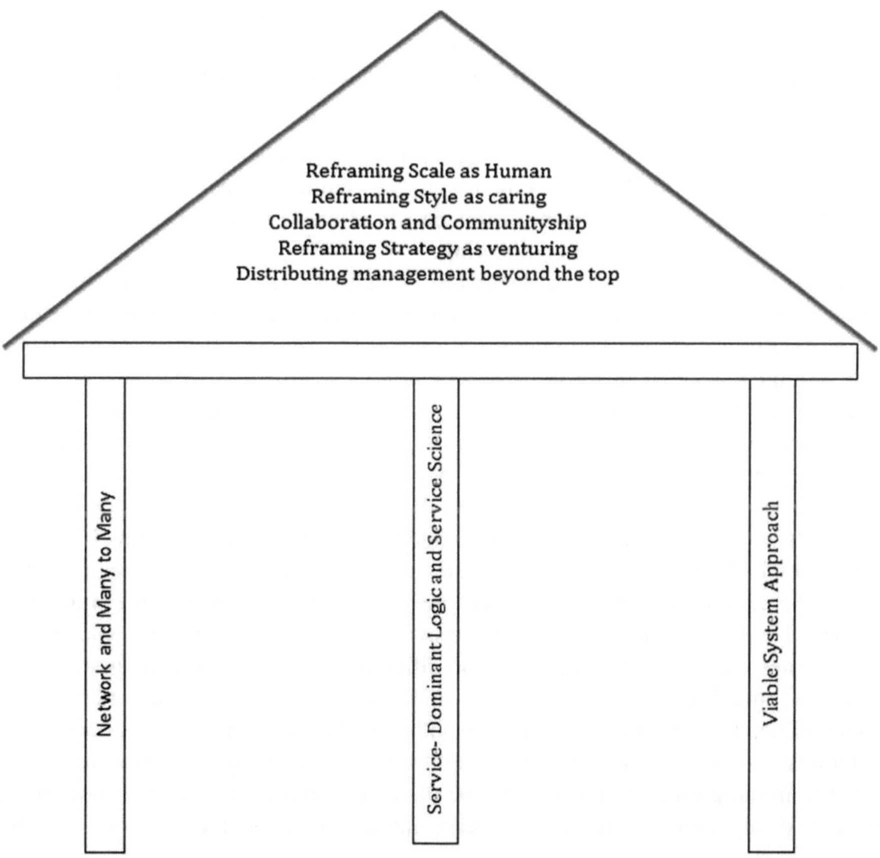

Fig. 12.1 Three theoretical pillars to overcome managerial myths in Italian Health care

The transition from a dyadic to a multiple view of relationships, in which the "many-to-many" connections contemplate the collaboration between managers and physicians, allows actualizing the new "management beyond the top" mindset. Besides, the adoption of such a holistic view allows increasing the autonomy, the consciousness and the effectiveness of managerial choices, thus facilitating a better implementation of policies.

Reconsidering each element of the market as a service, reinterpreting service logic shifting attention toward value, recognizing the importance of intangible resources and of the ability to enable them, rethinking customers' role in service design and provision, generating a concrete process of cocreation, necessarily required in Italian healthcare system

- a reformulation of the strategies, which should not only correspond to planning but should also be intended as emerging strategies;
- a reframing of the organizations, designed to encourage the surfacing of a distributed leadership and the collaboration among the various parts of the system;
- a rethinking of the managerial style adopted, which should be more and more oriented to meet patients' expectations;
- a reframing of the measurement scales, which should not only be numerical, but above all humanized.

Moreover, a point of great convergence between the suggestions proposed by Henry Mintzberg (2012) and Gummesson (see Gummesson contribution in this same book) seems to be the Henry Mintzberg's Myth #2 that the healthcare system can be fixed by clever social engineering.

According to the current mainstream, consultants, management experts, and strategic analysts, are the only ones who understand the problems of the health system: only these "detached engineers" Henry Mintzberg (2012, p. 4) can delineate strategies in order to fix it.

Henry Mintzberg (2012, p. 6) is very clear about this point: "If you want to understand what strategy means in a professional organization such as a hospital, stay away from almost all the strategy books […]. If strategy concerns the positioning of products and services for users, then in a hospital the services are specific kinds of treatments for specific diseases. And where do these come from? […] They come mostly from the venturing activities of professionals: concern about a new disease here, championing of a new treatment there. In other words, the strategy of a hospital is largely the sum total of the many ventures of its professional staff".

Gummesson, basing his arguments on different theoretical foundations—namely SDL, ST, and SS—similarly conclude that patients is the most important stakeholder of healthcare system: for this reason hospitals are not for administrators staff. Solutions and new ways of doing the right things necessarily in healthcare system come from the ground. For too long time the consultants postulated the adoption of an industrial logic in healthcare recognizing the fundamental role of cost accounting: now, it is time to overcome the model that led to the construction of "health factories" (see Gummesson contribution in this same book)!

The overcoming of the Myths of health care, and in particular of the Myth #2, can be pursued, recognizing the fundamental role of the two most important stakeholder of the system: the patient and the physician. Only their concrete interaction and a contextual reduction of the actual complexity and bureaucracy can lead to the introduction of self-learning practice to better cocreate the healthcare service. It is not a case that McColl-Kennedy et al. (2012, p. 375), studying healthcare customer value cocreation practice styles, remarked the relevance of interaction assuming that "Interactions are the ways individuals engage with others in their service network to integrate resources".

12.3.3 The Departure from Mainstream Logics in Italian Health care

The theoretical pillars discussed in the previous paragraph and elaborated from Gummesson's and Henry Mintzberg's contributions represent an adequate conceptual framework in analyzing the Italian context.

The Italian healthcare system is based on a mixed approach: on the one hand, it is mainly public in nature, and on the other hand it is characterized by a series of individualistic features that Henry Mintzberg (2012) attributes to the private approach, closely related to business organization. The reasons of this individualism are associated with the typical liberalism-statism deviation of the Italian context, based on the application of the liberistic logic to a statist system. Consequently, if on the one hand the guarantees of statism are respected, on the other hand the corresponding adhesion to economic risks is lacking.

A typical example of this Italian deviation could be found in the role of general managers, whose salaries should be reduced, thus erasing the Italian idolizing of senior positions. These figures are, in fact, the symbol of an excessively hierarchical vision of healthcare organizations, completely exemplifying the false myths of social engineering and of leadership introduced by Henry Mintzberg (2012).

In this way, general managers become expert supervisors controlling, commanding and solving problems through a top-down approach. In truth, rather than being efficient "dei ex machina", generally they are only the emblem of a kind of administration that, instead of supporting, tends to criticize and supervise, thus encouraging an onerous culture of control which fosters hypertrophic administrative systems. In so doing, these apparatus are incapable of understanding the concept of internal client and the improvements required in terms of compatibility among the various system departments and in terms of service and process quality.

In an attempt to remove the old rational culture focused on control in favor of the establishment of organizational models based on personal and professional responsibility, the reorganization of national healthcare system should be centered on the containment and on the reduction of verticalism and on the rediscovery of the polycentric logic associated with the diffusion of collaborative horizontal networks.

As Henry Mintzberg (2012) suggests, management should be redistributed beyond the top, empowering those organizational members who concretely deal with everyday challenges in the healthcare environment and are able to fully understand the characteristics of such challenges. For this purpose, general managers should not be involved in those tasks and roles that can be decentralized. The role of the middle line and of integrating managers should be emphasized, to promote a sensitivity for the engagement of all the specialists involved in the process of value creation in the healthcare ecosystem. As well, it is crucial to reduce the hypertrophic number of medical specialties, insisting on the general ones. The possibility of redistributing the initiative in a polycentric organization which sticks to a hub & spoke model requires a training which contemplates also managerial and organizational skills and enables physicians to manage groups, departments, and funds. In this way, homogeneous teams, which are able to achieve systemic efficiency on a large scale, can be created.

As Henry Mintzberg (2012) observes, health care, intended as a vocation, works better in units as small as technology allows. The ideal and natural scale of these units should depend on the efficiency of organizational systems, which basically consists of a network of services, physicians and patients. Lastly, all the reframes proposed by Henry Mintzberg, as underlined through the aforementioned examples, should be centered on a network logic and on SDL in which patients cocreate value, as highlighted by Gummesson (2010).

References

Adams RJ, Stocks NP, Wilson DH, Hill CL, Gravier S, Kickbusch I, Beilby JJ (2009) Health literacy-a new concept for general practice? Aust Fam Physician 38(3):144–147

Baker DW, Parker RM, Williams MV, Clark WS (1998) Health literacy and the risk of hospital admission. J Gen Intern Med 13:791–800

Baker DW, Wolf MS, Feinglass J, Thompson JA, Gazmararian JA, Huang J (2007) Health literacy and mortality among elderly persons. Arch Intern Med 167(14):1503–1509

Barile S (2009) Management Sistemico Vitale. Giappichelli, Torino

Botti A, Grimaldi M, Tommasetti A, Troisi O, Vesci M (2017) Modeling and measuring the consumer activities associated with value cocreation: an exploratory test in the context of education. Serv Sci 9(1):1–11

Barile S, Polese F (2011) Contributions to theoretical and practical advances in management: a viable systems approach (vSa). ASVSA—Association for Research on Viable Systems International Printing, pp 37–59

Butera N, Cosentini MA, Cotugno A (2004) Alcuni effetti dell'aziendalizzazione nella sanità pubblica. Psicobiettivo 1(1):65–84

Chase RB (1978) Where does the customer fit in a service operation? Harvard Bus Rev 56(6):137–142

DeWalt DA, Berkman ND, Sheridan S, Lohr KN, Pignone MP (2004) Literacy and health outcomes. A systematic review of the literature. J Gen Intern Med 19:1228–1239

Eichler K, Wieser S, Brügger U (2009) The costs of limited health literacy: a systematic review. Int J Publ Health 54:313–324

European Health Literacy Survey Project, Department of International Health, Maastricht University (www.inthealth.eu)

Freedman DA, Bess KD, Tucker HA, Boyd DL, Tuchman AM, Wallston KA (2009) Public health literacy defined. Am J Prev Med 36(5):446–451

Fullam J (2014) Conceptualisation, measurement, and exploration of health literacy in Ireland, PhD Thesis. School of Public Health, Physiotherapy, and Population Science. School of Business. University College Dublin

Glaser BG, Strauss AL (1967) The discovery of grounded theory. Aldine, Chicago, IL

Glouberman S, Enkin M, Groff P, Jadad A, Stern A (2006) Entrenched health care practices and complex systems. Aust Health Rev 30:7–11

Grönroos C, Gummerus J (2014) The service revolution and its marketing implications: service logic versus service-dominant logic. Managing Serv Qual 24(3):206–229

Gummesson E (2008) Quality, service-dominant Dominant logic and many-to-many marketing. TQM J 20(2):143–153

Gummesson E (2010) Lectio magistralis: reflections on health care systems. Paper presented at the conference The Health Care Service organized by the University La Sapienza di Roma, The University of Cassino and The University of Salerno. Salerno, 15 Oct 2010

Gummesson E (2012) The three service marketing paradigms: which one are you guided by? Mercati e Competitività 1:5–13

Gummesson E (2014) Reflections on health care systems. Stockholm University School of Business, Sweden

Gummesson E (2017) Case theory: reinventing case study research in business and management. Sage, London

Gummesson E, Grönroos C (2012) The emergence of the new service marketing: Nordic school perspectives. J Serv Manage 23(4):479–497

Health Literacy Conference Report (2008). European patients' forum spring conference. Brussels, 8–9 April

Holman H, Lorig K (2000) Patients as partners in managing chronic disease. Br Med J 320 (7234):526–527

Ishikawa H, Nomura K, Sato M, Yano E (2008) Developing a measure of communicative and critical health literacy: a pilot study of Japanese office workers. Health Promot Int 23(3):269–274

Joiner KA, Lusch RF (2016) Evolving to a new service-dominant logic for health care. Innov Entrepreneurship Health 3:25–33

Kickbusch I, Maag D (2008) Health literacy. In: Heggenhougen K, Quah S (eds) International encyclopedia of public health, vol 3. Academic Press, San Diego, pp 204–211

Koh HK, Berwick DM, Clancy CM, Baur C, Brach C, Harris LM, Zerhusen EG (2012) New federal policy initiatives to boost health literacy can help the nation move beyond the cycle of costly 'crisis care'. Health Aff 31(2):434–443

Levy M, Royne MB (2009) The impact of consumers' health literacy on public health. J Consum Aff 43(2):367–372

Lusch RF, Vargo SL (2006) Service-dominant logic: reactions, reflections and refinements. Mark Theor 6(3):281–288

Lusch RF, Vargo SL (2012) The forum on markets and marketing (FMM): advancing service-dominant logic. Mark Theor 12(2):193–199

Lusch RF, Vargo SL (2014) Service-dominant logic. Cambridge University Press, Cambridge, UK
Lusch RF, Vargo SL, O'Brien M (2007) Competing through service: insights from service-dominant logic. J Retail 83(1):2–18
Maglio P, Spohrer JC (2008) Fundamentals of service science. J Acad Mark Sci 36(1):8–20
Mancuso JM (2008) Health literacy: a concept/dimensional analysis. Nurs Health Sci 10(3):248–255
McColl-Kennedy JR, Vargo SL, Dagger TS, Sweeney JC, van Kasteren Y (2012) Health Care customer value cocreation practice styles. J Serv Res 15(4):370–389
Mele C, Polese F (2011) Key dimensions of service systems in value-creating networks. In: Demirkan H, Spohrer J, Krishna V (eds) The science of service systems. Springer, New York, pp 37–59
Michie S, Miles J, Weinman J (2003) Concepts of trust among patients with serious illness. Patient Educ Counselling 51:197–206
Mintzberg H (2009) Managing. Berrett-Koehler Publishers
Mintzberg H (2012) Managing the myths of health care. World Hosp Health Serv 48(3):4–7
Nielson-Bohlman L, Panzer A, Kindig D (2004) Health literacy: a prescription to end confusion. Institute of Medicine, National Academy of Sciences, Washington, DC
Nutbeam D (1998) Health promotion glossary. Health Promot Int 13:349–364
Nutbeam D (2001) Health literacy as a public health goal: a challenge for contemporary health education and communication strategies in the 21st century. Health Promot Int 15:259–267
Nutbeam D, Kickbusch I (2000) Advancing health literacy: a global challenge for 21st century. Health Promot Int 15(3):183–184
Parker RM, Williams MV, Weiss BD, Baker DW, Davis TC, Doak CC, Doak LG, Hein K, Meade CD, Nurss J, Schwartzberg JG, Somers SA (1999) Health literacy-report of the council on scientific affairs. J Am Med Assoc 281(6):552–557
Parker RM, Ratzan SC, Lurie N (2003) Health literacy: a policy challenge for advancing high-quality health care. Health Aff 22(4):147–153
Perotti R (2014) Alti dirigenti pubblici, tutti gli stipendi d'oro. Retrieved from http://www.ilfattoquotidiano.it/2014/01/20/alti-dirigenti-pubblici-tutti-gli-stipendi-doro/850407/
Ramaswamy V (2009) Leading the transformation to co-creation of value. Strategy Leadersh 37 (2):32–37
Rootman I, Gordon-El-Bihbety D (2008) A vision for a health literate Canada: report of the expert panel on health literacy. Canadian Public Health Association, Ottawa
Schau HJ, Muniz AM Jr, Arnould EJ (2009) How brand community practices create value. J Mark 73(5):30–51
Simonds SK (1974) Health education as social policy. Health Educ Monogr 2(suppl):1–25
Sørensen K, Van den Broucke S, Fullam S, Doyle G, Pelikan J, Slonska Z, Brand H (2012) Health literacy and public health: a systematic review and integration of definitions and models. BMC Public Health 12:80
U.S. Department of Health and Human Services, Office of Disease Prevention and Health Promotion (2010) National action plan to improve health literacy, May 2010
Vargo SL (2011) Market systems, stakeholders and value propositions: toward a service-dominant logic-based theory of the market. Eur J Mark 45(1):217–222
Vargo SL, Lusch RF (2004) Evolving to a new dominant logic for marketing. J Mark 68:1–17
Vargo SL, Lusch RF (2006) Service-dominant logic: what it is, what it is not, what it might be. In: Lusch RF, Vargo SL (eds) The service-dominant logic of marketing: dialog, debate and directions. M.E. Sharpe Inc., Armonk, pp 43–56
Vargo SL, Lusch RF (2008) Service-dominant logic: continuing the evolution. J Acad Mark Sci 36:1–10
Vargo SL, Maglio PP, Akaka MA (2008) On value and value co-creation: a service systems and service logic perspective. Eur Manage J 26(3):145–152

Vernon JA, Trujillo A, Rosenbaum S, De Buono B (2007) Low health literacy: implications for national health policy. George Washington University Medical Centre, School of Public Health and Health Services

Volandes AE, Paasche-Orlow MK (2007) Health literacy, health inequality and a just health care system. Am J Bioeth 7(11):5–10

Wieland H, Polese F, Vargo S, Lusch R (2012) Toward a service (eco) systems perspective on value creation. Int J Serv Sci Manage Eng Technol 3(3):12–24

Yost KJ, Webster K, Baker DW, Choi SW, Bode RK, Hahn EA (2009) Bilingual health literacy assessment using the Talking Touchscreen/la Pantalla Parlanchina: development and pilot testing. Patient Educ Counselling 75(3):295–301

Part III
Lessons Learnt

Chapter 13
Looking Through the Lens of the Complexity Paradigm

Paola Adinolfi and Elio Borgonovi

The contributions in this volume have offered separate insights and frameworks and, around these, a mosaic of specific indications and applications which remain irreducibly various. There are indeed some common points, which deserve to be highlighted.

The authors unanimously agree on the need for overcoming healthcare myths, which together constituted the intellectual framework of scientific management orthodoxy applied to health care. This was not obvious, since we stimulated a collective reflection polarized between equally passionate critics and supporters of Henry Mintzberg's theses.

Complexity is one of the major ideas that undermine the hegemony of health myths. Combined, the various contributions present a picture of health care as a complex system, where the main challenge is to inform, train and educate people to live and behave in an increasingly complex healthcare environment, rather than to try to reduce complexity or to manage it with tools and techniques.

As it is evident on consideration of the chapters of this volume, there is not an agreed definition of complexity or a single useful taxonomical classification. We underline in these few pages the different dimensions of complexity discussed by the contributors, as well as the related challenges and opportunities.

(1) The first dimension of complexity has to do with the model of medicine. The "scientific biomedical model," based on the application of the laws of physics, mechanics and chemistry to physiological processes, has traditionally dominated medicine and set the research agenda, leading to a spectacular progress in

P. Adinolfi (✉)
CIRPA (Interdepartmental Centre for Research in Economics, Law and Management of Public Administrations), University of Salerno, Fisciano, Salerno, Italy
e-mail: padinolfi@unisa.it

E. Borgonovi
Public Administration and Health Institute "Carlo Masini", University "Luigi Bocconi" of Milan, Milano, Italy
e-mail: elio.borgonovi@unibocconi.it

P. Adinolfi and E. Borgonovi (eds.), *The Myths of Health Care*,
https://doi.org/10.1007/978-3-319-53600-2_13

the last century and, particularly, in the last decade, to a huge increase in knowledge and competencies on anatomy, physiology, pathology. Currently, the scientific evolution, far from being completed and stabilized, is undergoing a process of "disruptive innovation," because traditional specialization of knowledge for diseases, organs, and diagnosis, cure and rehabilitation procedures, tends to be destroyed, notwithstanding professionals' or lobbies' defence of roles, organizational power and privileges. At the same time new, creative approaches for prevention, diagnosis and treatment based on new paradigms are required, allowing for the shift from cure to care.

The challenge of the emerging paradigm of medicine, which is highlighted in Chap. 4 (preventive, predictive, proactive, customized, participatory, specific) is to devise the development of anthropological-social reasoning on a par with the progress of technical-scientific reasoning. At a macro-level, this means, on the one hand, keeping the conquests of scientific progress, while on the other contrasting the "consumeristic" elements of hyper-medication, as well as, on the one hand, taking the new potential capacities of medicine while, on the other, redefining its limits, in the awareness that health determinants depend less and less upon the provision of Health Services and more and more on a mix of policies/trends/social behaviours, and that any intervention has to combine the resources of the State Health Services with the other resources available in society (as discussed in Chap. 9). It is useful to study and experiment health assistance models (public–private–third sector), in which public resources could become multipliers of the informal care resources which are present in community contexts, thus realizing the passage from an assistance model in which the State is exclusively entitled to produce health care, to a model in which the civil society is entitled to produce health, within a system of relationships which links together the various determinants of health.

(2) The second dimension of complexity is related to the evolution of health operating systems and professional responsibility. The traditional "biomedical model" defines professional responsibility for early diagnosis, diagnosis, cure and rehabilitation; so, according to his/her specific training and education, each professional has the autonomy to decide on the medical or nursing procedure in the context of the organizational model: ambulatory, hospital, medical lab, imaging unit, surgery unit, etc.

The new health conditions generate the need for coordination of medical, nursing and other professional activities in different settings, for example hospitals (inpatient, day-hospital and outpatient treatment), general practitioners and other nonhospital health delivery organizations. Multi-trauma, intensive care, chronicity, long-term care, homecare, gene and cell therapies, regenerative medicine and other advanced therapies, require approaches which are multidisciplinary (biomedicine, physics, engineering, informatics, etc.) and multi-professional or, better, interdisciplinary and inter-professional: different professionals must learn how to understand, interact and complement each other.

Two questions arise. Who is entitled to coordinate different people, respecting their own responsibility for medical or nursing procedures? What are the knowledge, the competencies and the skills he/she needs? No single discipline or profession is by itself entitled to coordinate multidisciplinary and multi-professional procedures. Any solution should guarantee the empowerment of the users and their families within the health value chain, as clarified in Chap. 12, in an organizational context in which hospital care does not serve chronic conditions (but only acute conditions), and residential care does not serve patients who could apply to home care.

The models to cope with the novel challenges cannot be designed by clever people, but should derive from rationality, intuition and adaptation suggested by day-to-day field experience, so as to conciliate the process of "disruptive innovation" of traditional medical specializations with the new emerging approaches, balancing the two opposite tendencies of specialization/integration.

(3) Such a balance can only be achieved if a coherent change takes place in the organizational structures and processes by which medical-health aims are accomplished, thus leading to the third dimension of complexity. At the organizational level, the challenge is to design structures which are able to balance a number of paradoxical tensions: not only specialization versus integration, but also economies of scale/specialization versus economies of proximity, automation versus innovation, stability versus change.

As regards the tension specialization/integration, on the one hand, the renewed attention to patient satisfaction calls for delayering and downsizing interventions; on the other hand, because of the disruptive innovation challenge related to the scientific progress, hospitals and other healthcare delivery organizations tend to be based, more and more, on big platforms, which connect doctors, nurses and many other professionals. Logistic platforms within and among hospitals and other delivery organizations can provide (in a short time and at lower costs) drugs, devices, other medical supplies and nonmedical goods and services. Centralized surgical platforms tend to be used by general surgeons, cardio-surgeons, neuro-surgeons, ophthalmologist surgeons and others, to guarantee better patient safety, higher productivity and lower costs. Technological platforms tend to be used to improve procurement, maintenance, substitution, updating of health equipment and other technologies. Facility management platforms can guarantee the quality of buildings and their adaptation to new environmental patterns. Integrated and interactive information systems, to which different professionals have access in real time, tend to be the common platforms for integrated care approaches.

This brings about the need to simultaneously accomplish economies of proximity and economies of scale/specialization, in relation to the trade-off between quality of services, patient satisfaction and costs, as discussed in Chap. 11. The balance can be found through internal differentiation: for subsystems where there is a high level of agreement among agents and certainty about what is required (for example, the functioning of a surgical theatre for routine operations, or the paths of standardized cycles of care), and for subsystems that can, for practical/political purposes, be treated in this way, a mechanistic model can be adopted, which applies economies of scale and work specialization based on pre-agreed roles. Also, this is true for back-office services (administration, accounting, procurement, information systems, logistics, technology maintenance, facility management, etc.), which could well be organized through centralized platforms. On the contrary, for issues characterized by a high degree of complexity—such as the development of clinical guidelines, the care of a patient with multiple clinical and social needs, or the coordination of educational and development initiatives throughout a department—organizational solutions could be explored by experimenting and working at the edge of knowledge and experience. The industrial districts celebrated by Marshall (1920) are an interesting model: the standardization takes place at the level of single components rather than whole structures, and the coordination of flexible networks of small specialized autonomous blocks organized according to a "hub & spoke" configuration is automatic, and in any case less costly than the one occurring between the big building blocks of a big organization. The latter entails the risk of managers being overwhelmed by coordination tasks, or, in other words, "of managers lying distracted in ditches considering how to manage," as from the following quotation reported by Henry Mintzberg (2009, p.157):

> The centipede was happy quite
> Until a toad in a fun
> Said: "pray, which legs goes after which?"
> That worked her mind to such a pitch,
> She lay distracted in a ditch
> Considering how to run.

This leads to further tensions, strictly intertwined with the previous one: automation versus innovation, stability versus change.

The two opposite drivers of automation and innovation could be dynamically framed and connected in a virtuous circle, by creating a learning organization where experiential learning allows for the construction of automatisms, which simplifies behaviours by offering a set of predefined possibilities, thus releasing time and energy for innovation and adaptation to the external environment. Also the stability/change dilemma could be conciliated within a time frame: the conflicting needs for stability and for change could be addressed by first attending to one and then attending to the other, back and forth in cycles of some kind. As observes Henry Mintzberg (2009, p.191), "in managing, as in the Bible, there can be a time to sow and a time to reap."

In any case, an important challenge is to design organizational solutions flexibly enough to spread the possibility/capability to care and to produce innovation throughout the whole healthcare system. In this perspective, it is not necessary to clearly separate knowledge innovation (limited mainly to universities and research hospitals or centres), knowledge and competencies diffusion (limited mainly to universities and other education institutions) and production and delivery of healthcare services. Nobody denies that in the future there will be the need to concentrate financial resources, teams of researchers and innovation efforts in some high level research-oriented institutions (public or private), but the mere transfer of standardized health approaches should be tackled and rejected.

More broadly, organizational solutions should go beyond the traditional vision of the value chain, which is typical of the industrial economy, by which healthcare providers deliver health services, suppliers produce products or services for the healthcare providers, university professors provide training and knowledge diffusion, researchers produce research, patients receive health assistance, and so on. A more complex approach could be adopted, according to which all the parts involved form a value-generating system, and ultimately a health-generating system: users and their families, suppliers, competitors, regulators, research institutions, universities. These apparently disconnected agents could be regarded as if they are part of a relational system (no matter which organization they belong to), albeit maintaining their specific assets and competences. Consequently, their assets acquire a specific positional value (which is different from the intrinsic value) in relation to their position in the time and space of the value chain.

As an example, the inclusion of pharmaceutical companies in the health value chain by favouring the possibility of experimenting clinical trials within hospitals, allows for adding value to the productive processes of healthcare organizations and to the informative fluxes on pathologies and therapies. In some countries, like Italy, there are few trials because of delays and complicated bureaucratic procedures, with consequent loss of resources and opportunities for innovation.

In a broader perspective, all the territorial actors linked to the idea of health could be regarded as nodes of the health value chain, so as to create health districts which, beyond the activities related to medical assistance, could integrate the process of creation of health with the infrastructures and the other productive sectors which concur to that process.

(4) The fourth dimension of complexity concerns the decision-making process. In the past, individual professionals (doctors, nurses, others) were the critical decision-makers, also on behalf of the patient, who had not the knowledge about his/her health or illness and was in a condition of psychological subordination. The evolution towards an *équipe* approach to the patient, discussed above, creates the paradoxical challenge of guaranteeing an acceptable balance between the joint decision-making process and the personal responsibility of each professional for his/her medical, nursing and other procedures. In addition, even when the multi/interdisciplinary and multi/inter-professional approach is the best way to provide high quality care, the patient needs a personal relationship with somebody. If the binomials joint decision-making/individual responsibility, as well as joint decision-making/individualized relationships are not conciliated, even high quality care can create a low level of satisfaction.

A further challenge is related to the introduction of "clinical decision support systems" and the evolution towards "clinical artificial intelligence." It means that big computers or computer networks are able to process, in a few minutes or seconds, thousands of clinical trial results, population studies, papers and official documents. In this situation, the decision-making process is the result of accumulated knowledge, analysis and interpretation competencies of doctors, nurses and other professionals, fine-tuned with their experience on the patient and their socio-economic environment, for example patient orientation towards health risks or towards the side effects of drugs. Patients are much more informed about their symptoms and so can interact with doctors for defining the treatment they are willing to accept. Doctors, for their part, have the professional knowledge to interpret the information and so can guarantee an added value for the patients. There is no doubt that, in this advanced information environment, the doctor–patient relationship is quite different from the past. Such relationship can be valued in the framework of an "ethic of care", envisioning both the parties, albeit asymmetric in power and resources, as interconnected and mutually dependent, as opposed to an "ethic of cure" conventionally assuming the parties as independent (Pettersen 2001, p. 55). Such a relational and reciprocal mode of thinking paves the way for a "mature care", conceptualized not as a mono-directional activity—something that is transferred from the carer to the cared-for—but rather as a relational process in which both the carer and the cared-for participate and which relies not only on rational calculation or rule-following, but includes taking experiences into account, exercising self-reflection and sensitive judgements where contextual differences are attended to.

(5) The fifth dimension of complexity concerns the regulation and the administrative system under which doctors, nurses, other professionals, hospitals and other providers operate. Because health is a unique need of the person and is considered a human right, there is no doubt that public rules to guarantee quality of care and patient safety are needed. Moreover, public rules must guarantee that healthcare services providers, both public and private, meet predefined structural (beds, buildings, equipment and technologies) and functional (manpower indicators, procedures for diagnosis and treatment, risk management procedures, cleaning procedures and others) standards.

Since the beginning of the twentieth century, public systems have been, and still are characterized, by the bureaucratic rationality that implies hierarchical command and control. Even when, from the late 80s of the last century, the new public management approach was introduced, the basic logic of command and control remained. Bureaucrats and managers tried to impose "scientific rationality" principles and criteria, which do not match the complex world of health care. This leads back to the tensions between rigid administrative/managerial procedures and the need for autonomy and adaptability, which can be framed in the above-mentioned dilemmas (automation versus innovation, stability versus change). The challenge is to maintain standards and procedures, but within rich and stimulating "federal contexts" (in turn located within non-degraded natural settings) where individuals can be active agents of the coevolution with their environment, rather than within "imperial contexts," where individuals are passive receivers of a systemic demand. In this scenario, we should consider Henry Mintzberg's idea that "engaged managers," able to involve people and liberate the energies naturally present in them, should replace the traditional "heroic managers", who formulate strategies and dominate from the top (Henry Mintzberg 2009, p. 186). As the frame of "mature care" should be applied to physicians who have lost the relational dimension, having become cold analysers of clinical tests and mechanistic executors of clinical protocols and guidelines, it should also be applied to managers, who have become cold examiners of financial data and detached deliverers of bureaucratic norms and procedures.

According to the authors of the volume (Chap. 6), the idea of engaging leaders should not be absolutized (Henry Mintzberg himself is not willing to do so); further efforts are needed to investigate how and in what circumstances this approach to leadership seems to be working best.

A challenge is to study and experiment recruitment and selection systems which allow for the assessment of managerial potential, training programs which are adequate to the complexity of health care (rather than prepacked programs inspired to the reductionist models of industrial management), evaluation and reward systems orientated to the development of personnel rather than to control.

(6) The sixth dimension of complexity concerns the measurement issue. For sure, measurement systems are helpful for improvement. In the last century, many measurement systems had been introduced and fine-tuned with regards to epidemiology, test results, any kind of treatment results, survival indicators after treatment. In the last three decades, also good and detailed financial and management measurement systems have been introduced. It can be said that, nowadays, many significant and critical measurements are available. Anyway, it must not be forgotten that the relations between measurements and improvements are very complex. The authors agree on the fact that it is mainly a question of selecting proper measurements and identifying the proper use of such measurements. A number of criticalities related to the inability of measurements to represent the complexity of health care, have been detected, such as:

   (a) Many health measurements are focused on inputs (number of doctors, nurses, beds and equipment), throughputs (quantity and quality of procedures accomplished), and outputs (quantity and quality of health services provided) rather than on outcomes (impact on patient wellbeing), and their uncritical use could cause unintended consequences of some sort, determining wrong decisions. For example, inadequate Diagnostic-Related Groups (DRGs) can orient hospitals to privilege inappropriate health treatments (high rate of caesarean sections vs natural childbirths, etc.).
   (b) Sometimes, there is no quality control of data, so information and decisions are distorted.

(c) Sometimes, ideological and political factors or bureaucratic/managerial rationality prevail on professional understanding of the actual needs of patients.
(d) Quality aspects cannot be measured, or if measured, are perceived and evaluated differently by patients, professionals, hospital bureaucrats-managers and health policy decision-makers.
(e) There is no differentiation between consolidated health treatments and innovative approaches to patient. For example, cost-accounting systems are not differentiated if used for comparing consolidated surgical procedures or inpatient–outpatient treatments, or for cost–benefit analysis or health technology assessment of a new drug or a new medical technology.
(f) Organizations or individual professionals often tend to take paths for granted, without questioning them through measurements (although these differ greatly among various organizations and even within the same organization). This precludes the identification, through experimental evidence-based studies, of what works best in specific contexts.

There is a certain convergence among the authors about the need to adopt an integrated approach that could lead to the achievement of key goals in the rethinking of health management. The challenge is to design systems which integrate data on costs, risks and outcomes over whole healthcare processes, through an evidence-based, experimental method which overcomes the myth of measurement (Chap. 10). As pointed out, it is important that these measurements are used to provide quick feedback for an evidence-based, learning approach, rather than for supporting a *command and control* style. They could also be linked to financing mechanisms related to patient paths or projects, rather than to medical treatments or episodes.

After having discussed the various dimensions of the healthcare system's complexity and related challenges, one key question arises: how can we deal with a complex health care environment?

The first step is to understand complexity. Health care cannot be reduced to deterministic cause–effect relations, as it is for other phenomena, such as technical industrial processes. The scientific approach to health and health care developed the "probability knowledge," and a number of theories on decision-making under conditions of uncertainty. In the last decades, chaos and other theories of the complexity sciences have been developed, which are slowly penetrating the field of management. These approaches offer a fecund opportunity for theory-building and have the potential of providing new ways of thinking and new tools for analysis. There is also the need for carefully crafted empirical studies, which enter into the details of how, in practice, organizations cope with the current challenges, and what the results are.

In particular, empirical research could focus on positive cases of organizations which have built a carefully selected set of systems and processes, that enables and encourages individuals to make their own judgements on how to divide their time between antagonistic demands. Research could also benefit from broader units of analysis that go beyond organizational boundaries, adopting techniques such as network analysis, and from narrower units of analysis than the organizational level (for example, a "practice- or process-centred approach"), which could provide the micro-foundations of successful organizational ambidexterity. Longitudinal studies could also be useful, focusing on how organizations coevolve dynamically over time with environmental changes.

Once the complexity of health care is understood, the possible reaction is twofold. One possibility is the case of the health myths commented in this book, which we would instinctively follow on the basis of our reductionist thinking: to neglect the real nature of complexity, break down the ambiguity, resolve any paradox and propose simple solutions to fix things. An evolution, embedded in the rational choice culture, is to govern complexity with more and more complicated measurement and decision-making systems. This is the stream of thoughts that connects the biomedical approach and the traditional Weberian bureaucracy to scientific managerialism and to the neo-Weberian models, to decision support information systems, to artificial intelligence.

There is indeed another possibility. Without refusing the scientific knowledge, this option entails accepting the challenge to be part of the complexity and adopting complex solutions. It implies going beyond *medical* and *managerial reductionism*, to enact a *New Healthcare Governance* which pursues a dynamic balance of the fundamental conundrums and paradoxes built into medical and managerial work: specialization/integration; automation/integration; stability/change; joint decision-making/individual responsibility; joint decision-making/individualized relationships; control/development of human resources. As Henry Mintzberg (2009, p. 192) points out, although the term "paradox" entered management literature in a way that indicates that it can be managed—and this is emblematic of the sense of omnipotence that characterizes traditional scientific management—these tensions could indeed be alleviated but never resolved: to try and escape them is to fall back into the *medical* and *managerial reductionism.*

The "anthropo-ecological" route to change, we have called *New Healthcare Governance,* could be framed philosophically as an *Aufhebung*, a concept of Hegelian inspiration—broadly translated in the handbooks as "all-inclusive overcoming," found on the post-modern capacity to accept ambivalence: overcoming while preserving the positive aspects of what has been overcome. How this could be operated in practical terms should be the object of future research, focusing on the declension of models of *New Healthcare Governance* applied to the various contemporary health contexts. All the research and experimentation initiatives should be framed as a system, and a choral effort on the part of all components of the health creation system should be made, with no supremacy of one over another and the availability of each of them to learn, unlearn and re-learn.

Our trip into healthcare complexity ends with no definitive answers, but many questions and ideas for research. We do share Minzberg's hope (expressed in his forward) that "we can continue to share our ideas in the future".

References

Coleman K, Austin BT, Brach C, Wagner EH (2009) Evidence on the chronic care model in the new millennium. Health Aff 28(1):75–85

Langton CG (1989) Artificial life. In: Proceedings of the Santa Fe Institute. Studies in the Sciences of Complexity, Vol. 6. Addison-Wesley, Redwood City, CA

Marshall A (1920) Principles of economics. Macmillan, London

Mintzberg H (2009) Managing. Berrett Koehler, Oakland

Pettersen T (2001) The ethics of care: normative structures and empirical implications. Health Care Anal 19(1):51–64

Erratum to: Myth #3: Healthcare Institutions as Well as the Overall System Can Be Fixed by Bringing in the Great Leader

Anna Maria Livia Colao, Pasquale Antonio Riccio, Antonio Botti, Aurelio Tommasetti, Massimo Sargiacomo, Antonio D'Andreamatteo and Luca Ianni

Erratum to: Chapter 6 in: P. Adinolfi and E. Borgonovi (eds.), *The Myths of Health Care*, https://doi.org/10.1007/978-3-319-53600-2_6

The original version of the book was inadvertently published with the following errors in Chapter 6, which now have been corrected:

Two of three contributing author names, "Antonio D'Andreamatteo" and "Luca Ianni" of Section 3, which were missing in the Table of Contents and the chapter listing, now have been included.

In Section 3, the incorrect author name "Ianni Luca" has been changed to read as "Luca Ianni."

The updated online version of this chapter can be found at https://doi.org/10.1007/978-3-319-53600-2_6

P. Adinolfi and E. Borgonovi (eds.), *The Myths of Health Care*,
https://doi.org/10.1007/978-3-319-53600-2_14

Erratum to: The Myths of Health Care

Paola Adinolfi and Elio Borgonovi

Erratum to: P. Adinolfi and E. Borgonovi (eds.), *The Myths of Health Care*, https://doi.org/10.1007/978-3-319-53600-2

In the original version of the book, the belated correction to update the affiliations of authors have to be incorporated in BookFrontmatter, Chaps. 4, 10 and 11. The erratum book has been updated with the changes.

The updated online version of these chapters can be found at
https://doi.org/10.1007/978-3-319-53600-2_4
https://doi.org/10.1007/978-3-319-53600-2_10
https://doi.org/10.1007/978-3-319-53600-2_11
https://doi.org/10.1007/978-3-319-53600-2

P. Adinolfi and E. Borgonovi (eds.), *The Myths of Health Care*,
https://doi.org/10.1007/978-3-319-53600-2_15

Index

P. Adinolfi and E. Borgonovi (eds.), *The Myths of Health Care*,
https://doi.org/10.1007/978-3-319-53600-2

MIX
Papier aus verantwortungsvollen Quellen
Paper from responsible sources
FSC® C105338
FSC
www.fsc.org

If you have any concerns about our products,
you can contact us on
ProductSafety@springernature.com

In case Publisher is established outside the EU,
the EU authorized representative is:
Springer Nature Customer Service Center GmbH
Europaplatz 3, 69115 Heidelberg, Germany

Printed by Libri Plureos GmbH
in Hamburg, Germany